Mothering in the Age of Neoliberalism

Mothering in the Age of Neoliberalism

Edited by
Melinda Vandenbeld Giles

Canada Council for the Arts   **Conseil des Arts du Canada**

The publisher gratefully acknowledges the support of the Canada Council for the Arts for its publishing program.

Demeter Press logo based on the sculpture "Demeter" by Maria-Luise Bodirsky <www.keramik-atelier.bodirsky.de>

Cover Artwork: Maya Vandenbeld Giles "Colours of the World," 2014
Printed and Bound in Canada.

Library and Archives Canada Cataloguing in Publication

Mothering in the Age of Neoliberalism / edited by Melinda Vandenbeld Giles.

Includes bibliographical references.

ISBN 978-1-927335-28-4 (pbk.)

1. Mothers–Social conditions–21st century. 2. Mothers–Economic conditions–21st century. 3. Working mothers. 4. Motherhood–Social aspects. 5. Motherhood–Economic aspects. 6. Mothers–Political activity. 7. Neoliberalism–Social aspects. I. Vandenbeld Giles, Melinda, 1973-, author, editor of compilation

HQ759.M884165 2014   306.874 3   C2014-900698-5

Demeter Press
140 Holland Street West
P. O. Box 13022
Bradford, ON L3Z 2Y5
Tel: (905) 775-9089
Email: info@demeterpress.org
Website: www.demeterpress.org

Table of Contents

Foreword: Countervisions   ix
   Christa Craven

Acknowledgements   xiii

Introduction: An Alternative Mother-Centred Economic Paradigm   1
   Melinda Vandenbeld Giles

Section I: Mothering and Neoliberal Labour

Flexible Labour and Care Work

1   Multiplying Mothers: Migration and the Work of Mothering
     in Canada and the Philippines   35
     Catherine Bryan

2   Across the Great Divide: Balancing Paid Work and Child Care
     in Neoliberal Times in Two Policy Jurisdictions in the Ottawa
     Valley, Canada   51
     *Patrizia Albanese, Megan Butryn, Louisa Hawkins and Court-
     ney Manion*

3   Mothers, Doulas, Flexible Labour and Embodied Care in the
    United States   75
    Angela Castañeda and Julie Searcy

The Entrepreneurial Mother

4   "Doing It All...and Making It Look Easy!": Yummy Mum-
    mies, Mompreneurs and the North American Neoliberal Crises
    of the Home   95
    Gillian Anderson and Joseph G. Moore

5   Eco-Diapers: The American Discourse of Sustainable Moth-
    erhood   117
    Chikako Takeshita

6   Negotiating Identities: The Case of Mompreneurs in Trinidad
    and Tobago   133
    Talia Esnard

Section II: Mothering and the Neoliberal State

Austerity and the Silencing of Mothers

7   Making Invisible: The Eradication of "Homeless Mothers"
    from Public Policy in Ontario, Canada   153
    Melinda Vandenbeld Giles

8   Neoliberalism and the De-politicising of Motherhood: Re-
    flections on the Australian Experience   169
    Joanne Baker

9   Austerity and Gender Neutrality: The Excluding of Women
    and Mothers from Public Policy in the UK   185
    Jane Chelliah

The Making of "Good" Neoliberal Mothering Subjects

10   Welfare Queens and Anchor Babies: A Comparative Study of
     Stigmatized Mothers in the United States   199
     Katrina Bloch and Tiffany Taylor

11   "Educating" Mothers through Media: The Therapy Market
     in South Korea and the Making of "Deviant" Children   211
     Jesook Song and Yoonhee Lee

12   "Education of Mothers" in Turkey: Discourses on Maternal
     Propriety and Neoliberal Body Politics on Motherhood   223
     Sevi Bayraktar

13   Affective Labour and Neoliberal Fantasies: The Gendered and
     Moral Economy of School Choice in England   237
     Andrew Wilkins

Section III: Neoliberalism and the Nuclear Family

14   Redefining Single Motherhood: The 1990s Child Support Dis-
     course and the Dismantling of the U.S. Welfare State   255
     Celia Winkler

15   "Who Is in Charge of the Family?": Religious Mothering, Ne-
     oliberalism, and *REAL Women of Canada*   279
     Vanessa Reimer

16   When Neoliberalism Intersects with Post-Second Wave Moth-
     ering: Reinforcing Neo-traditional American Family Config-
     urations and Exacerbating the Post-Second Wave Crisis in Fem-
     ininity   297
     Lynn O'Brien Hallstein

17   Deserving Children and "Risky Mothers": Situating Public
     Policy and Maternal/Child Welfare in the Canadian Context   315
     Pat Breton

TABLE OF CONTENTS

Section IV: Countering Neoliberalism Through Maternal Activism

18 Dancing without Drums: Using Maternalism as a Political
Strategy to Critique Neoliberalism in Ibadan, Nigeria   329
Grace Adeniyi Ogunyankin

19 Maternal Activism in the International Campaign for Justice
in Bhopal (ICJB), India   343
Reena Shadaan

20 It's Not the Meek Who Inherit the Earth: Low-Income Mothers Organize for Economic Justice in Canada   355
Katheryne Schulz

Epilogue   373
Jesook Song

List of Contributors   375

Foreword

Countervisions

CHRISTA CRAVEN

The advent of neoliberalism in the late 20th century brought with it a myriad of social, political, and economic shifts that have had profound effects on *all* of our daily lives.[1] Understanding mothering in this particular moment—where public services that previously benefited families and children are increasingly gutted and privatized, and efforts to introduce state supports are prevented by corporate interests—involves a keen attention to the lived experiences of mothers. As previous feminist ethnographic collections have demonstrated,[2] the fallout of neoliberalism has rested disproportionately upon mothers, often from racially and economically marked groups.

Indeed, although neoliberal public policy shifts have evidenced their deepest impact upon those struggling to survive within ever-widening economic gaps, *all* mothering has become complicated by a naïve trust in unbridled "choice" and the promotion of unfettered consumption and privatization as the antidote to social and economic inequity. While in some places, "consumer rights" for mothers are lauded as the ascendant strategy for achieving social change, and child-rearing strategies are increasingly managed and surveilled by judicial bodies when social safety-nets are eliminated, in other places, the concept of individual rights is lost as mothers become subsumed beneath financialized corporate imperatives.

It is more important than ever for feminist scholars to put our research to work in offering alternatives to the overwhelmingly market-driven approach of neoliberalism. In order to do this, feminist ethnography offers a particularly potent methodology to interrogate and challenge the wide-reaching effects of neoliberal policies and practices. As I have argued with Dána-Ain Davis previously, "feminist ethnography—which privileges particularity and the importance of individual experience, situated within uneven systems of power—can be central in uncovering how neoliberalist policies lurk in people's everyday lives" and offer compelling and innovative countervisions to neoliberalism's purportedly apolitical faith in the market to ameliorate social, political, and economic inequities (Craven and Davis 6).

Mothering in the Age of Neoliberalism offers thoughtful and thought-provoking new material to this sustained feminist critique by pairing detailed ethnographic analyses focused on women's intimate and highly politicized lives with sharp critiques of public policy throughout the globe that question neoliberalism's ascendency. Situated historically within the shifting political and economic landscape of neoliberalism at the turn of the 21st century, authors in this collection explicate the ways that class-based and racialized inequities create uneven terrain for mothers. In particular, they highlight ways that mothers frequently police other mothers in welfare offices and on nativist anti-immigration websites (Bloch and Taylor, this volume, 199), and how mothers are often "airbrushed" out of public assistance programs (Chelliah, this volume, 185), policies aimed at the homeless (Vandenbeld Giles, this volume, 153), and the harsh guidelines of Structural Adjustment Programs (Ogunyankin, this volume, 329).

While neoliberal policies disproportionately affect poor and racialized mothers, the collection effectively highlights how, despite popular media representations, neoliberalism infiltrates and negatively affects the lives of *all* mothers from a broad range of backgrounds and constituencies throughout the world. Authors highlight how neoliberalism has subtly (and oftentimes not so subtly) seeped into the norms and practices of motherhood among women in racially, ethnically, and economically dominant groups throughout the world. In particular, authors highlight the deployment of socially conservative public policies under neoliberalism (Baker, this volume, 169), the public valuation of a variety of experts advocating "effective" mothering (Song and Lee, this volume, 211), the advent of increasing flexible labour among mompreneurs in areas throughout the globe (Anderson and Moore, this volume, 95; Esnard, this volume, 133), and impossible efforts at "work-life balance" as mothers and those who support them negotiate between "flexible embodied care and market rationality" (Castañeda and Searcy, this volume, 90; see also O'Brien Hallstein, this volume, 297).

The authors in this collection seek to ground more abstract theoretical discussions of neoliberalism in sharply critical, often ethnographically specific analyses of public policy in areas throughout the world as it affects women's lived experience of mothering. Cumulatively, the authors also have several important lessons to offer continued feminist activist work into the 21st century, as well as movements toward social justice aims more broadly. Here they offer strong critiques, for instance, of recent debates over Momism and a neo-conservative "post-feminist" political climate under which "women's rights [have] become political points of negotiation" (Chelliah, this volume, 193); see also Baker, this volume, 169; Bloch and Taylor, this volume, 199; O'Brien Hallstein, this volume, 297). Others highlight how the narrow (if well-intentioned) foci of movements for the "rights of the child" (Breton, this volume, 315), ecologically driven "green" motherhood (Takeshita, this volume, 117), and the increasingly popular services of doulas in an age when medical provisions for mothers have been eroded (Castañeda and Searcy, this volume, 75) can silence structural problems that ultimately exclude many mothers from these "choices."

Situating neoliberal policies in their local context deconstructs their presumed homogenizing effects. For instance, while in North America, neo-traditional family configurations provide the policy antidote to swelling inequities (O'Brien Hallstein, this volume, 297), in the Philippines, mass migration and dispersed extended families provide the purported solution to impoverishment (Bryan, this volume, 35). In fact, as these chapters demonstrate, despite popular Euro-American conceptualizations of motherhood as biological (and perhaps adoptive), mothering frequently encompasses community engagement far beyond biological kinship structures. Yet, however motherhood is defined, these chapters draw important attention to how the unremunerated or poorly remunerated labour of mothers is so frequently left unacknowledged by policy makers, precisely because it remains so pivotal to the neoliberal paradigm.

In sum, this ensemble of detailed policy analyses and rich ethnographic work demonstrates eloquently that feminist social science is, in fact, poised to expose and challenge the encroachment of neoliberalism in mothers' daily lives—a task worthy and essential for feminist scholars to continue to foreground as we move forward in an era marked by heightened inequities on a global scale.

Christa Craven
Wooster, Ohio
September 2013

NOTES

[1]Many thanks to Dána-Ain Davis for her thoughtful critiques of several drafts of this Foreword and for always encouraging me to sharpen my feminist scholarship and activist work.
[2]See, for instance, Gunewardena and Kingsolver

WORKS CITED

Craven, Christa & Dána-Ain Davis. "Introduction." *Feminist Activist Ethnography: Counterpoints to Neoliberalism in North America.* Eds. Christa Craven & Dána-Ain Davis. Lanham, MD: Lexington Books, 2013. Print.

Gunewardena, Nandini and Ann Kingsolver. Eds. *The Gender of Globalization: Women Navigating Cultural and Economic Marginalities.* Santa Fe, New Mexico: School for Advanced Research Press, 2007. Print.

Acknowledgements

Mothering in the Age of Neoliberalism has meant so much more than creating a book—it has been about actively participating in the feminist demand for a new economic imaginary that prioritizes the needs of mothers and children and as such, many dedicated and inspirational individuals have contributed. First of all, without the contributors in this volume, the book would not exist. I am extremely indebted to the amazing researchers, academics, and writers who have shared their knowledge and experience within the pages of this book. *Mothering in the Age of Neoliberalism* is about exposing neoliberal failures toward mothers, but it is also about building community and revealing the multiple ways in which people can work together to establish collectivity.

I would like to extend an enormous thank you to the three reviewers. Your insightful and crucial comments helped shape this volume into what it is. This book would also not exist without the incredible support of Andrea O'Reilly. The work Andrea O'Reilly has accomplished through MIRCI (Motherhood Initiative for Research and Community Involvement) and Demeter Press publications is crucial to countering individualistic neoliberal narratives. Andrea has been so much more than an academic mentor; she is a close friend and feminist inspiration who has transformed the lives of many mothers. I am also enormously indebted to Jesook Song, whose continual support and demand for ongoing academic rigor have shaped the landscape of my academic theorizing, and Sandra Bamford, whose astute academic philosophical theorizing has reshaped my perceptions of the world.

Thank you must also be given to my editorial selection committee: Sandy

Oh, Kori Allan, Bess Doyle, Columba Gonzalez, and Ken Huynh. Meeting on a Friday morning to sort through over 100 amazing submissions shows true dedication. A further enormous thank you goes to my editorial committee: Sandy Oh, Kori Allan, Bess Doyle, and Anita Vandenbeld. Your support and friendship has been immeasurable through the process of editing *Mothering in the Age of Neoliberalism* and your comments have been crucial, particularly in the pre-production process. I would also like to thank Angie Deveau, for working away on MIRCI projects and Demeter Press titles and making sure everything happens when and where it should, including the production of this book. A huge thank you to my feminist sisters, Linn Baran and Renée Knapp, for always being so supportive; your knowledge, dedication, and enthusiasm are an inspiration.

I would like to conclude my acknowledgements by thanking my family—without your love and support none of this would be possible. Thank you to my sister, Anita Vandenbeld, not only for providing lived-experience knowledge of global political feminism as a member of the editorial committee, but for always being there for me providing support as a sister and friend. Thank you to my parents, Maria and Herman Vandenbeld, for providing endless love and support, and also for those crucial moments when the rigorous process of editing required additional child-care help. Given our current neoliberal context of few child-care supports, your help has been enormously appreciated. Thank you to my dear husband, Christian Giles—how can I possibly list the number of ways you have supported me—through endless political-economic discussions and editorial revisions, through chicken dinners and after-school pick-ups, and through laundry and sick days. Finally, thank you to my sweet seven-year-old daughter, Maya Vandenbeld Giles, whose inspirational and optimistic view of the world can now be revealed for everyone to see on the cover of *Mothering in the Age of Neoliberalism*, providing hope that a future in which the needs of mothers and children will predominate *is* possible.

Introduction

An Alternative Mother-Centred Economic Paradigm

MELINDA VANDENBELD GILES

Mothers are the primary producers, consumers, and reproducers of the neoliberal world. Yet, contrary to optimistic pronouncements regarding the ascent of women,[1] neoliberalism has produced a globalized space in which of the one billion people living in absolute poverty (less than one dollar US per day), seventy percent are women (Braedley and Luxton 21). The majority of those women living in absolute poverty are mothers. While there has been an increasing global interest in reducing childhood poverty and maternal mortality within an international right to health framework[2] (Breton, this volume), there has not been a corresponding economic acknowledgement of the centrality of mothers as essential to the neoliberal paradigm. This collection was created as a starting point in which to centralize the positionality[3] of mothers within the neoliberal global landscape.

"Mothering" and "neoliberalism" are terms weighted with presumed assumptions and political contestations. As such, both terms provide a potent discursive space within which to actively reconfigure ingrained normative understandings and thereby create new imaginaries. In *Fortunes of Feminism*, Nancy Fraser asks the question, "How does it happen, under conditions of domination, that people come together, arrange themselves under the banner of collective identities, and constitute themselves as collective social agents?" Fraser discusses the pivotal use of discursive formations in creating legitimation for circulating previously fragmented identities—particularly that of women—in establishing a political collectivity that can claim rights based on its created membership. Fraser goes on to discuss Gramsci's concept of hegemony as "the power to establish the 'common sense'" and thus producing "authoritative definitions of social situations and social needs...and the power to shape the political agenda" (Fraser 142). I borrow from Fraser's conceptualizations and claim mothering as a potent discursive space within which the creation of a global collectivity can provide a starting point to push for localized economic alternatives that prioritize the needs of mothers and children.

While I utilize the term mothering as a universal discursive device, it is with the recognition of the multiplicity of mothering practices and forms. My usage of the term mothering borrows from the anthropological understanding of mothering as being about "engaging acts of *mothering*, regardless of institutional involvement, biology, sex, and gender. More to the point, *mothering* occurs whether or not it is biologically, legally, and/or socially/culturally recognized as such" (Walks and McPherson x). Thus "mothering" refers to the work of primary caregiving, being responsible for the economic, educational, and social care of another human being. Such an expansive definition means fathers, grandparents, LGBTQ parents etc. can perform "mothering". However, the reality is that caregiving continues to be highly gendered, and while I acknowledge "mothering" occurs in many forms, it is also crucial to acknowledge that it is women who are globally performing the majority of this mothering work. Thus it is this highly gendered reality of mothering that is prioritized in this volume.

The value of subjective and detailed ethnographic accounts of mothering cannot be overestimated. A pivotal goal in this volume is to reveal the multiple ways in which various neoliberal policies and ideologies are conceptualized and enacted upon within the context of mothering, whether such mothering occurs in localized and/or transnational spaces. Thus, in the interest of creating an activist paradigm within which to claim mothering rights, it becomes imperative that a global collective be established. In this way, "mothering" becomes the heuristic tool within which mothers can claim their collective rights and thus actively oppose neoliberal initiatives.

Just as mothering has been a site of contestation, so, too, has neoliberal. My usage of the term neoliberal acknowledges the multiplicity of neoliberalisms globally. Borrowing from Kingfisher and Maskovsky, I acknowledge neoliberalism not as a totalizing global project but rather as a process in which "instabilities, partialities, and articulations with other cultural and political-economic formations" has made the neoliberal rise to global prominence incomplete (Kingfisher and Maskovsky 115). This volume prioritizes the need to situate neoliberal policies and discourses within their historical, cultural, political, and economic paradigms thereby destabilizing the presumed homogenizing effects of a singular neoliberalism. In this way, the fissures and cracks within the global economic system can be revealed providing opportunity for an alternative mother-centred economic paradigm. Each chapter situates the global by revealing the interconnections between mothering and neoliberalism within localized spaces.

Given the multiplicity of theorizing and popular usage of the term neoliberal, there has arisen a debate over whether neoliberal has become so diluted as to have lost its potential as a discursive device (Hilgers). I argue that while neoliberal may lose its relevance as a symbolic signifier in academic discourse, it becomes increasingly potent in global popular uprisings (Ayres). Thus, as Anna Tsing has revealed in *Friction* in her discussion of the potentiality within global circulating discourses, the universal has always had the power of both subjugation *and* emancipation (Tsing). If the goal is to create an alternative global economic paradigm in which the needs of mothers and children are prioritized, then "mothering" becomes the most effective discursive tool to counter "neoliberalism" and thereby make demands for social and material change.

FROM THE FEMINIZATION OF POVERTY TO THE EMANCIPATION OF WOMEN

"One of the central distinguishing features of neoliberalism is the gender regime that anchors it" (Braedley and Luxton 12). Indeed, inherent within neoliberalism is a morality that places mothers at its very core. And yet, while neoliberal philosophy prioritizes the role of mothers, it contradictorily recognizes only individual market actors. In this way, identifying mothering within a market realm appears to erase the public/private divide upon which liberal economics was based. This does suggest a fundamental difference between liberal and neoliberal philosophy in terms of gender. And yet, it must be acknowledged that this dichotomy was only made relevant for primarily white middle-class mothers. Thus, in many ways, the specific identification of mothering in the market realm only further entrenches dualistic conceptualizations of motherhood by creating an exclusive "working mother" categorization that does not incorporate reproduction or caregiving. Mothers must be neoliberal self-optimizing economic agents in the "public" realm *and* maternalist self-sacrificing mothers in the "private" realm. The more mothers become integrated within the market, the more do essentialist maternalist conceptualizations of mothering predominate.

"Unlike liberalism, which rested upon the legal subordination of women, neoliberalism assumes that the individual can be male or female (and perhaps trans). The result is a new gender regime; one that is a consequence of an economy in which men and women are income earners" (Braedley and Luxton 13). Despite theorizing indicating the end of traditional wage labour through the emergence of a knowledge economy (Beck) or a new global creative class (Florida), the suggestion that something is ending assumes it had already begun. However, as Wallerstein (22-24) indicates, within the historical capitalist system the concept of wage labour as the primary determinant of "value" is itself a construction. Yet, it is a construction that has held particular force regardless of economic paradigms ever since Adam Smith's *Wealth of Nations*. Thus, while those who are "privileged" may enter the global capitalist creative class, the majority must enter the increasingly poorly remunerated and precarious wage labour market in unprecedented numbers. And the majority of those entering this neoliberal global wage labour market are women and mothers.

Such a fundamental shift in gender conceptualizations has sparked a popular fascination with the "feminization of society." Framed within a "feminist" language of empowerment, this discourse can be highly persuasive: "The earth is shifting. A new age is dawning. From Kabul to Cairo to Cape Town and New York, women are claiming their space at home, at work and in the public square" (Armstrong 1). The United Nations Millennium Development Project claims that the status of women is directly related to the economy. "The World Bank asserts that if women and girls are treated fairly, the economy of a village will improve" (1). In Kevin Voigt's CNN article "Women: Saviors of the World Economy?" he writes "the largest growing economic force in the world isn't China or India—it's women" (Edgar 2). Women in the United States control 80 percent of all consumer purchasing decisions (and consumer purchases make up two thirds of U.S. gross domestic product) (2). According to the United Nations Development Fund for Women, women do 66% of the world's work (3). The United Nations World Food Programme reports that women in developing countries produce 80% of the food (3). "Furthering a woman's economic position directly affects her ability to purchase needed improvements in health, housing, and education; her bargaining position and power in the family; and her ability to act against violence in her home and in her world. Expanding economic opportunities for women decreases a woman's vulnerability to human trafficking, HIV/AIDS, and violence" (4).

While it is true that women and mothers form the productive, reproductive, and consumptive basis to ensure neoliberalization, mothers are still a long way from claiming collective power and material gain for themselves and their children. UN initiatives and global campaigns such as Because I am a Girl offer powerful images for reframing the global failure of neoliberalism toward a more positive opportunity for change. Indeed, "hope" has become a new mantra. However, such empowerment programs, while acknowledging material poverty, offer solutions that reside within the very framework upon which the poverty emerged. Thus, while these narratives reveal the failure of neoliberalism toward women and mothers, they do nothing to challenge the inherent political-economic basis upon which neoliberalism is built—the poorly remunerated labour of women and mothers.

In the *Feminization of the Labor Force*, Jenson, Hagen, and Reddy write, "One of the most dramatic changes in industrial societies in the postwar years has been the intensification of women's participation in the paid labor force" (3). And yet, women's work in the reproductive sphere as mothers and caregivers has equally increased in direct response to the reduction of government funding for social and community services. "Mothering/caring was being garnered as a means to fill in the gaps left by economic reform" (Simon-Kumar 147). Women who are caregivers in the home are placed within an essentialist maternalist framework of reproduction and given no state support. Yet, women performing care work in the marketplace (many who are also mothering transnationally), are placed within the neoliberal efficiency framework of production, as in the case of Filipina care-work migration (Bryan, this volume, 169). Such dualistic categorizations of "mothering" lead to massive structures of inequality that benefit neither mothers nor children. The marketization of mothering has also meant that reproduction itself becomes a commodity (Craven). Just as the bodies of individuals become identified in terms of economic potentiality, so, too, do the bodies of mothers become economized as experimental markets for pharmaceuticals, particularly contraceptives (Simon-Kumar 148).

"Neoliberalism's core theoretical premise and its practice...has resulted in a global decline in women's positions and material well-being" (Braedley and Luxton 13). Braedley and Luxton identify three important dynamics in how the neoliberal project has had global negative consequences for women: 1. Women's work is so poorly remunerated that women are the majority of poor people in the world. In many areas of the world, the promotion of international agribusiness has undermined women's subsistence farming thus affecting the survival of their households and communities. At the same time, while more waged labour opportunities arise, they are predominantly low paid and insecure. 2. While neoliberalism identifies women only as economic actors, the work of mothering must still be performed and is in fact integral to the reproduction of future neoliberal workers. However, due to the neoliberal commitment of reducing state expenditures such as paid maternity leave and child care, mothers are left with no support systems (15). 3. Despite the emancipatory potential within the "feminization of society," neoliberalism remains an inherently male paradigm in terms of who controls the capital assets. "So neoliberalism allows space for women who are willing or able to live like men, who present themselves as men do and who are able to compete as men do" (15).

Neoliberalism ensures mothers who are responsible for caregiving remain marginalized and thus dependent upon poorly remunerated wage labour, disenabling them from entering the "male" category of capital assets by eroding community and state caregiving structures and independent agricultural-based means for household survival (14). In this way, while a very few "privileged" mothers may "choose" to enter the neoliberal space of masculine virility by offloading the responsibilities of mothering onto other mothers and caregivers, for the majority, whether to perform labour in the "public" sphere *or* perform mothering work in the "private" sphere is not a question of "choice," but rather economic necessity. And even for those "privileged" few garnering success through becoming the ideal "male" neoliberal worker, there is no space in this patriarchal paradigm to be a mother. For those mothers attempting to merge the worker and maternalist spheres through part-time labour, working from "home" etc. (contradictorily encouraged given the lack of state support for child care), they are faced directly with the difficulties of merging two realms that have been constructed as diametrically opposed. Creating a divisionary paradigm in which mothers as economic agents becomes antithetical to mothering, ensures a maternal/child separation for *all* mothers. Far from creating more "choice," such a paradigm in effect takes all choices away by necessitating the majority of mothers either enter the poorly remunerated work sphere or become full-time caregivers due to lack of child-care supports. Neoliberal emancipatory social justice in which "everyone is equal under the law" obscures the structural realities of gender, race, and class, thus intensifying existent inequalities. The very magnification of such inequalities is the foundation upon which neoliberal capital relies. While the neoliberal paradigm theoretically creates spaces in which a few women and mothers can thrive, we cannot call neoliberalism a feminist emancipatory paradigm until *all* mothers, women, and children are able to thrive globally.

THEORIZING MOTHERING

Coinciding with this discussion of women in the global political-economic realm[4] has been a popular preoccupation with all things "mothering" (Kawash). A discussion of mothering paradigms is required to position the apparent disjunctive between popularized motherhood claiming emancipatory potential within an increasingly essentialist global material reality void of structural supports.

Until the 1970s, a discussion of mothering as an independent source of academic investigation did not exist. While the family has always been pivotal within anthropological discussions of kinship, the presumed assumption of biological motherhood was a given and thus mothering was only discussed within the context of economic exchange in small-scale societies (Lévi-Strauss). Mothering was (and continues to be) pivotal in psychoanalysis but within an essentialized and subjectivist paradigm (Freud). And sociological accounts of mothering place the mother within the institution of the family.[5] Thus, the 1970s second-wave feminist investigation into universal and biological conceptualizations of both the family and motherhood was pivotal.[6] The desire was to repudiate modernist functionalist and Freudian conceptualizations of naturalized motherhood that had dominated all discussions of mothering until that point.[7] Nancy Scheper-Hughes's publication of her 1985 article, "Culture, Scarcity, and Maternal Thinking: Maternal Detachment and Infant Survival in a Brazilian Shantytown" and subsequent 1993 book *Death without Weeping: Violence of Everyday Life in Brazil* brought the active debate regarding maternal instinct to the forefront (See Scheper-Hughes 1985; 1993). Such theorizing was essential in terms of deconstructing biological motherhood. However, during the 1980s and early 1990s, the focus on mothering was quickly subsumed within the context of increasing neoliberalization and identity politics. It was not until the late 1990s and 2000s that an academic discussion of mothering started to re-emerge.

It is no coincidence that the height of global neoliberal restructuring in the mid-1990s coincided with a returned interest in mothering given how the neoliberal paradigm necessitates mothers take on the primary role of caregiving with the depletion of state resources. And yet at the same time, women entered the labour force in unprecedented numbers. A number of factors including the deindustrialization of "traditional" well-paid male wage labour being replaced by increasingly feminized, precarious, and low-wage service-sector jobs led to an increasingly "feminized" workforce with global repercussions. However, given the cultural academic turn arising out of subjectivist philosophy in the 1960s becoming dominant in the social sciences and humanities from the 1980s to the early 2000s, the return of mothering within the academic sphere for the most part excluded systemic global political-economic analysis. Thus, despite the overt connection between popular and academic interest in mothering and neoliberal economics, the majority of theorists analyzing mothering did so within the cultural realm and the majority of theorists analyzing neoliberalism excluded any discussion of mothering.

The flurry of everything mothering arising in the mid-1990s and continuing to proliferate in the 2000s created renewed academic interest in kinship, the family, and reproduction. However, as Kawash writes in "New Directions in Motherhood Studies," motherhood is "frequently subsumed into discussions of women and work, migration, or reproduction (including abortion on one side and reproductive biotechnologies on the other)" (971). Within anthropology, the economic place of the family has always been of central concern.[8] While feminist deconstructions of the biological basis of motherhood and Schneider's deconstruction of the nuclear family created a temporary academic "crisis" (See Schneider 1980, 1984), it was in the 1990s when Kinship Studies started to move in several new directions, prompting new expanded understandings of what constitutes relatedness. Related research within anthropology and sociology includes the study of New Reproductive Technologies,[9] transnational kinship (i.e., international adoption, mail order spouses, foreign domestics, etc.),[10] and work regarding the non-biological basis of relatedness.[11] This research is pivotal in furthering our understandings of relatedness in a rapidly changing world, and more related research that specifically connects the subjectivities of mothers within the processes of neoliberal transformation is needed.

Feminist Political Economy has been pivotal in producing a sustained anti-capitalist critique.[12] However, there is little reference to mothering but rather social reproduction. Social reproduction provides an expansive analysis in terms of opening the space to a discussion of caregiving performed by all social actors and institutions including the state and NGOs rather than exclusively mothers. Bezanson and Luxton define social reproduction as "the processes involved in maintaining and reproducing people, specifically the labouring population, and their labour power on a daily and generational basis. It involves the provision of food, clothing, shelter, basic safety, and health care, along with the development and transmission of knowledge, social values, and cultural practices and the construction of individual and collective identities" (Bezanson and Luxton 4). However, the continued reality is that the individuals who are globally doing the majority of this work of social reproduction are mothers. Within a neoliberal paradigm in which gender is erased, it becomes even more necessary to actively acknowledge the specific positionality of mothers who collectively perform such labour.

In *Fortunes of Feminism*, Nancy Fraser discusses an emerging transnational feminism that has been pivotal in contributing to anti-neoliberal activism.[13] Feminism shifted from second-wave radicalism to cultural politics just as rising neoliberalism declared war on social equality. However, as neoliberalism has entered its current crisis, feminist radical second-wave potential is reviving, particularly given the neoliberal erasure of gender and race (Fraser 2). And yet, in Nancy Fraser's analysis of feminism, there is no mention of mothering. This is particularly striking given the increasing predominance of maternal activism as a global anti-neoliberal force (Ogunyankin and Shadaan, in collection).

MATERNAL STUDIES

Much of the maternal theorizing arising in the 1990s and continuing in the 2000s focuses on identifying what is termed Intensive Mothering.[14] Intensive Mothering involves positioning children as social capital to be "invested in." In "Why Can't a Mother Be More Like a Businessman?" Sharon Hays defines Intensive Mothering as "child-centred, expert-guided, emotionally absorbing, labor-intensive, and financially expensive" (Hays 414). Such analysis positions mothers within the cultural political economy, particularly Ann Crittenden's *The Price of Motherhood* (Crittenden) and Taylor, Layne, and Wozniak's edited collection *Consuming Motherhood*.[15] It has been crucial in revealing the inconsistency of a neoliberal paradigm necessitating economic actors yet demanding full-time motherhood. It has also deconstructed normative "good mother" conceptualizations to reveal how despite increasing popular focus on all things mothering, far from disentangling and reconstituting mothering away from biological conceptualizations, neoliberalism has further entrenched such ingrained understandings thus magnifying the Domestic Goddess image (Anderson and Moore, Baker, O'Brien Hallstein, Reimer, and Vandenbeld Giles, in volume).

Given the shift from Keynesian social democracy to neoliberal individual responsibility, there has been corresponding research in terms of how the erosion of the welfare state has had the most direct material consequences for women and mothers.[16] The idealization of the Domestic Goddess and the Intensive Mothering image only obscure the increasing feminization of poverty as a direct result of neoliberal policies eroding social supports for mothers. In addition, while the Domestic Goddess image idealizes biological motherhood, it provides no structural support for the increasing majority of working mothers. Thus, the "working mother" becomes de-gendered within a framework of "equality" while the mythical Intensive Mother becomes fixed within biological gendered assumptions. Within this paradigm, it becomes advantageous for the state to offload social reproduction onto the shoulders of mothers while simultaneously creating a "feminist" contradictory narrative of emancipation through "choice" (Albanese et al., Chelliah, Schulz, Takeshita, Vandenbeld Giles, Wilkins, and Winkler, in volume).

While neoliberal individualism appears to "emancipate" all people within a discourse of "equality", in reality it further entrenches inequalities by obscuring structural factors of poverty, gender, and race. Thus, such "good mothering" assumptions predicated on Anglo white-middle-class positionality further marginalize those who exist outside these normative categories, in particular resulting in the further erosion of welfare support through governance structures that implicate racialized and impoverished mothers as "undeserving" (Bloch and Taylor, in volume).

While there has been some research regarding the concept of Intensive Mothering in the global south (Donner), this is an area in dire need of further research. Given the rising influence of supranational organizations and global financing intersecting and colluding with local state imperatives, the degree to which "good mothering" ideals become implicated in global paradigms of aid and investment in determining those mothers "deserving" or "undeserving" of support is crucial. And since neoliberalisms are never totalizing, the multiple ways in which mothering subjectivities and material lives are formulated within these circulating discourses of "good" mothering must be explored in their local contexts (Bayraktar, Esnard, Song and

Lee, and Wilkins, in volume).

In response to the increasing "crisis of care"[17] as a result of multiple neoliberal policies since the 1980s eroding the welfare state, a global network of remunerated care work has arisen. There has been crucial interdisciplinary research studying the specifics of mothering and migration, domestic work, and the crisis of care.[18] Such work is pivotal in revealing the extent to which mothers are central in the global neoliberal nexus of care and reproduction. However, while such research often incorporates a discussion of mothers within a discussion of women and children, the focus is more on caregiving as a systemic political-economic issue, thus mothering in terms of situated meanings and practices is not often the principle site of investigation. More research uniting the cultural specifics of mothering with the political-economy of global care work and migration is required, particularly when considering the multiple ways in which neoliberalism has shifted entitled to merit-based citizenship delineated by "deserving" versus "undeserving" individuals based on categorizations of race and gender. One of the neoliberal paradoxes is that while gender and race become invisible in public policy, such ingrained conceptualizations are further entrenched in the popular imagination thus creating disjuncture between state rhetoric and lived realities. Additionally, the neoliberal push to prioritize individualized entrepreneurialism above family reunification has altered the landscape of migration globally. Given that it is women and mothers who are performing the majority of care work globally, they are thus primarily implicated in such policy change (Bryan, in volume).

Feminist anthropology has highlighted the sites of reproduction within a neoliberal context, thereby contributing enormously to expanding our understandings of reproductive justice in a neoliberal age.[19] Given the neoliberal prioritization of the family as the primary social reproducer of society, such research is particularly crucial. Additionally, such research defies neoliberal claims of market rationality by revealing a nexus of care and relationality not predicated upon market initiatives. A merging of this vital research within a larger framework of global mothering rights would provide a powerful space of contestation to neoliberal imperatives (Castañeda and Searcy, in volume).

This literature review, by no means complete, does reveal the enormous wealth and diversity within maternal studies and research related to mothering and neoliberalism. However, it also reveals the inconsistencies, erasures, and need for greater integration between the various disciplines to build a feminist mothering paradigm from an inclusive knowledge basis. MIRCI (Motherhood Initiative for Research and Community Involvement)—originating as ARM (Association for Research on Mothering) in 1998—provides a vital interdisciplinary space in which such diverse theorizations of mothering can merge. ARM and MIRCI have produced a vast array of pivotal mothering research through related journals and Demeter Press.[20]

NEOLIBERAL THEORIZING

Despite mothers providing the primary nexus of labour, consumption, and reproduction upon which global neoliberalism is reliant, mothering is peculiarly absent in neoliberal theorizing. Neoliberal philosophy is often attributed to the Austrian micro economist, Friedrich Hayek, and later neoliberal public policies are associated with the American economist, Milton Friedman. As director of the Austrian Institute for Economic Research between 1927 and 1931, the beginnings of Hayek's argument with scientific positivism began to emerge. Writing subjectivist economic theory at the height of modernist-Keynesian inspired discourse meant Hayek's arguments remained marginalized. Therefore, in 1956, the Institute of Economic Affairs was established specifically as a venue to promote Hayek's prolific publications (O'Brien and Penna 80). Hayek's philosophical orientation was a direct response to Keynes' economic theory, popular at the time of his early writing. Hayek continued his sustained critique of regulated markets by spending his entire life combating what he perceived as *The Errors of Socialism* (Hayek).

In *The Shock Doctrine* Naomi Klein identifies Hayek as "Friedman's own personal guru" (61). Friedman first joined with Hayek in 1947 to form the Mont Pelerin Society in Switzerland to provide a space for their then radical theorizing (Harvey 20). With memories of the market crash of 1929 and the Great Depression still fresh, popular opinion necessitated increasing market regulation during the 1930s-1950s, thus the laissez-faire economic theorizing of Hayek and Friedman was decidedly marginalized.

However, a growing resistance to Keynesianism emerged within the University of Chicago economics department during the 1950s. David Harvey refers to "the Chicago boys" (8) in *A Brief History of Neoliberalism* and Pinochet's Chile as the first testing ground for neoliberal policy. During the 1950s, the U.S. funded the training of Chilean economists "as part of a Cold War programme to counteract left-wing tendencies in Latin America" (8). Equally, Chicago-trained economists, immersed in neoliberal theorization of the laissez-faire market inspired by Friedman and his mentor Hayek, came to dominate the private Catholic University in Santiago, Chile (8). During the 1970s, business elites organized their opposition to then Chilean president Salvador Allende—who had nationalized industry through collectivization—through a group called the "Monday Club" and developed a working relationship with the Chicago School economists, even funding their work through research institutes (Harvey 8). Following the 1973 military coup led by Augusto Pinochet in which Allende was overthrown, in 1975 Pinochet brought these economists into the government where their first job was to negotiate loans with the International Monetary Fund (8). In the documentary film *Shock Doctrine*, there is video footage of Friedman meeting directly with Pinochet during his trip to Chile in March 1975 (Klein 93).[21] Neoliberal policies continued to erode the governments of Latin America during the 1970s and 1980s, including Argentina, Uruguay, Brazil (102), Nicaragua (161), Bolivia (169), and Mexico (103).

The direct association between neoliberal market ideology and Pinochet's Chile is often erased from the historical trajectory of neoliberal thought with Thatcher and Reagan providing the starting points. Indeed, Thatcher had been attempting a neoliberal imposition in the UK beginning with her 1979 election slogan "Labour isn't working" (160), although she did write a letter to Hayek indicating that a complete Chilean transformation would not work in a democratic society (161). However, as Klein writes in *The Shock Doctrine* in reference to the Falklands War, "Thatcher used the enormous popularity afforded her by the victory to launch the very corporatist revolution she had told Hayek was impossible before the war" (Klein 164).

Neoliberalism is most often associated with Ronald Reagan's 1980 victory, deregulation, tax cuts, budget cuts, and attacks on trade union and professional power in the United States (25); however, it was in the 1990s when neoliberal policies became globally predominate, particularly given the 1989 collapse of the Berlin Wall. During the 1980s, the free-market economist John Williamson coined the term "Washington Consensus" to indicate a global framework for free-market economic development to counter the previous highly regulated international developmentalist model (Steger and Roy 19). It is this free-market model that thereafter became the global articulation for neoliberalism.

This brief and extremely simplified foray into neoliberal political history only highlights the direct involvement of Hayek and Friedman within the political-economic structures of several nation-states. This by no means suggests a totalizing American "neoliberal invasion" of the world. How-ever, it does illuminate the need to directly connect philosophical theoriz-ing with political economy. Understanding the multiple political and eco-nomic forms in which neoliberalisms have arisen globally necessitates un-derstanding the basic philosophical premise. During the 1990s in which ne-oliberal policies were shifting the global landscape, there had not yet devel-oped a comprehensive popular terminology to define such radical change. In Aihwa Ong's 2006 publication *Neoliberalism as Exception,* Ong indi-cates how the term neoliberalism means different things depending upon one's vantage point: "American neoliberalism" defined post-Asian debt cri-sis as economic restructuring, "savage neoliberalism" in Latin America, or "radicalized capitalist imperialism" in reference to Iraq. However, "In the United States…neoliberalism is seldom part of popular discourse outside the academy" (1). Within the context of a post-2008 U.S. mortgage crisis sparking global recession, Ong's observation no longer holds. The term ne-oliberalism has become part of the American and global colloquial usage (Ayres).

While neoliberal philosophy and resultant public policies have increas-ingly dominated the global landscape since the 1970s, it is crucial to equally recognize the inconsistencies and impartialities within what we have termed the "neoliberal world". By situating neoliberal-driven policies within local-ized spaces, context breaks down the homogenized spectre of neoliberalism thereby revealing inherent contradictions. However, given that the social sciences and humanities for the past thirty years have been predicated upon a critique of modernity, investigating and critiquing neoliberalisms within localized spaces initially presented an unrecognizable challenge. In "Neolib-eralism and the End of Liberal Democracy" Wendy Brown writes, "We are not simply in the throes of a right-wing or conservative positioning within liberal democracy but rather at the threshold of a different political forma-tion, one that conducts and legitimates itself on different grounds from lib-eral democracy even as it does not immediately divest itself of the name" (12).

Thus even poststructuralist opposition to capitalism remains framed within the very same anti-enlightenment critique within which neoliberal subjectivist economics arose. As Swift writes in *At Risk: Social Justice in Child Welfare and Other Human Services,* "Neo-liberalism has benefitted from and perhaps is made possible by postmodern challenges to modernist forms of authority, challenges to the welfare state, and challenges to profes-sional expertise" (7). Wendy Brown discusses the need for devising "an intelligent Left challenge to the neo-liberal political-economic formation now taking shape and an intelligent left counter-vision to this formation." She goes on to write "...not only liberal democratic principles but democratic morality has been largely eviscerated" (13).

When economic theories such as neoliberalism become enshrined within the popular imagination, they are removed from their contextual source. Such de-contextualization creates a naturalization of knowledge, thereby making it extremely difficult to critique. However, by situating neoliberal philosophy within its historical space and thus revealing its inherent inconsistencies and theoretically questionable premise, this de-legitimates the apparent authority upon which it is based.

AN INTERDISCIPLINARY APPROACH TO THEORIZING MOTHERING AND NEOLIBERALISM

Just as mothering became a recognized space for interdisciplinary academic discussion in the 1990s, so, too, did neoliberalism. While social theorists had been actively theorizing globalization, identifying a separate thread of academic knowledge as neoliberalism did not fully emerge until the 1990s and has since become prolific. And yet, despite mothering and neoliberalism being intimately connected, they have remained predominately disconnected within the academy. In this way, this volume is particularly salient. Not only does it centralize the positionality of mothers within the neoliberal landscape, it also reveals a vast expanse of interdisciplinary knowledge regarding the subjectivities and material realities of mothers in a neoliberal age.

In order to explicate some methods in which mothering and neoliberalism can be further theorized, I will borrow from Hilgers and define three primary approaches to neoliberalism thus far: governmentality, culturalist and systemic (Hilgers 352). In the culturalist approach, "we treat neoliberalism as a cultural formation, a set of cultural meanings and practices related to the constitution of proper personhood, markets and the state" (Kingfisher and Maskovsky 120). Indeed, the concept of culture as a set of bounded practices has been subject to sustained critique.[22] Thus, identifying culture as a formation rather than a homogenized system is crucial to this approach. A culturalist perspective investigates how neoliberalism is altering our understandings of self, life, social relationships, and material realities thereby incorporating analysis of lifestyle, institutions, economic structures, symbols, and intergenerational relations.[23] Several authors in this volume have incorporated elements of a culturalist approach in which new economic, political, and social formations have altered understandings and practices of mothering (Anderson and Moore, Baker, Bryan, Esnard, and O'Brien Hallstein, in volume). In many ways, the increasing financialization of society has created an arbitrary postmodern realm in which realities are fragmented and meanings unclear thus potentially altering subjectivities and social relations (Castañeda and Searcy, in volume). However, the degree to which such fragmented identities are increasingly coalescing into collectivities must equally be considered (Reimer, and Takeshita, in volume). Such an approach is particularly conducive to ethnographic research in which the homogenous processes of neoliberalism can be located in specific spaces and places. This approach has been especially effective in highlighting the interconnections between culture and mothering subjectivity.

By positioning such research within specific localities, the particularities in which this potentially overarching concept of "neoliberal culture" can be further explored. The authors of this volume have located their research within particular locations to trace the historical, political, economic, and social trajectories of material and subjective change for mothers. However, these authors do not utilize singularly a culturalist approach. One of the expansive elements of this volume is that all of the authors utilize various aspects of interdisciplinary knowledge to illuminate their localized discussions of mothering. Thus, cultural texts and maternal subjectivities are analyzed within the larger spaces of political economy.

Another approach to understanding neoliberalism is through an analysis of governing structures. The governmentality approach draws inspiration from Foucault, particularly his 1978/79 lectures regarding biopolitics (Hilgers 358). Within the governmentality approach, neoliberalism is understood in terms of practice. How do technologies of neoliberal subjectivity encourage individuals to become self-optimizing subjects within a market economy based on competition? Additionally, how do technologies of subjugation regulate populations to ensure such optimal productivity?[24] Several of the authors in the volume utilize elements of a governmentality approach to better understand how mothers identify themselves within this individualized self-actualizing narrative, but also how they are identified by the state and other governing systems (Song and Lee, and Wilkins, in volume). How do such identifications lead to particularizing public policies that delineate "deserving" versus "undeserving" citizens in terms of specific supports? And how are such "undeserving" citizens made into appropriate self-optimizing neoliberal subjects through forms of regulation? (Bayraktar, in volume) Despite the optimistic neoliberal narrative of equality for all who can accomplish such self-maximizing behaviors and dispositions, such research is imperative in revealing the structural elements of sexism and racism implicit within such universalism (Bloch and Taylor, in volume). Ethnography is essential in preventing overarching rationalities such as governmentality to become decontextualized. By revealing the specifics in which governance occurs, some of the mystique of the neoliberal market can thus be explicated thereby losing its mythical persuasion. How do mothers identify themselves and how do they work and negotiate their lives and positionalities within these governance frameworks? Far more research connecting mothering to structures of neoliberal governance is required. The mythical image of the independent self-optimizing tax payer completely eliminates all aspects of mothering and communality. Given the centrality of mothering within neoliberalism in terms of social reproduction *and* production, it is imperative that governmentality theorists directly centralize further discussion of mothering.

A third approach to studies of neoliberalism is systemic. Within this approach, neoliberalism is described as "a system or structure constituting a network or relations between different positions in the social space" (Hilgers 355). Within this paradigm it is assumed there are certain patterns internal to the development of a neoliberal society.[25] Specifically, in certain industrialized nations, how did a shift from a nationalized Fordist manufacturing economy to a global service economy occur? What are the structures and patterns of capital accumulation and how have such patterns resulted in the "absurdity" of over-production (Marx and Engels 15) in the midst of famine? How has capital become so disarticulated from its productive source that we are now in the midst of an arbitrary financialized world in which entire cities of investment are built with no residents (Bar-On)? Several authors in this volume have illustrated through macro-level systemic political-economic theorizing the material consequences of neoliberalism on mothers' lives (Albanese et al., Breton, Chelliah, Vandenbeld Giles, and Winkler, in volume).

CONCLUSION

Mothering in the Age of Neoliberalism creates a vital starting point—a point from which future interdisciplinary research within the specific realm of mothering and neoliberalism can be centralized. Establishing mothers as pivotal to the neoliberal paradigm within academic discourse is a first step toward centralizing a discussion of mothering within the globalized political-economic realm. Mothers need to be framed beyond a dualistic maternalist caregiving or worker paradigm. A holistic approach integrates mothers as central to the neoliberal world. In this way, discursive legitimation leads to material change.

Recognizing the need for an integrative and holistic approach, while the book is divided into four main sections (Labour, State, Family, Activism), many of the chapters interweave their themes creating a diverse blend of analysis. The section on Labour includes a Marxist analysis of declining industrialization producing neoliberal forms of flexible labour alongside discussion of affective labour in care work. In the section on the State, the analysis includes discussion of the eroding welfare state alongside increasing biopower. The section on Family incorporates neoconservative religious ideology alongside nuclear-family based state policies. And finally, the section on Maternal Activism incorporates narratives of appropriating essentialized maternalism alongside mothers fighting for economic justice. While recognition of the dire consequences of neoliberal failures toward mothers is required and must be prioritized to demand material change, I end the collection not with despair, but rather with hope. Thus, the final three chapters (Ogunyankin, Schulz, and Shadaan, in volume) focus on the strength and resiliency of mothers around the world who are fighting for their rights, and the rights and livelihoods of their families.

The chaos of incorporating diverse methodologies and disciplinary perspectives is embraced within this volume, illuminating the potential of expanding beyond categorized or inscribed academic boundaries and allowing connections to be made through a more expansive knowledge basis. Given the range of disciplinary backgrounds, maintaining author voice was a priority in the editing process. Diverse methodologies and interpretations all provide critical and crucial analysis, thus illustrating the embracing of difference within the larger framework of mothering and neoliberalism.

By situating the material realities of mothers' lives within historical, political, economic, and social trajectories, this has the capacity to destabilize and de-legitimate the neoliberal narrative of mystical markets. While a discussion of discursive neoliberal maternal subjectivity and cultural formations are essential, such theorizing must always remain grounded within localized political-economic material realities. Equally, the power of systemic theorizing is lost should it become disconnected with the everyday subjectivities and experiences of mothering. In this way bringing together mothering and neoliberalism creates an imperative space in which the perceived dominant de-politicising neoliberal narrative can be grounded and thus destabilized. The homogenizing spectre of "equality" can be made accountable, and the massive failures of neoliberalism toward mothers can be made explicit.

NOTES

[1] For popular references regarding the neoliberal ascent of women see Armstrong; Mundy; and Sandberg

[2] For research regarding access to medicines and UN initiatives for maternal and child health see Forman and Kohler; and Toure et. al.

[3] I am using the term "positionality" in reference to Linda Alcoff's discussion in "Cultural Feminism versus Post-Structuralism: The Identity Crisis in Feminist Theory." Alcoff uses the term "positionality" to indicate how gendered subjectivities must be contextualized within particular social, historical, political, economic, and racialized frameworks. Yet, these frameworks are not determinant since women are also active subjects within such patriarchal paradigms.

[4] For reading regarding women and globalization see Blossfeld and Hofmeister; Cohen and Brodie; González and Seidler; Kelly, Bayes, Hawkesworth and Young; Miles; Mohanty; Mutari and Figart; and Razavi.

[5] See Durkheim; and Parsons

[6] For further reading regarding the deconstruction of biological motherhood see Chodorow; Firestone; Ortner; Rich; and Rosaldo and Lamphere

[7] See Ainsworth; Bowlby; Freud; and Parsons

[8] See Levi-Strauss; and Malinowski

[9] For further reading regarding new reproductive technologies see Franklin; Ragone; Strathern; and Thompson

[10] For further reading regarding transnational kinship see Colen; Friedman and Schultermandl; Gailey; Howell; Kim; and Modell

[11] For further reading regarding deconstructing biology see Bamford; Carsten; Collier and Yanagisako; Counts & Counts; Thorne and Yalom; Weismantel; Weston; and Yanagisako and Delaney

[12] For further reading regarding feminist political economy see Bezanson; Bezanson and Luxton; Braedley and Luxton; Brodie and Bakker; and Connell

[13] For further reading regarding transnational feminism see Dean; Fraser; and Mohanty

[14] For further reading regarding Intensive Mothering see Douglas and Michaels; Hays; Horwitz; Maushart; Morris; O'Reilly; Rubenstein; Thurer; Walkerdine and Lucey; and Warner

[15] See Taylor, Layne and Wozniak

[16] See Braedley and Luxton; Jenson, Hagen and Reddy; and Razavi

[17] See Baines, Evans and Neysmith; and Fine

[18] For further reading regarding globalization and care work see Chavkin and Maher; Ehrenreich and Hochschild; and Parreñas

[19] For further reading regarding anthropology and mothering see Craven; Davis-Floyd; Ginsburg and Rapp; Jordan; Kitzinger; Rothman; and Walks and McPherson

[20] For Demeter Press titles see Friedman and Calixte, O'Brien Hallstein and O'Reilly; O'Reilly; Reimer and Sahagian, Vandenbeld Giles; Walks and McPherson; and Warner

[21] See Whitecross and Winterbottom for reference to *The Shock Doctrine* 2009 documentary film

[22] For further reading regarding the deconstruction of "culture" see Abu-Lughod; Clifford and Marcus; Gupta and Ferguson; and Rosaldo and Lamphere

[23] For further reading regarding culturalist approaches to neoliberalism see Boltanski and Chiapello; Comaroff and Comaroff; Friedman, *Cultural Identity and Global Process*; Muehlebach; and Sennett

[24] For further reading regarding governmentality approaches to neoliberalism see Agamben; Foucault; Ferguson; Lazzarato; Li; Ong; Rose; and Song

[25] For further reading regarding systemic approaches to neoliberalism see Arrighi; Harvey; and Wallerstein

WORKS CITED

Abu-Lughod, Lila. *Writing Women's Worlds: Bedouin Stories.* Berkeley: University of California Press, 2008 (1993). Print.

Agamben, Giorgio. "Form-of-Life." *Radical Thoughts in Italy: A Potential Politics.* Eds. Paolo Virno and Michael Hardt. Minneapolis, MN: University of Minnesota Press, 1996. 151-156. Print.

Ainsworth, Mary D. Salter. "Attachment Theory and Its Utility in Cross-Cultural Research." *Culture and Infancy.* New York: Academic Press, Inc, 1977. 49-67. Print.

Alcoff, Linda. "Cultural Feminism versus Post-Structuralism: The Identity Crisis in Feminist Theory." *Signs* 13.3 (Spring 1988): 405-436. Print.

Armstrong, Sally. *Ascent of Women: Our Turn, Our Way—a Remarkable Story of Worldwide Change.* Toronto, ON: Random House Canada, 2013. Print.

Arrighi, Giovanni. *The Long Twentieth Century: Money, Power, and the Origins of Our Times.* New York, NY: Verso, 2002 (1994). Print.

Ayres, Jeffrey. "Framing Collective Action Against Neoliberalism: The Case of the 'Anti- Globalization' Movement." *Journal of World-Systems Research* x.1 (Winter 2004): 11–34. Special Issue: Global Social Movements Before and After 9-11. Print.

Baines, Carol, Patricia Evans and Sheila Neysmith. *Women's Caring: Feminist Perspectives on Social Welfare.* Toronto: McClelland & Stewart Inc., 1991. Print.

Bamford, Sandra. *Biology Unmoored: Melanesian Reflections on Life and Biotechnology.* Berkeley: University of California Press, 2007. Print.

Bar-On, Shachar. Producer. Lesley Stahl. Reporter. "China's Real Estate Bubble." *60 Minutes.* Aired March 3, 2013. Web.

Beck, Ulrich. *The Brave New World of Work.* Cambridge, UK: Polity Press, 2000. Print.

Bezanson, Kate. *Gender, the State, and Social Reproduction: Household Insecurity in Neo-liberal Times.* Toronto: University of Toronto Press, 2006. Print.

Bezanson, Kate and Meg Luxton. *Social Reproduction: Feminist Political Economy Challenges Neo-Liberalism.* Montreal and Kingston: McGill-Queen's University Press, 2006. Print.

Blossfeld, Hans-Peter and Heather Hofmeister. Eds. *Globalization, Uncertainty and Women's Careers: An International Comparison.* Northampton, Massachusetts: Edward Elgar Publishing Ltd., 2006. Print.

Boltanski, Luc and Eve Chiapello. *The New Spirit of Capitalism.* London and New York: Verso, 2005. Print.

Bowlby, John. *Attachment and Loss Vol 1: Attachment.* New York: Basic Books, 1969. Print.

Braedley, Susan and Meg Luxton. "Competing Philosophies: Neoliberalism and Challenges of Everyday Life." *Neoliberalism and Everyday Life.* Eds. Susan Braedley and Meg Luxton. Montreal and Kingston: McGill-Queen's University Press, 2010. 3-21. Print.

Brodie, Janine and Isabella Bakker. *Where Are the Women? Gender Equity, Budgets and Canadian Public Policy.* Ottawa, Canada: Canadian Centre for Policy Alternatives, 2008. Print.

Brown, Wendy. "Neo-liberalism and the End of Liberal Democracy." *Theory and Event* 7.1 (2003): 1-25. Web.

Carsten, Janet. Ed. *Cultures of Relatedness: Approaches to the Study of Kinship.* Cambridge: Cambridge University Press, 2000. Print.

Chavkin, Wendy and JaneMaree Maher. *The Globalization of Motherhood: Deconstructions and Reconstructions of Biology and Care.* New York, NY: Routledge, 2010. Print.

Chodorow, Nancy J. *The Reproduction of Mothering.* Berkeley: University of California Press, 1999 (1978). Print.

Clifford, James and George Marcus. Eds. *Writing Culture: The Poetics and Politics of Ethnography.* Berkeley: University of California Press, 1986. Print.

Cohen, Marjorie Griffen and Janine Brodie. Eds. *Remapping Gender in the New Global Order.* New York, NY: Routledge, 2007. Print.

Colen, Shellee. "Like a Mother to Them: Stratified Reproduction and West Indian Childcare Workers and Employers in New York." *Conceiving the New World Order: The Global Politics of Reproduction.* Eds. Faye Ginsburg and Rayna Rapp. Berkeley: University of California Press, 1995. 78-102. Print.

Collier, Jane and Sylvia Yanagisako Eds. *Gender and Kinship: Essays Toward a Unified Analysis.* Stanford: Stanford University Press, 1987. Print.

Comaroff, J. and L. Comaroff. "Millennial Capitalism: First Thoughts on a Second Coming." *Public Culture* 12.2 (2000): 291-343. Print.

Connell, Raewyn. *Confronting Equality: Gender, Knowledge and Global Change.* Cambridge, UK: Polity Press, 2011. Print.

Counts, D. and D. Counts. "Father's Water Equals Mother's Milk: The Conception of Parentage in Kaliai West New Guinea" *Mankind* 14.1 (1982): 46-56. Print.

Craven, Christa. *Pushing for Midwives: Homebirth Mothers and the Reproductive Rights Movement.* Philadelphia, Pennsylvania: Temple University Press, 2010. Print.

Crittenden, Ann. *The Price of Motherhood: Why the Most Important Job in the World Is Still the Least Valued.* New York: Metropolitan Books, 2001. Print.

Davis-Floyd, Robbie. *Birth as an American Rite of Passage.* Berkeley, California: University of California Press, 2003 (1992). Print.

Dean, Jodi. *Solidarity of Strangers: Feminism after Identity Politics.* Berkeley: University of California Press, 1996. Print.

Donner, Henrike. *Domestic Goddesses: Maternity, Globalization and Middle-Class Identity in Contemporary India.* Hampshire, England: Ashgate Publishing, 2008. Print.

Douglas, Susan J. and Meredith W. Michaels. *The Mommy Myth: The Idealization of Motherhood and How It Has Undermined Women.* New York: Free Press, a Division of Simon & Schuster, 2004. Print.

Durkheim, Emile. *The Division of Labour in Society.* London, England: Macmillan, 1984 (1893). Print.

Edgar, Stacey. *Global Girlfriends: How One Mom Made It Her Business to Help Women in Poverty Worldwide.* New York: St. Martin's Griffin, 2011. Print.

Ehrenreich, Barbara and Arlie Hochschild. Eds. *Global Woman: Nannies, Maids and Sex Workers in the New Economy.* New York, NY: Henry Holt and Company, 2002. Print.

Ferguson, James. *The Anti-Politics Machine: Development, Depoliticization and Bureaucratic Power.* Cambridge, UK: Cambridge University Press, 1990. Print.

Fine, Michael. *A Caring Society? Care and the Dilemmas of Human Service in the 21st Century.* New York, NY: Palgrave Macmillan, 2007. Print.

Firestone, Shulamith. *The Dialectic of Sex: The Case for Feminist Revolution.* New York: Farrar, Straus and Giroux, 1970. Print.

Florida, Richard. *The Rise of the Creative Class.* New York: Basic Books, 2012 (2002). Print.

Forman, Lisa and Jillian Clare Kohler. Eds. *Access to Medicines as a Human Right: Implications for Pharmaceutical Industry Responsibility.* Toronto, ON: University of Toronto Press, 2012. Print.

Foucault, Michel. *The Birth of Biopolitics. Lectures at the Collège de France 1978-79.* New York: Palgrave Macmillan, 2008. Print.

— *Discipline and Punish: The Birth of the Prison.* New York: Vintage Press, 1979 (1975). Print.

— *Technologies of the Self: A Seminar with Michel Foucault.* Eds. Luther Martin, Huck Gutman, and Patrick Hutton. Amherst: The University of Massachusetts Press, 1988. Print.

Franklin, Sarah. "Deconstructing Desperateness: The Social Construction of Infertility in Popular Representations of New Reproductive Technologies." *The New Reproductive Technologies.* Eds. Maureen McNeil, Ian Varcoe and Steven Yearley New York: St. Martin's Press, 1990. 200-229. Print.

Fraser, Nancy. *Fortunes of Feminism: From State-Managed Capitalism to Neoliberal Crisis.* London, UK: Verso, 2013. Print.

Freud, Sigmund. *Civilization and Its Discontents.* London: Hogarth Press, 1957. Print.

Friedman, May and Shana Calixte. *Mothering and Blogging: The Radical Act of the MommyBlog.* Bradford, ON: Demeter Press, 2009. Print.

Friedman, May and Silvia Schultermandl. Eds. *Growing Up Transnational: Identity and Kinship in a Global Era.* Toronto: University of Toronto Press, 2011. Print.

Friedman, Milton. *Capitalism and Freedom.* Chicago: University of Chicago Press, 1962. Print.

Friedman, Jonathan. *Cultural Identity and Global Process.* London: Sage, 1994. Print.

Gailey, Christine. "Ideologies of Motherhood and Kinship in U.S. Adoption." *Ideologies and Technologies of Motherhood: Race, Class, Sexuality, Nationalism.* Eds. Heléna Ragoné and France Twine. New York: Routledge, 2000. 11-55. Print.

Ginsburg, Faye and Rayna Rapp. Eds. *Conceiving the New World Order: The Global Politics of Reproduction.* Berkeley, California: University of California Press, 1995. Print.

González, Ana Marta and Victor J. Seidler. *Gender Identities in a Globalized World.* Amherst, New York: Humanity Books, 2008. Print.

Gupta, Akhil and James Ferguson. Eds. *Culture, Power, Place: Explorations in Critical Anthropology.* Durham: Duke University Press, 1997. Print.

Harvey, David. *A Brief History of Neoliberalism.* Oxford: Oxford University Press, 2005. Print.

Hayek, Freidrich. *The Fatal Conceit: The Errors of Socialism.* Chicago: University of Chicago Press, 1988. Print.

Hays, Sharon. *The Cultural Contradictions of Motherhood.* New Haven: Yale University Press, 1996. Print.

— "Why Can't a Mother Be More Like a Businessman?" *Maternal Theory: Essential Readings.* Ed. Andrea O'Reilly. Toronto: Demeter Press, 2007. 408-430. Print.

Hilgers, Mathieu. "The Three Anthropological Approaches to Neoliberalism." UNESCO. Oxford, UK: Blackwell Publishing Ltd., 2011. 351-363. Print.

Horwitz, Erika. "Resistance as a Site of Empowerment: The Journey Away from Maternal Sacrifice." *Mother Outlaws.* Ed. Andrea O'Reilly. Toronto: Women's Press, an imprint of Canadian Scholars' Press Inc., 2004. 43-57. Print.

Howell, Signe. "Kinning: The Creation of Life Trajectories in Transnational Adoptive Families." *Journal of the Royal Anthropological Institute* 9.3 (2003): 465-484, 2003.

Jenson, Jane, Elisabeth Hagen and Ceallaigh Reddy. Eds. *Feminization of the Labor Force: Paradoxes and Promises.* New York, NY: Oxford University Press, 1988. Print.

Jordan, Brigitte. *Birth in Four Cultures: A Cross-Cultural Investigation of Childbirth in Yucatan, Holland, Sweden and the United States.* Montreal: Eden Press, 1978. Print.

Kawash, Samira. "New Directions in Motherhood Studies." *Signs* 36.4 (Summer 2011): 969- 1003. Print.

Kelly, Rita Mae, Jane H. Bayes, Mary E. Hawkesworth and Brigitte Young. *Gender, Globalization and Democratization.* Oxford, England: Rowman and Littlefield Publishers Inc., 2001. Print.

Keynes, John Maynard. *The General Theory of Employment, Interest and Money.* London: Macmillan, 1973. Print.

Kim, E. "Wedding Citizenship and Culture: Korean Adoptees and the Global Family of Korea." *Social Text* 74, 21.1 (2003): 57-81. Print.

Kingfisher, Catherine and Jeff Maskovsky. "The Limits of Neoliberalism." *Critique of Anthropology* 28.2 (2008): 115-126. Print.

Kitzinger, Sheila. *Ourselves as Mothers: The Universal Experience of Motherhood.* New York: Addison-Wesley Publishing Company, 1995 (1992). Print.

Klein, Naomi. *The Shock Doctrine: The Rise of Disaster Capitalism.* Toronto: Knopf Canada, 2007. Print.

Lazzarato, Maurizio. "Neoliberalism in Action: Inequality, Insecurity and the Reconstitution of the Social." *Theory, Culture and Society* 26 (2009): 109-133. Print.

Lévi-Strauss, Claude. *The Elementary Structures of Kinship.* Boston, MA: Beacon Press, 1969 (1949). Print.

Li, Tania. *The Will to Improve: Governmentality, Development and the Practice of Politics.* Durham: Duke University Press, 2007. Print.

Malinowski, Bronislaw. *Argonauts of the Western Pacific: An Account of Native Enterprise and Adventure in the Archipelagoes of Melanesia, New Guinea.* London: R. Routledge and Kegan, 1922. Print.

Marx, Karl and Frederick Engels. *The Communist Manifesto.* New York, NY: International Publishers Co., 2007 (1948). Print.

Maushart, Susan. *The Mask of Motherhood: How Becoming a Mother Changes Everything and Why We Pretend It Doesn't.* New York: The New Press, 1999. Print.

Miles, Angela. Ed. *Women in a Globalizing World: Transforming Equality, Development, Diversity and Peace.* Toronto, Canada: INANNA Publications and Education Inc., 2013. Print.

von Mises, Ludwig. *Human Action: A Treatise on Economics.* U.S.: Yale University Press, 1949. Print.

Modell, Judith. *Kinship with Strangers: Adoption and Interpretations of Kinship in American Culture.* Berkeley: University of California Press, 1994. Print.

Mohanty, Chandra Talpade. *Feminism without Borders: Decolonizing Theory, Practicing Solidarity.* Durham, NC: Duke University Press, 2003. Print.

Morris, Anne. "Too Attached To Attachment Theory?" *Theorising and Representing Maternal Realities.* Eds. Marie Porter and Julie Kelso. UK: Cambridge Scholars Publishing, 2008. 107-118. Print.

Muehlebach, Andrea. "*Complexio Oppositorum*: Notes on the Left in Neoliberal Italy." *Public Culture* 21.3 (2009): 495-515. Print.

— *The Moral Neoliberal: Welfare and Citizenship in Italy.* Chicago, Ill: University of Chicago Press, 2012. Print.

Mundy, Liza. *The Richer Sex: How the New Majority of Female Bread-

winners Is Transforming Sex, Love, and Family. New York, NY: Simon and Schuster, 2012. Print.

Mutari, Ellen and Deborah M. Figart. Eds. *Women and the Economy: A Reader.* Armonk, New York: M.E. Sharpe, 2003. Print.

O'Brien, Martin and Sue Penna. *Theorizing Welfare: Enlightenment and Modern Society* London: Sage, 1998. Print.

O'Brien Hallstein, Lynn and Andrea O'Reilly. *Academic Motherhood in a Post-Second Wave Context: Challenges, Strategies and Possibilities.* Bradford, ON: Demeter Press, 2012. Print.

Ong, Aihwa. *Neoliberalism as Exception: Mutations in Citizenship and Sovereignty.* Durham: Duke University Press, 2006. Print.

O'Reilly, Andrea. *Rocking the Cradle: Thoughts on Motherhood, Feminism and the Possibility of Empowered Mothering.* Toronto: Demeter Press, 2006. Print.

Ortner, Sherry B. "Is Female to Male as Nature Is to Culture?" *Woman, Culture and Society.* Eds. Michelle Zimbalist Rosaldo and Louise Lamphere. Stanford: Stanford University Press, 1974. 67-87. Print.

Parreñas, Rhacel Salazar. *Servants of Globalization: Women, Migration and Domestic Work.* Stanford, California: Stanford University Press, 2001. Print.

Parsons, Talcott. *Family, Socialization, and Interaction Process.* Glencoe, Ill: Free Press, 1955. Print.

Ragone, H. *Surrogate Motherhood: Conception in the Heart.* Boulder: Westview Press, 1994. Print.

Razavi, Shahra. Ed. *The Gendered Impacts of Liberalization: Towards "Embedded Liberalism?"* New York, NY: Routledge, 2009. Print.

Reimer, Vanessa and Sarah Sahagian. Eds. *Mother of Invention: How Our Mothers Influenced Us as Feminist Academics and Activists.* Bradford, ON: Demeter Press, Fall 2013. Print.

Rich, Adrienne. *Of Woman Born: Motherhood as Experience and Institution.* New York: W.W. Norton & Company, Inc., 1986 (1976). Print.

Rosaldo, Michelle and Louise Lamphere. Eds. *Woman, Culture and Society.* Stanford: Stanford University Press, 1974. Print.

Rose, Nikolas. *Powers of Freedom: Reframing Political Thought.* Cambridge, UK: Cambridge University Press, 1999. Print.

Rothman, Barbara Katz. *Recreating Motherhood: Ideology and Technology in a Patriarchal Society.* New York: W.W. Norton & Company, 1989. Print.

Rubenstein, Carin. *The Sacrificial Mother: Escaping the Trap of Self-Denial.* New York: Hyperion, 1998. Print.

Sandberg, Sheryl. *Lean In: Women, Work, and the Will to Lead.* New York, NY: Alfred A.Knopf, 2013. Print.

Scheper-Hughes, Nancy. *Death without Weeping: The Violence of Everyday Life in Brazil.* Berkeley: University of California Press, 1993. Print.

—"Culture, Scarcity, and Maternal Thinking: Maternal Detachment and Infant Survival in a Brazilian Shantytown." *Ethos* 13.4 (1985): 291-317. Print.

Schneider, David. *American Kinship: A Cultural Account,* 2nd edition. Chicago: University of Chicago Press, 1980 (1968). Print.

— *A Critique of the Study of Kinship.* Ann Arbor: University of Michigan Press, 1984. Print.

Sennett, R. *The Culture of the New Capitalism.* New Haven and London: Yale University Press, 2006. Print.

Simon-Kumar, Rachel. "'Productive' Reproducers: The Political Identity of Mothering in Contemporary India." *Mothering and Poverty. Journal of the Association for Research on Mothering* 11.2 (2009): 143-152. Print.

Smith, Adam. *The Wealth of Nations.* West Sussex, UK: Capstone Publishing Ltd., 2010 (1779). Print.

Song, Jesook. *South Koreans in the Debt Crisis: The Creation of a Neoliberal Welfare Society.* Durham, NC: Duke University Press, 2009. Print.

Steger, Manfred and Ravi Roy. *Neoliberalism: A Very Short Introduction.* Oxford: Oxford University Press, 2010. Print.

Strathern, Marilyn. *Reproducing the Future: Essays on Anthropology, Kinship and the New Reproductive Technologies.* Manchester: Manchester University Press, 1992. Print.

Swift, Karen and Marilyn Callahan. *At Risk: Social Justice in Child Welfare and Other Human Services.* Toronto: University of Toronto Press, 2009. Print.

Taylor, Janelle, Linda Layne and Danielle Wozniak. Eds. *Consuming Motherhood.* New Jersey: Rutgers University Press, 2004. Print.

Thompson, Charis. "Strategic Naturalizing: Kinship in an Infertility Clinic." *Relative Values: Reconfiguring Kinship Studies.* Eds. Sarah Franklin and Susan McKinnon. Durham: Duke University Press, 2001. 175-202. Print.

Thorne, Barrie and Marilyn Yalom Eds. *Rethinking the Family: Some Feminist Questions.* New York: Longman Inc, 1982. Print.

Thurer, Shari L. *The Myths of Motherhood.* New York: Houghton Mifflin Company, 1994. Print.

Toure, Kadidiatou, Rotimi Sankore, Shyama Kuruvilla, Elisa Scolaro, Flavia Bustreo and Babatunde Osotimehin. "Positioning Women's and Children's Health in African Union Policy-Making Analysis." *Globalization and Health* 8:3 (2012): 1-15. Web.

Tsing, Anna Lowenhaupt. *Friction: An Ethnography of Global Connection.* Princeton, New Jersey: Princeton University Press, 2011. Print.

Vandenbeld Giles, Melinda. "Educating Our Children for the Future? The Shifting Tides of Maternal Pedagogy." *Mothering, Education, Maternal Pedagogies and Motherhood Studies. JMI (Journal of the Motherhood Initiative for Research and Community Involvement)* 4.1 (July 2013): 108-120. Print.

— "From 'Need' to 'Risk': The Neoliberal Construction of the 'Bad' Mother." *Mothers and the Economy: The Economics of Mothering. JMI (Journal of the Motherhood Initiative for Research and Community Involvement)* 3.1 (July 2012): 112-133. Print.

— "Living in Isolation: Motel Families in Ontario and the Neoliberal Social/Built/Physical Environment" *Mothering and the Environment. JMI (Journal of the Motherhood Initiative for Research and Community Involvement)* 2.1 (July 2011): 194-212. Print.

— "Feminism as Practice: Valuing a Feminist Motherline in the Age of Innovation." *Mother of Invention: How Our Mothers Influenced Us as Feminist Academics and Activists.* Eds. Vanessa Reimer and Sarah Sahagian. Bradford, ON: Demeter Press, Fall 2013. 36-47. Print.

Walkerdine, Valerie and Helen Lucey. *Democracy in the Kitchen: Regulating Mothers and Socialising Daughters.* London: Virago Press, 1989. Print.

Walks, Michelle and Naomi McPherson. *An Anthropology of Mothering.* Bradford, ON: Demeter Press, 2011. Print.

Wallerstein, Immanuel. *Historical Capitalism.* London, England: Verso, 2011 (1983). Print.

Warner, Judith. "The Motherhood Religion." *Maternal Theory: Essential*

Readings. Ed. Andrea O'Reilly. Toronto: Demeter Press, 2007. 705-725. Print.

— *Perfect Madness: Motherhood in the Age of Anxiety.* New York: Riverhead Books, a member of Penguin Group, 2005. Print.

Weismantel, M. "Making Kin: Kinship Theory and Zumbagua Adoptions." *American Ethnologist* 22.4 (1995): 685-704. Print.

Weston, Kath. *Families We Choose: Lesbians, Gays, Kinship.* New York: Columbia University Press, 1991. Print.

Whitecross, Matt and Michael Winterbottom. Directors. Naomi Klein. Writer. *The Shock Doctrine.* 2009 documentary film.

Yanagisako, Sylvia and Carol Delaney Eds. *Naturalizing Power: Essays in Feminist Cultural Analysis.* New York: Routledge, 1995. Print.

Section I: Mothering and Neoliberal Labour

Flexible Labour and Care Work

1.

Multiplying Mothers

Migration and the Work of Mothering in Canada and the Philippines

CATHERINE BRYAN

INTRODUCTION

The neoliberal "crisis of care" has produced a globalized space in which migrant mothers have shouldered the burden of eroding state support for social reproduction. Migrant mothering necessitates a new kind of flexibility vis-à-vis the manual, physical, emotional, and psychological work of motherhood, one that must take into account multiple time zones, competing schedules, and the uneven distribution of technology and resources. This chapter explores the increasingly globalized nature of mothering through the shared efforts of a group of women, migrants and non-migrants alike, whose lives and relationships have been significantly shaped over time by migration.

In many ways, this is the story of the Global Care Chain (Hochschild) as it was articulated nearly 25 years ago by Arlie Hochschild, in which the care labour of one woman is passed to another and another across circuits of migration and gendered lines of affinal responsibility. Yet, reflecting increasingly diverse pathways of migration and the ever evolving availability of communication technology, their labour is not simply transferred from sister to sister, daughter to mother. Instead, as their lives are organized according to logics both local and global, the daily labour of mothering and practices of motherhood become profoundly layered across time and space. Rather than merely symptomatic, this layering emerges as one of the central defining characteristics of their work as mothers. In this way, this chapter offers an expansion and nuancing of the Global Care Chain[1] thesis.

Situated practices and hierarchies offer insight into global dynamics (Glick Schiller). Given that the inherent connections between the local and global are best explored through the particulars of everyday life (Abu-Lughod), the chapter maps the quotidian and localized experiences of a group of women, all belonging to one family, as they navigate the temporal and physical displacement and reconfiguration of their mothering. This analysis is rooted in a particular approach to political economy that emphasizes the social and relational processes of capital accumulation—processes that despite their globalized qualities, are felt in immediate and visceral ways. It is this immediacy, this intimacy—embodied in the disparate actions of these women, reconfigured through migration, and transmitted through technology—that this paper aims to capture. What are the visceral and affective dynamics of neoliberal imperatives, and what are the resulting detrimental consequences for mothers within these migratory paradigms? Drawing on in-depth life history interviews, time allocation surveys, and participant observation in Manitoba, Ontario, and the Philippines (2012-2013), this is achieved through a textual oscillation between the immediately local and the ever-present global—relative positions occupied simultaneously by each of the women.

WHO IS DOING THE CARE WORK?

Women's unpaid labour as mothers and caregivers has long been the focus of feminist scholars seeking to better understand women's roles and positioning within societies and families.[2] However, over the past twenty years of increasing neoliberalization, this routinely localized labour (embedded in the daily activities of cooking, cleaning, and care) has become diffuse as mothers—responding to new social and economic realities—meet their reproductive responsibilities in ways that are as much globally, as they are locally derived. In the West, and in various post-colonial contexts such as the Philippines, the scholarship on migration and care labour has effectively interrogated women's shifting subjectivities and reproductive roles in relation to the processes of capital accumulation.[3] Reflecting correlated yet diverse neoliberal outcomes, new patterns of survival and care develop as people and families engage in a range of previously unimagined livelihood strategies.[4]

For a significant number of families in the Philippines, these strategies have culminated in domestic care labour migration as Filipino women, unable to secure local employment, draw on the gendered and increasingly racialized scripts of globalized care work in order to find work abroad (Barber). This move, now spanning a period of over 30 years, signals the overwhelming failure of the neoliberal state toward mothers. The increase in care labour migration is a direct result of failed capital investment and short-sighted structural adjustments. However, even more insidiously, it is an individual response to the uncertainties generated by neoliberal policy and practice producing a re-signification and reorganization of social relations within a globalized, neoliberal paradigm that is detrimental for mothers and children.

Concurrently, within the Philippines, there are a number of historical precursors to domestic care labour migration.[5] These examples of much more localized domestic labour migration provide insight into the infrastructure of care labour export, and also into the economy of care that has emerged in the absence of so many migrant mothers—an economy of care that disperses reproductive work between differently situated kin-members. Even as it draws on pre-existing structures of kinship, reciprocity, and obligation, this current iteration remains unique as the work of motherhood has, for so many, been reconstituted within the circuits of globalized capital, and the labour of mothers so dispersed between people and places and transnationally.

NEOLIBERAL RESTRUCTURING AND MIGRATION

The women at the centre of this work are members of one family. Judith, Ivy, Edith, and Maria are sisters. Judith and Edith live in the Philippines; Ivy and Maria in Canada. Their brother, RJ, lives in the Philippines with their mother, June, while their other brother, Edward, lives and works in Dubai. His wife, Kate, serves as primary caregiver for the family's youngest members. June's family traces its lineage to the shores of a small island—the site of one of the Philippine's most active volcanoes. June left the island in the mid-1940s when her parents and grandparents moved to the mainland.

It is from the mainland, thirty years later, that June and her husband would begin their lives as overseas domestic workers. Their decision was predicated on a convergence of pressures and emerging realties. In 1965, the volcano erupted, beginning a 12-year period of sustained volcanic activity and considerable social and economic upheaval. Their traditional means of subsistence disrupted, islanders and mainlanders became, for the first time, entirely dependent on the requirements of capital for their survival. At the national level, the 1960s saw increased involvement between the Philippine state and foreign and international financial institutions, notably the International Monetary Fund and the World Bank. In the 1970s, aided by rising world commodity prices, debt rescheduling, and IMF-sponsored stabilization programs, the country saw considerable economic growth. This, however, was accompanied by massive debt accumulation (Bello).

By 1981, the Philippines owed $21 billion dollars in foreign debt, and a new set of structural adjustment programs were initiated. Emphasizing economic liberalization, retrenchment of publicly funded services, and the privatization of national industry (including the sale of the state-owned water utility) (Bello), these programs reconfigured the relationship of the state to the market, and were heralded by the Philippine state as the means by which economic growth and development would be achieved. Of course, the history of the Philippines over the last fifty years (but particularly since the 1980s) has demonstrated otherwise. Nationally, almost half of the population lives on less than US $2 a day, and while the county's richest 10 percent holds over 40 percent of total income earned, the poorest accounts for less than 2 percent (Tyner). The country's debt, despite the imposition of an aggressive repayment schedule, continues to grow (Briones).

The purported prosperity of the 1970s never reached the barangay where June, her parents, and eventually her children would live. Instead, the area would be transformed by labour export policy—an attempt by the Philippine state to redress widespread unemployment and poverty, while doing nothing about social and economic disparity. Faced with the costs of feeding, clothing, and educating their six children but no local employment, June and her husband left the Philippines for Greece in the mid-1980s. They staggered their departures. June left first, following the growing number of Filipino women "deployed abroad" to work as domestic workers. A year later, she negotiated a position for her husband with her employer. She was the household's housekeeper; he was the gardener. Their children in the care of her mother, June and her husband remained in Greece until the graduation of their two eldest daughters from university. At that time, Judith and Ivy would assume responsibility for the family—their own children, their siblings, and their nieces and nephews. Judith would fulfill her role from the Philippines; Ivy, from Canada.

Almost 70 years after June's initial arrival on the mainland and 20 years after her return from Greece, very little in the barangay has changed but everything is different. In 2013, only a handful of formal employment opportunities exist in the town and only a small percentage of the population has managed to secure local income. In addition to these, less formalized forms of work are available. About 100 young men drive tricycles (public transportation). There are several *sari sari* stores (small scale family-run convenience stores where household products are sold for a small profit). And a number of women work as domestic labourers, often circulating between local households. These women cook, clean, do laundry, and provide multifaceted care, ranging from child- and elder-care to grooming and massage services. They are, perhaps, the least explicitly mobile in the barangay, their movement restricted to the town and surrounding area, but they are inextricably connected to the processes of globalization and neoliberalization; (Hochschild) they care for the dependents of migrants and their earnings are generated in globalized labour markets.

Despite the lack of paid work available locally, the barangay has grown; it has become, so to speak, developed: the palm nipa huts have been replaced with concrete houses; the mud roads have been paved. There is an elementary school. A community centre has been constructed with a basketball court and spectators' balcony. A small grotto has been built adjacent to the chapel. The barangay hall has been renovated. Prosperous in appearance, this incongruity is a typical one within the Philippines as the money required for these developments (and similar ones throughout the country) is earned abroad. The town is decorated with plaques referencing that reality. Listing the names of countless absent benefactors, the plaques reinforce the notion that opportunity, indeed, resides elsewhere. Many of the town's residences, eager to access the benefits of globalized capitalism while desperate to lessen its sting, engage in some kind of labour migration. Some travel back and forth to larger neighbouring towns, others have gone to Manila, and others to near-by provinces in search of factory work. A greater number, still, work outside of the Philippines.

MIGRATING MOTHERS (AND THOSE WHO MOTHER IN THEIR ABSENCE)

Kate's Story

In 2007, Kate, a 24-year-old university graduate, arrived in Taiwan to work on an assembly line in an electronics factory. Sometimes they would work seven days a week for weeks on end, beginning early in the morning and finishing late at night, but she liked it, she assured me: they were paid overtime. It was better than the similar position she had held in a neighbouring province in the Philippines where the work had been just as hard, the hours just as long, but pay insufficient to meet her needs and those of her family. By 2013, she had already spent four years in Taiwan and one year in Dubai. Life in Dubai, however, had been difficult, the conditions of her labour precarious and her wages low, and she had returned to the Philippines with the intention of going back to Taiwan. When we met, she was waiting to hear back from her Taiwanese employer. Once her contract was renewed, she would return to her life as an Overseas Foreign Worker (OFW).

In the small rural barangay of her in-law's in the Philippines, Kate's time and labour follows rhythms and patterns predicated on both the intimately present and the physically absent. Her day begins at 4am when she wakes up and makes her way to the family's laptop. The wireless signal is strongest at the desk under the window by the front door, and so most online activity takes place in that area of the house. In Dubai, it is one in the morning, where Kate's husband lies on his bed, a heavy arm resting on his pillow. His roommates are asleep; he is tired from staying awake, from waiting, after a long day of work. He watches his wife type a greeting.

While Kate is not a care labourer in the sense typically invoked in the feminist literature on women's migration, she has assumed a role of primary caregiver, of "mother", in relation to both her immediate kin and her in-laws. However, her role is constituted differently within each family-group; her waged labour in Taiwan (and later in Dubai) supports the reproductive efforts of her immediate family, while her unwaged labour in the household of her in-laws compensates for the absence of her husband and his sisters. She is the migrant at the head of one care chain and she is the "localized" unwaged caregiver at the tail end of another. Her role shifts as she transitions from migrant to non-migrant at various points in time. Yet, it remains tied to the increasingly multifaceted conceptualization of motherhood in the Philippines where, since the advance of neoliberalism in the 1970s, mothers have provided for their children from abroad and where women, like Kate, have assumed the responsibilities of motherhood in the absence of female-kin.

While she is in the Philippines, Kate cares for six children. The care Kate provides goes beyond the daily manual labour associated with raising children. While she cooks and cleans, she also attends parent-teacher interviews, she spends time with them, tending to their emotional needs, and, when necessary, disciplining them. Yet, this is her role in relation to all of the children, including those whose mothers are present. Migration, then, has established the relationship Kate has to the children, but not its defining features. Rather, the organization of care labour within the family, and indeed the boundaries of relatedness and obligation, are configured according to pre-existing and highly localized logics that dictate Kate's inclusion within the kin-group. And while this inclusion is not devoid of power and considerations of status, Kate moves within the family of her in-laws easily. She has grown to care for them as she cares for her own family. This is my family, she tells me; these are my sisters. It is not unexpected, then, that she cares for their children; this is a role she accepts. Four of the children Kate cares for are Ivy's.

Ivy's Story

Ivy, Kate's sister-in-law and the second eldest of June's children, has also forged her identity as a mother within this global context. So calibrated, her work as a mother has become increasingly flexible, not only in relation to earlier conceptualizations of the double-day and more contemporary gendered labour processes (the feminization of labour and survival) (Sassen), but in terms of how it is transmitted; how Ivy must overcome distance and time-difference in order to continue caring for her children. After having spent three years in Hong Kong, Ivy lives and works in Winnipeg, Canada. She has spent nearly seven years outside of the Philippines where she had mothered her children and practiced midwifery. Like her parents before her, she is a migrant domestic worker. Her labour, as it unfolds in Winnipeg and in the Philippines, can, perhaps, best be understood in relation to the transnational double-day (Barber)—the working day that stretches into the night as migrant mothers turn their attention to the needs and wants of their own kin abroad. In Winnipeg, work starts early. Ivy gets up. She gets ready. She feels lucky, she tells me, her room in her employer's house is big and comfortable; she has her own bathroom and a TV. Her employers have given her a laptop and she can easily get online. Perfect for chatting with her sister who is also in Canada; challenging when trying to connect with the Philippines. The internet at home, she tells me, cuts out when it rains.

Showered and dressed, she goes to the kitchen. With relative ease, she interacts with her employers. There is a closeness there, but Ivy knows well enough not to get overly attached. She cares for the children, but they are not her children. She is seriously considering moving to Ontario. In Ontario, she will be with her own family—her sister, Maria, who joined her husband and his family in Canada nearly six years ago. Maria is trained as an engineer. In Ontario, she is retraining to be a nurse. In this way, she has become integrated into the circuits of care labour migration. And in a manner similar to Kate, unexpectedly so. Yet, serving as a counterpoint to Kate's experience, whose care labour is predicated on her on-going mobility between the Philippines and Taiwan, Maria's care labour is highly localized, based on Canadian labour markets and situated within the context of her permanent settlement in Canada.

Ivy's employers leave for their day. She sets about cleaning. Her job description, despite the Live-in Caregiver Program's emphasis on care, includes light housekeeping. On paper, the Canadian state regards her as a professional caregiver, but more than caregiving, she is engaged in the labour of mothering; she tends to the physical (extending to their lived environment) and emotional well-being of her employers' children. Her education (though focused very explicitly on biological acts of reproduction) did not prepare her for this; rather, it was the highly gendered training she received as a child and young mother. Her female employer, a mid-career academic, has received similar training although she, by virtue of the availability of foreign domestic labour, does not draw so explicitly on it. Instead, like many women who employ live-in caregivers from the Philippines, she has assumed an almost managerial position in relation to the social reproductive labour done in her household. Much in the way Judith has in the Philippines.

Judith's Story

Judith, the eldest of her siblings, is the principal at the local elementary school. Although her monthly salary is low, Judith is positioned as head of the household in the Philippines; she is the local breadwinner and the legal guardian of the six children. Her husband, a seaman, has worked abroad for 15 years. He returns to his family once a year for a month. Without reliable internet service on the ship, his communication with his wife is limited largely to text messaging. With only a vague idea of where her husband is at any time, her sisters in Canada, her brother in Dubai, her own schedule, and the children to organize, Judith is always thinking somewhere outside of her immediate location. Her day, like Ivy's night and Kate's early morning, is shaped not only by "what happens here" but by "what happens there", by what people (her people) are doing somewhere other than where she is. She keeps track of their routines, their schedules. She is acutely aware of how many "minutes" she has left on her phone.

Edith's Story

Edith is the third of her siblings. She lives in her mother's house while her daughter, the eldest of the six children, spends most of her time next door with Kate, Judith, and her five cousins. About a year ago, Edith returned to the Philippines after three years in Greece where she worked as a domestic helper. When she talks about Greece, Edith echoes Kate's description of Taiwan: her life was difficult but fine; hard but unremarkable; she did it because she had to; there were no other options.

Edith is taking a telemarketing-English course to Americanize her inflection. She would like to find a job in the Philippines, but she is not overly optimistic. Most likely, she will go abroad again. With this in mind, her sister Judith retains legal guardianship of her daughter. Canada offers the most long-term promise, but she doubts she will meet the criteria of the Live-in Caregiver Program. Instead, following Ivy, she will go to Hong Kong, and after several years, she will apply from there. This plan is not without risk and considerable sacrifice. Ivy has not seen her children in over six years (her youngest has just turned seven). And Edith already feels that her connection to her daughter is strained; she goes more frequently to Judith with problems and appears more affectionate toward Kate.

THE MULTIFACETED REALM OF MIGRANT MOTHERING

At 5:30am Kate says goodbye to her husband, and she makes her way to the kitchen. Once breakfast is prepared and the children are up, Kate and Edith begin the morning chores. Kate sweeps inside the house, pushing the dust and dirt that accumulated the day before into the dirty kitchen. Edith sweeps outside, gathering all of the dry leaves that fell during the night. They will burn the leaves, as they do every day, with the trash. "There is no garbage pick-up", Edith explains to me as Kate lights the fire, "only re-cycling, and then we have to pay for it." By 9am, the slow burning fire has consumed the leaves, plastic wrap, soiled tissue, food scraps, food contain-ers; everything has been reduced to a near perfect circle of ash on the ground. In Winnipeg it is 8pm. Ivy is in her room. She sends a message to her eldest daughter. Marking the end of her localized working day, this is the first of countless messages that will be sent over the course of the evening and into the night.

Kate re-enters the house where she puts together a morning snack for the children. She brings them their sandwiches: baloney sent from Win-nipeg, fried with processed cheese, tomato, cucumber, and mayonnaise. Once the kitchen is clean, she runs a cloth along the window sills, moving from the dirty kitchen, to the interior kitchen, to the living room. She care-fully removes the dust from the figurines lining the shelves that flank the TV. She joins her nieces and nephews on the couch, her cell phone in her hand, just as they hold on to theirs. Ivy's eldest daughter receives a text. It is her mother. She replies: colon, closed round bracket. Everything is OK.

Ivy's life and her children's lives are connected despite her absence. They unfold simultaneously; they run, slightly askew in light of the 13-hour time difference, concurrently; and they are punctuated by sustained, yet spo-radic interactions that serve as a corrective to the challenges of separation. These interactions necessitate a near constant consideration and accounting of schedules and routines corresponding to different time zones and a near constant navigation of imperfect technology, itself unequally distributed between sites. It is midnight now. Ivy's phone is on her pillow. She will sleep while her family goes about their day. She is acutely aware of this real-ity. She waits for the phone to ring but hopes it won't (she is always partially in prayer). Who knows what will be on the other end: a crises, a request for money, some call to action. And then there's that volcano. The Philippines, she reminds me, is a dangerous place.

But from her bedroom in Winnipeg, she is largely helpless, unable to act. And so she leaves this responsibility to her sisters. Besides, she tells me, beyond her inability to "do much about anything", she lacks experi-ence—in Winnipeg, the children she cares for are two and four; the lives of her own children, teenagers, are somewhat mysterious to her although she does her best to guide them. Their relationship, then, comes to be enacted through a daily exchange of symbols—like the smiley face, brief greetings, simple reminders, and hypothetical questions:

Good night / be good / study hard / don't pester your brother / help your aunties/ Hello / what are you doing? / when are you coming home? / I had a good day / I miss you

Other than these interactions, Ivy's primary contribution to her family takes the form of remittances, the monthly money she sends to her sisters, and *Balikbayan* boxes, the dried goods, canned foods, shampoo, and soap she buys on sale in Winnipeg, packs, and then ships to the Philippines—the meat for the morning snack. Several weeks later, Kate's work visa is issued. Within the month, she will leave for Taiwan. In her absence, Judith will have to rely more heavily on her mother and she will have to hire a helper. This will require more money from Ivy—money that she may not, in the near future, have. Already the family employs two women to do the laundry. A huge undertaking involving an intricate system of cross-cutting clothes lines, plastic laundry baskets, and wash basins, strategically placed in relation to the single faucet and the small dual-washer-dryer unit Judith bought with remittances sent from her husband.

CONCLUSION

The material, manual, emotional, and relational work necessary for the maintenance and continuation of life, the work of mothering reflects the "everlasting nature-imposed condition of human existence" (Mies 52), common to every point in history, every social formation, and every economic system. Yet, this very essential need has a politics, one that is embedded in asymmetries of gender, class, ethnicity, and citizenship, and embodied in who does what for whom and where. These "inequalities of reproduction," (Kofman) while not historically identical, are historically situated: reflected in the subordination of reproduction to production, the sexual division of labour, and the increasingly dense social reproductive networks to which migrants and their non-migrant counterparts belong. At the same time, they dictate who does what, where, and for whom as differently situated women (migrants and non-migrants alike; kin-members, employers, and employees) all navigate and contend with the realities of neoliberalism in diverse ways.

The lives portrayed here are similar to the lives of many; yet, they are unique. They tell us something about the institutions and hierarchies that shape contemporary life, but they do not stand for them. Rather, in detailing the multifaceted labour of these women and how it comes to be modified through the experience of migration, this chapter emphasizes the centrality of mothering (in its various forms) to social, cultural, and economic processes while highlighting its socially constituted nature. Paralleling the argument offered by Maria Mies in her work on Housewifization (Mies), the women at the centre of this chapter have assumed identities and roles consistent with the requirements of globalized capital and those of the Philippine state; yet, they have done this in order to mitigate the crises of survival, in large part, engendered by those requirements. Their labour has become increasingly flexible, extending well beyond the status and condition of women's work, both paid and unpaid, to the very enactment of that work across time and space, and filtered through an increasingly unsustainable and expansive network of family members.

Globalization and the subsequent movement of people out of the Philippines since the 1970s has spurred this reality. It is a consequence of neoliberalism, but it is also the means by which individuals and families (in the Philippines but also in Canada) have been forced to navigate neoliberalism. Put differently, as the state retreats from the provisioning of basic services and as local employment becomes more and more flexible and precarious, collective and individual survival becomes contingent upon the incorporation of different people in various economic and reproductive activities. These activities may be formalized through pay or other kinds of exchange, but they engender and magnify within an economic paradigm existent structures of obligation and reciprocity. And within these structures of obligation and reciprocity, it is women, and specifically, mothers, who shoulder the burden of reproductive and productive labour. As is consistent with capital accumulation, such an elaborate system assumes the ongoing and willing provision of poorly or non-remunerated female labour for its functioning. The labour of Judith, Ivy, Edith, Maria, and Kate, indeed their survival and the survival of the neoliberal paradigm, have become contingent upon the labour and actions of multiple family members doing the work of mothering within an increasingly unsustainable neoliberal world.

NOTES

[1] See Manalansan; and Yeates

[2] See Collier & Yanagisako; Glenn; Ginsburg & Rapp; Moore; and Stolcke

[3] See Barber & Bryan; Bezanson; Chant & McIlwaine; Elson & Pearson; Eviota; and Mies

[4]See Bakker; Chin; Gamburd; LeBaron; Ong; Parreñas; Sassen; and Wichterich

[5]See Barber & Bryan

WORKS CITED

Abu-Lughod, L. "Writing Against Culture." *Recapturing Anthropology: Working in the Present.* Ed. R. G. Fox. Santa Fe, New Mexico: School of American Research Press, 1991. 137-162. Print.

Bakker, I. *The Strategic Silence: Gender and Economic Policy.* London: Zed Books, 1994. Print.

— "Neoliberal Governance and the Reprivatisation of Social Reproduction: Social Provisioning and Shifting Gender Orders." *Power, Production and Social Reproduction: Human In/Security in the Global Political Economy.* Eds. I. Bakker & S. Gill. New York: Palgrave MacMillan, 2003. 66-82. Print.

Barber, P. G. "Agency in Philippine Women's Labour Migration and Provisional Diaspora." *Women's Studies International Forum* 23.4 (2000): 399-411. Print.

— "Cell Phones, Complicity and Class Politics in the Philippine Labour Diaspora." *Focaal: European Journal of Anthropology* 51 (2008): 28-42. Print.

Barber, P. G. & Bryan, C. "'Value Plus Plus:' Housewifization and History in Philippine Care Migration." Eds. P. G. Barber & W. Lem. *Twenty-First Century Migration: Political Economy and Ethnography.* New York: Routledge, 2012. 215-235. Print.

Bello, W. *The Anti-development State: The Political Economy of Permanent Crisis in the Philippines.* New York: Zed Books, 2005. Print.

Bezanson, K. *Gender, the State, and Social Reproduction: Household Insecurity in Neo-Liberal Times.* Toronto: University of Toronto Press, 2006. Print.

Briones, L. *Empowering Migrant Women: Why Agency and Rights Are Not Enough.* Ashgate Publishing, 2009. Print.

Chant, S. & McIlwaine, C. *Women of a Lesser Cost: Female Labour, Foreign Exchange and Philippine Development.* London: Pluto Press, 1995. Print.

Chin, C. B. N. *In Service and Servitude: Foreign Female Domestic Work-*

ers and the Malaysian "Modernity Project". Columbia University Press, 1998. Print.

Collier, J. F. & Yanagisako, S. J. "Introduction." *Gender and Kinship: Essays Toward a Unified Analysis*. Eds. J. F. Collier & S. J. Yanagisako. Stanford, CA: Stanford University Press, 1989. 1-13. Print.

Elson, D. & Pearson, R. "The Subordination of Women and the Internationalisation of Production." Eds. K. Young et al. *Of Marriage in the Market: Women's Subordination in International Perspective*. London: CSE Books, 1981. 18-40. Print.

Eviota, E. *The Political Economy of Gender: Women and the Sexual Division of Labour in the Philippines*. London: Zed Books, 1992. Print.

Gamburd, M. G. *The Kitchen Spoon's Handle: Transnationalism and Sri Lanka's Migrant Housemaids*. Cornell University Press, 2000. Print.

Glenn, E. N. "Racial Ethnic Women's Labor: The Intersection of Race, Gender and Class Oppression." *Review of Radical Political Economics* 17 (1985): 86-108. Print.

Ginsburg, F. D. & Rapp, R. "The Politics of Reproduction." *Annual Review of Anthropology* 20 (1991): 311-343. Print.

Glick Schiller, N. "A Global Perspective on Migration and Development." *Social Analysis* 53.3 (2009): 14-37. Print.

Hochschild, A. "Global Care Chains and Emotional Surplus Value." Eds. A. Giddens & W. Hutton. *On the Edge: Living with Global Capitalism*. London: Jonathan Cape, 2000. Print.

Kofman, E. "Rethinking Care Through Social Reproduction: Articulating Circuits of Migration." *Social Politics* 19.1 (2012): 142-162. Print.

LeBaron, G. "The Political Economy of the Household: Neoliberal Restructuring, Enclosures, and Daily Life." *Review of International Political Economy* 17.5 (2010): 889-912. Print.

Manalansan IV, M. F. "Queer Intersections: Sexuality and Gender in Migration Studies." *International Migration Review* 40.1 (2006): 224-249. Print.

Mies, M. *Patriarchy and Accumulation on a World Scale: Women in the International Division of Labour*. New York: St. Martin's Press, 1986. Print.

Moore, H. L. *A Passion for Difference*. Bloomington: University of Indiana Press, 1994. Print.

Ong, A. *Spirits of Resistance and Capitalist Discipline: Factory Women in Malaysia.* Albany: State University of New York, 1987. Print.

Parreñas, R. S. "Migrant Filipina Domestic Workers and the International Division of Reproductive Labor". *Gender and Society* 14.4 (2000): 560-580. Print.

— *The Force of Domesticity: Filipina Migrants and Globalization.* New York: New York University Press, 2008. Print.

Sassen, S. "Notes on the Incorporation of Third World Women into Wage-labour through Immigration and Off-Shore Production." *International Migration Review* 18.4 (1984): 1144-1166. Print.

— "Women's Burden: Counter-geographies of Globalization and the Feminization of Survival." *Journal of International Affairs* 53.2 (2000): 503-524. Print.

Stolcke, V. "Women's Labours: The Naturalization of Social Inequity and Women's Subordination." Eds. K. Young, Wolkowitz, C. & McCullagh, R. *Of Marriage and the Market: Women's Subordination Internationally and Its Lessons.* London: CSE Books, 1981. 159-177. Print.

Tyner, J.A. *The Philippines: Mobilities, Identities, Globalization.* New York: Routledge, 2009. Print.

Wichterich, C. *The Globalized Woman: Reports from a Future of Inequality.* London: Zed Books, 2000. Print.

Yeates, N. "Global Care Chains." *International Feminist Journal of Politics* 6.3 (2004): 369-391. Print.

— "A Dialogue with 'Global Care Chain' Analysis: Nurse Migration in the Irish Context." *Feminist Review* 77 (2004): 79-95. Print.

— "A Global Political Economy of Care." *Social Policy and Society* 4.2 (2005): 227-234. Print.

— "Global Care Chains: A State-of-the-Art Review and Future Directions in Care Transnationalization Research." *Global Networks* 12.2 (2012): 135-154. Print.

2.

Across the Great Divide

Balancing Paid Work and Child Care in Neoliberal Times in Two Policy Jurisdictions in the Ottawa Valley, Canada

PATRIZIA ALBANESE, MEGAN BUTRYN, LOUISA HAWKINS AND COURTNEY MANION

INTRODUCTION

Spring 2010, Pontiac County, Quebec

Driving back from the local hardware store with 15 feet of heavy chain for my (first author's)[1] new fence in the back of my Jeep, my unemployed, 30-something year old neighbour and I chat about the state of the local economy. He says: "You know things are bad this year when the poutine stand has not opened yet." He lost his job at a unionized paper mill owned by a large international corporation over a year ago and has not found decent-paying employment since. He keeps busy, helping friends, family and neighbours with outdoor chores, renovations, and repairs—all stereotypically masculine pursuits—but while doing a bit more of the household work and child care, still doesn't seem willing or comfortable taking on more of the primary caregiving responsibilities within his family.

He's among one of the more "macho" working-class men that I know, but he too is changing.[2] In fact, I think sitting in the *passenger* seat beside his wife's female-friend (first quietly, uncomfortably, hands in his lap; minutes later relaxed and shooting the breeze about the local economy), was a novelty for him, in a town that for the most part is characterized by parallel but separate spheres for men and women. His life has undoubtedly changed, but so too has his wife's. Her own work as a caregiver, working shifts for a local social services agency has not changed much over the past few years, but her ability to contemplate a different career path, especially after completing more postsecondary education through distance education, her husband's respect for her financial contribution to the household, and her role and responsibilities within her household have changed, and not always for the better.

From my travels and interviews throughout the Ontario and Quebec sides of the Ottawa Valley, I have seen, heard and been touched by mothers' experiences of social change resulting from economic restructuring of rural and semi-rural economies. This chapter is about sharing some of what I've seen and been told from mothers of young children living and working on the two sides of the Ottawa Valley. It also makes a small attempt to dispel some of the myths about "stagnant" and "static" rural lives, relations, and economies.

THE NEOLIBERAL CONTEXT

Some have condemned small-town Canada for being a colonialist cultural relic—conservative, static and monocultural (Ibbitson). Others, however, note that in non-urban communities, "once traditional supports of the extended family and the close-knit community have been eroded" (Brownell 12). Although limited, research that has focused on gender roles and identities in contemporary non-urban economies has shown that rural restructuring is a growing reality.[3] That is, rural economies have been negatively affected by global economic shifts, first away from farming, and later away from manufacturing.[4] Furthermore, dependency of rural areas on the state for some of the better paid service jobs (education, health services, local bureaucracy and related state services) tend to make rural areas vulnerable to state retrenchment and downsizing (Leach). Job losses, state retrenchment, the rise of non-standard service jobs, and mounting insecurity are part of the consequences of living in neoliberal times in contemporary Canada, and this includes non-urban communities.

Neoliberalism involves the restructuring of local economies, driven by global capital's imperative for profit. On the ground, "jobs are structured to minimize costs and to maximize profit" with jobs becoming increasingly part-time and temporary, as "companies shift to 'no-commitment' hiring" (Kelly 84). As a result, the restructured economy makes increasing demands on workers, while providing fewer returns and increased insecurity.[5]

Neoliberalism has also meant that Canada's already miserly social policies have become even less generous over time, leaving Canada's social safety net threadbare. Efforts to support workers and families through access to health care, education, community services and welfare have been scaled back, hit by a tidal wave of neoliberal reforms.[6] And rural communities have not been spared. Leach's research in Ontario showed that despite first holding and then losing similar jobs in manufacturing, men and women had different experiences and outcomes following the restructuring (Leach). Some feminist researchers have argued that women's invisibility actually increased as their workloads changed.[7] At the same time, rural restructuring has forced many women to become even more creative in their strategies for meeting their own and their families' physical, emotional and economic needs (McKinley Wright). Research is making it increasingly clear that rural restructuring has resulted in limited employment opportunities for women, further away from home, with few options when it comes to child care.[8]

ECONOMIC CHANGE IN THE OTTAWA VALLEY

Communities in the Upper Ottawa Valley, in both Ontario and Quebec, were hit by cuts and job losses in the male-dominated forestry and logging industry even before the recent economic crisis hit other parts of Canada in 2008. [9] The economic downturn in 2008 simply made matters worse. By December 2009, monthly lumber production by sawmills decreased 14.3 percent compared to the same month last year, and saw a decline of 9.7 percent in one month alone—between November and December (Statistics Canada "Sawmills"). This resulted in the loss of some of the higher paying jobs found across all industries in Canada. For example, in 2008, average weekly earnings of those working in the forestry and logging industry were $935.84 (or $21.87 per hour), well above average weekly earnings of those in educational services ($862.64), and health care and social assistance ($743.94)—not surprising, both female-dominated industries.[10]

Job losses in the forestry and logging industry were slightly offset by gains in some service sector jobs, where average weekly earnings remain low (by comparison, average weekly earnings in retail trade were $475.17 or $13.09

per hour).[11] Customer service call centres, and other often low-waged and insecure feminized service sector employers have emerged to set up shop near the border, in Ontario, near a source of relatively cheap, bilingual, feminized labour (Akyeampong). Some have noted that when "families lost their good jobs, they also lost their ability to continue social and economic activities at their previous level" (Seiling 21). This chapter aims to document some of these changes, particularly as they impact upon the lives of employed mothers in the region, as they struggle with managing their childcare needs.

NEED FOR CHILD CARE WITH THE RISE OF WOMEN'S NON-STANDARD EMPLOYMENT

The proportion of women with young children in the labour force has been increasing steadily. By 2005, 81% of women ages 25 to 54 were in the labour force,[12] as were 71.9% of mothers with young children (Roy). Mothers' average time spent on paid and unpaid work also increased (Marshall). As noted above, this coincides with the rise of neoliberal governance, and the undervaluing and re-privatization of social reproduction.[13] Cuts to public expenditure and privatization meant that "good jobs" for women were replaced with insecure, low-waged employment.[14] In the Ottawa Valley, this coincided with the loss of well-paid, male-dominated jobs, forcing a larger proportion of families to increasingly depend on the wages of women for subsistence. This also resulted in women being forced to enter or re-enter the labour force soon(er) after the birth of a child, which also inevitably required them to find some form of non-parental child care.

A growing proportion of workers are also working rotating or irregular shifts and multiple jobs.[15] The 2005 *General Social Survey* shows that by that year, some 28 percent of the 14.6 million employed Canadians (a total of 4.1 million workers) worked shifts—something other than 9 to 5 (Williams 5). Men made up 63 percent of full-time shift workers, while women made up 69 percent of part-time shift workers (Vanier Institute of the Family 1). While some claim to be "choosing" shift work to help balance work and family obligations, research shows that shift workers report lower levels of satisfaction with their "work-life balance" compared to those working 9 to 5, and many find that child-care centres' (and some home day cares') hours of operation do not coincide with their actual, often rotating and shifting, child-care needs.

CHILD-CARE POLICY IN ONTARIO AND QUEBEC

Canada—and this is true for Ontario—has been classified as a 'liberal welfare state' (Esping-Andersen), which relies on the free market rather than solid state support to families through generous social programs. Canada's family policies are for the most part limited, targeted, and often not very family-friendly. Quebec, on the other hand, is closer to a social democratic model when it comes to social policies.[16] Since the mid-1990s, Quebec began transforming its policies, introducing more feminist-informed programs aimed at integrating paid work and family, promoting gender equity, and reducing family poverty.[17] One of the province's major policy reforms came in 1997, when it introduced $5/day (increased to $7/day in 2004) child care for children using child care at least 3 days a week, regardless of family income and employment status.[18]

Since the late 1990s, the federal, provincial, and territorial governments appeared to have been making progress towards improving access to quality child care across the country (the National Children's Agenda in 1997, the Federal/Provincial/Territorial Early Childhood Development Agreement in 2000 and the Multilateral Framework on Early Learning and Child Care, 2003).[19] However, after 2006, the Federal (Conservative) minority government replaced past funding commitments made by the Liberals, with their own "Universal Childcare Benefit," which gives families $100 monthly (before tax) for each child under age six, and professes to provide parents with "more choice in child care."[20] As a result, in most of the country, childcare spaces remain expensive and in short supply: since 2006, expansion of child care has slowed, with spaces for less than 20 percent of new-born to five year olds, and even then, fees range from $600 to $1,200 per month.[21] This marked the end of any hope—at least in the short-term—for a national child-care strategy. Any new developments and initiatives that have taken place in the area of early childhood education and care have happened at the provincial level. For example, Ontario has been making some changes to its early learning programs, as it began implementing full-day kindergarten for 4- and 5-year olds—part of the more comprehensive early learning plan for Ontario that was set in motion, following the June 15, 2009, release of what came to be known as the "Pascal Report" or the "Premier's Report on Early Learning" (Pascal). None of this, however, was even proposed when interviewing for this project began in late spring, 2009.

PROJECT APPROACH AND METHODOLOGY

This work is based upon the assumptions that: 1) the "distribution of paid work and caring work is inequitable" (between women and men) (Perrons 105), and increasingly so with economic globalization and neoliberalism;[22] 2) that rural economies are morphing under the weight of profound economic transformations; and 3) that the weight of this economic and state restructuring disproportionately burdens rural women.[23]

Using this framework, the project involved interviews with 55 women (22 in Quebec and 33 in Ontario[24]), mothers of young children currently living and employed in the Ottawa Valley.[25] This was a non-probability purposive (and snowball) sample of employed mothers working in and around two economically stagnant, small urban centres near the Ontario/Quebec border, in the Ottawa Valley. The interviews were conducted in the summer of 2009 in women's homes, a community centre, or neighbourhood coffee shops, in Renfrew County, Ontario, and the Outaouais, in Pontiac County, Quebec. Interviews were tape recorded, and about one-hour in length. Mothers were asked about their employment history/background, and the impact that they believed that their paid work had on their household work, and personal relationships. They were specifically asked about their child-care arrangements, and about how they managed child care in light of their own and/or their partners' changing work schedules and shifts. The interviews were transcribed in fall 2009 and winter 2010, and data analysis began in earnest, when some themes and patterns were identified and compared.

FINDINGS

Some Differences: More Job Losses in The Pontiac (Quebec), but More Reasons to Stay (Low-Fee Child Care)

Briefly, while the forestry sector on both sides of the Ottawa Valley continues to bleed jobs, the hit on the Quebec side seems more acute. Renfrew County, Ontario has about 500 small businesses that are wholly or partly dependent on forestry, and the economy in Renfrew County is more diversified, and the forestry industry there is made up of many small family-run, multigenerational businesses that have been in business for over a century. These were less likely to be unionized jobs and the closure of any one mill tended not to affect entire communities as drastically as in Quebec.

In contrast, while there are small mills and other forestry-related businesses on the Quebec side, the economy in the Pontiac was more firmly dependent on larger, unionized, nationally or internationally owned lumber and paper mills. Their closures—three in under a decade—resulted in the loss of many well-paid, men's jobs that required relatively little education. One mother shared the following:

> Well I'm in an elementary school now so I don't see much. I used to work at a Youth Centre though, and lots of the boys will just go straight from school to work, if they even finish high school, you know. Around here, the girls seem to [finish school]. I know my graduating class, all of the girls went on to I think, yah every one of us I think went on to college and all that and a lot of the guys stayed back and just started work right away.

A number of mothers pointed out, for every job lost in the mills, there were five job losses in the bush (logging), in trucking (more men's jobs), and in other services in the region that depended on the sector (including shops and restaurants—where many local women worked). Some men who lost $20+/hour jobs in the Pontiac took some of the few available $11/hour mill jobs in Pembroke and Eganville, in Ontario, over a 30 minute drive away. Some of the Pontiac's women found low-waged, shift work in retail or at a customer service call centre that was recently established in Ontario, also 30 minutes away. This resulted in considerably longer commutes to and from work for both men and women in the Pontiac, when jobs were actually available. Some women tried carpooling to work in Ontario, but shifting shifts and child care made this untenable.

When the customer service call centre opened in Ontario (around the time of the beginning of the mill closures), near the Quebec border, there was great optimism in the region and many women from the Pontiac applied for and got jobs there. As noted above, some carpooled to make the almost 100km round trip more economically feasible. For a number of reasons, including variations in child-care needs and arrangements, and variable shifts which forced some to wait around for others, the carpool arrangements became unsustainable. One young Quebecoise mother of two explained:

> Like there were three of us from [here], and we asked them for gas and stuff but the only thing is, if one of us wouldn't

go in [one of the drivers] the others would like stay home, or
they would waste a lot of time [waiting for each other's shift to
start or end] so they stopped. Nobody loved carpooling...but
now they stopped it, so a lot of people had to quit because they
couldn't drive there.

Renfrew's somewhat (relatively) healthier economy is counterbalanced
by Quebec's more family-friendly social policies and programs. That is,
Renfrew County has two smaller "urban" centres—Renfrew and
Pembroke—that are the hub of social services and retail for both Renfrew
County and the Pontiac; and act as a source of low-waged employment for
people on both sides of the border. Renfrew also has a more diversified
economy with some better paid jobs at the large military base in Petawawa,
at Atomic Energy of Canada in Deep River and Chalk River, and Algo-
nquin College in Pembroke.

On the other hand, as noted above, Quebec, since 1997, has been introducing a package of family-friendly policies and initiatives that include
more flexible and generous parental leaves, and ($7/day) low-fee child care
for families, regardless of their income or employment status. Ontario mothers, instead paid very high fees (between $30 and $40 per day per child), for
often unregulated, private child-care arrangements that at times were less
than ideal. One Ontario mother reflected on the challenges related to cost
that she faced:

> Well, I think number one [challenge] for me is financial, um,
> cause daily I sort of sit back and think: is this really worth it
> in the end you know? It's almost come down to a quality of
> life kind of thing because you know we're driving all the time
> and we really aren't making that much money, and you know,
> maybe I should just be staying at home with my kids. But
> how can we financially as a family do that? We can't, that's
> the point.

Low-fee child care in Quebec has kept some families that experienced
job losses *tethered* to the Pontiac. Families were tethered there because some
of the Quebecoise women interviewed talked about their unemployed partners seeking and finding employment very far from home, in the mines of
Northern Quebec, Ontario and Manitoba, and being absent for long periods of time—leaving women to tend to all matters at home. One mother
explained:

My husband in September decided that he wanted to go back into the mines [after working in the local mill for 8 years], so he was going to be gone most of the time during the week and stuff or more. So we tried it out for a month and a half, with him gone and me picking up everything around the house, taking care of our son, paying the bills, making sure everything functioned and me working full-time; it got to me. I wasn't always happy, and I wasn't spending that much time with my son, and I finally sat back and I said is this worth it, for the amount of money, is this worth travelling? So I asked to cut some of my hours from work, and then they were very, they didn't want me to go....

So rather than her husband returning to town, and giving up the better paid of the two jobs, she cut back her hours at the customer service call centre located 45 kilometres away, in Ontario. But the family remained in Quebec. Relatively cheap housing, cheaper child care, more generous family-friendly policies, and proximity to extended family networks kept some of these families in Pontiac County.

Cost of child care was clearly a major difference between Ontario and Quebec. One mother who was born and raised in Quebec, then lived and worked in Ontario for a time, and then returned to Quebec shared the following:

I worked there [in Ontario] for 8 years and I had three kids in the span of 4 years and two months. So I had three children and I needed day care because there's senior kindergarten. There [in Ontario] it's part-time, whereas ours [in Quebec] is full-time. So I had to have day care 5 days a week for three kids, and because one was, you know, young, one was a different fee—[for] the youngest. So, going back to work after her, I paid every two weeks, $1,094; and my pay every two weeks for 80 hours of work was $1,075. So working 80 hours, I lost $20 bucks. So then we had our name on a list here [in Quebec] for two years before we moved. When our name got on the top of the list, they phoned me to say: "are you moving yet, and we say "no" and she'd go "okay" and give it to the person under our name and she just left me at the top...and then we were finally, like my husband had to get a job that allowed us to move, so once he [her husband] got a job that allowed us to move, we moved…so I was able to go from full-time work to part-time work…and we have the same disposable income. I went from making a decent wage, to less, because you make less money here [in Quebec]; like I lost $5 an hour…[but] I was able to work less hours for less pay and still have the same amount of income.

Even with low-fee child care in the Pontiac, most of the women interviewed depended on a network of family, friends and sitters to coordinate shifting shifts, and/or long commutes related to paid work and child care. One mother of two explained:

I was scheduled like 9:30 to 6:00pm. By the time I got home, it was a quarter to seven and my parents were the ones watching my kids after day care…my husband works nights all the time, so like my parents watch them from the time they are done school and day care until I get home.

Another shared the following:

This will be really good for your study, I had three jobs. I was living in town and wasn't married or anything, anyways. I got up and we [her and her son] were out the door by 8 o'clock. His day care was on the way. So two days a week I either dropped him off there or I dropped him off at school (part-time kindergarten). Um, so by 8 o'clock we were out the door and I had to be at work by 8:30, or at school by 8:20, so either way, um I barely made it everywhere, I'd say. And I literally, had to be at my other job for um 3 o'clock. Anyways, school did not get out till 2:50. I had to drive probably 7 or 8 minutes out of town, pick him up, bring him back to my house in town, drop him off with another babysitter. Like I had two 16, 17-year-old girls babysitting. And then I left him there and I was always 15 minutes late for my job at the youth centre…and then I worked at a [fitness centre] for random shifts on weekends and stuff…sometimes my mom would take him. There was one time I took him with me, which probably wasn't allowed, but my boss was really good.

These were not unusual cases. Most Quebecoise mothers interviewed relied upon family, friends and sitters for some of their child-care needs, to patch a daily "care gap" between two partners' schedules, when shifts shifted, or on weekends or holidays when centres and family day cares were closed, but mothers still had to work (for pay). Quebec's low-fee child care was useful and appreciated by all mothers interviewed, but child care that ran from 6:30 or 7:00am until 4:00 or 5:00pm, from Monday to Friday was inadequate for most families dealing with multiple jobs and shiftwork.

This is not to say that the mothers interviewed in Ontario were not multiple job holders or did not struggle to pick up their children "on time." This was a chronic problem for almost all mothers on both sides of the provincial border, so they too often relied on others to "help out" with child care. However, because these Ontario mothers were paying higher fees, often outside of licensed child-care facilities (in private home arrangements), they were much more likely to seek out or negotiate child care that was more likely to fit their schedules. Clearly, despite differences, there were a large number of similarities in the experiences of employed mothers on the two sides of the provincial border.

Some Similarities...Change Is the Norm, but Some Change was Slow in Coming

One of the most obvious similarities between the experiences of mothers in Renfrew County, Ontario, and in the Pontiac, in Quebec, was that change, requiring considerable flexibility on the part of mothers, was the norm. Mothers on both sides told me about changes in residence, changes in their jobs or careers, changing shifts and schedules, changing caregivers...change was all around them. And they were constantly adapting.

First off, contrary to popular thinking about people moving out of rural areas and rarely moving into them, I found that over half the mothers I spoke to on both sides of the Ottawa River, but especially in Ontario, had relatively recently moved into their current community. Some in Ontario moved from one Renfrew County town to another; from Ontario cities to "the country:" or from parts of Quebec to Ontario.

The Quebecoise mothers I spoke to were much more likely to be originally from the Pontiac, moved away to urban areas in Ontario or Quebec for school or work, and then returned. Some were "from away," and some were locals who had not moved. Moves into and between rural areas, in both Ontario and Quebec, were very common in this sample. Mothers on both sides of the Ottawa River, and perhaps especially in Ontario spoke about changing jobs or careers or shifts, especially after becoming mothers; in many cases giving up higher status or higher paying jobs for lower ones. For example, one mother said:

> I'm no longer at work in the network. I recognized my limits, um, and, you know, with a bit of reservation, I have withdrawn my volunteer activity...I'm noticing that, I recognize, I have to, I have to set the limits. I just have to know my limits, and I'm tired, I'm exhausted. And, I keep telling myself this is temporary, and I'm not the first one that has gone through this...but I'm living it now and I'm having difficulty.

Another explained:

> Actually when I was working at Canadian Tire I had to give up a really great job because I didn't have child care. I couldn't afford to pay rent, pay a babysitter, and continue working that job and I mean back then it was, you worked at Canadian Tire you got like 8 bucks an hour, right. It wasn't glorified wages but I was doing the job I was doing.

A third said:

> I changed to four days a week; I used to work five days a week but I just, I thought it was best to do this, and originally the plan was to spend more time with my child but as it turns out, I spend more time in appointments with him but I mean, that's the luck of the draw eh?

Mothers on both sides of the border also seemed equally vocal and concerned about long child-care centre waiting lists, challenges finding appropriate care, travelling long distances to access work and child care, and going to great lengths to juggle and manage shifting work schedules and child care. The combination of these frustrated and exhausted many mothers. One Quebec mother who commuted close to 100km round-trip for low-waged work lamented:

> We don't see our kids. Other people raise our kids so that's hard cause like when I used to work till 6:30 pm I'd get home

at a quarter after seven and at 8 o'clock they would be in the bathtub and go to bed. I would see them for maybe half hour a day because when I get up in the morning to go, they are asleep, so that's the only thing I don't like [her husband who works nights sees that one child gets on the school bus and takes the other to day care]. Like if I'd be working here [in town]…I'd be home earlier…so I have the whole evening with them, which I like; so that's the part I don't like, being a working mom.

Another striking similarity was that despite the economic changes sweeping through the lives of mothers on both sides of the Ottawa Valley, gender ideologies, responsibilities and roles were considerably slower to change for these women in both Ontario and Quebec. First off, a number of these mothers seemed much more likely, and less reluctant, to take low-waged work, even when they were better educated than their husbands (not uncommon in this region)—while men held off for better-paying jobs and opportunities. With a few exceptions, women continued to take cuts and losses on the one hand, or put in more hours of both paid and unpaid work compared to their male partners. Some fathers were contributing, by either picking up or dropping off children at day care, but for the most part, it was still mothers who made the arrangements, managed the schedules, instructed their partners, etc.

One Quebecoise mother of three whose husband was a farmer, spoke of at one point working three jobs (8:30-2:00pm, 3:00-9:00pm and some weekends). She explained that on top of $7/day child care, she relied on her mother, mother-in-law, and two teenage baby sitters to manage her work schedules and child care. Almost as an afterthought she added:

Yeah, and I mean, Bob, if he could. But not too often. It's not like he could never like stay home on my sick [day] or something, you know what I mean? [But] like he's not in the house for the day, he's gone [into their fields/barns behind their home].

Similarly another mother, talking about her unemployed husband (who lost his job at the paper mill) said:

So he's presently at home to help us get going in the morning right now—which is nice. That makes a difference. Um, but he just assumes it would always be up to me.

Another Ontario mother admitted:

> So even though his wage isn't that much more than mine...He
> wouldn't jeopardize his job for anything. It would be mine
> that would take the back seat. I just don't see that being the
> right choice either.

Some mothers rationalized or worked hard to justify why their male partners did not do more. For example, it was not uncommon to hear things
like:

> My husband's hours [teacher] are more unpredictable than
> mine [retail management]. There's a lot of afterschool meet-
> ings and what not. I wouldn't want her stranded at the care-
> givers if her father has a meeting until 7 in the evening.

This Ontario mother actually told her employer to treat her like she was a
single mother, and not expect her husband to leave his job during the day
for emergencies. She warned her employer in advance, that if needed, she
would be the one missing work. She was not alone on this. On both sides
of the border, the phone call from the child-care centre or caregiver, alert-
ing mothers that their child was sick (a common occurrence for some) was
identified as a major challenge. It often meant scrambling to find someone to step in at work or in caregiving, and travelling long distances between work, the caregiver, alternative care, and sometimes back to work.
In sum, as noted above, mothers in Quebec seemed especially hard hit by
widespread job losses in the male-dominated forestry sector. Many of these
women were able to take on low-waged work, at times long distances from
home, but increasingly relied on family, friends and sitters to fill gaps between a low-fee child-care system that catered to almost non-existent 9-to-5
jobs, and the reality of their shifting shifts, often 7 days a week. Women in
Ontario struggled with high cost of care, often outside a regulated child-
care system, and long commutes. Navigating through difficult and changing times left many tired and frustrated, but not necessarily defeated. Times
changed, and they adapted. What was striking, however, was that despite
the economic and social change in the Valley, mothers' role as primary caregiver, and the primary managers of care, changed very little.

CONCLUSION

Although there continues to be the assumption that men are the primary income earners and women work in order to supplement family incomes, declining male wages have made a dual-earner model necessary for many families living through neoliberal times (Luxton, "Family Coping Strategies"), even in families and communities perceived to be rural and traditional. Women's incomes, in non-urban economies are often necessary for the survival and sustainability of their families. In response to recent economic changes, many women have turned to pursuing more education, usually part-time and/or through distance education, in order to access opportunities in health and education and other better paying and more stable service sector jobs. Women's pursuit of education (another growing reality in neoliberal times) has been occurring while also managing paid work and child care, thus leading to a "triple burden" for many women—paid work, unpaid care work and education.

Since economic restructuring has been taking place at the same time as the restructuring of the welfare state, local communities, and especially mothers have been doubly hit. Many of the services once provided outside of the home by the welfare state have been moved into the home, as the individual is now deemed responsible for such services and care. This often and inevitably places an extra burden on mothers to provide such services not only for themselves, but for their families and communities as well (Fox). Neoliberal downloading of state responsibility onto families and individuals has made finding accessible, affordable and flexible services such as child care very difficult, if not impossible to attain, especially outside Quebec (Ames et al.). State retrenchment has burdened mothers by making it even more difficult to navigate the needs and requirements of the paid labour market, unpaid household and caring responsibilities, and education—all of which are often experienced as incompatible.[26]

That said, as noted above, since the mid-1990s, Quebec has been transforming its once patriarchal and later pro-natalist policies (Albanese, "Addressing the Interlocking Complexity of Paid Work and Care") towards more feminist-informed programs. Despite the ongoing challenges that mothers in rural Western Quebec continued to experience, this reminds us that neoliberal restructuring can be somewhat kept in check through the introduction of more progressive family policies, such as low-fee child care. Again, despite some shortcomings, there are clearly lessons to be learned from Quebec as families trudge forward through neoliberal times.

NOTES

[1]"I" and "my" in this chapter refer to Albanese, the first author of the chapter, who lives part of the year in one of the communities cited in this study.
[2]Ironically, in 2012, he has a job as a caregiver—nobody would have believed it in 2010, including him—but he still does relatively little care work at home.
[3]See Cummins; Fitchen; Leach; Miewald and McCann for further discussion
[4]See Fitchen; and Leach
[5]See Connell; Duffy and Pupo; Kelly; Kelly and Shortall; and Leach and Winson for further discussion regarding economic restructuring and job loss
[6]For further discussion regarding neoliberal reforms see Bezanson; Little and Morrison; Luxton; and Warriner and Peach.
[7]See Heather et al.; Johnston; and Whitzman for further reading. Johnston noted that rural Canadians produce 40% of GNP but receive only 10% of services in health and education.
[8]See Fitchen; and McKinley Wright
[9]Albanese & Farr; Albanese; Dufour; HRSDC, Statistics Canada "OECD Regions at a Glance"; and Statistics Canada "Sawmills and Planing Mills"
[10]See Statistics Canada "Table: Earnings, Average Weekly, by Industry" and "Table: Earnings, Average Hourly for Hourly Paid Employees". Between 2005 and 2009, manufacturing sales in both Ontario and Quebec saw a sharp decline. In Quebec, manufacturing sales dropped from $139,556.4 million in 2005 to $128,2787.3 million in 2009, while in Ontario they dropped from $303,607.2 million to $223,257.4 million in 2009 (Statistics Canada "Table: Manufacturing Sales, by Province and Territory, 2005-2009.")
[11]See Statistics Canada "Table: Earnings, Average Weekly, by Industry" and "Table: Earnings, Average Hourly for Hourly Paid Employees"
[12]See Luffman; and Marshall
[13]See Albanese; Bezanson; Gill & Bakker; Perrons; and Stinson for further reference
[14]See Kelly; Leach; Statistics Canada "1996 Census: Labour Force Activity, Occupation and Industry, Place of Work, Mode of Transportation to Work, Unpaid Work"; and Stinson for further reference
[15]See Albanese; Robertson et. al.; Vanier Institute of the Family; and Williams
[16]See Albanese; Baker; and Krull

[17] See Albanese; Jenson; and Roy and Bernier

[18] See Albanese "Addressing the Interlocking Complexity of Paid Work and Care: Lessons From Changing Family Policy in Quebec"; Albanese "Small Town, Big Benefits: The Ripple Effect of $7/day Child Care"; Bégin et al.; Gov't of Quebec "Family and Childcare Services – Childcare Services"; Gov't of Quebec Development and Funding Scenarios to Ensure the Permanence, Accessibility and Quality of Childcare Services: Consultations 2003; and Tougas "Reforming Quebec's Early Childhood Care and Education: The First Five Years," "Quebec's Family Policy and Strategy on Early Childhood Development and Childcare."; "What we can Learn from the Quebec Experience." Quebec also negotiated its withdrawal from the national EI maternity-parental leave benefits program to offer its own system with two options to parents (effective Jan. 2006), both with more equitable eligibility criteria and more generous replacement rates than the national plan (Albanese "Addressing the Interlocking Complexity of Paid Work and Care: Lessons from Changing Family Policy in Quebec"; Ministère de l'Emploi, de la Solidarité sociale et de la Famille; and Phipps).

[19] Also see Government of Canada and Government of Quebec

[20] Government of Canada. "Universal Child Care Plan."

[21] See Beach et al.; and Friendly and Prentice

[22] See Bakker; Pearson; and Stinson

[23] See Albanese and Farr

[24] I (first author) was surprised to find that it was much easier to recruit women in Renfrew County, Ontario, than in the Pontiac County, Quebec. I believe this is the result of a few things: 1) I have conducted research with mothers and child-care providers in Quebec in the past, and did not want to tap into the same individuals and social networks; 2) I was greatly assisted by having access to a network of agencies and women's/mothers' groups through the Renfrew County Child Poverty Action Network; 3) Mothers in Quebec explained that they felt that "they were spoiled" in Quebec, and that they had less to complain about, so less incentive to volunteer to talk to me because of the government's low-fee child-care program; 4) Being Anglophone and conducting my interviews in English likely resulted in me missing a large number of Francophone mothers.

[25] I was interviewed by two reporters for two different regional newspapers (one in Ontario and one in Quebec), where I described the project and asked for volunteers. I placed a radio ad in a non-for-profit French and English community radio station in Quebec. I posted fliers at local child-care centres, at/through two agencies (Centres De Petit Enfance/CPEs in Que-

bec), and at organizations that were frequented by both licensed and un-licensed home day care providers. I was granted permission to post information about the study and my contact information on a child and family services website. Through the site and its connected listserv, the study information circulated through various networks across Renfrew County. I returned mothers' calls and set up appointments for interviews throughout the region.

[26]See Leach; and Luxton "Family Coping Strategies: Balancing Paid Work and Labour"

WORKS CITED

Albanese, Patrizia & Tanya Farr. "'I'm Lucky'...To Have Found Child Care: Evoking Luck While Managing Child Care Needs in a Changing Economy" *International Journal of Child, Youth and Family Studies* 1(2012): 83-111. Print.

Albanese, Patrizia. "Addressing the Interlocking Complexity of Paid Work and Care: Lessons from Changing Family Policy in Quebec" *A Life in Balance? Reopening the Family-Work Debate.* Eds. C. Krull & J. Sempruch. Vancouver: UBC Press, 2011. 130-143. Print.

— "$7/Day, $7/hour and 7 Days a Week: Juggling Commutes, Low-waged Shift Work and Child Care in a Changing ('New') Economy" *Women Across Borders.* Eds. Jeffery Klaehn and Jean Chen. Toronto: Blackrose Books, 2009. 26-40. Print.

— "(Under)Valuing Care Work: The Case of Child Care Workers in Small-Town Quebec" *International Journal of Early Years Education* 15.2 (2007): 125-139. Print.

— "Small Town, Big Benefits: The Ripple Effect of $7/day Child Care" *Canadian Review of Sociology and Anthropology* 43.2 (2006): 125-140. Print.

Akyeampong, Ernest B. "Business Support Services." *Perspectives on Labour & Income* (Statistics Canada) 6.5 (2005): 5-9. Print.

Ames, B. D., W. Brosi, & K.M. Damiano-Teixeira. "'I'm Just Glad My Three Jobs Could be During the Day': Women and Work in a Rural Community." *Family Relations* 55 (2006), 119-131. Print.

Baker, Maureen. *Restructuring Family Policies: Convergences and Divergences.* Toronto: University of Toronto Press, 2006. Print.

Bakker, Isabella, (ed.) *Rethinking Restructuring: Gender and Change in Canada.* Toronto: University of Toronto Press, 1996. Print.

Beach, Jane, Martha Friendly, Carolyn Ferns, Nina Prabhu and Barry Forer. *Early Childhood Education and Care in Canada 2008.* Toronto: Childcare Resource and Research Unit, 2009. Print.

Beck, Ulrich. *The Brave New World of Work.* Translated by P. Camiller. Cambridge: Polity Press, 2000. Print.

Bégin, Louise, L. Ferland, G. Girard, and C. Gougeon. *School Daycare Services.* Québec: Gouvernement du Québec. Cat. No. 2002-02-00121, 2002. Print.

Bezanson, Kate. "Child Care Delivered through the Mailbox: Social Reproduction, Choice, and Neoliberalism in a Theo-Conservative Canada." Eds. Susan Braedley and Meg Luxton. *Neoliberalism and Everyday Life.* Montreal: McGill-Queens University Press, 2010. 90-112. Print.

Bezanson, Kate. *Gender, the State & Social Reproduction: Household Insecurities in Neoliberal Times.* Toronto: University of Toronto Press, 2006.

— "Gender and the Limits of Social Capital." *Canadian Review of Sociology and Anthropology* 43.4 (2006): 427-443. Print.

Bezanson, Kate and Meg Luxton Eds. *Social Reproduction: Feminist Political Economy Challenges Neoliberalism.* Montreal: McGill-Queen's University Press, 2006. Print.

Braedley, Susan and Meg Luxton Eds. *Neoliberalism and Everyday Life.* Montreal: McGill- Queens University Press, 2010. Print.

— "Competing Philosophies: Neoliberalism and the Challenges of Everyday life." Susan Braedley and Meg Luxton Eds. *Neoliberalism and Everyday Life.* Montreal: McGill-Queens University Press, 2010. 3-21. Print.

Brownell, Barbara. *Task Force on Rural Child Care & Early Childhood Education.* Task Force on Rural Child Care & Early Education (TORC), 2000. Print.

Connell, Raewyn. "Understanding Neoliberalism" Susan Braedley and Meg Luxton Eds. *Neoliberalism and Everyday Life.* Montreal: McGill-Queens University Press, 2010. 22-36. Print.

Cummins, Helene. "Unraveling the Voices and Identity of Farm Women." *Identity: An International Journal of Theory and Research.* 5.3 (2005): 287-302. Print.

Duffy, A. & N. Pupo. "Employment in the New Economy and the Impact on Canadian Families." Eds. C. Krull and J. Sempruch. *A Life in Balance?*

Reopening the Family-Work Debate. Vancouver: UBC Press, 2011. 98-114. Print.

Dufour, D. "The Lumber Industry: Crucial Contribution to Canada's Prosperity." *Manufacturing Overview Research Papers.* (Cat. No031F0027XIE-No.01). Stats Canada, 2002. Print.

— *Sovereign Virtue: The Theory and Practice of Equality.* Cambridge: Harvard University Press, 2000. Print.

Esping-Andersen, Gosta. "Women in the New Welfare Equilibrium" *The European Legacy* 8.5 (2003): 599-610. Print.

— *Social Foundations of Post-Industrial Economies.* Oxford: Oxford University Press, 1999. Print.

— *Three Worlds of Welfare Capitalism.* London: Polity, 1990. Print.

Fitchen, J. *Endangered Spaces, Enduring Places: Change, Identity and Survival in Rural America.* Boulder, CO: Westview, 1991. Print.

Fox, B. Ed. *Family Patterns, Gender Relations.* Toronto: Oxford University Press, 2009. Print.

Friendly, M. and S. Prentice. *About Canada: Childcare.* Black Point, NS: Fernwood, 2009. Print.

Gill, Stephen and Isabella Bakker. *Power, Production and Social Reproduction: Human Insecurity in the Global Political Economy.* New York: Palgrave, 2003. Print.

Government of Canada. "Universal Child Care Plan." 2006. Retrieved November 22, 2006. http://www.universalchildcare.ca/en/faqs_benefit.shtml Web.

Government of Canada and Government of Quebec. "Canada-Quebec Agreement on Early Learning and Child Care, Funding Agreement." Toronto: Childcare Resource and Research Unit, 2005. Retrieved June 5, 2007. http://action.web.ca/home/crru/rsrcs_crru_full.shtml?x=82553. Web.

Government of Quebec. "Family and Childcare Services – Childcare Services" 2006. Retrieved June 4, 2007. http://www.mfa.gouv.qc.ca/thematiques/famille/services-garde/type/index$_e$n.aspW eb.

Government of Quebec. *Development and Funding Scenarios to Ensure the Permanence, Accessibility and Quality of Childcare Services: Consultations 2003.* Québec: Ministère de L'Emploi, de la Solidarité sociale et de la famille. Print.

Heather, Barbara, Lynn Skillen, Jennifer Young and Theresa Vladicka. "Women's Gendered Identities and the Restructuring of Rural Alberta." *Sociologia Ruralis* 45.1/2 (2005): 86-97. Print.

Human Resources and Skills Development Canada. "Wood Products Industry" Government of Canada, 2005. www.hrsdc.gc.ca/en/hip/hrp/sp/industry_profiles/woods.shtml. Web.

Ibbitson, John. *The Polite Revolution: Perfecting the American Dream.* Toronto: McClelland & Stewart, 2005.

Jenson, Jane. "Family Policy, Child Care and Social Solidarity—The Case of Quebec" Susan Prentice Ed. *Changing Child Care: Five Decades of Child Care Advocacy & Policy in Canada.* Halifax: Fernwood Publishing, 2001. 39-62. Print.

Johnston, Mary T. "Goin' to the Country: Challenges for Women's Health Care in Rural Canada." *Canadian Medical Association Journal* 159.4 (1998): 339-341. Print.

Kelly, E. Brooke. "Leaving and Losing Jobs: Resistance of Rural Low-Income Mothers." *Journal of Poverty* 9.1 (2005): 83-103. Print.

Kelly, Roisin and Sally Shortall. "'Farmers' Wives': Women Who Are Off-Farm Breadwinners and the Implications for On-Farm Gender Relations." *Journal of Sociology* 38.4 (2002): 327-343. Print.

Krull, Catherine. "Families and the State: Family Policy in Canada." Ed. David Cheal. *Canadian Families Today: New Perspectives.* Don Mills: Oxford University Press, 2007. 254-272. Print.

Leach, Belinda. "Transforming Rural Livelihoods: Gender, Work, and Restructuring in Three Ontario Communities." Ed. B. Fox. *Family Patterns, Gender Relations.* Toronto: Oxford, 2009. 509-522. Print.

Leach, B. & A. Winson. "Bringing 'Globalization' Down to Earth: Restructuring and Labour in Rural Communities." *The Canadian Review of Sociology and Anthropology* 32.3 (1995). 341-364. Print.

Little, Margaret Hillyard and Ian Morrison. "'The Pecker Detectors are Back': Regulation of the Family Form in Ontario Welfare Policy." *Journal of Canadian Studies* 34.2 (1999): 110-136. Print.

Luffman, Jacqueline. "Core-Age Labour Force." *Perspectives on Labour and Income* (Statistics Canada): 7.9 (2006): 5-11. Print.

Luxton, Meg. "Family Coping Strategies: Balancing Paid Work and Labour." Ed. B. Fox. *Family Patterns, Gender Relations.* Toronto: Oxford University Press, 2009. 453-473. Print.

— "Families and the Labour Market: Coping Strategies from a Sociological Perspective." *How Families Cope and Why Policymakers Need to Know.* Ottawa: Canadian Policy Research Networks & Renouf Publishing Co., 1998. 57-74. Print.

Luxton, Meg and June Corman. *Getting By in Hard Times: Gendered Labour at Home and on the Job.* Toronto: University of Toronto Press, 2001. Print.

Marshall, Katherine. "Converging Gender Roles" *Perspectives On Labour and Income* (Statistics Canada). 7.7(2006):6-17. Print.

McKinley Wright, Mareena. "'I Never Did Any Fieldwork, but I Milked an Awful Lot of Cows!' Using Rural Women's Experiences to Reconceptualize Models of Work." *Gender & Society* 9.2 (1995): 216-235. Print.

Miewald, Christiana and Eugene McCann. "Gender Struggle, Scale and the Production of Place in the Appalachian Coalfields." *Environment & Planning* 36.6 (2004): 1045-1064. Print.

Ministère de l'Emploi, de la Solidarité sociale et de la Famille. "Quebec's Parental Insurance Plan." 2007. Retrieved on July 9, 2007, http://www.rqap.gouv.qc.ca/a-propos-regime/caracteristiques_en.asp. Web.

Pascal, Charles. *With Our Best Future in Mind: Implementing Early Learning in Ontario* (Report to the Premier by the Special Advisor on Early Learning. Toronto: Queen's Printer for Ontario, 2009. Print.

Pearson, Ruth. "Beyond Women Workers: Gendering CSR." *Third Work Quarterly* 28.4 (2007): 731-749. Print.

— "The Social is Political." *International Feminist Journal of Politics* 6.4 (2004): 603-622. Print.

Perrons, Diane. "Care, Paid Work, and Leisure: Rounding the Triangle." *Feminist Economics* 6.1 (2000): 105-114. Print.

Phipps, Shelley. "Working for Working Parents: The Evolution of Maternity and Parental Benefits in Canada." *IRPP Choices* 12.2 (2006): 1-40. Print.

Robertson, N., H.C. Perkins, & N. Taylor. "Multiple Job Holding: Interpreting Economic, Labour Market and Social Change in Rural Communities. *Sociologia Ruralis* 48.4 (2008): 331-350. Print.

Roy, Laurent and Jean Bernier. *Family Policy, Social Trends and Fertility in Quebec: Experimenting with the Nordic Model?* Government of Quebec: Ministère de la Famille, des Aînés et de la Condition Féminine, 2007. Print.

Roy, F. "From She To She: Changing Patterns of Women in the Canadian Labour Force." *Canadian Economic Observer.* (Statistics Canada). Catalogues No. 11-010, 2006. pp. 3.1-3.10. Print.

Seiling, Sharon. "Changes in the Lives of Rural Low-income Mothers: Do Resources Play a Role in Stress?" *Journal of Human Behaviour in the Social Environment* 13.1 (2006): 19-41. Print.

Statistics Canada. "Sawmills." *Service Bulletin* (Cat. No. 35-003-X). 63.12 (2010): 1-22. Print.

— "Table: Manufacturing Sales, by Province and Territory, 2005-2009." Ottawa: Statistics Canada, 2010. http://www40.statcan.gc.ca/101/cst01/manuf28-eng.htm. Web.

— "Table: Earnings, Average Weekly, by Industry (All Industries)." Ottawa: Statistics Canada, 2009. http://www40.statcan.gc.ca/101/cst01\-/labr73a-eng.htm. Web.

— "Table: Earnings, Average Hourly for Hourly Paid Employees, by Industry (All Industries)." Ottawa: Statistics Canada, 2009. http://www40.statcan.gc.ca/101/cst01/labr74a-eng.htm. Web.

— "OECD Regions at a Glance." *The Daily,* Sept. 13, 2005. Ottawa. Print.

— "Sawmills and Planing Mills." *The Daily,* March 5, 2002. Print.

— "1996 Census: Labour Force Activity, Occupation and Industry, Place of Work, Mode of Transportation to Work, Unpaid Work" *The Daily,* March 17, 1998. Print.

Stinson, Jane. "We Need Feminist Organizing Now More than Ever." *Canadian Dimension* 41.2 (2007): 12. Print.

— "Impact of Privatization on Women." *Canadian Dimension* 40.3 (2006): 27-32. Print.

Tougas, Jocelyne. "Reforming Quebec's Early Childhood Care and Education: The First Five Years." Toronto: Childcare Resource & Research Unit, Centre for Urban & Community Studies, 2002. Occasional Paper 17. Print.

— "Quebec's Family Policy and Strategy on Early Childhood Development and Childcare." *Education Canada* 39.4 (2002): 20-22. Print.

— "What We Can Learn from the Quebec Experience." Eds. Gordon Cleveland and Michael Krashinsky. *Our Children's Future: Child Care Policy in Canada.* Toronto: U of T Press, 2001. 92-105. Print.

— "Child Care in Quebec: Where There's a Will, There's a Way" *Child*

Care Advocacy Association of Canada—Parent Voices. 2001. Retrieved June 4, 2007. http://action/web.ca/home/crru/rsrcs_crru_full.shtml? x=33518. Web.

Vanier Institute of the Family. "Families Working Shifts." *Fascinating Families* 26 (2010): 1-2. Print.

Warriner, William and Ian Peach. *Canadian Social Policy Renewal, 1994-2000*. Halifax: Fernwood, 2007. Print.

Whitzman, Carolyn. "At the Intersection of Invisibilities: Canadian Women, Homelessness and Health Outside the 'Big City.'" *Gender, Place and Culture* 13.4 (2006): 383-399. Print.

Williams, Cara. "Work-life Balance of Shift Workers" *Perspectives on Labour and Income*. Ottawa: Statistics Canada, 2008. Cat. No. 75-001-X. Print.

3.

Mothers, Doulas, Flexible Labour and Embodied Care in the United States

ANGELA CASTAÑEDA AND JULIE SEARCY

INTRODUCTION

Doulas, who provide support for mothers during birth, engage in care work that is increasingly embedded within discourses and practices of neoliberal flexible labour. This paper takes doulas, and the mothers who hire them, as a place to begin interrogating the relationship between mothering and what has been termed neoliberal logic. We conducted research in a small U.S. Midwestern town with a thriving doula community and a non-profit organization that supports women and their families in their transition to motherhood. Through participant-observation, interviews with twenty-five doulas and three focus groups with mothers, we consider the discourses and practices of care work as negotiated within the context of neoliberal labour. In our research we found that doulas experience tension between their conceptualizations of the embodied caring nature of "mothering the mother" and a neoliberal market that pushes them to professionalize. In this paper we privilege the voices of mothers and birth doulas as we interrogate how neoliberal market-based professional strategies influence the type of care doulas provide to mothers.

For many American women, doulas are becoming an integral part of their entry to motherhood. In her book *The Tender Gift*, Dana Raphael, a medical anthropologist, first applied the word doula to birth culture when describing the importance of "mothering the mother" during the fourth trimester to increase successful breastfeeding results. Yet, today we find doulas are increasingly active in all stages of this event from birth through postpartum. DONA International, the largest professional organization for doulas describes a doula as "a trained and experienced professional who provides continuous physical, emotional and information support to the mother before, during and just after birth".[1] Indeed, the field of doulas is growing, yet doulas work at the margins of a very established medical profession. They interact regularly with midwives, obstetricians, nurses and medical staff, but do not have medical training or licensure. Doulas enter the homes and intimate spaces of pregnant women and straddle the constructed boundaries between intimate and public in their work.

NEGOTIATING INTIMATE SPACES

In one ethnographic moment, Lisa sits in the warm sun of a coffee shop as she thoughtfully pauses, "I am trying to think about what's so . . . different about this work and how to describe it." Lisa is in her mid-thirties and has been working as a doula for a decade. After attending over one hundred and fifty births, she has recently taken a break following the birth of her first child. She said:

> I think it has to do with the way this profession defines boundaries. Being clear about what the doula-client relationship is and what the parameters of that are [is important]. I think that in any sort of caretaking helping profession, [these boundaries are] really important because we are involved intimately in people's personal lives.

Lisa points to a tension as she tries to articulate the kind of care provided by doulas. She describes the kind of intimate work doulas do; fielding phone calls at all hours of the night and seeing women and their partners in the intimate spaces of their homes as a birth unfolds. Yet this intimate care comes up against the push towards the professionalization of doula work.

As doulas explain their work, they describe two perceived competing logics: one influenced by embodied care and the other a neoliberal market. We describe embodied care as a lived experience that is "relational, fluid and processual" (Jaye 41). Doulas speak about their work, what we are calling "embodied care," in terms of a "doula spirit" that is performed, shared, and demonstrated through their interactions with mothers, fellow doulas, and other care providers. This form of care appears to compete with a neoliberal market model in which individuals see themselves as sets of skills that need careful marketing (Gershon 539, Harvey 42). In a neoliberal world, agents are expected to use market rationality to understand the social relationships around them and to draw on that same market rationality when they are considering what social strategies to use in those relationships (Brown 694, Gershon 539, Rose 240). It became clear through interviews that doulas articulate their work using the neoliberal frame for market agency while also struggling to configure relationships in ways that resist neoliberal constraints. As one doula explained, "We are the compassionate component to that business of birthing." Doulas often describe their work as "holding the space," their community as a "sisterhood ministry," and their presence at birth as "an honored guest." Yet doulas are also faced with pressure to legitimize their work via a process of professionalization that appears to conflict with the embodied care epitomizing a doula spirit.

METHODS AND FIELDWORK

This article is based on ten months of ethnographic fieldwork conducted with doulas and mothers in a thriving Midwest doula community from 2011-2012. The Midwestern town where we conducted this research is a unique place for doulas, in that many doulas are trained through a non-profit organization in town that serves area women and their families as they transition from birth to parenthood. For the size of the town, we believe it is fair to describe this place as a "thriving" doula community. There are monthly doula discussion nights where doulas gather to share their experiences, as well as a website and Facebook page for local doulas, where doulas seek advice and cultivate a community of support. We conducted twenty-five semi-structured interviews with birth doulas, each lasting between forty-five and ninety minutes. Interviews were conducted in a variety of settings from local restaurants to the public library, and all interviews were recorded, transcribed and coded for themes. We used Internet and local public directories to first identify practicing doulas. In addition, we utilized snowball sampling to compile a more extensive list of birth doulas. All of the twenty-five participants were currently practicing as birth doulas with the average number of years practicing at six. The average number of births attended on an annual basis was eight and the amount charged for doula services ranged from $100 to $700. All but seven participants had children, and eight had used a doula with the birth of their own children.

An analysis of the participant doulas reveals that the overwhelming majority are white, heterosexual, married and college educated. While not dismissing the power of this majority, we also recognize the presence of minority voices within the doula community. For example, four of the women identified as bisexual and two as queer. Our study confirmed that only seven doulas recorded an annual household income of less than $35,000. Given these results, it would appear that the desire to frame doulas in terms of unpaid "care work" is reserved for a privileged group. The issue of class conflict was discussed by several doulas such as Crystal who shyly admitted, "Sometimes it feels like it's just for the higher class, both the doulas and their clients...the whole atmosphere in general. And I feel like I stand out in terms of the group of doulas because everyone is so highly educated and I'm not. Everybody has these big degrees and it just makes me feel like an outsider." These results also raise questions on the economic viability of doula work and highlight the various ways that doulas perform flexible labour. With neoliberal policies eroding state provisions, the increasing prevalence of doulas is not surprising given the market imperative to offload state responsibility once again onto the shoulders of mothers.

Indeed, doulas themselves identified a tension surrounding the ethical nature of their work struggling between marketing their services while not appearing "greedy" in the eyes of other doulas and the larger culture in general. This point reflects how despite ever-present neoliberal pressure to identify oneself as an economic agent in the "public" sphere, contradictorily, in the "domestic" sphere, the dominant American society prefers to view women and mothers as essentialized maternalist caregivers, thus creating a culture uncomfortable with claiming high pay for assumed "maternal" duties. Shelly, a leader in the doula community, highlights some of these "maternal" duties ascribed to mothering the mother. "As a mother I can connect, manage the situation, anticipate needs, lift her (the labouring mother) up, and my maternal instinct offers me a deeper connection because I'm caring for this mother and family like I would care and protect my own kids."

Given their passion for doula work, nearly half of the doulas interviewed identified their current position as "doula" and saw doula work as an economically viable business when paired with other birth related activities such as teaching childbirth education classes, lactation consultation, or midwifery assistant, something incorporated by eleven of the twenty-five doulas in our study. Despite this passion, the majority of doulas cited their main form of employment something other than their doula work, such as nanny, massage therapist, social worker, and accountant. These women recognized that doula work alone was not an economically viable option. Arriving at this conclusion was often described as a process. One doula and mother, Missy, described changes to her doula work as a "journey" where "money went from not being important to now I'm charging a sliding scale from $300-500 a birth, and this became a joint decision with my husband because I realized I needed to be compensated for the time spent away from my family." And Shelly said she "realized I needed to charge more when in this one moment I had to step away from a family during a birth to pump milk for my own baby," and she decided, "This isn't worth it."

Decisions to change pricing or take a leave from doula work were often described as family decisions, where the role of a supportive partner or spouse was emphasized by several doulas. Doulas discussed the need for both emotional and financial support, citing their partner or spouse as someone with whom they could share confidential experiences. We heard stories of doulas nudging a sleeping spouse awake at 3am so they could share their experiences after a long and difficult birth. Partners and spouses were described as flexible, supportive, and understanding of doula commitments. Financially, doulas identified a dual-income household as a supportive element to their ability to engage in doula work, especially if the doula also identified as a mother, which was the case for eighteen of the twenty-five doulas. Child-care responsibilities and the support for such unexpected work schedules also fell to partners and spouses and in some cases to other doulas who creatively arranged child-care swaps with each other to support their doula activities and reduce the cost of child-care expenses.

In addition to the twenty-five interviews, we also conducted three focus groups with twelve mothers who used a birth doula. Advertisements for the focus groups were displayed at the public library, preschools, and churches as well as posted with a local nonprofit organization and new moms' group. Children often accompanied mothers to the focus groups, which were conducted at the public library and in a local residence. The age of participating mothers ranged from twenty-six to forty years old. Only four mothers had more than one child, and all but three mothers had unmedicated vaginal births. The mothers reported paying between $250 and $500 for their birth doula. All but four mothers had completed either a Master's or Doctoral degree, and they listed current occupations ranging from student and stay at home mom, to minister and grant writer. Given the size and nature of this site and the fact that this work represents traditional ethnographic research based in a single community, we have changed the names of all participants to protect their identities.

TO MOTHER THE MOTHER

"She was my connection to a world that I didn't know, the world of motherhood."

Recent scholarship on consumption and motherhood suggests that mothering and neoliberalism are becoming entwined.[2] Rothman calls this the "consequences of capitalism for motherhood" as she describes the way commercial relationships become central to childbirth and mothering (279). Christa Craven and Robbie Davis-Floyd both write about how women and midwives have used neoliberal logic to position midwives as a consumer choice.[3] In light of this valuable scholarship, we were surprised to hear mothers in our focus groups describe their memories of their doula based solely on the embodied care they provided. Reassuring, confident, supportive, calm, engaged, knowledgeable, observant, caring, compassionate, selfless, and motherly. All of the mothers in our focus groups spoke about the importance of hiring a doula for the information, physical and emotional support they provided. Research gathered from mothers demonstrated the role of doulas as advocates and integral team players who built relationships with clients that extended beyond a business model.

The majority of mothers discussed hiring a doula for her experience. Mothers expressed wanting someone "with the right information," "who knew the medical environment," and "who could remain thoughtful during a process when I couldn't remain in control." Often times mothers emphasized the difference between a doula and their own biological mother as described here, "I wanted more confidence and a mother figure with more experience than my own mother would have been." Certification was not an important criterion for any of the mothers. As one mother admitted, "I don't even know what the training includes," and another mother commented, "I would have been hesitant to hire someone with no training, but now I have come to realize [that] the training is significant, but the hands on experience is far superior." All of the mothers emphasized the importance of personal contact and experience over certification.

Advocacy is an integral role for a birth doula. DONA International, the largest professional organization for doulas, states, "The doula advocates for the client's wishes as expressed in her birth plan, in prenatal conversations, and intrapartum discussion, by encouraging her client to ask questions of her caregiver and to express her preferences and concerns."[4] This is best illustrated by one young mother who recalled, "I was at the hospital at thirty-eight weeks, and they threatened pit [Pitocin]. My doula was there with me, and she was the advocate. She encouraged me to ask questions, and finally I asked if I could go home, and I did." For this mother, the doula gave her encouragement to ask for additional information that ultimately helped her avoid an unnecessary induction. Yet the advocacy role described by some mothers went beyond the professional standards of practice as outlined by DONA. Another mother described how her doula responded directly to hospital staff, "During my labour at the hospital a group of trainee nurses came in and asked 'Can we watch?' And I remember my doula saying vehemently 'No, you cannot. This is not a theatre.'" In this case, the doula advocated for her client's privacy and right to labour unobserved.

In all of our conversations with mothers, they expressed an appreciation for the information and the way it was provided by their doulas. Mothers recalled their doulas as "cheering them on," and one mother even described working with her doula as "almost like working with a personal trainer." Through their advocacy work, mothers also recognized the role of doulas in building relationships and acting as mediators between mothers and their partners, husbands, family, and care providers.

For many mothers, it was important to have a doula who could work in harmony with both care providers and partners. Mothers talked about doulas as team players: "supporting my husband and I together" and "working as part of the professional team." In this role as a team player, the doula complemented existing support systems. This sentiment was echoed by one mother who shared, "I wanted a doula for the professional aspect of it. She didn't replace family, instead she was the experience, not my mom who had been at three births of her own, but a doula who had been at one hundred and fifty births." Doulas were described as not only supporting the mothers, but also the spouses and partners, as illustrated in this example:

> My doula made me trust in my body and what was happening, and trust in the baby. There was this special moment during

labour when I was already six centimeters open, but I felt disappointed, and I remember her saying to me, "Six centimeters is wonderful. Now you can take a shower, and it is going to go quickly from here." So my confidence was back and after that, she explained to my husband how to relieve my pain, and they worked together to make a wonderful team.

Even prior to the birth, the role of a doula was described as integral in building a stronger relationship between mothers and partners. One mother described how her doula helped her learn more about her partner:

I found my prenatal appointments useful... when she asked us if we had any fears, my husband shared his fears about a previous surgery I had, and I had no idea he was scared or even still thinking about that experience which, thanks to my doula, I now know was traumatic for him.

In this example, the doula mediated the relationship between the mother and partner, and by strengthening their trust in one another; the doula was building a stronger birth team. And finally in one particular case, a mother shared how her faith influenced the relationship between herself, her husband and her doula:

Part of being a Christian doula is honoring and supporting that relationship between husband and wife. My doula shared my view that by allowing your husband to be strong then you can draw from his strength. It's like the husband is building a house and she is standing there handing him the tools.

In this role, the doula recognizes and shares the belief system of her clients and is able to harness this energy in her birth work to strengthen the bond between husband and wife.

While the mothers in our focus groups ranged from a few weeks to several years postpartum, all of the mothers described maintaining a continuing relationship with their doula. Mothers described this lasting relationship by noting, "she is an important person in our family," "it didn't feel like a business deal, or there was an end," and "she has become a permanent part of our lives." While they recognized the monetary exchange involved with the experience of hiring a doula, mothers instead focused on the quality of care provided by doulas. As one mother shared, "Completely apart from the fact that we paid her and hired her, I feel like we have an advocate and a friend for life. It never felt like a business type relationship at all." Mothers expressed being mothered by doulas as an experience marked by advocacy and teamwork. These mothers seemed to value most the embodied care doulas provided for them before, during, and after their births. In the following section we relate the stories told by doulas that work to balance professional standards with mothers' expectations for embodied care.

EMBODIED CARE

"A calling is the spirit, the doula spirit. It means this is what you were meant to do."

The term embodied care describes the kind of work doulas do; doulas build relationships, work with flexibility as a woman's needs change, and see birth as a transformative process. Doula work is often described as "mothering the mother," and it emphasizes a connection between women, which is physical, emotional and spiritual. Doulas talk about embodied care as a "doula spirit" that is performed, shared, and demonstrated through their interactions with mothers, fellow doulas, and other care providers. Many doulas speak with a kind of reverence about the work they do. As Ruth, a seasoned doula, explained:

> [When you are giving birth] you don't get any of the coverings that regular life allows you. You are completely and utterly vulnerable. To have a woman there who is compassionate, loving, intuitive, knowledgeable about birth and has your best interest at the centre of her heart...that's part of what I do. To have that person with you makes that woman come out of the process more whole and not more harmed. No matter what the outcome [of the birth] is.

Most doulas also said that their relationships with clients extend past the postpartum visit, as one doula noted, "I keep in touch with all of my clients well beyond the birth. I don't think you can be at someone's birth and then just disappear from their life. My clients and I feel a connection that goes beyond what they've hired me to do." This relational work allows a doula to provide intimate support during birth, but for some doulas it also extends beyond the mother-doula relationship to one that includes special attention to the partner, husband and with care providers, in particular labour and delivery nurses. Several doulas in our study described working as part of a team with care providers. As Maria commented:

> When I'm at a birth, I tend to make really good connections with the nurses because I'm willing to do stuff on my own. I try not to make [my presence an] inconvenience for them. I'm [like] "Oh I'll take care of this, I'll get my own sheets.".…And if I know that they are going to have the monitor on, I will have it laid out on the bed, and they're like "That's nice." Then they don't have to do it. It is that type of thing that [I do] to make them feel like I care.

It is this relational work that so many doulas and mothers find deeply satisfying.

While a small portion of the doulas interviewed regularly attend homebirths, the large majority interact primarily with obstetricians at the local hospital. Indeed, "rather than distancing themselves from medicalized birth, doulas have elected to operate within the system" (Norman and Rothman 257). Working within the dominant medical system forces doulas to construct different strategies of approach. From their chapter "The New Arrival" Norman and Rothman appropriately describe doulas as "chameleons" (262), a description that echoes the experiences often heard from doulas commenting on the unpredictability of birth work. "When we walk into a birth space, there is no way to predict what we might be doing over the next hours. I have found myself in the strangest positions. I have twisted my body into odd shapes, slept in weird chairs, dirty danced with a labouring woman, gotten in the shower fully clothed and stood on a hospital bed" (Beyers 23). To provide continuous support during a birth, doulas commit to staying with the woman from whenever she calls requesting the doula's help until the baby is born and has successfully breastfed. This can mean six hours or it can mean three days. Ultimately, their work is grounded in a doula's fluid ability to see what a woman in labour might need and to offer it to her in a way that is helpful for that particular woman and birth.

The last component to an embodied model of care is addressing how doulas saw their work as part of a larger process; for them birth itself was a transformative process for both the mother and the doula. In fact, many women came to doula work because of their own experiences with birth. As Maria, a young doula, revealed:

I was always terrified of childbirth myself since I was little because I thought it would be super painful. Since then I have only witnessed [one person in my family give birth] and it was really scary for me because I didn't understand it and nobody explained it to me... so I was always really terrified of [birth]...also I was a victim of sexual abuse so that kind of played into it as well. But since becoming a doula I have seen amazing things and I just have no doubts in my mind about what my body is capable of, so for me personally it has been transformative in terms of my own confidence about birth.

Doulas build relationships with the women who hire them, their families and other care providers they work with, they provide flexible services as they help during labour, and they understand birth to be a process that shapes all those who participate. These three elements reflect what we call embodied care, the kind of work doulas saw as encompassing the doula spirit. In describing this embodied care doulas saw themselves providing support and services that would make a lasting difference for families in transition, and it was this embodied care that gave doulas the most satisfaction in their work. And yet doulas also described their work in other terms, terms that better matched a presumed neoliberal market model of rationality.

NEOLIBERALISM AND THE PROFESSIONALIZATION OF DOULA WORK

"I feel like there are other things I have to seek out or offer that make me more of an 'in demand' doula, otherwise I feel like I just look like another doula. There are tons of pregnant women out there, but how do I get to those pregnant women? How do I market myself without looking greedy?"

Doulas also described their work in terms of market rationality; training, certifications, and marketing. David Harvey describes neoliberal market policies as those that advocate universal market principles through deregulation and privatization (Harvey 3). Many scholars have pointed to the way these policies come with new ideas about what it means to be an individual and an agent.[5] Most of this literature focuses on the way that people are expected to organize themselves according to neoliberal logics; people should see themselves as a bundle of skill sets seeking to form alliances with other bundles of skill sets (people) under market principles (Urciuoli). Agents are expected to use market rationality to understand the social relationships around them and to draw on that same market rationality when they are considering what social strategies to use in those relationships. Ultimately, neoliberalism can shape the way people see themselves operating in the world in regards to others.

Within the context of such presumed neoliberal logic, a concern about "professionalism" becomes apparent in the doula community. For doulas describing their work, "professionalism" seemed to index the need to operate under market principles in ways that often appeared to contradict the essentialized "mothering the mother" care they also described. Creating a false divide between "maternalism" on the one hand and "market rationality" on the other inevitably led the doulas interviewed to experience disjuncture—a constructed contradiction only reinforced by normative and essentialized conceptions regarding "mothering" in American society. All of the doulas we interviewed were asked about certification and professionalization. Nearly all of the doulas agreed on the importance of training with a professional organization and most felt certification was critical to be seen as professional. One doula said, "I felt like I had to be certified in order to work as a doula because I worried that people wouldn't hire me if I didn't have that certification even though I had the training and lots of experience." Certification was important even when choosing which professional organization to align with. One doula said she decided on CAPPA (Childbirth and Postpartum Professional Organization) as opposed to DONA certification because they offered multiple certifications, and she felt the more certifications she had the more professional she would appear to clients.

Many doulas saw professionalization as becoming a member of an organization that established rules for how doulas should be "engaged in the exchange of goods and services" they offered (Craven 701). As one doula shared, "It became really important to have a legit organization guiding me in what I should know and do and backing me up so that my clients know that I'm not just this island." Certification and professional affiliation was clearly an important part of acquiring the kind of bundled skill-set that neoliberal market logic requires. Working within this neoliberal logic, doulas saw themselves as a "collection of assets that must be continually invested in, nurtured, managed and developed" (Martin 582). Other examples of skill-sets and assets identified by doulas included: placenta encapsulation, prenatal and birth photography, yoga and massage therapy, aromatherapy, belly casting, cloth diaper and babywearing education, and additional lactation certification.

Some women commented on the way in which they saw a shift in the "doula spirit" or embodied care illustrated in this emphasis on marketing. Jane, an experienced doula, said:

> I see newer doulas entering the work with a completely different frame. They are more entrepreneurial; this is really a business for them and that was never the case 12 years ago when I started doing this work. It was not about business, it was not about money and it was not about how to market yourself. It was about the mothers and their families. I see that as a real change in doula work.

Michelle, another doula who trained over ten years ago, said, "It makes me sad to see all the new marketing techniques doulas use; doula contracts, webpages, Facebook, business cards, blogs...that was never the case earlier." Both Michelle and Jane express anxiety also felt by other doulas about the way professionalization affects doula spirit. However, newer doulas saw their marketing work as an essential part of their doula work necessary to "grow their business" and even expressed some "resentment" about having to do births for free, a practice that many older doulas saw as an essential part of training.

A decade makes an enormous difference in terms of the American economy and perceptions regarding the availability of work and the ability to maintain a decent standard of living through wage labour. As full-time jobs with benefits are increasingly being replaced by flexible labour, the position of the "doula" becomes a perceived "entrepreneurial labour opportunity" rather than "a way of giving back to the community." Within this neoliberal logic, "giving back to the community" cannot be legitimated unless it is quantified thus revealing the tensions between new and more experienced doulas. And yet, while doulas are increasingly relied upon to fill the state gap in provision of care, those providing this care are equally part of the larger flexible labour market in which appropriate pay for care work is devalued in society.

Such tension is revealed when Maria recounted an exchange with another doula scheduled to provide backup for her, a precautionary measure typically used by birth doulas. Maria wanted to reimburse the backup doula and recalled the following exchange:

> "No, no I don't need the money," she said. "No, I want to give you the money. I want to do that," and then she said, "I'm not doing this for the money. None of us are doing it for the money," and I said, "Well I am." I almost felt guilty when I said that. Don't tell anyone, but I am doing it for the money...And she looked at me like what is wrong with you.

Maria reiterated strongly after telling this story that she saw nothing wrong with doing doula work as a business. In fact, she saw doula work as requiring a monetary exchange in order to keep it from devaluing both the work she was doing and the person whom she was working for. The exchange between Maria and her backup doula represents the kinds of competing understandings of what it means to "mother the mother" in doula work. We heard doulas emphasizing both the embodied care that accompanied their work and the marketing and professionalization they saw as central to their ability to continue their work.

CONCLUSION

> "My role is to walk the tightrope...It's living on the edge of the boundaries and that's what makes it [doula work] a powerful role, and the best births occur when the tension is held among all those things and something new emerges. That's the beauty of it. That's the spiritual practice of it. That's the thing that cannot be captured in either the nurturing model or maybe the entrepreneurial model, because you can't classify it."

This research illustrates how doulas engage in an embodied model of care that balances honoring what the mother wants and needs while negotiating their own personal and professional obligations. We argue that while doulas recognize and identify with embodied care, they must also work within the increasing demands of a neoliberal flexible labour market. Given that the "doula spirit" is placed within an essentialized framework of "maternalism," professionalization thus creates a tension between the kind of "mothering the mother" or embodied care that doulas value. We return to Lisa, the doula we heard from first, who acknowledged this tension, stating:

Another problem about professionalism is walking the balance of honoring this work as important work that deserves financial compensation and respect and also honoring the emotional, spiritual intensity of it. And I feel like I see people swing both ways, where it's like this work is so amazing, and I'm so privileged to do it that I will just do it for free, and that doesn't honor the energy exchange that is required and that burns people out. Nobody can sustain that for very long, and on the flipside I've seen some doulas more recently who really want to do it as a job, and it lacks something deeper. Ultimately it's a hard balance to strike.

Another doula, Helen, commented on this tension by identifying "a huge conflict between the business mind versus the mothering mind." She went on to say, "The conflict is: why am I charging to do something women have been doing for thousands of years? It should just be a given, but I think the reason I'm charging is because the world has changed. And the birth culture has changed." Doulas exist at the very intersection of the neoliberal "mother" versus "worker" construct where women are expected to identify in terms of economic agency while also maintaining essentialist conceptualizations of mothering. In their efforts to negotiate these two constructed contrasting logics, doulas turn to professional organizations and marketing techniques in an effort to find spaces that help regulate and mediate the conflict of interest inherent in neoliberal alliances. Lisa recognizes this saying, "I think that is why it helps to have a professional organization and either be a member, or certified, or whatever. But not because certification itself is necessarily important, but because it provides a context for figuring out that professional role." Lisa did not see a conflict between growing your business as a doula as long as you didn't lose the "doula spirit." She said, "I feel like there is kind of a lack of self-awareness amongst some of the doulas, and a little bit more ego than I would like to see...one of the things that will change as the profession becomes broader, there maybe will be less soulfulness and heart in it."

Here Lisa makes clear that balancing embodied care in the context of a neoliberal logic requires a kind of self-awareness and heart. In our research, we saw doulas managing to foreground embodied care at certain moments of their work as a doula, and to foreground marketing and professionalism at other moments. Some doulas did this more adroitly than others, some doulas rejected the neoliberal framework completely suggesting that it undermined the kind of work doulas stood for, and other doulas firmly positioned themselves within a neoliberal market rationality, seeing even the kind of embodied care they provided through this lens.

The ability of doulas to negotiate between their conceptualizations of flexible embodied care and market rationality reflects their own economic position in a neoliberal world. As mentioned earlier, most of the doulas in this community come from dual-income households, many with supportive partners. None of the participants make a living wage based on their doula work alone, and since conducting our initial interviews, five doulas have stepped away from doula work due to the need for a more reliable and substantial income. However, doulas' desire to frame the care they offer as a "privilege" or "honor" also speaks to their own ambivalence about the kinds of constraining value they believe neoliberal logic imposes on their work. Many doulas seemed to recognize that within a neoliberal market, economic compensation pointed to validation for the care they provided. Others expressed ambivalence about this economic validation, as if embodied care was a more valuable skill, which exceeded the boundaries of a metric provided by market regulations.

This raises larger questions: doulas and mothers both express their work as one of constant giving that often requires a sublimation of self. How does this care translate into a presumed market logic, and what is lost in that translation? How can we account for the different frames embodied work and care necessitate? As doulas negotiate this and many other questions, they represent a community where we can turn as scholars to think through the disjunctures inherent in the process of neoliberalism and what it means for the kind of work mothering entails.

NOTES

[1] See DONA "What Is a Doula?" http://www.dona.org/mothers/index.php, accessed July 4, 2012.
[2] See Craven; Rothman; and Taylor et al.
[3] See Craven; and Davis-Floyd
[4] See DONA "Standards of Practice for Birth Doulas."
[5] See Brown; Gershon; and Rose 240

WORKS CITED

Beyers, Julie. "Doula Performance Anxiety." *International Doula* 20.1 (2012): 23. Print.

Brown, Wendy. "American Nightmare." *Political Theory* 34 (2006): 690-714. Print.

Craven, Christa. "A 'Consumer's Right' to Choose a Midwife: Shifting Meanings for Reproductive Rights under Neoliberalism." *American Anthropologist* 109.4 (2007): 701-712. Print.

— *Pushing for Midwives: Homebirth Mothers and the Reproductive Rights Movement.* Philadelphia: Temple University Press, 2010. Print.

Davis-Floyd, Robbie. "Qualified Commodification: Consuming Midwifery Care." *Consuming Motherhood.* Eds. Janelle Taylor, Danielle Wozniack, and Linda Layne. New Brunswick: Rutgers University Press, 2004. 211-248. Print.

DONA. "Standards of Practice for Birth Doulas." 2012. http://www.dona.org/aboutus/standards_birth.php accessed May 1, 2012. Web.

— "What Is a Doula?" 2012. http://www.dona.org/mothers/index.php, accessed July 4, 2012. Web.

Gershon, Ilana. "Neoliberal Agency." *Current Anthropology* 52.4 (2011): 537-555. http://www.jstor.org/stable/10.1086/660866, accessed February 25, 2012. Web.

Harvey, David. *A Brief History of Neoliberalism.* Oxford: Oxford University Press, 2005. Print.

Jaye, C. "Talking Around Embodiment: The Views of GPs Following Participation in Medical Anthropology Courses." *Medical Humanities* 30 (2004): 41-48. doi: 10.1136/jmh.2003.000146, accessed March 16, 2012. Web.

Martin, Emily. "Mind-Body Problems." *American Ethnologist* 27.3 (2000): 569-590. Print.

Norman, Bari Meltzer and Barbara Katz Rothman. "The New Arrival: Labor Doulas and the Fragmentation of Midwifery and Caregiving." *Laboring On: Birth in Transition in the United States.* Eds. Wendy Simonds, Barbara Katz Rothman and Bari Meltzer Norman. New York: Routledge, 2007. 251-281. Print.

Raphael, Dana. *The Tender Gift: Breastfeeding.* Englewood Cliffs, NJ: Prentice-Hall, 1973. Print.

Rose, Nikolas. *Governing the Soul: The Shaping of the Private Self.* London: Routledge, 1990. Print.

— "Genetic Risk and the Birth of the Somatic Individual. Special Issue on Configurations of Risk." *Economy and Society* 29.4 (2000): 484-513. Print.

Rothman, Barbara Katz. "Caught in the Current." *Consuming Motherhood.* Eds. Janelle Taylor, Danielle Wozniack, and Linda Layne. New Brunswick: Rutgers University Press, 2004. 279-288. Print.

Taylor, Janelle, Linda L. Layne, and Danielle F. Wozniack, Eds. *Consuming Motherhood.* New Brunswick: Rutgers University Press, 2004. Print.

Urciuoli, Bonnie. "Skills and Selves in the New Workplace." *American Ethnologist* 35.2 (2008): 211-228. Print.

The Entrepreneurial Mother

4.

"Doing It All...and Making It Look Easy!"

Yummy Mummies, Mompreneurs and the North American Neoliberal Crises of the Home

GILLIAN ANDERSON AND JOSEPH G. MOORE

INTRODUCTION

Neoliberalism in North America has not only restructured the public sphere, it has engendered a troubling "crisis of home" (Duyvendak). Longer work hours, the erosion of collective supports and heightened consumption expectations have intensified the burden of social reproduction shouldered primarily by women as mothers. This chapter examines the emergence of Anglo North American "Yummy Mummy" and "Mompreneur" discourses as a cultural response to this "crisis of the home." Content analysis of a Canadian parenting magazine alongside a growing scholarship on this "new Momism"[1] reveal seductive stories of women who reconcile the "new reality" of neoliberal economies with their mothering largely through the pursuit of self-employment and entrepreneurial work. These "hip," confident, stylish, and business-savvy Moms can "d[o] it all...and mak[e] it look easy."[2]

And so it seems, at least at first glance, that these mothers have all on their own resolved the "crises of home." Faced with normative expectations of the "good mother," a lack of standard work, and the retreat of the state, self-employment and entrepreneurship may indeed be attractive, viable and profitable options for some women. Yummy mummy narratives, however, mask as much as they reveal. While the exit of relatively privileged mothers from standardized work is celebrated, the temporal and spatial extension of women's (un)paid labour remains hidden and the outsourcing of "mother-work" (Ladd-Taylor) to less privileged women and mothers is left unchallenged. Narratives such as these not only deepen structural inequalities, but also impart forms of "flexible reproduction" into the home.

Our aim is to both critique and contrast this flexible restructuring of the home with more sustainable alternatives that not only exist outside the commodified, market-based forms favoured by neoliberal models, but ones that are sensitive to mothers' ongoing struggle to "earn" and "care enough" (Jenson). The contradictions of the existing system are what make it untenable over the long term, and emerging alongside this instability is a sense of hope that other mothering ideologies and practices are possible.

NEOLIBERALISM AND SOCIAL REPRODUCTION: LESSONS FROM FEMINIST POLITICAL ECONOMY

While much of this chapter will focus on the description and critique of contemporary cultural representations of motherhood, we do so with a firm recognition that these representations are produced, consumed and resisted within the material and historical context of neoliberalism. As Harvey argues, neoliberalism is an ongoing political project of a ruling class (Harvey). State powers are directed towards the extension of markets across the globe, into areas of social and ecological reproduction (land, water etc.), and deeper into everyday life. In Canada and the U.S., as state involvement in social provision is withdrawn, neoliberalism violently overturns both formal political and economic institutions, and also "ways of life and thought, reproductive activities, attachments to the land and habits of the heart" (Harvey 3). Here the growing body of literature, especially that of feminist political economy (FPE), which has explored the politics of home in neoliberal states, is particularly informative.

FPE has identified neoliberal economic and social policy with the twin, and often contradictory processes of familialization[3] and defamilialization. Neoliberal policies have offloaded the costs and responsibilities of social reproduction onto families, women, and especially mothers. In Canada and the U.S, as workplace benefits, rewards and state supports have been eroded, families and communities have been forced to "take up the slack." Yet, these same policies and conditions have encouraged women's increased dependence on paid labour and increasingly women, like men, are viewed, and valued, primarily as worker-citizens. The processes of familialization/defamilialization and their inherent tensions must, according to FPE, be understood within the context of both existing patterns of racial and class inequality and the tendency for economic polarization across neoliberal states. Particular attention has been drawn to the limited and unsustainable coping strategies available to low-income, single and racialized mothers who find themselves working long hours in deregulated labour markets at the very moment when collective supports developed to make such participation possible have been lost.[4] However, others have noted that middle-class coping strategies, including increased personal debt and the outsourcing or purchase of social reproduction services and goods, depend upon and reproduce precarious work performed largely by working-class women and create further unsustainable market-dependencies.[5]

In this study, we build on this literature by critically engaging with what are largely middle-class Anglo North American narratives of motherhood in popular media. By many accounts (though few of them scholarly), the rise of the yummy mummy persona and mompreneur discourses have largely been stoked by media interest in hot Hollywood Moms and a general fascination with celebrity motherhood.[6] Following O'Donohoe, the term appears to have "emerged with a new generation of celebrities who retained their glamour (and regained their figures) after giving birth" (O'Donohoe). Think Angelina Jolie, Katie Holmes and Sarah Jessica Parker, among others. In Canada, O'Donohoe points to former Much Music VJ Erica Ehm. Ehm has "gone from rock'n roll to rocking the cradle."[7] As the creative voice of "YummyMummyClub.ca" her website "speaks to the woman in every mom struggling with the reality of being a modern parent" and in doing so she "has become the passionate voice of a whole new generation—Yummy Mummies."[8]

Mainstream media and pop culture have played a major role in epitomizing the yummy mummy as the success story of modern motherhood, completely eviscerating all structural realities. While the "privileged" yummy mummies who "have it all" are celebrated, mothers who are struggling are often faulted, and even blamed for being unable to do the same. In her *Atlantic Monthly* article, "Why Women Still Can't Have it All," Slaughter writes, "The women who have managed to be both mothers and top professionals are superhuman, rich, or self-employed…making millions of women feel that *they* are to blame if they cannot manage to rise up the ladder as fast as men and also have a family and an active home life (and be thin and beautiful to boot)."[9]

While scholars and activists have expressed reservations about emphasizing cultural imagery at the expense of structural inequalities and political struggle, FPE acknowledges the dialectic of structural and cultural moments, highlighting the ways in which cultural texts generally, and media images in particular, are integral to the reproduction of patriarchal capitalism. In our analysis, we seek to better understand the rise of a new "Momism"[10]—the yummy mummy/mompreneur, and what this means for those of us living under neoliberal regimes. We question the representativeness of these narratives and the extent to which they mediate or reinforce the tensions and crisis tendencies of neoliberalism in English-speaking North America.

YUMMY MUMMIES (YMS) AND WEST COAST MOMS (WCMS)

Since its launch in 2007, eight to ten times a year, *Yummy Mummy, This Time It's All About You!* magazine[11] was published inside *West Coast Families* magazine, a Vancouver, BC-based parenting magazine.[12] During the course of our data collection, in February/March 2010 *Yummy Mummy* was rebranded as *West Coast Mom.* Our study centres on the YM Profile which became the WCM Cover Mom profile, a short one-to-two page interview-style article and an accompanying photograph. We draw on *Yummy Mummy/West Coast Mom* profiles from 28 issues published between November 2007 and July/August 2011, yielding a convenience sample of 32 yummy mummies. All of the profiles have been openly coded and analyzed following a grounded approach[13] that is focused on making comparisons and noting emergent issues and themes. Demographic data was gathered and analyzed with respect to characteristics such as age, race, marital status, employment status and number of children.

While there is some diversity in the profiles (see Table 1), they generally reflect two images of modern motherhood, the "yummy mummy" and the "mompreneur." As Richardson and Laser note, the term "yummy mummy" refers to "an attractive, confident, and well-groomed or expectant mother, a woman who 'manages to glide through pregnancy and motherhood with the style and composure she possessed pre-conception,' (qtd. in O'Donohoe: 41) or 'a mother, of any age, who does not identify with the traditional, dowdy image of motherhood'" (qtd. in O'Donohoe: xvii). A "mompreneur" meanwhile refers to a mother "who has decided to take on the role of an entrepreneur, with the business itself being directly linked to either being a mom (via a product or service targeted at that market), or running a company in which the role of mom can be incorporated (i.e. working from home, flexible hours) into the business" (Buckworth).

The demographic profile of these yummy mummies/mompreneurs is hardly representative of most "west coast mothers." These mothers are overwhelmingly white, married, heterosexual, self-employed, middle-class women in their childbearing years, with one or two children under the age of ten. Our sample then reflects the racial and economic factors that others who have studied this cultural meme have noted. Douglas and Michaels indicate the contrast between media coverage of celebrity mothers versus welfare moms, the former "are perfect, most of them white," while welfare mothers are "usually Black or Latina—as if there were no white single mothers on the dole—poor, miserable and out of control" (qtd. in Jermyn 166). Further, "[u]nderplayed but nevertheless evident here is the sense in which the premise of the yummy mummy is, like the celebrity mom, arguably predicated on a degree of considerable economic privilege and is an inherently (middle-)classed concept" (Jermyn 166). As such, the struggles and coping strategies of yummy mummies/ mompreneurs are also particular to and reflective of their relatively privileged socio-economic position and family situation.

NARRATIVES OF MODERN MOTHERHOOD: THE BUSY, BLISSFUL LIVES OF YUMMY MUMMIES AND MOMPRENEURS

An overarching theme evidenced in these mothering narratives is the successful navigation of the multiple roles expected of women as "good mothers" in contemporary western societies. While struggles to manage the dual demands of (un)paid work are not altogether ignored, the clear intent of these women's profiles is to celebrate the possibility that mothers might simultaneously carve out a rewarding life, forge stable family relationships, engage in personally rewarding, socially useful paid work, and yet still embody expectations of physical beauty, a sense of self and opportunities for self-care.

Mothers are portrayed as successful career women with flourishing businesses and satisfying work. A ballet school director describes herself as "very fortunate to be able to pass on my years of experience as a dancer" (September 2010: 25), while a radio host feels "lucky to have been given the op-

Marital Status	N
Married	23
Engaged	1
Long-term relationship	1
Missing	7

Number of Children	N
One	8
Two	20
Three	1
Missing	3
Adopting	2

Race	N
Dominant Group	27
Visible Minority	5

Employment Status	N
Self-employed	19
Employed Full-time	7
Employed Part-time	4
Stay-at-Home Mom	2

Table 1: Demographic Characteristics ($N = 32$)

portunity to do this work, which I am truly passionate about" (April 2011: 27). An owner of a business providing education and networking services boasts, "We've only been around for two years, but we've got eight chapters across B.C. and Ontario" (October 2009: 33) and another sums up success as, "now that my business is up and running, I still have stressful days and sometimes I mess up, but most days are really great. I get to do what I love, and I get to be here for my family" (April 2009: 32). None of the profiles mention failed ventures or repetitive, menial or dangerous work. In addition to productive careers, these mothers epitomize domestic bliss. Of the eight issues analyzed in 2010 for example, all but one of the yummy mummies was "happily," "joyfully," or "blissfully" married, and many say they are "fortunate" or "lucky" to have such "supportive," "help[ful]," and "incredible" husbands. Few yummy mummies are single mothers, only two of the 32 cover moms or roughly 6% are single (of which, one at the time of publication mentioned a long term partner, while another spoke of "an amazing fiancé who is so supportive of [her] and [her] business" (July/August 2011: 26), and none are reportedly divorced. Children are inevitably described as "precious" (January/February 2011), "wonderful" (April 2011), "extraordinary" (May 2010), and the focal point of their lives. All of the yummy mummies' narratives centralize their role as mothers and their love for their children. Typical is the sentiment of a mother who said, "I have enjoyed every stage of my children's lives more than the last one… [n]othing puts life more in perspective than spending time with children" (February/March 2010: 37).

These mothers do express concern about the difficulties of balancing paid work and family life, however their profiles go to great lengths to suggest that they are "good mothers," and while they may get help from their male spouses, they also are still most likely to be the primary caregiver. One yummy mummy explains, "I would drop everything that I'm doing right now if they needed me… [b]eing a mom is the most important thing that I do" (December 2007/January 2008: 36). And yes, these moms value looking great while at home and work, or so it is suggested. Several of the women profiled extol the physical and mental benefits of exercise and healthy eating. One suggests, "the thing that makes me a 'Yummy Mummy' the most is making sure that no matter what, I get out of my PJs in the morning, jump in the shower, put on some make-up, dress in a cute outfit and get some fresh air… sometimes, this is an effort, but it is so well-worth it" (April 2008: 38). Taken together these themes culminate in the narrative of one recently featured mom who says "thank God I have an amazingly supportive husband and community of friends, a delightful son, and a career that I love; joy and a sense of calling in these things is what sustains me" (March 2011: 27).

STRUGGLES OF YUMMY MUMMIES: THE ELUSIVE SEARCH FOR WORK/LIFE BALANCE

If the narratives in *Yummy Mummy/West Coast Mom* are to be read as "success stories," these successes rarely emerge without an element of struggle. Though ultimately prevailing, yummy mummies invariably describe their daily lives as replete with challenge—especially the challenge of balancing paid work, unpaid domestic labour and personal well-being. Struggling to meet the demands of the "double day" (Luxton) many women spoke of the time stress they routinely encounter. One "joyfully married, mother of two precious boys and a part-time grade two and dance teacher" reflects:

> One of my challenges in day to day life—common to all work-ing moms—is juggling family and career. There are certainly days, where I feel that I am neglecting my family for career or career for family. There are many times when I work late into the night planning lessons and preparing for the next day. As well, there are those days when my husband or boys require my undivided attention. (January/February 2011: 25)

Similarly, a co-owner of a photography business laments:

> It's a challenge finding the balance, staying focused, wearing all the hats a business owner has to wear. It's hard being a mom, new wife and business owner who wants to be great at all of them, at times it feels like something has to give. Espe-cially finding time to exercise and take care of myself. (July/Au-gust 2011: 26)

And a married, mother of two, radio producer shares:

> I think one of the biggest challenges for any mom is to find a balance between family, career and self. It's not an easy for-mula to figure out, you have to find whatever works for you. Right now I have the luxury of being on maternity leave, so it makes things a little easier. It'll be a whole new ball game when I'm back at work next year. (At least motherhood will give me a ton of things to talk about on air!). (October 2010: 25)

This "whole new ballgame" is one of intense busyness where mothers are expected to have successful careers, run thriving businesses, be primary caregivers, and contribute to community. As one mother to an 18-year-old son and two daughters aged 16 and 10, an elected school board official, and former private practice dietician reveals, "I am very busy balancing my role as mother, elected official, and daughter of a mother who needs more and more care...I am on to go all the time." (February/March 2009: 32)

GETTING IT (EVERYTHING) DONE: YUMMY MUMMIES' COPING STRATEGIES

Taken together, these themes present not simply a metanarrative of success, but of good mothering in the face of many challenges. There is, of course, significant tension between these elements—one that cannot be sustained without further analysis of the strategies, resources and actions that might account for relative success in the face of adversity. Upon closer examination of their coping strategies, the yummy mummies' stories become more complex and ultimately reveal the normative expectations and contradictions of mothering under neoliberalism in Canada and the U.S.

How do they do it? There is no single coping strategy. One mom noted "I feel very lucky to have a part-time career and be at home with my boys. I get to experience the best of both worlds" (January/February 2011: 25). However, retreating from paid labour was rare. The vast majority of yummy mummies are either self-employed or work full-time. Many mothers run their own businesses or have otherwise crafted independent entrepreneurial careers. Mompreneurship is presented as a means to an end—income is rarely mentioned. Self-employment, these narratives suggest, is the preferred coping strategy. Flexibility is a key theme related to self-employment. A social worker noted her private practice allows her to "work independently and flexibly around child care" (May 2011: 27). Another mother who, following the birth of her second child took a buyout from her company and reinvented herself as a "family-focused strategic marketing specialist", describes working from home, the "flexibility" and "the ability to pick up and go" as influencing her decision and central to her happiness (July/August 2010: 27). Perhaps most tellingly, an owner of a travel company and "media personality" who "missed out on traditional perks, such as maternity leave" insisted that her "job has allowed for more flexibility and more fun with the kids" (December 2007/January 2008: 37).

Self-employment does not necessarily entail less paid work, but rather work that might better be scheduled around unpaid labour. As one mom describes, being a mompreneur "does not mean I work less—in fact, I am working more than I have in the past! However, I do it on my terms and have the flexibility to take the kids to preschool in the morning, attend their field trips, take them to all of their appointments and play hooky from time to time to hang out with them on a sunny afternoon" (May 2010: 33). What self-employment affords these women is flexible, paid work that can be done outside the time they remain primarily responsible for domestic tasks.

One mom describes her situation as follows: "I do take business calls during the day but it is understood that the person on the other end may hear one of my children in the background—that is just the reality of it. For the most part, however, I do my business during the evenings and week-ends" (October 2009: 32). Another mom explains working late or long hours as follows, "I paint when the boys are at school; I paint when Fred [my husband] takes them to the movies; I paint when they are all tucked up in bed asleep" (November 2008: 35), while another says "my kids barely think I work because when I leave I'm either taking them to school first or backing out of the driveway as they're going to school." Commenting on writing her first book, she further notes her "kids hardly think [she] wrote a book." Apparently, she spent most of her time "writing while her kids were off skiing during the weekends and after they went to bed in the evenings." She was determined to ensure her new venture did not disrupt family life (December 2007/January 2008: 37).

If self-employment offers flexible-scheduling and the ability to work in and around unpaid work, it is also suggested that productive labour and so-cial reproduction can in fact be merged. Here the ultimate flexibility comes not from doing paid work late at night or when children are at school, but when mothers work concurrently. A "blissfully married mom of two and self-employed sales and marketing professional specialist" notes:

> I have been known to make business contacts at the farmer's market and answer emails well into the wee hours of the morn-ing! I tend to work 24 seven… I love the flexibility my busi-ness gives me. Being able to work from my son's football game, while on a weekend away with my husband or at my daugh-ter's tennis lesson is pretty amazing. To me there is nothing better than spontaneous time with my family, so the ability to pick up and go at a moment's notice is invaluable to me (July/August 2010: 27).

If home and family spaces become places to work, workspaces are (re)-made to incorporate familial activities. This same mother states "one key solution for me has been making my office kid friendly. I have as much art and craft supplies in my office as I do files. This allows my daughter and me to 'work' together" (July/August 2010: 27). An organic bedding retailer mentions that her children hang around her showroom and "my boys even go to business meetings with me … I definitely keep them close and am so grateful that my work…allows me to do so" (April 2010: 34). Strategic multitasking—performing paid work alongside domestic duties—is not only made possible and encouraged by self-employment, but by information and communication technologies: ubiquitous internet connectivity, smart phones, and computers. It is no coincidence that many yummy mummies include among their "must-haves" "my shiny new iPhone, iPad & WiFi connectivity" (May 2010: 33), "my Blackberry/cell phone and my car" (February/March, 2009: 32) or most blatantly, "a Blackberry so that I can be at the park with my kids and still feel in touch with my work" (December/January 2010: 31). While there are fleeting moments of ambivalence, the mothers profiled generally and uncritically accept the limited and porous boundaries between their work and home lives. For yummy mummies, being tech-savvy, connected and willingly fusing the spheres of home and work are simply strategies to assist their search for work/life balance.

One strategy not entirely absent, but seldom articulated, is the sharing of unpaid labour. Only a lesbian couple explicitly mentioned the equal sharing of childcare (May 2011), while a business owner with grown children acknowledged, "I have been fortunate to have a true partner in life who shares everything and believes in equality and respect" (November/December 2010: 40). Most of the women do refer to their partners or husbands as "supportive," but just what this support entails is left unsaid. For instance, a co-owner of a company that provides services to entrepreneurial mothers notes she has "a very supportive husband who enables me to juggle various roles" though she is typically vague on whether this directly involves a sharing of domestic labour (December/January 2010: 31). Another woman listed among her "must haves" a husband who "took a month off when Sam and Lucy were born and it was so nice to have him around all the time" (October 2010: 26). This same mom was one of few who mentioned extended family, and one of the only who suggested family (tellingly her sister and mother) helped care for her newborn twins. Finally, a married mompreneur who loves the flexibility of being self-employed remarks:

> On the home front, the workload has increased as well because I now have to think of and consider every aspect of the kids' lives and make sure no balls are dropped. Did I sign the kids up for soccer? Did I fill out the permission slip? Did I get the school photo forms back on time? Is the paperwork filled for kindergarten? Are the kids' shots up to date? (May 2010: 33)

Men and fathers' participation in these labour intensive aspects of social reproduction are virtually absent and/or unquestioned, reinforcing and naturalizing the gendered division of labour in nuclear families and societal expectations that it is women as mothers who are primarily responsible for undertaking the mental and socio-emotional labour involved in caregiving. In one of the few very clear descriptions of the division of household labour, one business owner and married mother of two young children explains, "I have the immense privilege of being the one to be here and raise them. It is the biggest reward ever" (October 2009: 33). Another time-saving strategy rarely voiced is the purchase of goods and services, including domestic services. Many mothers listed consumer technologies as "must haves." One mentioned employing a personal trainer and several others "treat themselves" to massages, facials and health and beauty services. However in these narratives there are no nannies, day cares, tutors, cleaners, or meals to go. This absence is particularly notable given that their profiles are commonly surrounded by ads for "Top Model Birthday Parties ... promot[ing] positive self-image, creativity and lots of girlie fun" (October 2009: 33), children's fitness centres, synchronized swimming classes, pre-schools, music classes, and assorted purveyors of loot bags, children's performers etc. Moreover, mompreneurs are often involved in businesses that sell similar goods and services to other mothers.

Mothers are more likely to regularly report sacrificing personal time in order to "get everything done." When asked "Do you take time out for yourself? If so, what does that entail?" their answers were sometimes surprisingly blunt. One self-employed craftsperson was quite straightforward when she said, "I don't take time for myself—no, I don't" (November 2009: 32). A radio show host sarcastically replied, "Does watching recordings of Top Chef while folding laundry in the middle of the night count?" and added "Actually, I am pretty lucky because I get a wee bit of time to myself. Still I wish I could be in two (or three) places at once because it never feels like enough" (April 2011: 28). As a university professor put it, "This is a real challenge for me at the moment, as forty hours of work time plus forty hours of child care barely leaves enough time to empty the dishwater" and that for her the commute to work by bicycle counted as personal time because it allowed for "good time for reflection" (May 2011: 28). While a few yummy mummies "indulgences" include online shopping or meeting friends, those that do find time for themselves often exercise. Revealingly, in at least two cases exercise is explicitly linked to being more productive at work, while others more vaguely characterize exercise as rejuvenating and energizing (presumably needed to manage their long days). As one self-employed mother said, "I am reenergized [sic], excited and ready to take on the day after I leave the gym. It's a great way to get rid of stress—plus the best ideas come to me while I'm on the treadmill!" (October 2009: 33).

There is a marked similarity in the coping strategies evidenced in these narratives. Mothers faced with reconciling the competing demands and desires of paid work, maintaining and developing personal and family relationships, and retaining child-care responsibilities simply work longer hours, work more intensely, and sacrifice personal time. Through entrepreneurial endeavours and long hours in paid labour, these women are embedded into markets as owners and workers, and yet their narratives are curiously silent about how market goods and services enable them to cope with the "time bind" (Hochschild) central to their struggles. While professing their attachment to both spouses and children, if these mothers get any assistance it remains for the most part hidden or unarticulated.

To would-be readers, not to mention most mothers, these coping strategies raise as many questions as they answer. The tension between the successes and struggles of yummy mummies are never fully resolved, their explanations partial and vague. This ambiguity is not a consequence of the inaccuracy of the stories per se, though much remains unspoken, rather it is a consequence of how well these stories reflect the coping strategies of a select group of mothers attempting to find a way to succeed under the terms and conditions of a neoliberal state—a subject to which we now turn.

PROBLEMATIZING YUMMY MUMMY/MOMPRENEUR DISCOURSES

Given the lack of representation, naturalizing of women's roles in social reproduction, and unrealistic expectations, popular cultural narratives of motherhood have long been subjected to feminist criticism. As feminist political economists, we are interested in several related, but distinct questions including: how do these (mis)representations reflect the tensions and contradictions inherent within neoliberalism; how do such (mis)representations serve to sustain patriarchal capitalist forms; and how might they inform the struggle for more just economic and familial relations? Answers to our questions, in part, can be found in the gaps or silences in the yummy mummy narratives.

These are overwhelmingly the stories of married, middle-class, white women. Reading these narratives is an exercise in forgetting the diverse experiences of working-class mothers, mothers dependent on social assistance, and mothers living in poverty. Less advantaged, low-income, single, racialized mothers struggle with many of the same problems of busyness and balancing paid and unpaid work as those published in *West Coast Mom*. They struggle, however, without the support of a partner's income and in poorly compensated and alienated paid work and increasingly with the loss of social programs and community based supports. As Bezanson (Bezanson, *Gender, the State and Social Reproduction: Household Insecurity in Neo-liberal Times*) argues, the coping strategies of vulnerable mothers who lack representation here and elsewhere are clearly unsustainable.

Not only are the lives of working-class, low-waged and socially excluded mothers overlooked, the relation between these women and the success of yummy mummies is ignored. There is ample evidence to suggest a principal coping strategy of dual-income families involves using purchasing power to buy services and reducing time spent on unpaid labour.[14] Many middle-class and professional women use their greater earnings to buy more supports, increasing demand for domestic services such as house cleaning and child care. If this strategy goes unstated here, we might speculate it has more to do with the ubiquitous nature of such commodification and consumption, rather than any overt attempt to conceal. However, we acknowledge that the successful coping of yummy mummies/mompreneurs owes much to the low-paid, precarious work of nannies, tutors, service workers and children's party performers.

Relatedly, the *Yummy Mummy/West Coast Mom* profiles misrepresent the reality of self-employment as experienced by most women. As the availability, security and rewards from "regular" paid work have been eroded, those that can have turned to self-employment. However, there are good reasons to question the rosy picture of self-employment gracing the pages of *Yummy Mummy and West Coast Mom*. While some good, well-remunerated self-employment exists and women often choose self-employment for its flexibility, self-employment remains highly gendered, often poorly compensated and in many cases accentuates the gendered wage gap.[15] Perhaps the most significant silence in these narratives is reference to any non-market, cooperative solutions to the time bind. There is no mention of child care (socialized or even market based), labour market regulation, unionization, collective agreements or feminist struggles to redistribute responsibilities for unpaid domestic work (save for one exception: lesbian parents struggling for better parental leave for parents of twins).

Granted the problem may not reside in the mothers' narratives per se, but in the attempt to tell/sell a universal story of success under neoliberal conditions that create ever more unequal and disparate life conditions for many women as mothers. While neoliberal projects rely on an ideological claim of universal benefit, the resulting economic and political inequality has been particularly hard on working-class, racialized and single mothers. If the editors of *Yummy Mummy/West Coast Mom* magazine want to describe the coping strategies of "successful" mothering, where success is measured by good work and healthy families, it could be argued a group of middle-class, white women with professional jobs or who own their own businesses might be representative. That said, the stories of single mothers working low-wage service sector jobs, of racialized minorities in precarious work and unemployed women must be overlooked if we are to speak of mothers "having it all."

That the narratives of motherhood in a magazine delivering audiences to advertisers directly avoid confronting systemic problems within the neoliberal order is not terribly surprising. What is remarkable, however, is the extent to which these narratives reveal as much as they do about the contradictions of mothering for some of the most advantaged women. The "success" of these mothers comes primarily through individualized means, which involves withdrawal from traditional employment arrangements whose rewards and conditions have been eroded, adopting grueling work schedules, the interpenetration of paid work and home life, and the sacrifice of personal time.

It is telling that most mompreneurs reject part-time work as a viable solution as partially extricating oneself from neoliberal markets might offer middle-class mothers a way to balance personal well-being, paid and unpaid work. However, the maternal "choice" of part-time work is for most women a fiction (Webber and Williams 757). Deregulated labour markets have created much part-time work, but it is often precarious and for this reason, the chosen strategy of management.[16] Precarious work lowers women's current and future earnings, limits career possibilities, and fails to challenge men's participation in domestic tasks.

Still, the perceived more lucrative and rewarding self-employment celebrated in *Yummy Mummy/West Coast Mom* is hardly ideal. Aside from the flexibility and control that mompreneurs obviously value, many find themselves working more not less, and given the hyper-competitiveness of the markets they serve, including competition from other women seeking to do the same, this is unsurprising. Even in the idealized accounts of comparatively advantaged women, the idea that "mompreneurship" and the blending of unpaid and paid work provides freedom in anything but the narrowest sense is questionable. Accounts of family life marked by multi-tasking, planning and intense scheduling are suggestive of the self-discipline of flexible production in traditional workplaces (Hochschild). The mom-preneurs' workday has been reframed, but the boundaries have been ex-tended and/or have been redrawn under neoliberalism, pushing work-like principles into familial space(s).

That these mothers readily admit to ignoring themselves in terms of personal time is perhaps the most troubling feature of their narratives—and most destabilizing to the notion that these are, in fact, "success" stories. De-spite claims that they "wouldn't have it any other way," these are stories of self-sacrifice. Unveiled here is the fact that neoliberal conditions cou-pled with existing patriarchal societal forms means even the most advan-taged women must choose between personal time, paid work and caregiv-ing. This admission raises, if not answers, our question about the sustain-ability of yummy mummies' coping strategies. However, despite the con-tradictions inherent within these narratives, they do provide a point of anal-ysis from which a feminist discussion regarding alternative possibilities can occur.

CONCLUSION: RESISTANCE AND POLITICS OF HOME

Resistance can and is being built around the frustrations, hopes and dreams of mothers who insist that they, their children, families and communities should indeed "have it all." The material crisis of the home and the ten-uousness of popular narratives that attempt to resolve these crises while problematic, also provide opportunities to carve out other discursive and community-based spaces to locate resistance (Cossman).

But what might a progressive politics of home entail given the current state of affairs? At the very least said politics must address existing tensions between the paid work and family lives of mothers that do not depend on the embedded market or the exploitation of precarious labour. Projects to establish and extend job-sharing, flex-time, parental leaves, leaves of absence and compassion[17] must become central political programs of trade unions and progressive political parties. State policies and union contracts that en-courage shorter working hours and "good," non-precarious part-time work are also critical. At the neighbourhood and city level there is much room for a grassroots politics that builds community and non-commodified forms of family life. Community gardens and kitchens, shared parenting, and reclaimed streets for unstructured play are all sites of political awakening and organizing that potentially offer alternative venues for ensuring families are better able to meet their day to day and intergenerational needs.

However, none of these struggles will be sufficient if gender ideologies, roles and identities related to masculinity, men and fathers remain unchallenged. As has become clear in European social democracies, state policies that allow more time away from paid work, ensure non-precarious, part-time work options, provide socialized child care and more cohesive neighbourhoods and communities are crucial. Such supports make it more possible for women to juggle paid work and family life. But the fact remains that it is mothers who most often must juggle, thus gender inequity in the household must also be addressed. In the end, a progressive politics of home is imperative to free mothers from the burden of this balancing act, and to establish true social and economic value for mother-work (Ladd-Taylor).

NOTES

[1] See Douglas and Michaels

[2] See Yummy Mummy Magazine, December/January 2007/2008: 33

[3] See Fudge and Cossman

[4] Benzanson 187 *Social Reproduction: Feminist Political Economy Challenges Neo-Liberalism*; and Leach and Yates

[5] See Albo, Gindin, and Panitch; and Harvey

[6] See Jermyn; McRobbie; O'Donohoe; and Pitt, n.d.

[7] See http://www.yummymummyclub.ca/blogs/erica-ehm-exposed, last accessed January 1, 2014

[8] See http://www.yummymummyclub.ca/erica-ehm, last accessed February 21, 2013

[9] See http://www.theatlantic.com/magazine/archive/2012/07/why-women-still-cant-have-it-all/309020/, last accessed February 21, 2013

[10] See Douglas and Michaels; and Wylie

[11] In February/March 2010 *Yummy Mummy* was rebranded as *West Coast Mom* with little to no fanfare. The editor's note simply bids farewell to *Yummy Mummy* magazine and welcomes readers to "its re-incarnation, *West Coast Mom*" (February/March, 2010: 8). The name change was noted on the cover in very small font and read as follows: "yummy mummy is now West Coast Mom". Every issue published since only reads *West Coast Mom*. However, it is worth noting that the average number of pages and in-text

advertisements declined following the renaming of the magazine in February/March 2010. More recently, The West Coast Families website notes, "Each issue of WestCoast Families includes WestCoast Mom… which turns to WestCoast Dad or WestCoast Grandparents from time to time to ensure we are including all family members! This important section features a profile of a local parent along with events and information relevant to our readers." (http://westcoastfamilies.com/about/)

[12] See http://www.yummymummymag.com/
[13] See Glaser and Strauss
[14] See Luxton and Corman
[15] See Budig; and Hughes
[16] See Leach and Yates
[17] See Luxton and Corman

WORKS CITED

Albo, Greg, Sam Gindin and Leo Panitch. *In and Out of Crisis: The Global Financial Meltdown and Left Alternatives.* Oakland, California: PM Press, 2010. Print.

Bezanson, Kate. *Social Reproduction: Feminist Political Economy Challenges Neo- Liberalism.* Montreal, QC: McGill-Queen's University Press, 2006. Print.

— *Gender, the State and Social Reproduction: Household Insecurity in Neoliberal Times.* Toronto: University of Toronto Press, 2006. Print.

Buckworth, Kathy. "Do You Have What it Takes to be a Mompreneur?" 2012. As seen on sympatico http://www.westcoastmoms.ca/wcm.ca/-article2.html, last accessed February 21, 2013, July 23, 2012. Web.

Budig, Michelle J. "Gender, Self-employment, and Earnings: The Interlocking Structures of Family and Professional Status." *Gender & Society* 20.6 (2006): 725 –753. Print.

Cossman, Brenda. "Family Feuds: Neo-Liberal and Neo-Conservative Visions of the Reprivatization Project." *Privatization, Law, and the Challenge to Feminism.* Eds. Judy Fudge and Brenda Cossman. 169-217. Toronto: University of Toronto Press, 2002. Print.

Douglas, Susan and Meredith Michaels. *The Mommy Myth: The Idealization of Motherhood and How It Has Undermined All Women.* New York, New York: Free Press A Division of Simon & Schuster, Inc., 2004. Print.

Duyvendak, Jan Willem. *The Politics of Home: Belonging and Nostalgia in Europe and the United States*. Hampshire, UK: Palgrave Macmillan, 2011. Print.

Ehm, Erica. http://www.yummymummyclub.ca/erica-ehm, last accessed February 21, 2013. Web.

— http://www.yummymummyclub.ca/users/erica-ehm, last accessed February 21, 2013. Web.

— http://www.yummymummyclub.ca/blogs/erica-ehm-exposed, last accessed January 7, 2014. Web.

Fudge, Judy and Brenda Cossman. Eds. *Privatization, Law, and the Challenge to Feminism*. Toronto: University of Toronto Press, 2002. Print.

Glaser, Barney G and Anselm L. Strauss. *The Discovery of Grounded Theory: Strategies for Qualitative Research*. Chicago: Aldine Publishing Company, 1967. Print.

Harvey, David. *A Brief History of Neoliberalism*. Oxford, UK: Oxford University Press, 2007. Print.

Hochschild, Arlie R. *The Time Bind: When Work Becomes Home and Home Becomes Work*. New York: Metropolitan/Holt, 1997. Print.

Hughes, Karen. "Gender and Self-employment Trends in Canada: Assessing Trends and Policy Implications." CPRN Study No. http://cprn.org/documents/ACFHIvato.PDF, 1999. Web.

Jenson, Jane. New Realities of Earning and Caring. Presentation and Keynote Speech Prepared for the Special Meeting of the Provincial and Territorial Labour Market and Social Services Ministers: "A Labour Market in Tune with Families" organized by Ministère de l'Emploi de la Solidarité sociale et de la Famille of Quebec on August 23-24, 2004, in La Malbaie, Quebec. http://cprn.org/documents/32636_en.pdf, last accessed October 30, 2011, 2004. Web.

Jermyn, Deborah. "Still Something Else Besides a Mother? Negotiating Celebrity Motherhood in Sarah Jessica Parker's Star Story." *Social Semiotics* 18.2 (2008): 163 –176. Print.

Ladd-Taylor, Molly. *Mother-work: Women, Child Welfare, and the State, 1890-1930*. Urbana, IL: University of Illinois Press, 1995. Print.

Leach, Belinda and Charlotte Yates. "Gendering the Concept of Social Cohesion through an Understanding of Women and Work." *Solidarity First: Canadian Workers and Social Cohesion*. Ed. Robert O'Brien. Vancouver, BC: UBC Press, 2008. 21- 37. Print.

Luxton, Meg. *More Than a Labour of Love.* Toronto: Women's Educational Press, 1980. Print.

Luxton, Meg and June Corman. "Families at Work: Individual Versus Collective Strategies." *Canadian Families. Diversity, Conflict and Change* 4th Edition. Eds. Nancy Mandell and Ann Duffy. Toronto: Nelson, 2011. 211-242. Print.

McRobbie, Angela. "Yummy Mummies Leave a Bad Taste for Young Women: The Cult of Celebrity Motherhood Is Deterring Couples from Having Children Early. We Need to Rethink the Nanny Culture." 2006. http://www.guardian.co.uk/world/2006/mar/02/ gender. comment, last accessed February 21, 2013. Web.

O'Donohoe, Stephanie. "Yummy Mummies: The Clamour of Glamour in Advertising to Mothers." *Advertising & Society Review* 7.3 (2006) http://muse.jhu.edu/journals/advertisingandsocietyreview/summary /voo7/7.30donohoe.html, last accessed June 27, 2012. Web.

Pitt, Nicola. n.d. "'Yummy Mummies': Angelina Jolie and Early 21st Century Representations of Mothering." http://www.tasa.org.au/uploads/ 2011/05/Pitt-Nicola-Session-10-PDF.pdf, last accessed February 25, 2013. Web.

Slaughter, Anne-Marie. "Why Women Still Can't Have It All." http:// www.theatlantic.com/magazine/archive/2012/07/why-women-still-cant-have-it-all/309020/, last accessed February 21, 2013.

Webber, Gretchen and Christine Williams. "Mothers in 'Good' and 'Bad' Part-time Jobs Different Problems, Same Results." *Gender & Society* 22.6 (2008): 752 - 777. Print.

Wylie, Phillip. *A Generation of Vipers.* Dalkey Archives Press, 2nd Edition, 1942. Print.

WCM Profile

"West Coast Mom." *West Coast Families* February/March 2010: 36-37. Print.

— "West Coast Mom." *West Coast Families* April 2010: 34. Print.

— "West Coast Mom." *West Coast Families* May 2010: 33. Print.

— "West Coast Mom." *West Coast Families* July/August 2010: 27-28. Print.

— "West Coast Mom." *West Coast Families* September 2010: 25-26. Print.

— "West Coast Mom." *West Coast Families* October 2010: 25-26. Print.

— "West Coast Mom." *West Coast Families* November/December 2010:

40. Print.

— "West Coast Mom." *West Coast Families* January/February 2011: 25-26. Print.

— "West Coast Mom." *West Coast Families* March 2011: 25-27. Print.

— "West Coast Mom." *West Coast Families* April 2011: 27-28. Print.

— "West Coast Mom." *West Coast Families* May 2011: 27-28. Print.

— "West Coast Mom." *West Coast Families* July/August 2011: 26. Print.

YM Profile

"Yummy Mummy Magazine." *West Coast Families* December/January 2007/2008: 33— 37. Print.

— "Yummy Mummy Magazine." *West Coast Families* April 2008: 38. Print.

— "Yummy Mummy Magazine." *West Coast Families* November 2008: 35. Print.

— "Yummy Mummy Magazine." *West Coast Families* February/March 2009: 32. Print.

— "Yummy Mummy Magazine." *West Coast Families* April 2009: 32. Print.

— "Yummy Mummy Magazine." *West Coast Families* October 2009: 32— 33. Print.

— "Yummy Mummy Magazine." *West Coast Families* November 2009: 32—33. Print.

— "Yummy Mummy Magazine." *West Coast Families* December/January 2010: 30—31. Print.

5.

Eco-Diapers

The American Discourse of Sustainable Motherhood

CHIKAKO TAKESHITA

INTRODUCTION

"Cloth diapering makes me feel like a Super Mom! A super-green-awesome-loving mom!"

— J.A. Phoenix, Arizona (Wels 127)

Neoliberal capitalism has given rise to ever-expanding "green" businesses in America, including those run by mom-entrepreneurs, whose products and services appeal to the sensibilities of fellow parents' environmental consciousness. In an interview with Fox Business, Kim Graham-Nye, co-founder and president of gDiapers, stresses that industrially mass-produced disposable diapers are landfilled by the millions. Noting, "that's not really a sustainable solution," she explains that her company emerged out of her and her husband's pursuit of an alternative diapering solution for their first baby. Graham-Nye, who was named one of the Fortune Magazine Top 10 Women of 2011, sells biodegradable diapers that decompose rapidly, and thus have a less lasting impact on the environment. Flushable gDiapers can be composted in home gardens or be flushed down the toilet, thus "no land-fills [are] required."[1] While products such as gDiapers and reusable cloth diapers are currently unconventional, these "environmentally friendly" options are becoming trendy among consumers who imagine themselves to be mindful parents who simultaneously care for the earth and their babies. For avid supporters of alternative diapering, the products they use are at the core of their self-identification as environmentally friendly, smart, and caring mothers.

This chapter critically appraises the discourse of "green moms" by examining the co-construction of eco-diapers and sustainable motherhood as a gender-specific and individualistic environmentalism in a neoliberal society. I offer two interpretations of the "green mom" identity: first, as what Anthony Giddens called a reflexive project of self-making in late modernity and the second, as what Timothy Luke called an ecological subject of neoliberal green consumerism. I argue that an enthusiastic green lifestyle politics based on consumption of green goods silences the structural problems that exclude many parents from alternative diapering practices. I explore the ways in which "unsustainable" motherhood is constructed as well as ignored in the American discourse of green mothering. In the concluding section, I contemplate the possibility of making sustainable motherhood an option for women in the United States who currently do not have access to the privileges of using eco-diapers.

ECO-DIAPERS

Kelly Wels's colorfully illustrated 2012 book, *Changing Diapers: The Hip Mom's Guide to Modern Cloth Diapering*, walks the readers through the A to Z of cloth diapering.[2] Wels is a cloth diaper expert who once owned two popular online diaper stores and now dedicates her time to advocating for "diapering change." She uses mom-friendly pitches such as "it's best for the baby," "you can save big bucks," "despite what you think, cloth is convenient," and "it's fun for many moms" to promote cloth diapers. She also places an emphasis on environmental concerns as a significant cause to convert to cloth. The first words Wels's reader sees in the Foreword written by Heather McNamara of the Real Diaper Association are: "The numbers are bleak: approximately 90 percent of Americans use throwaway diapers. Single-use diapers are generating 7.6 billion pounds of garbage yearly. Choosing 100 percent reusable cloth diapers sets a valuable precedent for reuse for your family, conserving precious natural and family resources and keeping environmental toxins out of your home" (qtd. in Wels i). Echoing

McNamara, Wels quotes cloth diapering mothers throughout the book to convey how supporting the environment can make people feel good.

Once ubiquitous in the United States, cloth diapers and diaper services fell to the wayside as convenient disposable diapers displaced them during the 1970s. The convenience that throwaways offer has been undeniable, particularly as more women entered the workforce. Cloth diapers reemerged during the 1990s, but it is in the last ten years that we have seen a spike in cloth diaper manufacturers, distributors, and services.[3] A quick Google search under "eco-diapers" easily yields 200 hits consisting of websites that offer products and services and articles on cloth and biodegradable diapers. These websites promote the usual advantages associated with alternative diapering, such as cost savings and keeping toxins away from baby's skin. Most online stores offer attractively designed diaper covers, turning cloth diapers into a fashion item. Many also appeal to the rising consumer interest in green goods. Site addresses such as GoGreenPocketDiapers.com, EcoBuns.com, and Sustainablebabyish.com reflect this trend.

Disposable diapers such as Pampers, Huggies, and Luvs, however, are the established norm in American society. Cloth diaper enthusiasts turn to the virtue of reusability in order to claim its distinct advantage over disposables. Thanks to energy efficient washers and dryers, they argue, the environmental impact of cloth diapering is minimal. In comparison, the energy and other natural resources used and the pollution generated to produce, package, and transport millions after millions of disposable diapers are gargantuan. Furthermore, the amount of waste they turn into is astronomical. References to the horrifying mountains of baby waste punctuate cloth diaper advocates' representation of the offence that conventional diapers commit on the environment. As we have seen, Graham-Nye and McNamara are quick to draw attention to the everlasting landfill. Their followers also bring up the subject time and time again. The construction of disposable diapers as ecologically "unsustainable" underpins the rhetoric of eco-diapering as the "sustainable" alternative for baby waste management.

SUSTAINABILITY, CAPITALISM, AND GREEN BUSINESSES

Adjectives "sustainable" and "alternative" are often used interchangeably to suggest that environmental consciousness is still something extraordinary. Sustainability as a concept, however, is not very radical: it has been mainstreamed in such a way that it is compatible with neoliberalism. Long before the term "sustainability" became widely popular, it had become apparent by the 1970s that unrestrained industrial development was leading to a dangerously swift depletion of natural resources and high levels of pollution. Pressure to reverse this trend gave rise to a variety of ecological philosophies and movements, including those that suggested slowing down industrial development in favor of conserving nature and indigenous communities. World leaders agreed that reckless exploitation of natural resources and unchecked contamination of air, water, and land were clearly no longer acceptable. But, they were reluctant to suspend capitalist expansion and revisit the fundamental problems behind the environmental crisis. In this context, the World Commission on Environment and Development in 1987 defined *sustainable development* as "development that meets the needs of the present without compromising the ability of future generations to meet their own needs."[4] This statement was then interpreted in mainstream discourses to mean that economic expansion and environmental protection are compatible, rather than in conflict as some ecologists claimed. In other words, industrial countries did not need to compromise the current standard of living and developing countries could continue modernization in order to preserve resources for the future and keep the environment clean. "Sustainability," thus, has a history of being a capitalist friendly term.[5]

Committed environmentalists nonetheless still use the concept to represent a philosophical position that supports a more holistic approach to cohabiting with nature. Their cohorts are generally critical of capitalism. After a quarter of a century, however, "sustainability" has become an omnipresent catchall phrase with watered down meaning. The word is used to refer to everything from renewable energy sources such as solar and wind power to carbon emission reduction, and from recycling cans and bottles to washing with chemical-free shampoo. Terms such as "sustainable society" and "sustainable living" have been coined to envision the development of energy efficient communities and lifestyles that diminish the environmental impact of everyday activities. Solutions for accomplishing these visions are predominantly offered in the form of "sustainable" and "eco-friendly" products and services. Repeated exposure to ads that present "greenness" as a desirable trait has cultivated consumer desire to "live sustainably." And green consumerism has enabled "sustainability" to be implemented in a way unthreatening, even beneficial, to capitalist expansion.[6] Eco-diapers owe their popularity at least in part to the thriving green market.

THE CONSTRUCTION OF AMERICAN SUSTAINABLE
MOTHERHOOD

While green living appears to be a gender-neutral concept, Sarah Jacquette Ray notes that because mothers make decisions on what to buy for the household, they have been specifically targeted by green products (Ray). Furthermore, Ray observes that environmental cleanup has been bound up with mothering through housework and the care they provide to maintain the health of family members. The term "Mother Nature" also intensifies the association between mother and nature by suggesting that earth is like a mother on whom we depend for survival. Ray argues that "Mother Nature" has been used as a rhetorical device to encourage us to feel an ethical obligation to protect her. Wels, too, reminds the readers that "Mother Nature" is the one who "will have to deal with...the byproducts of industrial mass production" (43). Reminiscent of the ecofeminist claim that women are in much better touch with nature than men, the eco-diapering discourse presumes that it is natural for mothers to feel empathetic toward Mother Earth and have a desire to nurture it.

The eco-diaper discourse also frequently evokes mother-to-mother comradeship. "Throughout human history," writes Wels, "moms have struggled to contain and control the peeing and pooping until baby is fully trained to 'go' in an appropriate place" (13). With statements like this one, diapering is set up as a common problem that all mothers share. A cloth-diapering mother of three, Wels is immediately granted the status of an experienced expert and a trustable steward of cloth diapering. Most of the eco-diaper innovators and online distributors are mothers who have their own stories about how they started their businesses out of their own needs as a parent, and passion for offering environmentally friendly diapering options to other moms. These mompreneurs are celebrated as heroines who challenge mega-corporations that manufacture disposable diapers. A sorority-like bond gets established between mothers as this comment shows: "I think the best part is the camaraderie that you feel with other cloth diapering moms. It's like you are in a secret club that promotes healthy things for both your children and the planet!" (45)

Analyzing the green mothering discourse, Ray also notes that mothers are being charged with the responsibility to protect their children from toxic environments because of weak government regulations favored by the neoliberal economic system. In some cases, such as communities that "live downstream" of industrial toxins, motherhood is used strategically to challenge large companies because asserting their objections as mothers is the only means for political mobilization. Even though they do not face an immediate threat such as a neighboring polluting factory, the eco-diaper discourse reflects the assumption that mothers must be the ones to protect their children from environmental hazards. According to Wels, "many moms decided to use cloth diapers because they believe it to be in the best interest of their baby's health." She quotes a mother in Georgia who explains: "My biggest reason for making the switch [to cloth diapers] was that I started finding the gooey gel crystals in my baby's diaper area. I started thinking about all the chemicals and stuff they make those disposables with and it creeped me out!" (20) Wels points out how disposable diapers contain dioxin, a known carcinogen, and sodium polyacrylate, which has been linked to toxic shock syndrome in tampon users. She suggests that these chemicals might be absorbed through the baby's skin during the long exposure. She also cites a study done on mice, which shows that being around disposable diapers causes asthma-like reactions in the animals. While there are no definitive scientific studies that show disposable diapers carry health risks, mothers who are worried about the potential ill effects of toxic chemicals find cloth-diapering reassuring, as a mother in California writes: "I love knowing that I can keep chemicals away from my baby's bum" (21).

Environmental concerns and good mothering are further intertwined by a maternal obligation to make sure that her children will not have to suffer from the environmental damage caused by their parents' generation. "Cloth diapering feels like I'm making a positive impact on my child's well-being and his environment," (42) says one mother, while another declares, "I like it that my kids' poop won't be preserved for 500 years in a landfill. That's not a legacy I think they would like!" (69). The discourse of sustainable motherhood is thus constructed by effortlessly intertwining reusable diapering, caring for the baby, protecting the earth, and uniting mothers while meshing together familiar ideas about motherhood and the new norms around eco-friendliness.

"GREEN MOM" AS A REFLEXIVE SELF IDENTITY

Many women who choose cloth diapering adopt a "green mom" identity. Identification of the self that pertains to a style of living corresponds to what Anthony Giddens calls the reflexive project of self-making in late modernity. The reflexive project of the self "consists in the sustaining of coherent, yet continuously revised, biographical narratives" and "takes place in the context of multiple choices as filtered through abstract systems" (5). According to Giddens, "finding oneself" is a social condition enforced on those who live in a fluid society built on a dynamic economic system sustained by continuous demands for new products and services. "How should I live?" is a day-to-day decision that we are faced with because the perceived choices are infinite, granted that one has access to the necessary resources. The popularity of "guide to living" books is a "symptomatic social phenomenon" of American society in which people are always in search for an answer to this question (2). Selectively adopting a child-rearing philosophy and choosing baby products that reflect a particular mothering style are now integral to a mother's identity project. There are numerous handbooks on parenting, and ideas from these guides help women with newborns craft their own self-narratives as mothers. In this regard, Wels's *Changing Diapers* serves as a "how-to-live" guidebook that not only lays out a roadmap for a woman who wants a non-conventional diapering option, but also provides a narrative of eco-conscious mothering to someone who is engaged in constructing a green self-identity.

The "green mom" identity also involves being a kind of activist. "You'll be part of a grassroots movement," Wels writes, "backed by hundreds of thousands of moms around the world who have set out to do what's right for their babies, their wallets, and their planet" (15). This statement seems to imply that an aggregate of individual lifestyle changes can become part of a solution to complex and enormous environmental issues. Critical theorists, however, would maintain that such an assumption requires careful investigation. The next section will explore the nature of the eco-diaper "movement."

SUSTAINABLE MOTHERING AS A POLITICAL MOVEMENT

Is sustainable motherhood simply a form of self-expression that has more to do with building camaraderie? Or is it a legitimate political expression that turns mothers into political agents? Giddens would likely argue that green mothering qualifies as a reflexive self-identity project grounded in taking a political stance, and that sustainable motherhood can be conceptualized as *life politics*. Life politics, according to Giddens, is the "politics of a reflexively mobilized order,... which on an individual and collective level, has radically altered the existential parameters of social activity" (214). Elaborating on the relationship between self-actualization and life politics, Giddens explains that "globalizing influences intrude deeply into the reflexive project of the self" while the "process of self-realization [conversely] influence global strategies" (214). In other words, using Giddens's framework, sustainable motherhood can be viewed as a process of self-actualization in which lifestyle choices are made in response to a said global condition or the call to save the earth. Giddens concedes that a global environmental crisis "is bound to demand coordinated global responses on levels far removed from individual action" (222). Nonetheless he believes that in order to effectively counter environmental problems, "reaction and adaption on the part of every individual" is necessary (222). For him, then, the moral and existential questions raised in the alternative diapering discourse and the life processes of achieving a "green mom" self are the very building blocks for global change.

Giddens's optimism gives hope to anyone who alters their lifestyle for an abstract goal. Critics, however, argue that individual conversion-based environmentalism has serious limitations as a political movement. Feminist theorists Martha McCaughey and Christina French[7] make a similar point about the potentials and drawbacks of feminist political projects based on individual cultural critique. An interesting parallel can be drawn between the eco-diapering movement and the women's sex-toy parties that McCaughey and French analyze. In a private home gathering, an experienced hostess/saleswoman leads women in a discussion aimed at raising awareness of gender hierarchy in sexual relationships. Participants are nudged to engage in a reflexive self-making project that involves a new consciousness about their sexuality and relationships. McCaughey and French observe that sex-toy parties may qualify as a feminist project aimed at subverting male-centric assumptions about sexuality and empowering individual women with tools and knowledge to pursue pleasure on their own terms. Yet, they also caution that isolated emancipations that depend on women's subversion, or on each woman to improve her relationship with a partner one by one, are far less effective than an organized feminist movement that challenges patriarchy as a system.

McCaughey and French also express apprehension about feminist body projects being packaged and offered as sex-toy parties. Giddens himself has noted that one dilemma of life politics is that it is sometimes commodified or marketed as a fashionable lifestyle. Genuine reflexivity is absent when self-making is purchased in the form of goods and services ready to be consumed. The feminist authors warn that sex-toy parties encourage consumption-based women's liberation that may only result in a capitalist containment of feminist political expression. Eco-diapering might fall into similar dangers whereby sustainable motherhood becomes mainly about the consumption of fuzzy diapers, a practice that is contained in the private spheres of the home. While individual mothers may feel empowered, their "movement" may prove to be insufficient to de-normalize disposable diapers in a culture that heavily depends on one-time-use goods.

Activists who promote healthier and environmentally friendlier alternatives to industrially produced food have also struggled to make a larger impact beyond changing consumption habits of some. The organic food movement emerged out of concerns over ingesting food contaminated with pesticides. Its proponents promoted tastier and healthier options grown mainly by small farms, and harshly criticized industrial agriculture for contaminating the earth with chemical fertilizers, herbicides, and pesticides, hogging scarce water supplies, exploiting farm workers, treating animals inhumanely, and burning large quantities of fossil fuels in the production, distribution, and the storage of farm products. To the chagrin of small organic farmers and their supporters, corporations soon began producing "Big Organics" or industrially mass-produced organic products for what they perceived as a new niche market. While some view the shift positively as an improvement in the accessibility of organics, others lament that the organic movement has turned into another profit seeking venture and co-opted by corporate capitalism. The alternative diaper movement might find itself in a similar situation if, for instance, Procter & Gamble decided to sell biodegradable flushable diapers. The wider availability of eco-friendly diapers might allow more parents to give up conventional disposables. At the same time, however, what are now innovative and virtuous small-business products may be taken over by a powerful corporation.

Cloth diapers are likely to remain in the hands of smaller businesses since they do not entail long-term repeated purchasing by the customers like throwaway products do, and are thus unattractive for the paper product industry. Small and strong cloth diapering communities are perhaps comparable to the local food movement, which replaced the organic movement as an alternative food activism in recent years. Locavorism subverts industrial agriculture by sourcing food from independent nearby producers. Local food activism not only changes individual eating habits, but also builds community and stimulates the local economy. Critical theorist Chad Lavin, however, points out that localism does little to induce changes in the U.S. agricultural industry and the majority of Americans who continue to eat what is made available to them by large corporations. From Lavin's perspective, locavorism represents a retreat from a larger political movement

(Lavin). His critique parallels McCaughey and French's dissatisfaction with feminist political expressions that are contained in intimate settings, and thus do not lead to organized efforts to transform broader socio-cultural conditions that are biased against women. Similarly, while the growth in cloth diapering communities may make modest incremental changes, the more serious environmental impact from the disposable diaper industry would most likely remain intact.

Critical theorist Timothy Luke also contests Giddens's optimistic view that reflexive green self-identities make political subjects who become the engines of globalized change. Luke contends that environmental ideologies that used to press for deeper and broader changes in human values and practices have been domesticated by green consumerism. Green consumerism is welcome from a capitalist point of view because it stimulates economic activities. But, this neoliberal environmentalism also shifts the responsibility of saving the planet to individual consumers from corporations and politicians. Instead of pressing for a total reconstitution of modern industrial practices by means of systematic political transformation, this green "movement" relies on individuals and households to assume the role of an "ecological subject." Ecological subjects, who act on their own desire to practice green living, now serve as the "nonpolitical, nonsocial, noninstitutional solution to environmental problems" (119). Eco-diapering mothers fit this description of an ecological subject, who acts as the willingly responsible party and as a proud solution for the earth's ecological problem. The sense of empowerment felt by green moms is simultaneously self-actualizing as it is pre-programmed to entice individuals to assume the role of an ecological subject.

Giddens might still argue that individual conversions and life politics are essential to incremental improvement and cultural change. Eco-critics such as Luke and Lavin, however, are skeptical that personal lifestyle choices amount to fundamental changes because they are co-opted by, rather than working to overthrow, the system that essentially values economic growth over the health of humans and ecosystems. Individualist environmentalism that does not problematize the fact that not everyone has the capacity to "do the right thing" is insufficient. The current discourse of eco-diapering assumes that the choice of sustainable motherhood is made based on personal values and preferences, which obscures the structural and systemic barriers that restrict most parents to an "unsustainable" motherhood.

THE STRUCTURE OF UNSUSTAINABLE MOTHERHOOD

Eco-diaper advocates often qualify themselves saying that what they do is "not for everyone." This is perhaps a gesture to show that they are not being judgmental about those who, for whatever reason, do not practice alternative diapering. It could also indicate some kind of exclusivity. Although cloth diapering may save money in the long run, it requires substantial upfront financial investment, which may be prohibiting for many families. According to a popular website, the startup cost for the most basic diapers that require folding, pinning, and a cover much like our grandmothers' is about $200. For more sophisticated and convenient types of diapers, such as the cover-and-diaper-in-one and diaper liners that snap or velcros into fancy covers, the startup costs range between $400 and $600.[8] Extra accessories such as diaper pail, diaper sprayer, and wet totes for handling, cleaning, and carrying cloth diapers increase the expenses. Parents will also need access to at least a washing machine, if not also to a dryer. In addition, the family must be able to keep up with the laundry while juggling parenting, domestic tasks, and personal and professional commitments. Biodegradable diapers require less work, but are generally more expensive than conventional diapers, and since they are not found on many storefronts they require Internet access and a credit card to purchase. Eco-diapering is thus a class-specific practice that excludes those without adequate resources.

The discourse of green moms, however, is oblivious to class privileges. The presumption is that educated and conscientious mothers would make the "right" choice and those who do not are either uninformed, do not ascribe to the same values, or simply "cannot" do it. While alternative diapering advocates regularly point fingers at mega-corporations that flood the market with "unsustainable" diapers, they shy away from explicitly referring to the people who support their businesses by consuming these products. "Unsustainable" mothers are nonetheless implicated by the repeated assertion that conventional diapers are environmentally atrocious. These "other" parents, who casually pollute the earth and ruin it for their own babies' future, loom as a shadowy figure in the discourse that celebrates green living and demonizes disposable diapers.

For most Americans though, disposable diapers are not a matter of choice but a necessity. According to The National Diaper Network, one in three American families struggle to even afford the basic diapers for their children. Some families are compelled to cut down on other necessities such as food, while others cope by leaving their children in soiled diapers longer than they would otherwise. Since many day-care programs will not accept children without a supply of disposable diapers, some parents are forced to forgo employment or educational opportunities.[9] For low-income mothers, alternative diapers are quite frankly out of reach if it means that one needs to purchase an entire set of cloth diapers up front and own a washing machine. For most working mothers, the obstacle might be finding the time and energy to carry out alternative diapering. Diaper services, which pick up soiled diapers, launder them, and deliver fresh ones, may be the answer, but they are not universally available. Lack of resources, money, and time, not ignorance or indifference, present the biggest hurdle to expanding sustainable motherhood. These obstacles are structural issues that render poor and working mothers socially and economically unsupported.

The ideology of freedom of choice and individual rights masks the fact that not everyone has access to so-called options. What Giddens fails to examine closely is how unequal access to resources make certain lifestyles class-specific and particular self-making projects unattainable for the under-privileged. Neoliberal individualism, to which his ideas acquiesce, tends to hold each person responsible for his/her ill fate without accounting for social disadvantages that may have left him/her in an inescapable situation. Similarly, the discourse of eco-diapers focuses on individuals making good "choices," while not paying sufficient attention to the social structure that hinders sustainable motherhood from spreading. It occasionally hints that the true obstacle that lies between eliminating diaper landfill waste and the majority of the population is insufficient resources such as money, access to equipment, and time to practice cloth diapering. It is rarely acknowledged, however, that in order to spread green mothering to collectively save the planet, the economic gap between the affluent and the poor needs to be closed. If advocates wish to spread eco-diapers in order to protect the environment, they must look beyond converting individual mothers and start building a good support structure for mothers who currently do not have access to them.

There are a few existing efforts to make cloth diapering affordable. The Real Diapers Association, for instance, has been in operation for about ten years in the U.S., serving as a central resource organization for cloth diaper advocates who work in local communities to change diapering practices "one baby at a time." To offset the cost, a circle of my friends has been sharing sets of small, medium, and large cloth diapers over seven years among six babies who were born several months to years apart from one another. Internet based Cloth Diaper Network loans donated cloth diapers to families who cannot afford the startup cost. More can be attempted to build community-based support programs. A co-op, from which underfinanced parents can lease cloth diapers for a small fee on a monthly basis, might be a possibility. Day-care centres might investigate switching to cloth diapers whereby they carry their own supplies, do the laundry on site, and eliminate all disposable diaper wastes from the infants and toddlers they care for. The National Diaper Bank Network and regional diaper banks currently assist parents in need by giving away disposable diapers. At some point in the future, diaper banks may be able to distribute less expensive biodegradable diapers and then collect and compost them in local community gardens.

CONCLUSION: SUSTAINABLE MOTHERHOOD FOR ALL

Eco-diapering thrives under the ideal of sustainable living. It produces self-"empowered" mothers like the one from Indiana who writes: "Cloth diapering makes me feel empowered, earthy, crunchy, loving, frugal, happy, healthy, smart, and amazing!" (Wels 36). However, alternative diapering, which purportedly saves money, raises a healthy baby, protects the environment, and is also fun for mothers who enjoy the fluffiness of her baby's bottom and cute diaper covers, is a privilege reserved for those who have the resources. The discourse of sustainable mothering also perpetuates the notion that we each can protect the earth by changing our day-to-day practices. This is inspiring, but it is also illusory. While it may help the economy by driving green consumption and entrepreneurialism, individualist environmentalism can only do so much to transform large-scale industrial polluters and challenge social inequality that make green living out of reach for the majority of Americans. Before we despair, however, more steps can still be taken to unseat disposables from dominance. Alternative diapering advocates can work toward making eco-diapering a real and adoptable option for everyone, including low-income mothers. They can also start urging self-identified green moms to support this effort. This will require transforming the discourse of sustainable motherhood from an individualistic "do-your-part" scenario to one that is reflexive of the role we play in a neoliberal system, and proactively addresses "unsustainable" motherhood that is often silenced by the enthusiasm for green mothering.

NOTES

[1]See Graham-Nye. Interviewed by Fox Business

[2]The narratives in Wels's book typify the kinds of dialogues exchanged between cloth diaper advocates and their avid followers on various Internet sites of online stores, support organizations, and personal blogs. Throughout this paper I use Wels and the people she quotes as representatives of the larger alternative diapering community.

[3]Unofficial history of cloth and disposable diapers can be found on Internet sites such as http://www.diaperjungle.com/history-of-diapers.html and http://disposablediaper.net/general-information/disposable-diaper (Accessed July 2012)

[4]See UN Documents

[5]For critiques of the capitalization of "sustainability," see Sachs; and Visvanatha

[6]See Luke for a discussion on green consumerism.

[7]See McCaughey and French

[8]Data obtained from diaperdecisions.com (Accessed July, 2012)

[9]The National Diaper Bank Network (diaperbanknetwork.org: Accessed July, 2012)

WORKS CITED

Giddens, Anthony. *Modernity and Self Identity: Self and Society in the Late Modern Age.* Stanford: Stanford University Press, 1991. Print.

Graham-Nye, Kim. Interviewed by Fox Business. http://video.foxbusiness.com/eco-friendly-diaper-business-growing-rapidly (accessed June 15, 2012): n. pag. Web. 3 October, 2011. Web.

Lavin, Chad. "A Year of Eating Politically." *Taking Food Public: Redefining Foodways in a Changing World.* Eds. Psyche Williams-Forson and Carole Counihan. New York: Routledge, 2012. 576-591. Print.

Luke, Timothy. *Ecocritique: Contesting the Politics of Nature, Economy, and Culture.* Minneapolis: University of Minnesota Press, 1977. 115-136. Print.

McCaughey, Martha and Christina French. "Women's Sex-Toy Parties: Technology, Orgasm, and Commodification." *Sexuality and Culture* 5.3 (2001): 77-96. Print.

Ray, Sara Jaquette. "How Many Mothers Does It Take to Change All the Light Bulbs?: The Myth of Green Motherhood." *Journal of the Motherhood Initiative for Research and Community Involvement* 2.1 (2011): 81-101. Print.

Sachs, Wolfgang, ed. "Global Ecology and the Shadow of 'Development.'" *Global Ecology and a New Era of Political Conflict.* London: Zed, 1993. Print.

UN Documents: Gathering a Body of Global Agreements. *Report of the World Commission on Environment and Development: Our Common Future.* http://www.un-documents.net/wced-ocf.htm (Accessed July 2012) 1987. Web.

Visvanathan, Shiv. "Ms.Brundtland's Disenchanted Cosmos." *Alternatives* 16.3 (1991): 377-384. Print.

Wels, Kelly. *Changing Diapers: The Hip Mom's Guide to Modern Cloth Diapering.* Waterford, Maine: Green Team Enterprises, 2012. Print.

6.

Negotiating Identities

The Case of Mompreneurs in Trinidad and Tobago

TALIA ESNARD

INTRODUCTION

This chapter interrogates the meanings and experiences of mompreneurship in Trinidad and Tobago to problematize the ways in which mompreneurs understand and negotiate their gendered identities while working within the competing domains of work and family within a neoliberal flexible labour market. In so doing, the chapter draws on the multiple ways neoliberal imperatives have created a globalized work space in which the ever-increasing demands of accumulated capital and flexible labour necessitate the configuration of mothers as economic agents (thus requiring female entrepreneurialism), *and* the continuation of their "traditional" roles of mothering. Yet the role of mothers in entrepreneurial processes remains peripherally positioned within orthodox economically centred entrepreneurial research and a growing yet under-researched gendered discourse on entrepreneurship. Moreover, while there have been notable advances in research on entrepreneurship as a gendered space,[1] there remains a dearth of international data and an invisibility of Caribbean research that seeks to deepen our understanding of the ways in which mompreneurs negotiate gendered discourses and conflicts in the formation of their identities within a neoliberal context.

CONTEXTUALIZING MOMPRENEURSHIP IN TRINIDAD AND TOBAGO

Trinidad and Tobago is considered to be a high income (Harriott et al.), multi-racial twin island republic located at the most southern end of the Caribbean with a population of approximately 1.3 million people (Government of Trinidad and Tobago). The race and sex distribution of Trinidad and Tobago shows that the three largest groups are East Indians (35.4%), Africans (34.2%) and mixed (22.8%) with women representing 49.8% and males 50.2% of the population (Government of Trinidad and Tobago). In terms of economic orientation, Trinidad and Tobago ranked 6th out of 24 efficiency driven economies in the Total Entrepreneurship Activity (TEA) measure for the 2010 Global Entrepreneurship Monitor (GEM) survey with indications of a narrowing gender gap with 15.68% male involvement in early stage entrepreneurial activity compared to 14.31% of their female counterpart (Murdock et al.). However, while the data points to increased labour force participation, gender gap assessments point to persistent gender inequalities with Trinidad and Tobago ranking 43rd out of 135 countries and 47th in terms of women's economic participation and access to opportunity (Hausmann et al.).

One emerging yet underexplored paradox that speaks to the persistence of gender inequality in Trinidad and Tobago is that while mothers increasingly engage in economic opportunities, they continue to be constrained by normative understandings of femininity including the centrality of childbirth and childrearing.[2] Caribbean scholars link this contradiction not only to neoliberal restructuring processes since the 1980s, which affected a greater proportion of women than men (some of whom were propelled into entrepreneurship) but also to continued threads of normative gender stereotypes and structural practices of unequal participation and remuneration.[3] Within the past ten years, increasingly participation has also been fueled by deliberate neoliberal policies and initiatives aimed at promoting entrepreneurship throughout various sectors of the local economy.

Thus, in *Reconciling Work and Family in Trinidad and Tobago*, Reddock and Bobb-Smith argue that while the "rapidity and complexity of industrial and technological change that surrounds the building of households have resulted in the modification of family traditions and structures (forcing women to find new ways of coping with work and family)…it has not lessened their expected roles as nurturers" (75). Given such contradictory contexts, Bailey and Ricketts argue that "Caribbean countries…still experience gender vulnerabilities in areas of economic participation and empowerment with women in the region being at greater disadvantage than men" (50). Thus, understanding the gendered realities of mompreneurs in Trinidad and Tobago requires a movement away from narrow considerations of the sexual division of labour in the market, to a discussion of the entrepreneurial and mothering experiences as they are shaped by normative social and economic structures and their respective discursive contexts.

MOTHERING AND THE FLEXIBLE LABOUR MARKET

The growing significance of new venture creation as a perceived means of attaining individual freedom,[4] and the global increase in female entrepreneurship has spiraled investigations into the challenges of work-family conflict and work-family integration.[5] At the centre of these concerns is the recognition in the entrepreneurship literature that gender role expectations and identities (albeit differently for men and women) continue to mediate the nature, direction, and outcomes of the relationship between work and family life.[6] Increasing demands of flexible labour has created a shift in work practices where flexible labour necessitates a worker subject whose work-family boundaries and times are fluid. In locating this discussion in the Caribbean, Freeman's examination of *"Femininity and Flexible Labor in Barbados"* suggests that women make integral connections between the demands of economic flexibility and that of flexible gender identities.[7] It is, therefore, necessary to examine the effects of this labour and gender shift by better understanding the complexity of entrepreneurial mothers' lives.

In understanding the complicated "maze of motherhood" (Horwitz), many researchers exploring the specific relationship between work and mothering illuminate the contradictions, incompatibilities (Shelton), stresses and anxieties that accompany any effort aimed at circumventing the challenges of integrating motherhood and entrepreneurship. Despite such advancing in the literature, one central question that remains is: how do mothers who occupy these two spaces respond, if they do, to dominant societal "good" motherhood discourses? Simon-Kumar contends that neoliberal ideals intensify contradictions and indirectly render invisible the "relevance of mothering within the discourse of cost-effective society" (qtd. in Horwitz 40), thus making the study of entrepreneurial mothers' experiences and identity negotiations all the more integral.

METHODOLOGY

Embedded in case study research is the constructivist paradigm[8] that seeks to understand the ways in which contexts shape a given phenomenon. As an interpretative or critical approach (Willis), it allows "one to gain tremendous insight into a case by way of providing rich data on the 'why' and 'how' of a given phenomenon while taking into consideration the ways in which this phenomenon is influenced by the context within which it is situated" (Baxter and Jack 556). This approach allows the researcher to gain a deeper understanding of the dialectical frameworks within which mompreneurs engage, and which shape negotiations of identities.

Purposive sampling was used to conduct repeated in-depth interviews (for an average of one hour each) with three Afro-Trinidadian female entrepreneurs who owned and managed between two to three small to medium-sized enterprises within the urbanized East-West corridors of Trinidad and Tobago, had five to ten years of establishment and who were also mothers. Interviews sought to delve into their perceptions and experiences of negotiating identities. This involved questions on the what, when, why, and how of the meanings, practices, activities and routines of their daily lives that are (re)created,[9] while situating them within wider relational, temporal and socially constructed contexts. Although this focus on mompreneurs does not explore the comparative nature of lived experiences of male entrepreneurs who are also fathers, it stimulates needed theorizing on mompreneurs' negotiations of the dialectical dynamics of space, place and time in their everyday experiences.

Interviews were transcribed, manually coded, inductively (Reissman) and thematically analyzed[10] around the contextual and cognitive approach of the paper. For the purpose of enhancing the dependability and comparability of the interpreted versus the implied meanings of the data, the researcher also engaged in a verification process within which transcriptions were shared with interviewees. This allowed the researcher to discuss and clarify some of the interpretations as well as encouraged participants to elaborate on certain issues that remained unclear in the initial recording and sharing of the data. Applying the principles of idea convergence and confirmation of findings[11] the researcher also conducted comparative empirical reflection and analysis.

MOMPRENEURSHIP AS SITUATED, COMPLEX, AND SHIFTING

Although it is widely established in the entrepreneurial literature that gender remains integral to work and family,[12] the performative aspects of such phenomenon remains under-explored in a neoliberal context. In tracing configurations of gender at work, findings revealed that these mompreneurs were actively aware of, tolerant of, and in other cases resistant to the gendered and neoliberal discourses that continue to shape their experiences.

All three mompreneurs pointed to the opening up of perceived opportunities within the economy, and the need for autonomy, flexibility, and increased survivability of their families as key factors in the entrepreneurial journey. For instance, Angel, a 35-year-old mompreneur with two boys (three and five years) and two related ventures in accounting and catering drew attention to the need for her to "get into the [economic] system... support [her] husband...and move from the thinking that women don't have a purpose and [that] their only job is to take care of the home." Here, Angel embraces a complex and fluid notion of a woman's identity; one that captures ongoing modes of continuation and change in her acceptance of her contribution to the home but also promotes privileging of women in the economy. Similarly, Martha, a 45-year-old mompreneur with three ventures (electronics and fruit vending) and three boys (ages six, eight and eleven), suggested that "my first ventures emerged out of a need to help financially and to do something of my own." On the other hand, Giselle, a 29-year-old mompreneur with four children, married, and with three ventures in film, catering and fashion design prioritizes her obligations to her children over that of her interest in business; a practice that remains consistent with the dominant discourse of "good" mothering in Trinidad and Tobago in which mothers are assumed to place the needs of their child/children first.

The stories of these mompreneurs also unveil how gendered episodes infiltrate their ongoing entrepreneurial experiences. Angel recollected a troubling conversation with a potential male client who insisted that she was unsuited for the entrepreneurial world since she "does not wear a suit...does not have the right color...does not wear [specific] kind of shoes...[and her] hair is natural [without chemical enhancers]." For the client, her hair has to be "straight so that she has the right image." This conforming image of a female entrepreneur is reflective of the cultural importance placed on women's femininity in their presentation of selves both within and out-

side of the home. Such images remain consistent with semantic representations of selves as traced to legacies of colonialism, and more specifically
European ideals of beauty as indicative of social and occupational mobility
in the Caribbean (Braithwaite). Angel's narrative mirrors a growing concern for the inseparability of socio-historical expectations of gendered configurations of *"place"* with the growing entrepreneurial *"space"* as advanced
through the expansion of private enterprise.

Angel further disclosed that this cultural notion of the public female
persona resulted in this potential client's withdrawal and conclusion that
"she does not understand her place;" a statement she resented and perceived
as "backward," and suggestive of an essentialist need for her to "present
herself in a way that is fitting." This notion of "place" is what Schultze
and Boland refer to as the experience of *being* in a bounded locality where
traditions serve as a central stimulus for human behavior. In this context,
such notions are to some extent in unison with conventional expectations
of professional mirage (Freeman, "Femininity and Flexible Labor: Fashioning Class Through Gender on the Global Assembly Line."), and with traditional stereotypes surrounding women in and outside of the home.[13]

This time-space configuration of place, in which Angel is expected to
transfer the unchanging gendered representation of self into the entrepreneurial space that she occupies, points to embedded yet questionable notions and interpretations of change as restricted. Angel's use of the word
"backward" brings into disrepute not only the relevance of time-space configurations of place to her entrepreneurial identity, but also the ability of
contemporary socio-economic changes to mitigate the weight of such situated contexts on the experiences of mompreneurs. For Bayes et al.,[14] this
interplay of economic and social projects continue to (re)produce contradictions in the lives of women within "sites of contestations," where social
and economic demands of these two competing spaces collide and foster
intensified challenges to established gender regimes.

Thus, in negotiating these situated conflicts, Angel attempts to draw
more on the time-space demands of her entrepreneurial engagement than
on the traditional peculiarities of place. Angel lamented that "it's a business I'm running (laughs,) I ain't have time to do all them [sic] kind of
thing". She reiterated that, beyond her position, the temporal and adapt-
able demands of her entrepreneurial ventures dictated that "femininity has
no place in business". Angel was adamant that "my work must stand
out...not how I look or what race I belong to...." Angel's resistance hints
at the need for future research in what Halford and Leonard describe as

the fluid yet complex nature of gender and the ways in which "it intersects with other aspects of identity, including race, class, ethnicity, age, sexuality and physical ability" (12). Angel contended that "we need to remove ourselves from that stigmatism that when you're talking about a business woman, [that] you must see her in a suit and she must be looking dandy [with] the 'right' pump shoes and 'right' hairstyle...that's not what business is about." However, despite this oppositional stance, Angel recognizes the demand for more accommodating entrepreneurial identities that overlap with complex yet shifting images of professional representations, and the ongoing nature of this challenge in the process of (re)negotiating her entrepreneurial identity. For now, she discusses her struggles of *becoming* a professional female entrepreneur; that is, a woman who can do the job despite the colour, length, and texture of her hair or clothes.

While Angel rejects the penetration of gendered identities into entrepreneurial expectations, she strongly identifies with dominant idealizations of "good" motherhood as all-encompassing and the resultant peripheral placement of her entrepreneurial activities. As such, Angel rationalizes that "children are God's gifts...and I have to treasure them...with a certain amount of responsibility...importance, and most of all love". Such a concept of all-encompassing motherhood has been much discussed within maternal theorizing in reference to Euro-American mothering paradigms.[15] In particular, what Hays defines as "intensive mothering" became the predominate "good" mothering paradigm in North America arising in the 1990s in response to the neoliberal erosion of the welfare state and increasing privatization of responsibility within the family (Hays). Given the cultural, ethnic and historical realities of Trinidad and Tobago in addition to other stratifying factors including religion, race, class and gender, it is clear neoliberal policies in Trinidad and Tobago are equally reconfiguring dominant "good" mothering ideals, particularly in the realm of mompreneurs. It is apparent that the space of mothering and associated gendered assumptions is currently in flux where "traditional" conceptualizations of motherhood collide with new economic realities.

When speaking with Martha regarding her daily negotiating of gendered associations, she expressed concern over the inclination for some male clients and business associates to engage in sexualized discussions more than impending business transactions, and the ways in which these often overshadowed attempts at becoming a successful female entrepreneur. In the case of her fruit vending establishment, Martha described the frequent use of sexual language to refer to the "attractiveness and size of her 'fruits'"; as a comparative image of the fruits that she sells and "her own". Thus, she explained that "you have male customers that come in and they have to be smutty with it…they don't deal with you serious[ly] and do not treat women with respect" but use these utterances as bargaining strategies in the price reduction of intended purchases thereby trivializing her entrepreneurial venture. This language for Halford and Leonard "reinforces this [gendered] performance, with heavily sexualized metaphors being used to describe both the work and those successful at it" (9).

As a strategic response, Martha shared her attempts to capitalize on such sexualized metaphors (through her non-dismissive performance) and its potential role in her entrepreneurial performance. Thus, she declared that:

> well of course I have a big bottom…[that is] the attraction… everybody would talk about that and sometimes it works. Other times, I would say "So all that talk for nothing? Buy something!" You know…[but] he would buy the cheapest thing-something [for] two dollars. I'd say "You're a waste of time… waste of breath."

This mixed response to her strategizing has led a partially frustrated Martha to think of such male clientele as culturally helpless in that whether or not they acquire an item, they "feel that…if you say good morning, they must respond with some smuttiness after it." For Martha, unlike Angel, this sense of inescapability from the binds of femininity—or what Epstein[16] refers to as the cultural walls that shape master narratives and affect the global subordination and dismissal of women—cripples her ability to challenge it in her entrepreneurial practices. In a sense, her narrative points to a passive commoditization of her sexual identity within her entrepreneurial venture in response to similar growing trends within the marketplace. This highlights the need for research that situates actors within social and economic processes that are central to globalization (Freeman, "Is Local: Global As Feminine: Masculine? Rethinking the Gender of Globalization").

Martha also argued that the direction of her response is not only dependent on the intensity of these discursive contexts (*place*), but also on the penetration and acceptance of these into her entrepreneurial *spaces*. Thus, she uttered that "in my other company [electronics], I am more humble because my husband rules the nest…I met him as a business person so it's just a matter of me getting into the system." At one end, this positionality and acceptance of gendered hierarchies for Martha comes from her confidence in her husbands' entrepreneurial background; her expectation for transferability of that "expertise" through their collaboration and her entrepreneurial expansion and success. At another end, Martha's equation of this electronically oriented space to that of a masculine *place* also reflects her internalization and acceptance of the masculine nature of entrepreneurship (Ahl) as an extension of historical male privileging within economic spheres, and the processes by which authority and spatial relations are framed within such gendered assumptions and socially situated practices. Thus, in responding to these gender stereotypes within such situated contexts, she explained that:

> Here [in the electrical business] is men...my husband appreciates [the need for respect for his wife]...they call him Roger but me Mrs. Andrews [my husband's last name]....so, when it comes to money he wouldn't want to give them.... he's say go check Mrs. Andrews but then they wouldn't come, you know and so he appreciates when the big bad wolf have to operate and I kind of don't like that... but if it's a quality that's going to help and it's going to bring a balance...then so be it.

Thus, as gendered discourses continue to affect entrepreneurial activities,[17] Martha shared her need to be tolerant of these in framing her entrepreneurial identity despite the fact that her "husband does not reciprocate with his support at home [be] cause he thinks that is [her] space;" and justifies her more passive role in the electronic venture as a guarantee for greater "flexibility" when dealing with the ongoing demands of childrearing for which she remains primarily responsible. This lack of reciprocity for Martha remains a "sting in the tail;" and "an ongoing issue" that she is yet to come to terms with. It also points to the persistent state of powerlessness in her attempt to navigate the sometimes oppositional demands of work and family, and the social and economic ideologies that underlie them.

Giselle conceived of these ideologies as both disabling and enabling. In the case of the former, Giselle remains troubled by the continued centrality of childrearing and its effects on her entrepreneurial activities. In telling her story, she often cited conversations with her husband in which he emphasized the need "to put her children first". For instance, Giselle reported the apprehension and reprimand of her husband who often asked her "is something wrong here?" at times when a business transaction required the assistance of her sister in caring for her four children. This fragile situation for Giselle intensified with the growth of her entrepreneurial ventures and led to her husband's rejection of the use of what Edwards (qtd. in Horwitz 11) noted as "other mothering practices" in the provision of care from her family network. Her husband requested that she create a "boundary between her work and her family." This boundary for Giselle meant "letting go of business opportunities if it compromises what my husband sees as my responsibility to care for my family."

In crafting unique coping strategies in the formation of her identity as a mompreneur, Giselle sees the process as enabling in as far as it allows her to find creative ways of negotiating her complex identities. As such, Giselle revealed that "I try to balance the two but often realize how difficult that is...how I have no time to do all." Here, Giselle attempts to strike a balance by "squeezing time"[18] between demands of work and family. Yet, it is the very dialectical nature of the temporal demands of these *place-space* dynamics that produces a sense of failed time performativity and a reformulation of the maternal identity for these mompreneurs. In Giselle's case, her frustration with balancing these demands resulted in her modification and reconfiguration of her maternal practices from one that is self-sacrificing to one that is self-reliant; a change she acknowledged that allows her increased flexibility and autonomy in her entrepreneurial space. She disclosed that "I had to see things differently...make him [husband] see that while it is important to give a child a proper foundation...you must not completely sacrifice yourself...you need to teach [them] some independence." In this context of neoliberal reforms, Schild[19] argues that citizenship becomes synonymous with notions of self-reliance. This suggests the need to rethink and (re)conceptualize notions of flexibility within the market to include the integration of embedded socio-cultural understandings of mompreneurs in Trinidad and Tobago.

CONCLUSION

Despite the recognition that "the expansion of women's employment make it more likely that most young women will seek to combine child bearing with...personal autonomy and economic self-reliance" (Damaske and Gerson 245), balancing work and family remains a daunting challenge. In looking at these discursive and contextual conflicts, findings point to the perceived clash between individualized-economic projects of self-reliance, and institutionalized ideological (moral and cultural)-projects of gender relations and identities in Trinidad and Tobago. As part of negotiating these competing landscapes, these mompreneurs actively craft fluid, complex responses including those of conformity, modification, and rejection in the formulation of their entrepreneurial and maternal identities. Such findings reveal the need for further research that continues to explore the structural and cultural contours of gender discourses, questions the presumed unconditional acceptance of the "traditional" ideologies that lie therein, and theorizes the processes by which mompreneurs are (re)constituted by the contemporary landscapes of neoliberalism and prevailing cultural mindscapes that shape mothering practices.

NOTES

[1] See Eddleston and Powell; and Marlow et al.

[2] See Mohammed and Perkins

[3] See Bailey and Ricketts; Barriteau; and Seguino

[4] See Eddleston and Powell; and Reynolds and Renzulli

[5] See Damaske and Gerson; and Gregory and Milner

[6] See Emslie et al.; Greenhaus and Parasuraman; Korabik, McElwain and Chappell; and Reynolds and Renzulli

[7] See Freeman "Femininity and Flexible Labour: Fashioning Class through Gender on the Global Assembly Line"

[8] See Stake; and Yin

[9] See Halford and Leonard, citing Crossley

[10] See Creswell; and Marshall and Rossman

[11] See Knafl and Breitmayer

[12] See Ergeneli et al.; Emslie et. al.; Greenhaus and Parasuraman, and Gupta et al.

[13] Bailey and Ricketts; and Seguino

[14] Bayes et. al.

[15] See Douglas and Michaels; Hays; O'Reilly; and Thurer

[16] Epstein

[17] Eddleston and Powell; and Salmenniemi et al.

[18] See Offer and Schneider

[19] See Schild

WORKS CITED

Ahl, H. "Why Research on Women Entrepreneurs Need New Directions." *Entrepreneurship Theory and Practice* 30.5 (2006): 595-622. Print.

Barriteau, E. "Women Entrepreneurs and Economic Marginality: Rethinking Caribbean Economic Relations." *Gendered Realities: Essays in Caribbean Feminist Thought*. Ed. P. Mohammed. Kingston, Jamaica: University of the West Indies Press, 2002. Print.

Bailey, B. and H. Ricketts. "Gender Vulnerabilities in Caribbean Labour Markets and Decent Work Provisions." *Social and Economic Studies* 52.4 (2003): 49-81. Print.

Bayes, J. H. and R.M. Kelly. "Political Spaces, Gender, and NAFTA." *Gender, Globalization, and Democratization*. Eds. J. H. Bayes, R. M. Kelly, and M. Hawkesworth. Lanham, MD: Rowman & Littlefield Publishers, 2001. 147-170. Print.

Baxter, P. and S. Jack. "Qualitative Case Study Methodology: Study Design and Implementation for Novice Researcher." *The Qualitative Report* 13.4 (2008): 544-559. http://www.nova.edu/ssss/QR/QR13-4/baxter.pdf Web.

Braithwaite, L. "Social Stratification in Trinidad. Institute of Social and Economic Research" (ISER). Kingston, Jamaica: University of the West Indies, 1975. Print.

Creswell, W. J. *Qualitative Inquiry and Research Design: Choosing among Five Traditions*. Thousand Oaks, CA: Sage, 1998. Print.

Damaske, S. and K. Gerson. "Viewing 21st Century Motherhood through a Work-Family Lens." Eds. K. Korabik, D. S. Lero, and D. Whitehead. *Handbook of Family Work Integration: Research, Theory and Best Practices*. London: Academic Press, 2008. 233-248. Print.

Douglas, S. J. and M.W. Michaels. Eds. *The Mommy Myth: The Idealization of Motherhood and How It Has Undermined Women*. New York: Free Press, 2004. Print.

Eddleston, A. K. and G.N. Powell. "Nurturing Entrepreneurs' Work-Life Balance: A Gendered Perspective." *Entrepreneurship Theory and Practice* 36.3 (2012): 513-541. Print.

Emslie, C., K. Hunt, and S. Macintyre. "Gender, Work-Home Conflict, and Morbidity amongst White-Collar Bank Employees in the United Kingdom." *International Journal of Behavioral Medicine* 11.3 (2004): 127-134.

Print.

Epstein, F. C. "The Cultural Cognitive and Social Bases of the Global Surbordination of Women". Eds. H. Lune, E.S. Pumar and R. Koppel. *Perspectives in Social Research Methods and Analysis: A Reader for Sociology,* CA: Sage, 2010. 25-48. Print.

Ergeneli, A., A. Ilsev, and B. P. Karapinar. "Work-Family Conflict and Job Satisfaction Relationship: The Roles of Gender and Interpretive Habits." *Gender, Work and Organization* 17.6 (2010): 679-695. Print.

Freeman, C. "Femininity and Flexible Labor: Fashioning Class Through Gender on the Global Assembly Line." *Critique of Anthropology* 18.3 (2012): 245-262. Print.

— "Is Local: Global As Feminine: Masculine? Rethinking the Gender of Globalization." *Journal of Women in Culture and Society* 26.4 (2001): 1007-1037. Print.

Government of Trinidad and Tobago [GOTT]. Trinidad and Tobago 2011 Population And Housing Census: Demographic Report, Port of Spain: Central Statistics Office, 2012.

Gregory, A. and S. Milner. "Editorials: Work-life Balance: A Matter of Choice?" *Gender, Work and Organization* 16.1 (2009): 1-13. Print.

Greenhaus, H. J. and S. Parasuraman. "Research on Work, Family, and Gender: Current Status and Future Directions." Ed. G. N. Powell. *Handbook of Gender and Work.* Thousand Oaks, CA: Sage, 1999. 391-412. Print.

Gupta, V.K., D. Turban, S.A. Wasti, and A. Sikdar. "The Role of Gender Stereotypes in Perceptions of Entrepreneurs and Intentions to Become an Entrepreneur." *Entrepreneurship Theory & Practice* 33.2 (2009): 397-417. Print.

Halford, S. and P. Leonard. Eds. *Negotiating Gendered Identities at Work: Place, Space and Time.* Great Britain: New York, Palgrave MacMillan, 2006. Print.

Harriott, A, H. Munoz, F. Justiano, N. Fabiancic, and L. Mercado. Eds. *Caribbean Human Development* Report. New York: United Nations Development Program, 2012. Print

Hausmann, R., D. L. Tyson, and S. Zahidi. "Global Gender Gap Report, World Economic Report." Geneva: World Economic Forum, 2012. Print.

Hays, S. *The Cultural Contradictions of Motherhood.* New Haven, CT: Yale University Press, 1996. Print.

Horwitz, R. *Through the Maze of Motherhood: Empowered Mothers Speak.* Bradford, Ontario: Demeter Press, 2011. Print.

Knafl, K. and B. J. Breitmayer. "Triangulation in Qualitative Research: Issues of Conceptual Clarity and Purpose." Ed. J. Morse. *Qualitative Nursing Research: A Contemporary Dialogue.* Rockville, MD: Aspen 1989. 193-203. Print.

Korabik, K., A. McElwain, and B. D. Chappell. "Integrating Gender-Related Issues into Research on Work and Family." Eds. K. Korabik, D. S. Lero, and D. Whitehead. *Handbook of Family Work Integration: Research, Theory and Best Practices.* London: Academic Press, 2008. 215-232. Print.

Marlow, S., C. Henry, and S. Carter. "Exploring the Impact of Gender upon Women's Business Ownership: Introduction." *International Small Business Journal* 27.2 (2009): 139-148. Print.

Marshall, C. and G. B. Rossman. Eds. *Designing Qualitative Research.* 3rd edition. Thousand Oaks, CA: Sage, 1999. Print.

Mohammed, P. and A. Perkins. *Caribbean Women at the Crossroads: The Paradox of Motherhood among Women in Barbados, St. Lucia and Dominica.* Kingston: Canoe Press, 1999. Print.

Murdock, A. K., C. McDonald, J. Joseph, A. Edwards, and G. M. Carillo. "Global Entrepreneurship Monitor: Trinidad and Tobago Report." Port of Spain: European Union, 2010. Print.

Offer, S. and B. Schneider. "The Emotional Dimensions of Family Time and Their Implications for Work-Family Balance." Eds. K. Korabik, S. L. Donna, and D. Whitehead. *Handbook of Family Work Integration: Research, Theory and Best Practices.* London: Academic Press, 2008. 177-190. Print.

O'Reilly, A. *Mother Outlaws: Theories and Practices of Empowered Mothering.* Toronto, ON: Demeter Press, 2004. Print.

— *Rocking the Cradle: Thoughts on Mothering, Feminism and the Possibility of Empowered Mothering.* Toronto: Demeter Press, 2006. Print.

Reddock, E. R. and Y. Bobb-Smith. "Reconciling Work and Family: Issues and Policies in Trinidad and Tobago." NO. 18 International Labour Organization, Geneva, International Labour Office, ILO. 2008. Print.

Reissman, C. K. *Narrative Analysis.* Newsbury Park, CA: Sage, 1993. Print.

Reynolds, J. and L. A. Renzulli. "Economic Freedom or Self-Imposed Strife: Work-Life Conflict, Gender and Self-Employment." Ed. L. A. Keister.

Entrepreneurship: Research in the Sociology of Work 15 (2005) :33-60. UK: Elsevier Limited. Print.

Salmenniemi, S., P. Karhunen, and R. Kosonen. "Between Business and Byt: Experiences of Women Entrepreneurs in Contemporary Russia." *Europe-Asia Studies* 63.1 (2011): 77-98. Print.

Schild, V. "New Subjects of Rights? Women's Movements and the Construction of Citizenship in the 'New Democracies.'" Eds. S. Alvarez, E. Dagnino, and A. Escobar. *Cultures of Politics and Politics of Culture. Revisioning Latin American Social Movements.* Boulder: Westview Press, 1998. Print.

Schultze, U. and R. J. Boland, Jr. "Place, Space and Knowledge Work: A Study of Outsourced Computer System Administrators." *Accounting, Management and Information Technology* 10 (2000): 187-219. Print.

Seguino, S. "Why Are Women in the Caribbean So Much More Likely than Men to be Unemployed?" *Social and Economic Studies* 52.4 (2003): 83-120. Print.

Shelton, M. L. "Female Entrepreneurs' Work-Family Conflict, and Venture Performance: New Insights into Work-Family Interface." *Journal of Small Business Management* 44.2 (2006), 285-297. Print.

Stake, R. E. *The Art of Case Study Research.* Thousand Oaks, CA: Sage, 1995. Print.

Thurer, S.L. *The Myths of Motherhood: How Culture Reinvents the Good Mother.* New York: Penguin Books, 1994. Print.

Willis, J. W. *Foundations of Qualitative Research: Interpretative and Critical Approaches.* CA: Thousand Oaks, 2007. Print.

Yin, R. *Case Study Research: Design and Methods* (4th Ed.). Thousand Oaks: Ca: Sage, 2009. Print.

Section II: Mothering and the Neoliberal State

Austerity and the Silencing of Mothers

7.

Making Invisible

The Eradication of "Homeless Mothers" from Public Policy in Ontario, Canada

MELINDA VANDENBELD GILES

INTRODUCTION

A young homeless mother gives birth in a Toronto hospital on a Friday afternoon, loses custody of her baby, and is back on the street the next day. This is not an isolated or individualized occurrence. That particular moment cannot be understood unless it is placed within the larger social structure of which it is intrinsically a part. This chapter merges the particulars of human experience—mothers experiencing homelessness in Ontario—with the macro concepts of social change, specifically the emergence of what has been termed neoliberalism. By examining the places of disjuncture, a framework can be provided to better comprehend and create visibility regarding the contemporary state of Canada's social welfare system, thereby producing social policies that are relevant for the homeless mothers they purport to represent.

Homelessness in Canada is gendered in a particular way. Since the 1993 dismantling of the national housing program, there has been an unequivocal increase in homelessness for families, the majority of which are female-led (Layton 50). According to the Wellesley Institute Report, there are over

22,500 children currently homeless in Canada (Sky). Cathy Crowe, a Toronto street nurse and author of *Dying for a Home: Homeless Activists Speak Out,* says she has seen a shift in the demographics of homelessness over the past 15 years. "Across the country, the fastest-growing group of homeless people is families with children" (Banks). As of December 31, 2012, there were 158,445 households on the rent-geared-to-income waiting list in Ontario. Many families are waiting up to ten years for subsidized housing (ONPHA). And as of 2011, there were 882 shelter beds occupied nightly in the Toronto shelter system by families, a number that continues to rise every year (City of Toronto Social Housing).

THE STRUCTURAL CAUSATIONS FOR HOMELESSNESS IN CANADA

From WWII until 1993, Canada had a national housing program responsible for building 650,000 units and housing two million Canadians (Layton x). Consistent with the post WWII Keynesian focus on federal funding for urban infrastructure, the Central Mortgage and Housing Corporation was established in 1946 (now known as CMHC: Canada Mortgage and Housing Corporation) as a crown corporation to administer on behalf of the Canadian government federal participation in housing as described by the 1944 National Housing Act (xxvi). CMHC played an integral role in creating new affordable housing across Canada. However, in the 1980s, the federal Conservative government began the process of slowly eroding the federal housing program by cutting almost $2 billion in housing spending, and then in 1993 canceling funding for new social housing. In 1995, the Ontario Conservative government made policy changes to "liberate" the private rental housing market from rent control as part of Ontario Premier Mike Harris's "common-sense revolution" (138). In the 1996 federal budget, most of the national housing programs were downloaded to the provinces (xxvii). In 1996, the United Nations Centre for Housing and Human Settlements recognized Canada's co-operative housing program as a "global best practice" (7). A decade later, in May 2006, the United Nations Committee on Economic, Social and Cultural Rights recommended homelessness and inadequate housing in Canada be addressed as a "national emergency" (United Nations).

THE CANADIAN SOCIAL WELFARE SYSTEM

The extreme funding cuts to Canadian social housing programs in the mid-1990s coincided with the larger picture of neoliberal initiatives directly targeting social welfare globally. I will borrow from Jesook Song's definition of neoliberalism in *South Koreans in the Debt Crisis: The Creation of a Neoliberal Welfare State.* "Neoliberal is defined as an advanced mode of social governing that idealizes efficiency and productivity by promoting people's free will and self-sufficiency. Thus, both liberalism and neoliberalism do not just refer to political economic principles but to social ethos" (x). The loss of a national housing program in 1993—of which the effects are being felt today—needs to be positioned within this larger global neoliberal narrative. The increasing financialization of society has led to a marketization of nearly every aspect of social/cultural life. The state's regulatory role becomes one of promoting the free market to ensure its unhindered functioning. The market then becomes the defining element of society.

The direct impact of neoliberal policies were definitively felt during the 1990s Ontario Harris Conservative government, particularly in terms of the erosion of the social welfare system. The 1990 neoliberal welfare reforms in Ontario consisted of "the dislocation of the 'public' in favour of 'private support' in the family" (Gavigan and Chunn 64-65). The neoliberal extreme focus on individual freedom promoted by the concept of the individual as consumer necessarily created a shift in societal thinking from public to private.

Given the neoliberal anti-state agenda, it is no surprise the CAP (Canada Assistance Plan)—the policy introduced in 1966 that established national standards for welfare programs—was replaced in 1996 with the Canada Health and Social Transfer. In "Intimate Intrusions: Welfare Regulation and Women's Personal Lives," Janet Mosher writes, "The demise of CAP also signaled a new era of decentralization, from the federal government to the provinces, and subsequently from the provinces to local municipalities" (168). This policy shift resulted in a 30% decrease of federal transfers to the provinces between 1995 and 1998. And yet, while privatization and decentralization became primary, so, too, did the concept of "welfare fraud". "Neo-liberals do not claim that the market can do everything—for example, there remains a role for the state in providing national security" (O'Brien and Penna 213-214). Indeed, the welfare reforms of the late twentieth century shifted the state's role from "beneficently meeting the needs of citizens, and further toward that of disciplining and reforming these flawed citizens" (Mosher 165).

If we move ahead to the 2000s, we can further examine the erosion of the Canadian social welfare state as a direct consequence of neoliberal inspired "non-interventionist" philosophy. Prime Minister (elected 2006) Stephen Harper's Master's Thesis, written while he was at the University of Calgary in 1991, is titled "The Canadian Business Cycle and Fiscal Policy in Canada" in which he renounces the theoretical and fiscal basis of Keynesian economics in favor of New Classical Theories of government "non-intervention." Harper argues that Keynesian macro-economics ignores the unintended consequences of individual "rational self-interested" actors such as politicians, voters, and business actors who are *not* motivated by the "social optima" (iii) upon which enlightenment-inspired Keynesian economics is predicated. Harper proceeds to reveal through an analysis of the Canadian economy from 1953-1990 the extent through which business and electoral cycles influence fiscal policy thus skewing the results of a Keynesian intervention model and thereby suggesting such intervention effects harmful constraints upon an otherwise presumed self-regulating market.

Harper's neoliberal philosophical basis has been grounded in Canadian public policy in terms of the erosion of social supports for mothers and children and the defunding of research related to gender equity. The operating budget of the Status of Women Canada (SWC) has been cut and the Policy Research Fund (PRF) was terminated in 2006. In the PRF Report, *"Where Are the Women? Gender Equity, Budgets and Canadian Public Policy"*, Janine Brodie and Isabella Bakker write, "... the ascendance of neo-liberal thinking in political and policy circles... have been accompanied by the progressive disappearance of the gendered subject" (Brodie and Bakker 7). The erasure of gender has severe implications for maternal and childhood poverty since the mother and child become segregated in terms of public policy initiatives. As protection of the child is elevated, protection of the mother becomes irrelevant.

The increasing situation of familial homelessness in Canada is a direct consequence of neoliberal policies and practices of government offloading fiscal and social responsibility. The consequences of government "non-intervention" and austerity measures in terms of the Canadian child welfare system are best revealed by Karen Swift, a York University professor in the School of Social Work, who points out in her book, *Manufacturing "Bad Mothers": A Critical Perspective on Child Neglect*, "Each child welfare worker has the well-known problem of case overload, each organization is chronically underfunded, crises abound, virtually everyone involved complains of feeling ineffective, and many have come to feel that the system does not work" (4).

THE NEOLIBERAL DISJUNCTIVE: BUREAUCRATIC INSTITUTIONS IN A NEOLIBERAL SOCIETY

In *The Theory of Social and Economic Organization,* Weber writes, "Bureaucratic administration means fundamentally the exercise of control on the basis of knowledge" (339). This concept of expert knowledge arises within enlightenment assumptions regarding the human subject as rational and functioning within a collective of like-minded fellow citizens. However, since the 1970s, anti-science, anti-rationality, anti-expert and anti-bureaucracy philosophies have been popularized through the ascendancy of media as a prominent disseminating "knowledge" source. The result: individuals inspired daily by postmodern concepts of individual "choice" and "freedom" forced to work within rigidly defined yet underfunded bureaucratic systems. Bureaucratic systems require an ideology of compliance and collectivity, alongside enormous financial and human resources—elements lacking in a neoliberal ethos of individualized market actors.

NOTES FROM THE FRONT-LINES

Since May 2010, I have been conducting interviews with social service coordinators and public policy makers, organizing focus groups with nurses and social workers, attending community and faith-based meetings, touring women's shelters, detox centres, women's resource hubs and visiting families living in motels, in an effort to better understand the daily lives of mothers experiencing homelessness in Ontario and those with whom they interact. There has been remarkable synchronicity in what individuals working and living within the homelessness sector have said: the need to "work outside the system" and to "be creative", the recognition of the slow process of social change; the underfunding, the instability of short-term projects and pilot programs, and the need for integration of resources. It is not surprising that within such a dysfunctional environment, individuals are forced to "be creative". They are forced to "creatively" subvert the ingrained bureaucratic logic requiring evidence in exchange for neoliberal short-term and immediately pleasing results. Yet, as Weber writes in *Bureaucracy,* the bureaucratic system cannot be so easily subverted. "Where administration has been completely bureaucratized, the resulting system of domination is practically indestructible" (487).

In "*Complexio Oppositorum:* Notes on the Left in Neoliberal Italy" Andrea Muehlebach writes, "Neoliberalism is often better understood as a form that can contain the oppositional...and fold them into a single moral order" (495). In other words, as bureaucratic systems become increasingly vilified in popular discourse and thus underfunded, so, too, do they become increasingly regulatory. Thus, social workers and public health nurses must conform to increasingly stringent guidelines and surveillance requirements demanding "accountability" while simultaneously being told to be "innovative" and "take the initiative" in devising work strategies to cope with increased workload and decreased labour power.

A discussion with four Public Health nurses who work directly with women who are pregnant and homeless in Toronto allows insight into how bureaucratic elements remain deeply entrenched within the policies and practices of Children's Aid Societies in Toronto. Since child apprehension is often a potential factor when working with individuals categorized as "at-risk", the nurses often work directly with social workers from the Children's Aid Societies. As one nurse says:

> Oh, CAS is complicated. I have a sixteen year old right now, but because she's sixteen she has her own worker because she's a Crown Ward. While she was pregnant, she had the PAC (Children's Aid Pregnancy After-Care Worker) coming out to see her. And then when the baby was born, now the baby has a worker and a high-risk nurse so she's seeing four different CAS workers, one for herself and three for the baby. I don't even know who to call. No wonder these clients are so overwhelmed. They have so many workers. Why can't the worker that's for her baby be her worker? But they don't do it that way. It's confusing. So they can have multiple workers throughout their lives. And then depending on where they are living in the city, it's a different office. And if they move during the pregnancy, then they get another new worker. They can't continue with the same worker. —Saleha, Public Health nurse

This lack of service coordination arises often during the interviews. The sad death of baby Jordan Heikamp in 1997 due to chronic starvation while under the care of Children's Aid sharply revealed the extent to which division and segregation of resources and services had become amplified, both in the Children's Aid Societies and in the Toronto shelter system. Funding requirements that demand increasing competition for scarce resources only serve to further exacerbate these silos. This initiated a Coroner's inquest that resulted in the Chief Coroner's Report[1] containing recommendations, many of them implemented, regarding the Children's Aid Societies, the Ministry of Community and Social Services, and Toronto Public Health. A number of programs, particularly in Toronto Public Health, received increased funding or were initiated as a direct result of this inquest. There are a number of excellent programs in Toronto Public Health targeted specifically to young pregnant women experiencing homelessness or marginal housing, such as the Young Parents No Fixed Address Program and the St. Michael's Hospital Passport Program. And the HARP (Homeless At-Risk Prenatal Program) run by five nurses who help women at any age who are pregnant and experiencing homelessness, is another excellent program initiated as a direct result of this inquest.

However, rather than being evidence-based, the Coroner's Report is filled with subjective and ideological statements recommending increased division between the mother and child in Children's Services and increased surveillance of "lying" and "manipulating" young people who reside or have resided in shelters (No. 27 Coroner's Report). Instead of investigating an entire dysfunctional system in an effort to create structural change, the Coroner's Report provided a convenient and politically expedient launching point for particularized short-term initiatives with no guarantee of long-term funding. While the programs mentioned above are beneficial, the increased surveillance and regulatory requirements within Children's Aid were not. And even the benefit of the above programs is mitigated by the constant instability of funding.

According to the University of Toronto Centre for Urban and Community Studies "A Visceral Grief: Young Homeless Mothers and Loss of Child Custody" report, "A major constraint on providing services for young homeless pregnant women or mothers in Toronto is the lack of stable funding for agencies… With reduced government funding and an emphasis on temporary project funding, agencies struggle to maintain their core services and meet administrative costs. Without stable funding, more projects and programs are short-term, making it more difficult to maintain service coordination" (Novac et al. 28-29).

Demanding bureaucratic procedures without proper funding or labour power inevitably produces a system made irrational through its redundancy. Duplicate fail-safe measures lead to increasing paperwork that in effect erases the initial purpose for the safety measures. "Success" is then defined according to the perimeters of the initial assessments rather than what they purport to be assessing. Bureaucratic demands for "accountability" in effect eradicate all accountability by diffusing responsibility. Paperwork becomes prioritized over people. Systems become represented as "accountable" while social supports are eliminated leaving homeless mothers without appropriate shelter. The most detrimental result of this neoliberal disjunctive is the way in which mothers experiencing homelessness have been systematically eradicated from the bureaucratic public policy realm, in effect leaving them and their children with no social supports.

NEOLIBERALISM AND INTENSIVE MOTHERING

The height of neoliberal public policy in Canada during the mid-1990s coincided with what has been termed Intensive Mothering. This involves positioning children as social capital to be "invested in." In "Why Can't a Mother Be More Like a Businessman?" Sharon Hays defines Intensive Mothering as "child-centred, expert-guided, emotionally absorbing, labor-intensive, and financially expensive" (414). The current singular focus on productivity and the increased demand on the family, specifically mothers, to reproduce socially appropriate neoliberal subjects is consistent with the free-market focus on choice and individual responsibility. State responsibility becomes private familial responsibility. Homeless mothers with their children represent an aberration of the neoliberal promise of success and advancement. Spatially, their segregation into overcrowded shelters and undesirable and marginal motel strips ensures their invisibility. Socially, the individualized discourse of pathology constructs homeless mothers as "bad" mothers and through this Othering process, enables the rest of society to feel justified in their marginalization.

When speaking with individuals working directly with mothers experiencing homelessness in Ontario, many commented on how the current neoliberal focus on "good motherhood" as defined by white, middle-class consumption, does not apply for those mothers living on the margins. Many social policies effectively render their capacity to emulate "good mothering" practices negligible, thereby guaranteeing their societal condemnation and social exclusion. Valerie, a researcher manager whose work focuses on issues of homelessness and women's rights says, "The ideal mother, that breastfeeding is the best thing, that mother-child bonding is best, the most important thing is attachment—all of these discourses determine if someone is a good mother or not, and that all just falls by the wayside. All of those idealized things...all of that stuff doesn't apply to mothers at the margins, whether it's good or bad, regardless of what kind of mothers they would be." Many of the public policies pertaining to homeless mothers necessitate work requirements and maternal/child separation that invalidate the claims of Intensive Mothering thereby de-legitimating and visibly removing mothers experiencing homelessness from the discourse itself.

According to Janice, a Toronto public health manager who has coordinated a number of programs for mothers experiencing homelessness in Toronto, "I don't think there's been enough of a focus on homeless women issues. I think as a society, we just don't want to acknowledge it or see it or admit it. And there aren't as many visibly homeless women as there are visibly homeless men." As she goes on to say in reference to the "My Baby and Me" Infant Passport Program (Moravac) at St. Michael's hospital that enrolled 101 pregnant women experiencing homelessness between July 2005 and October 2007, "St. Michael's was interested in looking at pregnant homeless women because it's one of those things where they're marginalized and you don't necessarily hear a lot about it, or all negative if you do, always focusing on something terrible without realizing that there are some people who are actually making amazing changes in their lives to be able to achieve a healthy pregnancy." As Valerie says, "If a mother living in poverty who is single is made visible in the mainstream media, you will immediately find this backlash, and it's all the same messages, they're all prostitutes, they're drug addicts. It arises in relation to poverty, welfare, and housing issues."

Mothers experiencing homelessness are not only rendered invisible through a lack of societal recognition other than condemnation; they are made invisible through statistical categories that do not even acknowledge them as mothers. These statistical categories in turn lead to invisibility in terms of public-policy making. In terms of statistical categorization in The Toronto Report Card on Homelessness 2001, there are existent categories for Single Persons, Couples, Two Parents with Children, and Single Parent with Children. The number of homeless single persons is by far the largest category at 81.3%, but as the Centre for Urban and Community Studies "Better Off in a Shelter?" paper states, "Many seemingly 'single' homeless women are in fact mothers separated from their children" (Paradis et al 2). In the course of the study, one-quarter of the mothers lived separately from their children. However, if a mother is not directly with her child—occurring for a number of reasons, including having an older son who is not eligible to live in a women's shelter—the mother statistically becomes a "single person," thereby erasing her motherhood status.

> Think about it. You see these homeless women on the street, you find out that they've had five or six pregnancies in their life…has anybody ever seen a mother standing on the corner? We don't even consider them a mother because they don't have their kid. You know, it's just something I wonder about some-times, how many of the women living in these shelters that are called "depressed" are actually suffering postpartum de-pression that has never been diagnosed or treated. —Janice, Toronto Public Health Manager

In "Who's Counting? Marilyn Waring on Sex, Lies and Global Eco-nomics"—a National Film Board of Canada documentary regarding the in-visibility of domestic labour in national accounting—Waring says, "It's per-fectly obvious that the people who are visible to you as contributors to the economy are the people who will be visible when you make policy. And if you're not visible as a producer in a nation's economy, then you're going to be invisible in the distribution of benefits" (Nash). In other words, the way in which productivity is statistically determined will construct those who are rendered visible as productive or alternately as dependent. Regardless of whether a mother is actively working to sustain the livelihood of her chil-dren and perhaps also engaging with the informal labour market, she will be statistically identified as "dependent". But for the mothers who have lost custody of their children, because they have been statistically eradicated as "mothers", they become only visible as single dependents thus eliminating all access to familial resources. Waring's pivotal book *If Women Counted*, reveals the extent to which statistical categorizations determine redistribu-tion. As Waring writes, "The system cannot respond to values it refuses to recognize" (Waring 4). How can a mother regain custody of her children if she is allotted housing based on her "single status" yet must have familial housing to regain custody?

MOTHERS EXPERIENCING HOMELESSNESS AND LOSS OF CHILD CUSTODY

If we return to the discussion of a young homeless mother who gives birth in a Toronto hospital on a Friday afternoon, has her baby apprehended, and is back on the street the next day, we can now begin to position this narrative within the larger structural and ideological framework within which it is intrinsically embedded. According to the "A Visceral Grief" report, "There is no more disenfranchised group in the child welfare field than parents whose ties with their children have been permanently severed" (Novac et al. 11). The report goes on to state, "Our literature and document search identified some programs to assist pregnant homeless women, but almost none to help homeless mothers or birth parents at risk of losing custody of their children" (22-23). The report quotes Teresa Hinton, who wrote *Forgotten Mothers: Meeting the Needs of Homeless Women Who Have Lost Their Children.* "The category 'single homeless woman' obscures the fact that many women who are homeless have had children and lost custody of them to adoption, fostering and the care system. The impact of this stays with women throughout their lives and their invisibility as mothers has an additional emotional impact" (18).

> Many of the women who are not accompanied by children are actually mothers. And a lot of services are only for women accompanied by children. For me, one of the starkest things is the apprehension at birth by default. It's one of those examples where everyone agrees it's not ideal for the newborn. And it just happens almost for administrative reasons. It can be related to what kind of day the birth takes place on, whether it's a weekend or a holiday. — Valerie, Policy Research Manager

> There hasn't been funding available to develop many programs to the capacity that they need to be developed, including our own, which is restricted by whether or not we have children involved. What is hugely lacking are bereavement, grief and loss programs for this population. You might be in a shelter, then you deliver the baby, you're going to a different shelter and they wouldn't even know that you had a baby. And it's nobody's fault. It's just the way things are set up to deal with either single people or with children. — Janice, Toronto Public Health Manager

During the afternoon focus group session with four Toronto public health nurses who work directly with homeless mothers, many of the comments reiterated the above points:

"The whole grief after baby is apprehended is something that's not really talked about very much."

"One of my clients said that when her baby was taken away from her it felt like her soul was being ripped out of her."

"It's just such an untouched subject and we always say there's no support afterwards for these women. It's just such a common occurrence and there's no follow-up. It's terrible, the process they go through. Their baby's apprehended, they have to be in court within five days and retain a lawyer. They have to apply for a legal aid certificate. It's just insane."

"A lot is expected out of a woman after they give birth."

"Everyone gets on board if they keep their baby, but if not..."

The situation of a young mother having her newborn baby apprehended can now be positioned within a much larger underfunded bureaucratic reality that demands immediate results and preventative measures without time or funding for proper assessment and follow-up. The result is that these mothers are literally abandoned by current social policy—not because of a lack of concern or initiative on the part of Public Health Workers—but because the demands of an underfunded, under-resourced bureaucratic system require a convenient slot within which such mothers can be legibly identified. Without such bureaucratic identification, they become invisible.

THE SPACE OF UTTER NEGLECT

In *Economies of Abandonment: Social Belonging and Endurance in Late Liberalism,* Elizabeth Povinelli writes:

Any form of life that is not organized on the basis of market values is characterized as a potential security risk. If a social welfare program, for instance, can be shown to lengthen life and increase health, but cannot at the same time be shown to produce a market value, this lengthened life and increased health is not a value to be capacitated. Indeed, it is a value to be actively attacked and rooted out of the state and national psyche. (22)

The neoliberal paradigm is more insidious than creating legibility for "deserving" versus "undeserving" individuals. For those labeled "undeserving" the repercussions are increased surveillance and regulation, as evidenced in research regarding homeless shelters in North America.[2] However, there exists an additional space outside even these categorizations—the space of utter neglect. These mothers are not only "undeserving," they do not exist. Once a person ceases to be legible within the rigidly bureaucratic confines of the currently eroded social welfare system, they cease to be.

CONCLUSION

It is within the words of these women that we see the direct impact of neoliberal-inspired public policy. The demands of bureaucratic philosophy combined with the neoliberal market imperative for immediate results has created a particularly potent framework within which public policies emphasizing political expediency and representation become prioritized above long-term structural change. Procedure and regulatory administrative requirements become prioritized above the meeting of material human need. Decreased funding and job instability lead to a corrosive environment in which individuals are overworked, under-resourced, and forced to comply with increasingly stringent administrative requirements of "accountability."

Within such a de-centralized framework, mothers experiencing homelessness who lose custody of their child/children fall through the cracks of the underfunded administrative system and thereby are "erased" from the public policy framework itself. Creating contextualization for the social, political, economic, and historical influences of public policy initiatives enables the language of discussion to shift away from particularizing, individualized, short-term, funding-driven imperatives and toward long-term policies that render visible the individuals whom such policies purport to be representing—mothers who are experiencing homelessness in Ontario.

NOTES

[1]See Coroner's Report
[2]See Bridgman; Hopper; and Lyon-Callo

WORKS CITED

Banks, Wendy. "Middle-Class Families Join the Homeless." *National Review of Medicine* 1: 4. Interview with Cathy Crowe. Feb. 28, 2004. Print.

Bridgman, Rae. *Safe Haven: The Story of a Shelter for Homeless Women.* Toronto: University of Toronto Press, 2003. Print.

Brodie, Janine and Isabella Bakker. *Where Are the Women? Gender Equity, Budgets and Canadian Public Policy.* Ottawa, Canada: Canadian Centre for Policy Alternatives, 2008. Print.

City of Toronto Social Housing. Toronto Social Housing by the Numbers. Toronto: City of Toronto. May 2011. Print.

City of Toronto Report Card on Homelessness. Toronto: City of Toronto, 2001. Print.

Coroner's Report. Report on the Inquest into the Death of Jordan Desmond Heikamp. Toronto: Office of the Chief Coroner, September 2002. Print.

Gavigan, Shelley and Dorothy Chunn. "Women, the State and Welfare Law: The Canadian Experience." *The Legal Tender of Gender: Law, Welfare and the Regulation of Women's Poverty.* Eds. Shelley Gavigan and Dorothy Chunn. OÑATI International Series in Law and Society. Oregon: Hart Publishing, 2010. 47-72. Print.

Harper, Stephen. "The Canadian Business Cycle and Fiscal Policy in Canada" University of Calgary: MA Thesis, Department of Economics, 1991. Web.

Hays, Sharon. "Why Can't a Mother Be More Like a Businessman?" *Maternal Theory: Essential Readings.* Ed. Andrea O'Reilly. Toronto: Demeter Press, 2007. 408-430. Print.

Hopper, Kim. *Reckoning with Homelessness.* Ithaca: Cornell University Press, 2003. Print.

Layton, Jack. *Homelessness: How to End the National Crisis.* Toronto: Penguin Canada, 2008. Print.

Lyon-Callo, Vincent. *Inequality, Poverty, and Neoliberal Governance: Activist Ethnography in the Homeless Sheltering Industry.* Peterborough, ON: Broadview Press, 2004. Print.

Moravac, C, M Little, A Gorman, R Nisenbaum, D Dzendoletas, and R Fortin. "Evaluation of 'My Baby and Me' Infant Passport for Young Pregnant Homeless Women in South East Toronto." Toronto: Toronto Public Health, August 2009. Print.

Mosher, Janet. "Intimate Intrusions: Welfare Regulation and Women's Personal Lives." *The Legal Tender of Gender: Law, Welfare and the Regulation of Women's Poverty.* Shelley Gavigan and Dorothy Chunn Eds. OÑATI International Series in Law and Society. Oregon: Hart Publishing, 2010. 165-188. Print.

Muehlebach, Andrea. "*Complexio Oppositorum:* Notes on the Left in Neoliberal Italy." *Public Culture* 21.3 (2009): 495-515. Print.

Nash, Terre. Director. Kent Martin. Producer. "Who's Counting? Marilyn Waring on Sex, Lies & Global Economics." Montreal, Quebec: National Film Board of Canada. 1995. Documentary.

Novac, Sylvia, Emily Paradis, Joyce Brown and Heather Morton. "A Visceral Grief: Young Homeless Mothers and Loss of Child Custody." Research Paper 206. Toronto: Centre of Urban and Community Studies, University of Toronto, October 2006. Print.

O'Brien, Martin and Sue Penna. *Theorizing Welfare: Enlightenment and Modern Society.* London: Sage, 1998. Print.

ONPHA (Ontario Non-Profit Housing Association) Report on Waiting Lists Statistics for Ontario. "Waiting Lists Survey 2013." ONPHA, Oct. 2013. Accessed Nov. 29, 2013. Web.

Paradis, Emily, Sylvia Novac, Monica Sarty and David Hulchanski. "Better Off in a Shelter? A Year of Homelessness and Housing among Status Immigrant, Non-Status Migrant, and Canadian-Born Families." Research Paper 213. Toronto: Centre for Urban and Community Studies, University of Toronto, July 2008. Print.

Povinelli, Elizabeth. *Economies of Abandonment: Social Belonging and Endurance in Late Liberalism.* Durham, N.C.: Duke University Press, 2011. Print.

Sky, Laura. Film Director. Cathy Crowe. Executive Producer. "Home Safe Toronto." Toronto: SkyWorks Charitable Foundation, 2009. Documentary.

Song, Jesook. *South Koreans in the Debt Crisis: The Creation of a Neoliberal Welfare Society.* Durham, NC: Duke University Press, 2009. Print.

Swift, Karen. *Manufacturing 'Bad Mothers': A Critical Perspective on Child Neglect.* Toronto: University of Toronto Press, 1995. Print.

United Nations Economic and Social Council. Committee on Economic, Social and Cultural Rights. Thirty-sixth session. "Consideration of reports submitted by states parties under articles 16 and 17 of the covenant: concluding observations of the Committee on Economic, Social and Cultural Rights." Geneva, May 1-19, 2006. Web.

Waring, Marilyn. *If Women Counted: A New Feminist Economics.* Toronto: Fitzhenry & Whiteside. 1988. Print.

Weber, Max. *The Theory of Social and Economic Organization.* New York: Simon and Schuster Inc., 1947. Print.

8.

Neoliberalism and the De-politicising of Motherhood

Reflections on the Australian Experience

JOANNE BAKER

INTRODUCTION

This chapter considers mothering in Australia, where neoliberalism has exerted an increasingly pervasive influence over the past three decades. Neoliberalism here refers to the dismantling of the welfare state, the privatization of publicly owned resources and state-run services, and the expansion of global free trade. Since the early 1980s, successive Labor and Conservative Australian governments have adopted neoliberal economic and social policies, primarily in a quest for increased international competitiveness. The traditionally protectionist approach to trade and industrial relations has receded in favour of a minimalist state and the expansion of private markets. The scale and scope of this ideological shift has had profound implications for many areas of social protection. Specifically, this essay will consider the policy areas of child care, parenting payments, and paid maternity leave under the Howard Coalition Government of 1996-2007. While these areas of policy bear the imprint of neoliberal ideology, they are also marked, some-what contradictorily, by socially conservative understandings of mother-ing.

In addition to influencing the design and outcomes of policy, neoliberal ideology can also be understood as involving the extension of individualist and market principles beyond social and economic policy into other areas of human life, including subjectivity.[1] The extension of market values and rationality to other areas of life underscores the significance for social and cultural analysis of the contemporary experience of motherhood in Aus-tralia. Therefore, this chapter will consider the incursions of neoliberal doc-trine into both the material and subjective experiences of Australian moth-erhood. Mothering under neoliberalism will be considered in connection to the "post-feminist" environment and contemporary forms of maternal femininity. It will be argued that the regulatory dimensions of neoliberal-ism interact with post-feminism to create an updated and complex environ-ment in which to navigate motherhood. The increasingly individuated and privatized notion of mothering in this climate privileges a decontextualized and de-politicised emphasis on personal responsibility and an undermining of collectivist social responses to the care of children.

FEMOCRATS AND THE AUSTRALIAN STATE

Feminist scholars of motherhood have long noted that women's dispropor-tionate responsibility for domestic and caring work compromises their par-ticipation in paid work and limits their economic independence. Changes to the nature of the Australian family, combined with widened social roles for women and their increased participation in the paid workforce have raised the need for public policies, such as the provision of non-parental child care and maternity leave. Indeed, until the mid-1990s, Australia had been lauded for its progressive approach to women's policy. This was at-tributed in great part to the feminist bureaucrats who were part of the Women's Movement—femocrats—who entered political life in significant numbers from the mid-1970s when the sympathetic, social democratic Aus-tralian Government led by Gough Whitlam was in power (1972-75). In this conducive political climate, femocrats were able to redefine matters of par-ticular significance to women as mainstream rather than marginal issues. A women's policy machinery unit, the Office of the Status of Women was es-tablished in the central position of Department of the Prime Minister and Cabinet in 1974 and proved crucial to the establishment of space and legitimacy for gender analysis expertise and the securing of funding and support for women's movement initiatives and organizations (Eisenstein). These achievements brought a range of benefits to Australian mothers; services for women, delivered by women such as women's health centres, a comprehensive, national child-care system and domestic violence refuges/shelters.

However, such achievements have been significantly eroded during the four consecutive terms of conservative Coalition Governments led by John Howard between 1996 and 2007. Despite the winding back of many of the achievements of the femocrat era, detailed below, the Howard Government took up a progressive posture with the female electorate. In the first year of the Howard administration, Jocelyn Newman, Minister Assisting the Prime Minister for the Status of Women, announced the Government's policy focus on "more choice for women" (Australian Department of Social Security). The rhetoric of choice has increasingly characterized government addresses to women. It suggests a break with fixed gender norms and signals the arrival of sexual equality which allows women to pursue their desires unhindered by previous constraints. In the following interview excerpt, Prime Minister Howard is thus able to invoke feminism, in order to indicate its contemporary redundancy for women, and to offer "choice" as its legacy and alternative:

> We are in the post-feminist stage of the debate. The good thing about this stage is that I think we have broken through some of the old stereotypes. I find that for the under-30s women... the feminist battle has been won. That is not an issue. Of course a woman has a right to a career. Of course, women are as good as men. Of course, they are entitled to the same promotion and they can do it as well. Of course. That is accepted and what they are looking for now is a set of circumstances and a range of policies that allow them to exercise the choices they want. (qtd. in Hewett 45)

The apparently enlightened mantra of "more choice for women" coexisted with the rapid and robust dismantling of women's policy mechanisms and processes established in the femocrat era. This included cutting the budget of the Office for Women and moving it from its prominent position in the Prime Minister's Department to the very large Department of Families, Community Services and Indigenous Affairs; reducing funding and support for women's movement initiatives and organizations (the task of women's generalist representation was given to three conservative peak bodies; the National Council of Women, Young Women's Christian Association and the Australian Federation of Business and Professional Women), and the de-legitimizing and marginalization of gender expertise within policy discourse.[2] The Howard Coalition Government's treatment of some specific policy areas of particular significance to Australian mothers will now be considered.

CHILD CARE, MARKETS, AND CHOICE

Child care[3] in Australia had been almost entirely operated on a not-for-profit basis until the early 1990s. Child-care services developed as a result of feminist-inspired demands for equal opportunity policies that enabled mothers to take up employment. Since then, policy shifts have prioritized the incorporation of market forces into child-care provision. This has included the removal of operational subsidies to not-for-profit services in 1997, and the replacement of operational subsidies to child-care centres with the Child Care Benefit in 2000 (a fee subsidy directly payable to parents using services that have met national accreditation standards, rather than to the services themselves).[4] Such changes signaled the Coalition Government's commitment to competition, consumer choice, and reducing the state's direct provision of services in favour of private-sector expansion (although part-funded and regulated by the state). Australian child-care scholar Deborah Brennan has criticized the commodification and corporatization[5] of this core public service, calling the Howard Government's privatization of child care "a bonanza for business" (214, "The ABC of Child Care Politics") because government child-care subsidies have been used by child-care companies to stimulate record profits.

The wisdom of relying on the "superiority" of market forces to provide accessible, affordable, and safe quality child care has been questioned by critics.[6] In particular, the notion of choice has been questioned due to a scarcity of available and suitable placements in some areas. For mothers living in rural and remote areas of Australia, the notion of making a *choice* about child care is nonsensical in small, poorly serviced communities. For-profit providers are free to target demographic areas likely to bring the greatest profits, leaving not-for-profit providers to concentrate on demographic areas of no interest to for-profit companies. However, parents' experience of child care in metropolitan Australia is not unproblematic. The cost, quality and difficulty in securing a place at the child-care centre of choice and for the hours needed are frequent and significant problems (Cassells et al. 129-131). Additional critiques of the marketization of child care in Australia have pointed to the lack of financial incentive to improve the quality of services. Because income from government subsidies is the same regardless of the quality of the service, once accreditation has been achieved, child-care companies are only responsible for maximizing returns for their shareholders.[7] The introduction of market forces as a way of expanding choice has also been questioned by Deborah Brennan (217 "The ABC of Child Care Politics"), who observes that a potentially problematic concentration of ownership has characterized the child-care market rather than diversification. Indeed, in 2008, the consequences of market failure were keenly felt when ABC Learning (which occupied a dominant position in the market and provided more than 30% of all Australian child-care places) collapsed, owing debts of over one billion Australian dollars and was bailed out by the Rudd Labor federal government, which succeeded the Howard regime (Penn 157-158).

As Cribb and Ball have noted, the effects of privatization are widespread. Not only does it change the conditions under which services are provided, "it also changes how we think about what we do, and how we relate to ourselves and significant others" (121). Deborah Brennan has documented the features of the community-based child-care movement in Australia, describing its development of neighbourhood connections and support networks through the task of working together in a shared endeavour.[8] Critics argue that it is this kind of social fabric that diminishes when community-based approaches to child care are undermined.

PRO-NATALISM AND ITS CONTRADICTIONS

In contemporary Australia, and particularly during the Howard era, mothers have primarily received policy attention through the neoliberal imperative of labour market flexibility and the spectre of an ageing population with declining fertility rates. However, contradictory responses to these issues emerged due to the government's orientation to neoliberal policy settings and the influence of the Prime Minister's socially conservative Christianity.[9] Howard had a well-documented and longstanding commitment to breadwinner (heterosexual, two-parent, single income) families. Thus, the broad thrust of the Howard Government's family support policy was to discourage the employment of mothers of young children, unless they were sole parents. This was evidenced through changes to family support payments; family tax benefits (previously called family allowance payments) introduced high marginal tax rates (tax payable and benefits withdrawn) for secondary earners. These changes made it financially advantageous for a family to rely on a single income rather than to share paid work and caring for children between parents.[10] Meanwhile, sole parents reliant on parenting payments were added to those benefit recipients subject to "welfare to work" requirements. From mid-2006, such parents were moved to a lower level of income support payment and required to demonstrate specific work-seeking activities or to undertake at least fifteen hours of paid work each week. The extension of the welfare to work regime to sole mothers operated in conjunction with the Workplace Relations Amendment Act of 2005 (popularly known as WorkChoices) to facilitate a coerced, increasingly casualised and under-protected source of low-paid labour.[11] Work-Choices increased restrictions on industrial action, expanded company exemptions from unfair dismissal laws, and created five minimum workplace conditions; effectively reducing penalty rates and other protections for many workers.

Feminist history has documented the state's periodic concern with falling birth rates (Bryson 12-23). In Australia in the early 2000s, concern about falling birth rates and the implications of an ageing population made declining fertility a significant public policy issue. Based on an understanding that women's reproductive decisions were influenced by the tension between family care and employment demands, feminist groups and trade unions had been lobbying for a comprehensive, national paid maternity scheme to facilitate mothers' continuing attachment to the workforce and their ability to provide post-pregnancy care for their baby. Until 2011, Australia, along with the United States, was one of only two OECD (Organization for Economic Cooperation and Development) countries without a national paid maternity leave scheme. Although a signatory to the United Nations Convention on All Forms of Discrimination Against Women (CE-DAW), the Australian Government had entered a reservation on its article, which requires its parties to provide maternity pay. However, the Howard Government steadfastly opposed this and held on to its commitments to mothers out of the paid workforce. In lieu of paid maternity leave, a "baby bonus" scheme[12] was introduced in order to encourage women ("families" in the preferred gender-neutral language of the government) to have more children. Indeed, the Treasurer Peter Costello drew on the pro-natalist, nationalist exhortation for women to have "One for the mother, one for the father and one for the country" (McGrath). It is worth noting one of Brennan's reservations about the rise of for-profit child care here; improvements to the availability of paid maternity through the introduction of a national scheme conflict with the interests of private child-care providers, who profit on the financial imperative for (some) women to return to employment.

NEOLIBERALISM AND THE SUBJECTIVE EXPERIENCE OF MOTHERING

Having discussed state responses to mothers through public policy instruments, this chapter now turns to consider some of the ways in which contemporary, neoliberal subjectivities associated with motherhood are experienced in Australia. Feminist theorizing about mothering since the early 1970s have exposed the regulating discourses of "good" mothering.[13] Despite significant changes to the institutions and experiences of motherhood as a result of feminist challenges to its traditional social norms, regulating discourses of "good" mothering endure and "saturate everyday practices and interactions" (Goodwin and Huppatz 1, "The Good Mother in Theory and Practice"). The regulation of mothering alters with changing social and cultural conditions, the most recent being the pervasive influence of neoliberalism over the past thirty years.

Neoliberalism has come to be understood as an ideology that promotes an individualized form of citizenship, which emphasizes personal responsibility and self-reliance (Rose). Such self-reliant individualism revolves around the fulcrum of individual choice. Understanding women's lives primarily through the prism of choice is compatible with the contemporary post-feminist context. Cultural theorist Angela McRobbie understands the "post-feminist" era as one in which feminism has been "taken into account" through challenges to imposed restraints on women and is positioned as no longer relevant (McRobbie 255, "Post-feminism and Popular Culture"). Rosalind Gill has also described the present-day post-feminist sensibility that emphasizes individual autonomy, choice and empowerment, and is thus intimately connected to the logics of neoliberalism (260). Indeed, she notes the striking congruence between the autonomous post-feminist woman and the self-responsible subject demanded of neoliberalism. Thus, the regulation of women, and of course mothers, is now achieved through their self-governance rather than the overt imposition of constraint. Such neoliberal ideology conveniently exonerates the state from the provision of social welfare and ensures individuals are held accountable by their own measures of self-worth segregated from economic circumstances.

THE CONTEMPORARY INTENSIFICATION AND
EMBODIMENT OF MOTHERING

The notion of 'intensive mothering' has been articulated most prominently by Sharon Hays (8) as a contemporary American expression of mothering, which is characterized by its rigor and dedication. It is expressed through an explicit child-focused orientation and the input of extensive amounts of time, emotional, and monetary resources, commonly guided by expertise about children's care and their development. Such 'intensive mothering' has also come to define Australian conceptualizations of "good" mothering and is frequently cited in academic literature as a way of understanding contemporary mothering practices. The mainstream Australian mothering context has drawn heavily on its British colonial roots and has been characterized by patriarchal, heterosexual nuclear family structures and the male breadwinner model that organizes work in the public and private spheres. Communal approaches to child-rearing favored in Australian Aboriginal cultures have been de-centred and devalued following colonization (Moore and Riley 192). It is no coincidence that the ideals of "intensive mothering"—where women, and specifically birth mothers, are seen as inherently best suited to look after babies and children and required to be unconditionally available—became popularized in Australia at the height of state retrenchment from providing support to mothers.

These contemporary features of mothering have implications for the kinds of mothering behavior now routinely expected of women (by others and themselves), at a time when they are more likely to be employed as well as raising children. While there is some evidence in the Australian context that fathers have increased their participation in child care in recent decades, mothers have also increased their average care time.[14] Although gender equality in heterosexual parenting may now be a more widespread social goal, this has coincided with heightened expectations of what now constitutes "proper" parenting or its gendered reality, "good" mothering; particularly for those who are highly educated and socio-economically advantaged (Craig 553-554, "Parental Education").

The emphasis on mothers' provision of more intensive levels of emotional support for children could be considered to sit at odds with the self-optimizing rationality and competitive individualism associated with neoliberal ideology. Certainly, there is a tension between the self-abnegating demands of "intensive mothering" and the individualistic pursuit of self-interested endeavor. However, the ethos and demands of "intensive mothering" are compatible with the entrepreneurial neoliberal subject who bears responsibility for being the best "self" they can be through transformative behaviors, self-scrutiny, and monitoring.

In addition to the intensification of mothering, there are changed expectations associated with the physical presentation of pregnant and child-rearing women. The aspirational figure of the "yummy mummy" is recognizable by her tasteful and stylish modes of consumption both in dress and the accoutrements of mothering (such as prams and other nursery items). She is also increasingly required to maintain a "fit" (athletically toned)[15] and sexy[16] pregnancy and post-pregnancy body. Although subject to scholarly critique,[17] the yummy mummy motif continues to hold considerable sway in Australia. Australians consume more magazines per capita than the United States and Britain (FIPP) and this form of consumption may account for some of its endurance. It is a term that also continues to be heavily used to brand businesses targeting the lucrative pregnancy and postpartum markets; pregnancy day spas, maternity products, and pre and post natal fitness centres.

This new set of aesthetic pressures co-exists with the financial and time demands associated with "Intensive mothering," and represent an inherently classed set of practices.[18] This highly popularized representation of modern motherhood can be identified as a post-feminist trope because it purposefully resists the notion of motherhood as necessarily un-empowering or lifestyle-inhibiting (Baker 277, "Young Mothers"). Many feminist theorists[19] note that the fascination with affluent and chic mothering has flourished alongside the widespread attacks on "welfare mothers", and has served to legitimize the escalation of their punitive treatment by the state, as discussed further below.

MANAGING DIFFICULTY AND DISADVANTAGE: THE HYPER-RESPONSIBLE MOTHER

This popularized form of aspirational, empowered motherhood is not an unproblematic position for women in Australia. It overlays traditional mothering ideology and is therefore vulnerable to accusations of selfishness. However, it is seductive and represents a dangerous redefinition of motherhood for young women, because "maternity is thus fully incorporated into the language of self-perfectibility" (McRobbie 23, "Yummy Mummies"). Although it is evident that such a position is a privileged and classed one, it is commonly represented as universal and attainable for all—or at least for those who are ready and able to acquire the necessary expert knowledge and put in the requisite self-discipline (Ringrose and Walkerdine 228-230). Indeed, there are published manuals to achieving this celebrated status, such as *The Yummy Mummy's Survival Guide.*[20]

As discussed in the first section of this chapter, new responsibilities of citizenship are now attached to those sole mothers in receipt of government income support. This is no longer received on the basis of their responsibility for care work, but the demonstration of their work-seeking or work-readiness activities (Blaxland 143). The scapegoating of sole mothers as irresponsible, lazy and a drain on the welfare state ("dole bludgers" in Australian parlance), has shored up support for this policy shift, and for Aboriginal mothers such vilification is racialized.[21]

If prosperity and success derive from being the right kind of transformative and autonomous individual, then poverty and disadvantage can increasingly be associated with poor self-management. This makes critique of the gendered experience of motherhood difficult. One of the features of contemporary, post-feminist motherhood is that it is predominantly understood as a chosen rather than imposed state, and articulating the difficulties of an experience that is deemed to have been "chosen" is replete with challenges.[22] However, as Ann Crittenden[23] has argued, while women may choose to be mothers, they do not choose the adverse consequences of that decision. Of course, motherhood is not always planned, can bring unanticipated life changes, material hardship, and may co-exist with male violence. Nonetheless, having a well-planned and successful life is now a norm of modern femininity, and those who don't manage this may be singled out for more forceful disparagement. Therefore, it is incumbent on those who do not fit easily into these new categories of female achievement and success to make sense of—and justify—their experience of motherhood in relation to these new norms.[24] Baker argues that in the neoliberal, post-feminist climate, this is more likely to involve strategies that emphasize personal choice, volition, and disavow any notion of structural, gendered disadvantage.

CONCLUSION

Cultural values and social structures of family and workplace have not changed at the same pace as women's needs and expectations.[25] They continue to be constrained by traditional gender role ideologies and inadequate public policies. As the example of child care in Australia demonstrates, these policies have seen the erosion of state welfare through the privatization of community and government services. Such changes have privileged corporate interests and single-earner heterosexual families.

Furthermore, coinciding with the loss of gendered state supports is an insidious recalibration of the rights and responsibilities associated with motherhood in the private sphere. This has involved responsibility for the conditions of motherhood being increasingly attributed to the individual rather than the socio-economic system/s in which it is experienced, conveniently exonerating the state from social responsibility. The regulation of mothering under neoliberalism continues to promote the investment of women's identities in child-rearing, although through updated and intensified guises. What has changed is the achievement of this, not through coercion, but through the internalization of ideological forces associated with neoliberalism. Thus, these de-politicising forces prioritize a singular focus on individual mothering practices rather than a collectivized focus on structural deficiencies.

NOTES

[1] For further reading regarding the regulation of neoliberal subjectivity see Brown; and Rose

[2] Refer to Eisenstein; and Summers

[3] Child care is defined as formal, regulated, non-parental care for children, away from their home. It includes before and after-school care, long day care, family day care and occasional care.

[4] Refer to Summers; and Sumsion

[5] "Corporatization" here refers to the "rapid expansion and escalating market share of child care services owned and/or operated for profit by public companies listed on the Australian Stock Exchange" (Sumsion 100).

[6] Refer to Brennan "The ABC of Child Care Politics"; Harris; and Penn.

[7] Refer to Brennan "The ABC of Child Care Politics"; and Sumsion.

[8] Refer to Brennan "Childcare and Australian Social Policy."

[9] For an analysis of Prime Minister John Howard's socially conservative Christianity and its influence on government policy, see Maddox.

[10] Refer to Brennan "Babies, Budgets, and Birthrates: Work/Family Policy in Australia 1996–2006"; and Summers.

[11] Refer to Peetz.

[12] In its initial 2004 form this comprised a one-off "bonus" non means-tested payment of 5,000 Australian Dollars paid upon birth of a baby.

[13] For further reading regarding constructions of "good" mothering see Oakley; and Rich.

[14] Refer to Craig, *Contemporary Motherhood: The Impact of Children on Adult Time*; and Craig and Bittman.

[15] Refer to Nash, " 'You Don't Train for a Marathon Sitting on the Couch': Performances of Pregnancy 'Fitness' and 'Good' Motherhood in Melbourne, Australia" and "Weighty Matters: Negotiating 'Fatness' and 'In-Betweenness' in Early Pregnancy."

[16] Refer to Tyler

[17] Refer to Jermyn; and O'Donohoe

[18] Refer to Goodwin and Huppatz, "Mothers Making Class Distinctions"

[19] Feminist theorists include Douglas and Michaels; and McRobbie, "Post-Feminism and Popular Culture" and "Yummy Mummies Leave a Bad Taste for Young Women."

[20] Refer to Fraser

[21] Refer to Cutcher and Milroy

[22] Refer to Baker, "Claiming Volition and Evading Victimhood: Post-Feminist Obligations for Young Women"

[23] Refer to Crittenden

[24] Refer to Baker, "Claiming Volition and Evading Victimhood: Post-Feminist Obligations for Young Women," and "Young Mothers in Late Modernity: Sacrifice, Respectability and the Transformative Neoliberal Subject"

[25] For further reading see England; Gerson; and Summers

WORKS CITED

Australian Department of Social Security. "More Choice for Women." Statement by Jocelyn Newman, Minister for Social Security and Minister Assisting the Prime Minister for the Status of Women. Australian Government Publishing Service, 1996. Print.

Baker, Joanne. "Claiming Volition and Evading Victimhood: Post-Feminist Obligations for Young Women." *Feminism and Psychology* 20.2 (2010): 186-204. Print.

—"Young Mothers in Late Modernity: Sacrifice, Respectability and the Transformative Neoliberal Subject." *Journal of Youth Studies* 12.3 (2009): 275-288. Print.

Blaxland, Megan. "Mothers and Mutual Obligation: Policy Forming the Good Mother." *The Good Mother: Contemporary Motherhoods in Aus-*

tralia. Eds. S. Goodwin and K. Huppatz. Sydney, NSW: University of Sydney Press, 2010. 131-152. Print.

Brennan, Deborah. "Babies, Budgets, and Birthrates: Work/Family Policy in Australia 1996–2006." *Social Policy* 14.1 (2007): 31-57. Print.

—"Childcare and Australian Social Policy." *Children, Families, and Communities: Contexts and Consequences.* Eds. J. Bowes and A. Hayes. Melbourne: Oxford University Press, 2004. 210-227. Print.

—"The ABC of Child Care Politics." *Australian Journal of Social Issues* 42.2 (2007): 213-225. Print.

Brown, Wendy. "Neo-liberalism and the End of Liberal Democracy." *Theory and Event* 7.1 (2003): 1-19. Print.

Bryson, Lois. "Motherhood and Gender Relations: Where To in the Twenty-First Century." *Just Policy* 24 (2001): 12-23. Print.

Cassells, Rebecca, Justine McNamara, Rachel Lloyd and Ann Harding. "Child Care Affordability and Availability." *Agenda* 14.2 (2007): 123-139. Print.

Craig, Lyn. *Contemporary Motherhood: The Impact of Children on Adult Time.* Aldershot: Ashgate, 2007. Print.

—"Parental Education, Time in Work and Time with Children: An Australian Time-Diary Analysis." *British Journal of Sociology of Education* 57 (2006): 553–575. Print.

Craig, Lyn, and Michael Bittman. "The Effect of Children on Adults' Time-Use: An Analysis of the Incremental Time Costs of Children in Australia." *Feminist Economics* 14 (2008): 57–85. Print.

Cribb, Alan, and Stephen Ball. "Towards An Ethical Audit of the Privatisation of Education." *British Journal of Educational Studies* 53.2 (2005): 115-128. Print.

Crittenden, Ann. *The Price of Motherhood.* New York: Metropolitan Books, 2002. Print.

Cutcher, Leanne, and Talila Milroy. "Misrepresenting Indigenous Mothers: Maternity Allowances in the Media." *The Good Mother: Contemporary Motherhoods in Australia.* Eds. S. Goodwin and K. Huppatz. Sydney, NSW: University of Sydney Press, 2010. 153-174. Print.

Douglas, Susan and Meredith Michaels. *The Mommy Myth: The Idealization of Motherhood and How It Has Undermined Women.* New York: Free Press, 2004. Print.

Eisenstein, Hester. *Inside Agitators: Australian Femocrats and the State.*

Philadelphia, PA: Temple University Press, 1996. Print.

England, Paula. "The Gender Revolution: Uneven and Stalled." *Gender and Society* 24.2 (2005): 149-66. Print.

FIPP Worldwide Magazine Media Association. *World Magazine Trends in Australia 2012-13*. London: FIPP, 2013. Print.

Fraser, Liz. *The Yummy Mummy's Survival Guide*. London: Harper-Collins, 2006. Print.

Gerson, Kathleen. *The Unfinished Revolution: How a New Generation Is Reshaping Family, Work and Gender in America*. New York, NY: Oxford University Press, 2010. Print.

Gill, Rosalind. *Gender and the Media*. Cambridge: Polity, 2007. Print.

Goodwin, Susan, and Kate Huppatz. "The Good Mother in Theory and Practice; An Overview." *The Good Mother: Contemporary Motherhoods in Australia*. Eds. S. Goodwin and K. Huppatz. Sydney, NSW: University of Sydney Press, 2010. 1-24. Print.

—"Mothers Making Class Distinctions: The Aesthetics of Maternity." *The Good Mother: Contemporary Motherhoods in Australia*. Eds. S. Goodwin and K. Huppatz. Sydney, NSW: University of Sydney Press, 2010. 69-88. Print.

Harris, Nonie. "Child Care Is Not a Women's Issue!: A Feminist Analysis of Child Care Subsidy Policy." *Just Policy* 44 (2007): 45-50. Print.

Hays, Sharon. *The Cultural Contradictions of Motherhood*. New Haven: Yale University Press, 1996. Print.

Hewett, Jennifer. "The Mothers' Club." *Sydney Morning Herald,* September 7-8, 2002: 45 and 50. Print.

Jermyn, Deborah. "Still Something Else Besides a Mother? Negotiating Celebrity Motherhood in Sarah Jessica Parker's Star Story." *Social Semiotics* 18.2 (2008): 163-176. Print.

Maddox, Marion. *God Under Howard: The Rise of the Religious Right in Australian Politics*. Crows Nest, NSW: Allen and Unwin, 2005. Print.

McGrath, Catherine. "Costello Comments on Ninth Budget." Transcript from PM, Radio National, http://www.abc.net.au/pm/content/2004/\-s1106275.htm, accessed 25 July 2012. (2004). Web.

McRobbie, Angela. "Post-Feminism and Popular Culture." *Feminist Media Studies* 4.3 (2004): 255-264, 2004. Print.

— "Yummy Mummies Leave a Bad Taste for Young Women." *The Guardian,*

March 2, 2006. Print.

Moore, Jane and Lynette Riley. "Aboriginal Mother Yarns." *The Good Mother: Contemporary Motherhoods in Australia.* Eds. S. Goodwin and K. Huppatz. Sydney, NSW: University of Sydney Press, 2010. 175-194. Print.

Nash, Meredith. " 'You Don't Train for a Marathon Sitting on the Couch': Performances of Pregnancy 'Fitness' and 'Good' Motherhood in Melbourne, Australia." *Women's Studies International Forum* 34.1 (2011): 50-65. Print.

— "Weighty Matters: Negotiating 'Fatness' and 'In-Betweenness' in Early Pregnancy." *Feminism and Psychology* 22.3 (2012): 307-323. Print.

Oakley, Ann. *Becoming a Mother.* Oxford: Martin Robertson, 1979. Print.

O'Donohoe, Stephanie. "Yummy Mummies: The Clamor of Glamour in Advertising to Mothers". *Advertising & Society Review* 7.3 (2006): 1-21. Print.

Peetz, David. *Brave New Workplace: How Individual Contracts Are Changing Our Jobs.* Crows Nest, NSW: Allen & Unwin, 2006. Print.

Penn, Helen. "Gambling on the Market: The Role of For-Profit Provision in Early Childhood Education and Care." *Journal of Early Childhood Research* 9.2 (2011): 150-161. Print.

Rich, Adrienne. *Of Woman Born: Motherhood as Experience and Institution.* London: Vintage, 1977. Print.

Ringrose, Jessica, and Valerie Walkerdine. "Regulating the Abject: The TV Make-Over as Site of Neo-liberal Reinvention Toward Bourgeois Femininity." *Feminist Media Studies* 8.3 (2008): 227-246. Print.

Rose, Nicholas. *Powers of Freedom: Reframing Political Thought.* Cambridge: Cambridge University Press, 1999. Print.

Summers, Anne. *The End of Equality: Work, Babies and Women's Choices in 21st Century Australia.* Milson's Point, NSW: Random House, 2003. Print.

Sumsion, Jennifer. "The Corporatization of Australian Childcare: Towards an Ethical Audit and Research Agenda." *Journal of Early Childhood Research* 4.2 (2006): 99-120. Print.

Tyler, Imogen. "Pregnant Beauty: Maternal Femininities under Neoliberalism." *New Femininities: Postfeminism, Neoliberalism and Subjectivity.* Eds. R. Gill and C. Scharff. Basingstoke, UK: Palgrave Macmillan, 2011. 21-36. Print.

9.

Austerity and Gender Neutrality

The Excluding of Women and Mothers from Public Policy in the UK

JANE CHELLIAH

INTRODUCTION

This chapter provides an analysis of the impact of austerity cuts in the UK on women, particularly mothers. Despite austerity cuts having the most direct negative affect on women and mothers, the landscape of equality in the UK has been re-cultivated in accordance with a neoliberal framework that disregards female representation in society. The current austerity program gas of 2014) was implemented by the coalition government, consisting of the Conservative Party and the Liberal Democrat Party, when it came into power in 2010. The government's objective is to achieve a cyclically adjusted current balance by 2015-2016 through lowering government spending on public services, welfare, and social benefits. The total effect of these austerity measures on women's lives is disproportionate. According to the report titled "The Impact of Austerity on Women" by the Fawcett Society, it is anticipated that 710,000 jobs in the public sector will be lost by 2017. Women currently hold 40% of these jobs and account for 64% of the total workforce

(6). However, rather than recognizing how such measures affect women's lives, and mothers in particular, the government utilizes a rhetoric of fear to convince citizens of the necessity of austerity.

The feminization of poverty—the disproportionate burden of austerity upon women—has resulted in mothers feeling as if they are not only sacrificing hard-won feminist rights, but their children's present chances and future opportunities as well. According to the Trade Union Congress (TUC), some of the specific cuts affecting mothers are the abolition of the "Health in Pregnancy" Grant—a universal payment of £190 for pregnant women who are 25 weeks pregnant and have received health advice from a medical professional—and a three-year freeze on child benefit from 2011 to 2014. As a result of the freeze, a family with two children will see the amount they receive in child benefit for their first child frozen at £20.30 per week until 2014, and the amount they receive for their second child frozen at £13.40 per week until 2014. The TUC states that the average family with two children has suffered a cut in real-terms of £57.20 in 2011/2012, will lose a further £153.40 over the course of 2012/2013 with the largest amount being lost in the 2013/2014 duration with the figure of £197.60 (Trade Union Congress). Given the context of rising food costs and decreasing stable employment, benefits and wages, such austerity measures only increase poverty at a time when families most definitely need the assistance.

THE NEOLIBERAL POLICY FRAMEWORK IN THE UK

Margaret Thatcher introduced neoliberalism as a political project when she was elected as the first female British prime minister in 1979. She adopted the policies implemented by Paul Volcker (head of the US Federal Reserve), which were to promote business interests through the use of financial and social policies. Thatcher was a believer of Friedrich Hayek's (often referenced when discussing neoliberal philosophy) micro-economic policies. Hayek encouraged her to embrace neoliberalism citing Augusto Pinochet's success in Chile. In a letter addressed to Hayek dated February 17, 1982, Thatcher described Chile as a "striking example of economic reform from which we can learn many lessons" (Margaret Thatcher Foundation website). While putting up some resistance to turning the UK into another Chile (because she was worried that the methods would not accord with the British traditions and Constitution) Thatcher, instead, amplified the neoliberal basis of property ownership. One of Thatcher's enduring legacies was to introduce the Housing Act 1980, which gave tenants living in state-owned properties (council homes) the right to buy their homes. This move satisfied the neoliberal ideal of individual property ownership being a vehicle for so-called personal freedom. However, the properties that were sold were not replaced with a construction program to build new social housing. As a result, the lasting effect has been a continuing serious shortage of social accommodation (Meek). Thatcher also weakened the unions and undermined labour law and social policy (Stanford). She deregulated industry and financial markets and praised wealth creation. However, Thatcher did not address issues of rape, domestic violence, child care, benefits for single mothers, discrimination, or sexual harassment and sexual inequality.

A subsequent Conservative government (1990-1997) led by John Major, instigated a "Back to Basics" campaign that praised the role of the nuclear family and introduced further privatization measures and more deregulation of the financial markets. Subsequently, a Labour government led by Tony Blair (1997-2007) took over. Feminists who had held placards during Thatcher's era with the words, "We want women's right, not a right-wing woman" (Penniman 155), wrote about their expectations for the return of collective activism that would advance women's causes. Blair's political belief system was called "Third Way" and attempted to capture the centrism ground through social policies that prioritized equal opportunities. Blair's government introduced the National Child Care Strategy, extended maternity and paternity rights, introduced the working families tax credit and the minimum wage (Blair). But the neoliberal emphasis on responsibility and personal accountability remained predominate.

Gordon Brown, another Labour Prime Minister from 2007 to 2010, was scathing of Thatcher and wrote in 1989 that "the distribution of income in Britain has now become so unequal that it is beginning to resemble a Third World country" (Brown, "Where There's Greed: Margaret Thatcher and the Betrayal of Britain's Future"). However, he later contradicted himself during his premiership by courting big businesses and championing their interests through the setting up of an International Business Advisory Council. At the 2008 International Women's Day celebration held by ActionAid, Brown said that the left-leaning stewardship of women's rights was "one of the biggest challenges to social justice in our time" (Brown, 2008 International Women's Day celebration held by ActionAid).

PRESENT CHALLENGES FOR WORKING MOTHERS IN THE UK PUBLIC SECTOR

The working environment in the civil service during the Labour years of 1997 to 2010 has been defined as "family-friendly." However, social policies that were of direct benefit to working mothers are currently (as of 2014) being reappraised as a social benefit standing in the way of productivity. The civil service has been asked by the coalition government to "re-examine" the terms and conditions of civil servants, which include flexible working, emergency leave, and subsidized child care that is provided during all school holidays and home working. Female public sector employees, and particularly mothers, are being adversely affected in multiple ways. The Fawcett Society report titled "The Impact of Austerity on Women" refers to these as the "triple jeopardy:" 1. Women are being hit hardest by cuts to public sector jobs, wages and pensions; 2. Women are being hit hardest as the services and benefits they use more are cut; and 3. Women will be left filling the gaps as state services are withdrawn (5).

Approximately 500,000 women face redundancy in the civil service, local government, as nurses, as teachers, as council workers, as school dinner ladies, as public nursery workers, and in the sectors that support women such as domestic violence. Many women work in low-paid and insecure public sector jobs and are struggling to pay bills and make ends meet. A two-year pay freeze was introduced in the 2010 government budget for all public sector workers earning over £21,000, and in the 2013 budget a cap of an average 1% rise till 2015/2016 (11). Given the rising costs of child care, transport, energy bills, and food bills, it becomes increasingly difficult to live on a low wage. Since 2008, actual incomes have risen much more slowly than minimum income requirements. The required earnings for families with children has not risen in line with price increases and, on the contrary, has risen by 16% above inflation since the start of this recession (Joseph Rowntree Foundation). Thus, a two-year pay freeze imposed by the coalition government in 2010 only serves to widen the gap between income and the ability of many to maintain a decent standard of living.

According to the Fawcett Society, the lack of affordable high-quality child care in the UK is currently a major barrier to a mother's full and productive engagement in the labour market (Fawcett Society, "Budget 2013: Helping or Hurting Women?"). The Women's Budget Group (WBG) is an independent organization consisting of women from academia, non-governmental organizations and trade unions who use economic policy to promote gender equality. The WBG's response to the 2013 budget states that "Children are poor because their mothers are poor, and mothers are often poor because raising children in the UK can entail huge losses in earnings and opportunities" (WBG, "Further Commentary on Budget 2013"). The Daycare Trust has published figures on its' website which show that the average nursery cost for a child under two has risen by 4.2% to £106.38 per week for a part-time place (25 hours); a full-time place costs £11,000 for a year. Costs for children over two years old have gone up by 6.6% to an average of £103.96 per week for a part-time place (Daycare Trust). If you consider that most of the low-paid work is done by women with 63% earning £7 per hour or less, the burden of child-care costs is brought into sharper focus (Resolution Foundation).

The Chancellor of the Exchequer, George Osborne, said that every job loss in the public sector is offset by three created in the private sector (Osborne speech, *The Telegraph*). However, the WBG asserts that only 37 out of 100 private sector jobs has gone to women and these are likely to be lower paid, less secure and part-time (WBG, "The Impact on Women of the Coalition Government's Spending Round 2013"). The increased usage of Zero-Hours contracts in the private sector and in public sector work that is now being contracted out (care work) has increased a working woman's professional insecurity. Variable hours, uncertain earnings, and having to work at short notice are factors that weigh heavily on a woman's ability to manage her work-life balance and manage household expenditure (Resolution Foundation, "A Matter of Time"). The Government's emphasis on investment in physical infrastructure rather than social infrastructure has meant that mothers are left out of any investment dividends because of the lack of spending in the fields of health care or child care.

THE EXCLUDING OF MOTHERS FROM PUBLIC POLICY

There is a gradual "airbrushing" of women, especially mothers, out of the new national landscape that is emerging in austerity ridden Britain. In the neoliberal quest for individual action, previous government assistance is either being eradicated or remolded to fit into a privatization program. The lack of affordable child care has become the biggest barrier to a mother either being able to find employment or being able to climb the career ladder. "Sure Start" was an initiative launched by the Labour government in 1998 to offer free and low-cost support services in the areas of early education, health, and family support services to children and parents. Sure

Start centres were set up around the country. Although the present government promised to contribute to spending on Sure Start, over time the funding has merged into other programs (Daycare Trust, Sure Start Campaign). Any woman who has special needs faces further challenges in getting assistance. The female voluntary sector represents the collective interests of all women in the areas of violence against women, health services, minority women, disabled women, and mental health among many others. Due to a lack of government financial support, huge gaps are being left in the representation and advocacy of women. The National Society for the Protection of Children (NSPCC) estimated that spending on children's social care was reduced by 24% in 2011-12, which includes services such as Sure Start and child protection (National Society for the Protection of Children).

Neoliberal ideologues claim individuals must work out their own problems within the sphere of the nuclear family because it is too expensive for the government to provide provision for the wellbeing of people. Thus, a mother's unpaid work of caregiving becomes integral to the functioning of the neoliberal state. Jo Swinson, a female Liberal Democrat minister, spoke at the Liberal Democrats autumn 2012 conference and said that the government was struggling to fill the spaces left by working women (Swinson). Mothers still do the majority of domestic work despite their employment status outside the home. Mothers do two hours more unpaid work a day than men and that amount increases during the weekends and in school holidays (OECD). Consigning women to the domestic sphere where they will act as informal and unpaid government agents only serves to further embed the neoliberal agenda at the cost of advancing women's equality.

THE BRITISH WELFARE SYSTEM

The British welfare system was launched in 1945 to assist with post-war reconstruction. The Liberal politician, William Beveridge, identified conditions which, he said, needed addressing in order to make Britain more productive. These were: poverty, disease, ignorance, squalor, and idleness. Beveridge introduced the welfare state as a means of achieving this. The welfare state would provide social security, a free health service, free education, subsidized housing, and full employment (Beveridge). Almost seven decades later, we are witnessing radical reform. The Welfare Reform Act 2012 has brought about the greatest change in the welfare system since 1945. The changes will be phased in over 10 years and will limit the rights to a number of benefits, incentivise employment including for those who are sick and disabled, and will introduce a Universal Benefit system that will streamline benefits. Inherent in all these policies is a culture of "blame", and the basis for this blame is unemployment. Being employed is a new rite of passage into respectable society despite the increasing lack of job availability.

Single mothers are particularly stigmatized for drawing welfare benefits. Single women, according to the Fawcett Society, are set to lose a greater proportion of their income than other households, such as single men or couple households. Lone mothers can expect to lose the equivalent of one month's income a year by the time all the cuts are implemented (Fawcett, "What about Women in London?"). Single parents who are not working and whose youngest child is under five years old are no longer entitled to claim Income Support. Instead, they need to claim Jobseeker's Allowance, which pays less, as part of the government's plan to incentivise people into work. The harsh reality is that many single mothers are already struggling to find child friendly employment (Gingerbread). The costs associated with finding work—travelling to interviews, buying work clothes—often leave them worse off. Taking the first job that comes along is not a route out of poverty. The treatment of single mothers as "welfare scroungers" masks the material realities of their lives.

The unions have organized marches and demonstrations that are well attended, but there is still a strong polarization in attitudes towards welfare. Although unemployment could strike anyone in the current economic climate of uncertainty, government austerity measures are often supported by a hardening of public attitude towards welfare. In a 2012 survey conducted by an organization called British Social Attitudes on whether the government should spend more money on welfare benefits for the poor, 28% thought the government should spend more while 39% disagreed (British Social Attitudes).

NEOLIBERAL IDEOLOGY

Naomi Klein, in her book *The Shock Doctrine*, describes how neoliberalism came to take root in countries where upheaval had occurred. People with vested capitalist interests, organizations, and governments seized the opportunity to undertake what Klein refers to as, "Orchestrated raids on the public sphere in the wake of catastrophic events combined with the treatment of disaster as exciting market opportunities, disaster capitalism" (6). The banking crisis of 2008 shook the economic system and gave the incoming coalition government a blank page on which to create a free market economy fashioned from awarding the delivery of public services to private contractors, creating schools free from government control, privatizing the health service and helping businesses grow through deregulation and less stringent employment rights. The Chancellor of the Exchequer, George Osborne, at a party conference speech in 2012, said that, "Beneath the sound and fury of daily debate a quiet revolution is taking place... I am the Chancellor who is cutting the size of government faster than anyone in modern times" (Osborne). When juxtaposed against unemployment statistics, Osborne's statement becomes even starker. According to figures from the Office for National Statistics (ONS), as of April 2013, there were 2.56 million people unemployed in Britain (Office for National Statistics).

David Harvey, in *A Brief History of Neoliberalism* states that for any thought to become dominant a "conceptual apparatus" has to be designed that is appealing to people (Harvey). The conceptual apparatus utilized in the UK today to advance neoliberalism is a supposed British values-based system that harks of nostalgia, a social policy that pushes an agenda of individual responsibility but saves the concept of collectivism in references to the family, an economic policy that favours the male, right-wing think tanks run by conservatives that push the government's policies, and a government that uses a utilitarian appeal to the "greater good of the country" to justify cuts.

A common thread running through all these apparatus is the concept of the sacrificial mother as a married dependent in the domestic sphere (home), able to replicate the 1950s housewife desiring nothing more than to serve her family. This supports the neoliberal demand that families take more responsibility for their own wellbeing because the state cannot afford to care for each and every person. Women's unpaid labour is a crucial component in keeping the free market going. The Minister for Universities, a member of the Conservative Party, wrote in his book *The Pinch* that feminism was the "single biggest factor" for the lack of social mobility in Britain because women who would otherwise have been housewives had gone to university and taken well-paid jobs that ambitious working-class men would have taken (Willetts). These attacks on mothers are being challenged by women's interest groups. The Fawcett Society states that women continue to face persistent structural inequality and disadvantage as mothers.

CONCLUSION

The neoliberal agenda raises crucial questions about the intersection between feminism and the everyday lives of mothers in the UK. Feminism is about jobs, social care, the workplace, welfare benefits and single motherhood. Recasting social security as "welfare dependency" downgrades women's place in society. Women's rights become political points of negotiation as the free enterprise market demands increasing flexibility in an effort to compete with emerging Asian markets through supply side policies. The specific needs of mothers and children become silenced within ambiguous and gender-neutral public policies that fail to acknowledge that it is women and mothers who are principally affected by austerity in the UK. Thus, feminist collective activism provides a powerful force in calling for a new social contract recognizing mothers as essential in the running of a neoliberal economy and demanding appropriate compensation.

WORKS CITED

Beveridge, William. "Social Insurance and Allied Services: The Beveridge Report." His Majesty's Stationery Office, 1942. Print.

Blair, Tony. *The Third Way: New Politics for the New Century*. London: Fabian Society, 1998. Print.

Braedley, Susan and M. Luxton. Eds. *Neoliberalism and Everyday Life*. Canada: McGill-Queen's University Press, 2010. Print.

British Social Attitudes: "Anxiety Britain: Worries on Cuts and Public Services Present Big Challenges for Cameron's Coalition." 2012. Print.

Brown, Gordon. "Where there's Greed: Margaret Thatcher and the Betrayal of Britain's Future." Mainstream Publishing. May 3, 1989. Print.

— "Why the Right Is Wrong." *Fabian Ideas 626*. Fabian Society. London 2010. Print.

— International Women's Day celebration held by ActionAid, 2008. Speech.

Daycare Trust. "Childcare Costs in 2013". www.daycaretrust.org.uk. Web.

Fawcett Society Policy Briefing. "The Impact of Austerity on Women". UK: Fawcett Society, March 2012. Print.

—"Budget 2013: Helping or Hurting Women?" UK: Fawcett Society. March 2013. Print.

—"What about Women in London?" UK: Fawcett Society. May 2012. Print.

Gingerbread. www.gingerbread.org.uk. "It's Off to Work We Go?" May 21, 2012. Web.

Harvey, David. *A Brief History of Neoliberalism*. New York: Oxford University Press, 2005. Print.

Joseph Rowntree Foundation. "A Minimum Income Standard for the UK in 2012" July 10, 2012. Print.

Klein, Naomi. *The Shock Doctrine: The Rise of Disaster Capitalism*. USA: Penguin Books, 2007. Print.

Margaret Thatcher Foundation website: http://www.margaretthatcher.org. Web.

Meek, James. "Where Will We Live?" *London Review of Books* 36.1. (Jan 9, 2014): 7-16. Print.

National Society for the Protection of Children. www.nspcc.org.uk. "Smart Cuts? Public Spending on Children's Social Care". November 2011. *Occupied Times of London*. Editorial. February 8, 2012. Web.

Office for National Statistics. "UK Unemployment Rises by 7,000." April 17, 2013. Print.

OECD. Organization for Economic Cooperation and Development. "Gender Publication- Closing the Gender Gap: Act Now." December 17, 2012. Print.

Osborne, George. Chancellor of the Exchequer. Party Conference Speech, 2012.

— *The Telegraph*. Spending Review 2013. Speech. Web.

Penniman, Howard Rae. Ed. Britain at the Polls, *1979: A Study of the General Election*. American Enterprise Institute for Public Policy Research, 1981. Print.

Resolution Foundation. "Beyond the Bottom Line." January 20, 2013. Print.

— Resolution Foundation. "A Matter of Time: The Rise of Zero Hours Contract." June 2013. Print.

Stanford, James. *Economics for Everyone: A Short Guide to the Economics of Capitalism*. UK: Pluto Press, 2008. Print.

Swinson, Jo. Speaking at the Liberal Democrat Conference. September 2012. Speech.

Trade Union Congress (TUC) "Child Benefit Freeze Will Cost Two-Child Families Over £400." November 1, 2012. Print.

Willetts, David. *The Pinch: How the Baby Boomers Took Their Children's Future and Why They Should Give It Back.* UK: Atlantic Books, 2011. Print.

Women's Budget Group (WBG). "The Impact on Women of Budget 2013." April 2013. Print.

— "Women's Budget Group Further Comments on Budget 2013." July 2013. Print.

— "The Impact on Women of the Coalition Government's Spending Round 2013." June 2013. Print.

The Making of "Good" Neoliberal Mothering Subjects

10.

Welfare Queens and Anchor Babies

A Comparative Study of Stigmatized Mothers in the United States

KATRINA BLOCH AND TIFFANY TAYLOR

INTRODUCTION

In this chapter we explore the relationship between mothering and neoliberal ideology using a comparative case study of nativist (anti-immigrant) websites based in the United States and a welfare office in rural North Carolina. Neoliberalism in this context refers to a reduction in economic and social intervention by the state, a deregulation of labour markets, and the globalization of commerce and investments (Navarro). Unlike past liberalism regimes in the U.S. that encouraged laissez-faire free markets, U.S. neoliberalism that emerged in the 1980s and 1990s worked to actively create market ideologies through the erosion of social services and workers' rights (Navarro; and Soss, Fording and Schram).

Through this market ideology the U.S. government began to police individual behavior to reward "good citizens" for being rational "self-reliant market actors" and to punish "bad citizens" for "personal choices" that lead to "mismanaged lives" (Soss 22-23). Thus, the ideology, or interpretive framework supporting this inequality structure (Gramsci), took on a particular

focus on individualism and self-sufficiency to support the neoliberal policies of the 1980s through the 2000s. In turn, we argue this ideology and
conditions of a so-called "free market" result in the devolution of policing
"good citizens" to policing "good" and "bad" mothers. Since the emergence
of the neoliberal state in the U.S., the work of policing mothers has devolved
further from the state to other women and mothers thereby further eradicating state responsibility for social welfare.

THEORETICAL FRAME

Given that dominant nationalist ideology in the U.S. structures and supports the passage of neoliberal policies that negatively affect *all* mothers,
immigrant, poor and nonwhite mothers become disproportionately disadvantaged even more. Idealized images of mothers of which no mother can
replicate are constructed within this national framework.[1] While women
with race and class privilege are encouraged to focus almost solely on self-
sacrificial caregiving and are assumed to be wed mothers, the ideology of
intensive mothering (that children are a full-time "investment") does not
apply to marginalized women who are expected to be unwed, single parents who have made selfish, poor choices if they are not actively involved in
the labour market.

Neoliberal ideology that frames all individuals in terms of wealth accumulation further accentuates already existent raced, gendered and classed
notions of "good" and "bad" mothers, conditioning individual worth specifically around the perceived rational economic actions of working and paying taxes. Within the dominant neoliberal paradigm in the U.S., while some
mothers are encouraged to construct themselves as superior and worthy
of privilege through their actions of privatized self-sacrificing motherhood,
others are actively marginalized. State responsibility to provide resources to
all mothers is thus alleviated. And for immigrant and poor mothers—whose
livelihood and the livelihoods of their children—are dependent upon state
support, the consequences are detrimental.

DATA

In this chapter, we examine the construction of "good" and "bad" mothers through a comparative case study of immigrant mothers and mothers
receiving cash assistance ("welfare mothers"). The first study is a content

analysis of 91 U.S anti-immigrant organizations' websites and three discussion forums. The second is an ethnographic study of a rural welfare-to-work office in the southeastern United States.

ANTI-IMMIGRANT DATA

The first data come from a study of U.S. anti-immigrant activism on the internet. The data consists of 91 websites including 52 websites for organizations labeled "nativist extremist" by the Southern Poverty Law Centre, 17 organizations identified by Sohoni[2] as nativists on the internet, and 22 anti-immigrant groups were located through web search engines. We also analyze samples of threads from the online forums of three nativist organizations: Americans for Legal Immigration Political Action Committee (ALIPAC), the Minuteman Civil Defense Corps (MCDC), and the Indiana Federation for Immigration Reform & Enforcement (IFIRE).

WELFARE DATA

The second data come from a case study of a rural county welfare office in the southeastern U.S. conducted between June 2006 and July 2007. In this case study, the second author reviewed archival documents, including welfare policy history and current policy manuals. Secondly, she conducted formal and informal interviews with the entire office unit of 13 caseworkers and four supervisors. Finally, with varying levels of participation, she conducted observations in a number of settings, including inter- and intra-office meetings, unit office cubicles, client home visits, job readiness classes, and during eligibility interviews with clients. Field notes were taken during and after observations, interviews were recorded and transcribed immediately, and all data were open and then focus coded consistent with the grounded theory method.[3]

RESULTS AND DISCUSSION

From our analysis, we draw parallels in the neoliberal nationalist discourse that constructs immigrant mothers and welfare mothers as undeserving of rights associated with citizenship. Comparing our data, we find that raced, gendered, and classed discourses are used to stereotype immigrant mothers and welfare mothers as fraudulent and lazy. Immigrant mothers are said to have "anchor babies" to stay in the United States while welfare mothers supposedly have children to get cash assistance. The belief that these mothers have inferior cultural beliefs and values legitimates neoliberal policies that deny structural explanations for the status of the women. Instead, policies and the related discourse focus completely on personal responsibility. Below, we first examine how this is prevalent in the nativist discourse and then turn to the similar discourse among welfare caseworkers. Finally, we show how this system results in women policing other women. For the nativist movement, we document the visibility of anti-immigrant women activists policing immigrant women. In terms of welfare, the data show devolution of regulating power from the federal level, to the state, then county, and ultimately into the hands of other marginalized women working as caseworkers.

This devolution must be understood within the context of several shifts in both welfare and immigration policy beginning in the mid-1990s. The Personal Responsibility and Work Opportunity Reconciliation Act (PRWORA) and The Illegal Immigration Reform and Immigrant Responsibility Act (IIRIRA) both passed in 1996 were part of the devolution of welfare (specifically cash assistance) policy and immigration policing powers. These laws shift regulation power from the federal government to state and local governments for immigration (Varsanyi) and welfare.[4] Thus poor, vulnerable women who do not fit the national ideal face heightened exploitation while state and federal governments have eradicated responsibility for entitled social supports (Varsanyi).

FRAUDULENT AND LAZY MOTHERS

Both nativist websites and the rural welfare office workers constructed marginalized mothers as fraudulent and lazy. For the nativists, this was accomplished through the perception of immigrant women becoming mothers solely as a means to stay in the United States. To further stigmatize and dehumanize undocumented immigrant mothers the nativists used the term "anchor" baby. The Colorado Alliance for Immigration Reform website provides the following definition of an anchor baby: "Babies born to undocumented alien mothers within U.S. borders are called anchor babies because under the 1965 Immigration Act, they act as an anchor that pulls the undocumented "alien" mother and eventually a host of other relatives into permanent U.S. residency." This definition is consistent with how the term is used by other nativist websites and forum members.

Forty-two forum threads and 24 websites contain the term "anchor baby." Below are illustrations of how websites and forum members discuss the term. The first quote discusses "anchor babies" as commodities that undocumented immigrants use to gain access to monetary resources and citizenship. The second quote uses the term "anchors" in relation to claims that undocumented immigrants have abnormally high fertility rates.

> Many illegal aliens are known to exploit their children born here by using welfare funds to which their "anchor babies," as citizens, are entitled to support their families with food stamps, funds from Aid to Families with Dependent Children (AFDC) and WIC program funds. In addition, these children will continue to cost taxpayers billions of dollars in welfare and educational support for many years to come.
>
> Border Solution Task Force

> Illegals will outnumber citizens in this state soon. They are breeding like rabbits and their anchors already outnumber the children of citizens.
>
> TrueTexan post in the MCDC forum

The term "anchor baby" is used purposefully to control how people conceive of an immigrant's child. Discussing an "anchor" elicits different meaning than discussing an "infant." It also controls the emotional response connected to the phenomena. Instead of feeling sorry for the child or parent, it dehumanizes both parties and encourages a response of anger or injustice. Controlling the meaning of a child born to undocumented immigrants is a way for organizations to strengthen arguments that the children of undocumented immigrants should not automatically become U.S. citizens. The nativists dehumanize the mother (calling her "alien" and describing immigrant mothers as "breeding like rabbits") and the baby ("anchor" baby) and likewise imply that undocumented immigrants do not value their children as human beings, but instead "exploit" them like resources or commodities.

The first and second quotes state that undocumented immigrants use the child in order to receive "government benefits." This perception violates the patriarchal ideology of mothering where mothers should be caretakers and self-sacrificing as opposed to self-serving (Rothman). The quote from the Border Solution Task Force identifies immigrant mothers' motives for having children to receive food stamps, AFDC (a program that ceased to exist in 1996), WIC, and a free education. This demonstrates how nativists adhere to a neoliberal ideology of meritocracy. Hard work and not having babies should lead to resources. True Texan furthers this argument by complaining about undocumented immigrants' fertility rates. True Texan stigmatizes the sexuality and reproduction of undocumented immigrant mothers by bemoaning the increases in children born to immigrants. The statement suggests that undocumented immigrants have uncontrollable, even animalistic sexuality. This racializes Latina mothers as animals, suggesting that these women are either incapable or unwilling to regulate sexuality in order to work hard and follow the rules (Romero).

Similar to immigrant mothers, welfare mothers are also perceived as lazy and fraudulent. Caseworkers in the study gave accounts of why clients need cash assistance that present them as lacking a work ethic. For example, one of the caseworkers, Angela, describes Supplemental Security Income (SSI) as:

> ...welfare for people who have never worked. And there are a few honest to God good reasons that people get that, but if you've got momma and grandma getting a SSI check of $600 a month, an 18 year old daughter has got a baby and she's only getting $100 to $236. She [the daughter/participant] has not had the backbone in the household, the ethics of getting out and working and earning your own money. So sometimes we're the first time they ever heard that. There is pride working. There is pride in earning your paycheck.

In this quote, Angela is drawing from a "culture of poverty" ideology that suggests that welfare recipients are poor because of an inter-generational cultural deficiency of "dependency" instead of a work ethic. In fact, a common response to the direct question of what caseworkers saw as major barriers to clients, caseworkers often responded with similar explanations. For example, Joslyn stated:

> ...motivating them or them getting self-motivated. Some of these participants—their parents were on assistance, they instill them into their children and instill them in their children. So it is like a cycle. So the biggest barriers to having them open their minds and say "okay, I can go out into the real world. I

can get a job. I can become self-sufficient. I can take care of my family myself."

So, like nativists' attitudes towards undocumented immigrants, welfare case-workers view welfare participants as lazy (lacking "ethics" or "motivation") and many described clients as fraudulent and even claimed clients knew more about the policies (so they could cheat the system) than the caseworkers.

The shift from AFDC (Aid to Families with Dependent Children) through the PRWORA was a significant example of mid-1990s neoliberal policy whereby welfare participants were forced to work in order to receive cash assistance. After decades of attempting to mandate workfare, the U.S. federal government was finally successful in forcing states to mandate clients into the labour market. The change from AFDC to our current welfare system also included time limits to discourage long-term welfare assistance and family caps that prohibit additional funds if a participant becomes pregnant while receiving cash assistance. Similar to the way immigrant mothers who are charged with having babies purely to stay in the country (and use resources), the family cap responds to the stereotype that welfare mothers also have babies purely to gain cash assistance. In this sense both welfare and immigrant mothers are perceived as viewing children as commodities.

MOTHERS AGAINST MOTHERS

Yuval-Davis argues that women's reproduction is central to the reproduction of a nation (Yuval-Davis). In different time periods and geographic locations, this has meant encouragement or coercion in regards to having more or fewer children. While nonwhites and immigrants are marginalized within the nation, white middle-class women are expected to protect the sanctity of the home as a haven and carry on the nation's blood line of white babies. One organization in particular, Mothers Against Illegal Aliens (MAIA) and its leader Michelle Dallacroce, exemplify how mothers, and the symbol of "good" mothering are rooted in and simultaneously reinforce neoliberal ideology. Romero argues that MAIA and Dallacroce stereotype Latina immigrants as selfish and criminal "breeders," while constructing white mothers as idealized Madonnas (Romero). MAIA members construct themselves as "good" mothers by attempting to protect their white children from immigrants, whom they perceive as dangerous predators.

The frame of vulnerable children is consistent with strong cultural schemas that define childhood as a time of innocence that requires a mother's full devotion to the well-being of her child[5] —an idealistic construction increasingly impossible within the neoliberal context even for middle and upper class, disproportionately white women who have epitomized this fantasy. Undocumented immigrant mothers are constructed as not just bad mothers to their children, but as women whose actions presumably put the well-being of citizen-born children in jeopardy, particularly given the erosion of social supports for all mothers. Calavita argues that the recent focus of anti-immigrant sentiment on immigrants' use of social welfare resources derives from a "balanced-budget conservatism" propelled by deindustrialization and economic decline (285). Fear and anger about economic uncertainty lead individuals to resent taxes and treat recent immigrants as scapegoats. The media and political actors argue that immigrants drain scarce resources to the extent that there will not be enough resources available for U.S. citizens (Calavita). A MAIA member writes:

> A child being used by a mother to "steal" from the mouths of "legal children" in the USA should be charged with child abuse for attempting to benefit from their crime and profiting from additional actions while within the interior of the USA.

The statement constructs undocumented immigrant mothers as bad mothers who exploit their own children and steal "from the mouths of legal children." Here we see racialized and class beliefs that white children deserve the disproportionate access to resources that U.S. policy has traditionally provided, leaving nonwhite and poor children marginalized and expendable, open to the whims of the neoliberal market (Collins). These notions of defending scarce resources from bad mothers, and the concept of personal responsibility, were also evident in the welfare case study.

The second author was struck in her field research about how similarly situated the caseworkers were to their welfare clients. These women were often class marginalized women, some of which had previously been welfare recipients themselves. About half of the caseworkers were also women of color. In the rural area where the research was conducted, decent job opportunities were very slim, especially for those with limited education. Because of this, these women perceived their jobs, which were poorly paid and emotionally draining, as good jobs. None of the caseworkers were professional social workers and many of these caseworkers had worked in retail, restaurant, call centres, or third shift jobs prior to becoming caseworkers. The neoliberal practice of devolution in the "free market" created a situation where these caseworkers were called on to police and sanction women who were somewhat more marginalized than themselves. This often resulted in caseworkers having conflicted understandings of their clients and role as a caseworker, oscillating between sympathy for their clients, many of whom they knew from church or school, and a contradictory understanding of their comparative (though limited) privilege in terms of their own personality traits. This tension is heightened in the poor job market in this county where caseworkers realize they are a pink slip away from cash assistance themselves. In sum, they do what they need to do to keep their jobs.

Like many working women, these mothers left a difficult and stressful job to go home to a second shift of making dinner, cleaning house, and child care. Some caseworkers even did this work for grandchildren as their children went off to work second shift paid jobs. One of the implications of caseworkers balancing work and family is that they expect participants to be able to do the same. They often take on an "If I can do it, they can do it" attitude. In fact, several caseworkers expressed this to the second author explicitly. For example, Julie, a married mother, stated:

> But it's hard to justify giving a benefit to a person who is 37 years old and had two jobs in their life and worked one hour at one place and a week at the other. You know, okay. So if she gets another job she'll probably quit anyway.... Because I'm 30 years old and I been making it somehow. What happened that you haven't been working? What were you doing before?

Julie had previously discussed with the second author how important it was to not be judgmental. However, here she expresses her frustration with participants not working. After all, she seems to say, she has had to work and provide for her family and she has made it work.

In another example the instructor of the county job readiness class described to students what it meant to be a mother and to make sacrifices. The job readiness instructor spoke to the class about her 16-year-old son and having to provide for him. She told a story of applying to a fast food restaurant to be a biscuit maker from 5am until 2pm. An employee at the fast food restaurant told her she had too much education to work there. She said she wanted to cry, and did cry once she left. But she said she responded in pride, "Thank you Miss, have a nice day." She said she needed a job and a paycheck and it did not matter what that job was. She would make biscuits and sweep the parking lot if that was what it took. She told the students she would be proud to have a paycheck at the end of every two weeks. Then she said, "You gotta step up to the plate and take it like a woman. You gotta be mama and woman. It's not what you want. It's what you have to do to provide." Thus, we can see in both the nativists and the caseworkers that their own conceptions of being good mothers shape their desire (in the case of the nativists) or willingness (caseworkers) in policing who they perceive to be bad mothers. In both instances, the construction of a bad mother as a type of bad person is consistent with the seemingly stricter laws and policing of both immigrant and welfare mothers.

CONCLUSION

From our comparative case study of nativist websites and welfare casework-ers, we can see how neoliberal politics are structured from and reinforce patriarchy and capitalist ideologies of motherhood (Rothman). Neoliberal ideology in the United States has led to policies that call for personal respon-sibility while freeing the state of accountability. While neoliberal policies are in theory gender-neutral, neoliberal politics have led to an overall wors-ening of the position of women and mothers (Connell). Neoliberal policies have resulted in a decrease in welfare expenditures for programs dispropor-tionately used by women and simultaneously shrunk public sector jobs that women are most likely to hold. Further, it has led to a decrease in spending on education, a major path to women's advancement.

In conclusion, we find that the raced, gendered, and classed nature of neoliberalism and nationalism in the U.S. welfare state support policies that disadvantage all women, and particularly marginalize poor, nonwhite and noncitizen women and their families. Drawing from beliefs of meritocracy, women constructed as "privileged" by the nationalist ideology become rei-fied as "good" mothers to justify denying resources to women perceived as "bad" mothers. Thus, the way that nationalism shapes neoliberal policy re-mains invisible, with inequity in the distribution of resources explained by individual personality traits or lack of personal responsibility. In this way, the state can withhold all accountability and responsibility while simulta-neously ensuring the constructed false divides between "good" and "bad" mothers prevent all mothers from working together to access equitable re-distribution for themselves and their children.

NOTES

[1] See Collins; Skocpol; and Yuval-Davis
[2] See Sohoni
[3] See Charmaz ; and Glaser and Strauss
[4] See Handler and Hasenfeld
[5] See Blair-Loy; and Hays

WORKS CITED

Blair-Loy, Mary. *Competing Devotions: Career and Family among Women Executives.* Cambridge: Harvard University Press, 2003. Print.

Border Solutions Task Force. http://thorin.adnc.com/ bstf/. Retrieved 12/10/2007. Web.

Calavita, Kitty. "The New Politics of Immigration: 'Balanced-Budget Conservatism' and the Symbolism of Proposition 187." *Social Problems* 43.3 (1996): 284-305. Print.

Charmaz, Kathy. *Constructing Grounded Theory.* London: Sage Publications, 2006. Print.

Collins, Patricia Hill. *From Black Power to Hip Hop: Racism, Nationalism, and Feminism.* Philadelphia, Temple University Press, 2006. Print.

Colorado Alliance for Immigration Reform. http://www.cairco.org/. Retrieved 12/10/2007. Web.

Connell, R.W. *Masculinities* 2nd edition. Berkeley, CA: University of California Press, 2005. Print.

Glaser, Barney and Anselm Strauss. *The Discovery of Grounded Theory Strategies for Qualitative Research.* Chicago: Aldine, 1967. Print.

Gramsci, Antonio. *Selections from the Prison Notebooks.* New York: International Publishers, 1971. Print.

Handler, Joseph and Yeheskel Hasenfeld. *Blame Welfare, Ignore Poverty and Inequality.* New York: Cambridge University Press, 2007. Print.

Hays, Sharon. *The Cultural Contradictions of Motherhood.* New Haven: Yale University Press, 1997. Print.

Minutemen Civil Defense Core. http://www.minutemanhq.com. Retrieved 12/16/2007. Web.

Mother's Against Illegal Aliens. http://www.mothersagainstillegalaliens.-org/ Retrieved 12/15/2007. Web.

Navarro, Vicente. "Neoliberalism as a Class Ideology; Or, the Political Causes of the Growth of Inequalities" *Neoliberalism, Globalization and Inequalities: Consequences for Health and Quality of Life.* Eds V. Navarro. New York: Baywood Publishing Company, Inc., 2007. 9-23. Print.

Romero, Mary. "'Go After the Women': Mothers Against Illegal Aliens' Campaign Against Mexican Immigrant Women and Their Children." *Indiana Law Journal* 83.4 (2008): 1356-1389. Print.

— "Constructing Mexican Immigrant Women as a Threat to US Family." *International Journal of Sociology of the Family* 37.1 (2011): 49-68. Print.

Rothman, Barbara. *Recreating Motherhood.* New York: Routledge Press, 2000. Print.

Skocpol, Theda. *Protecting Soldiers and Mothers: Political Origins of Social Policy in the United States.* Cambridge, MA: The Belknap Press of Harvard University Press, 1995. Print.

Sohoni, Deenesh. "The 'Immigrant Problem': Modern-Day Nativism on the Web." *Current Sociology* 54.6 (2006): 827-850. Print.

Soss, Joe, Richard C. Fording, and Sanford F. Schram. *Disciplining the Poor: Neoliberal Paternalism and the Persistent Power of Race.* Chicago: The University of Chicago Press, 2011. Print.

Varsanyi, Monica W. "Rescaling the 'Alien,' Rescaling Personhood: Neoliberalism, Immigration, and the State." *Annals of the Association of American Geographers* 98.4 (2008): 877-896. Print.

Yuval-Davis, Nira. *Gender and Nation.* London: Sage Publications, 1997. Print.

11.

"Educating" Mothers through Media

The Therapy Market in South Korea and the Making of "Deviant" Children

JESOOK SONG AND YOONHEE LEE

INTRODUCTION

This chapter examines the South Korean TV program U-A-Dal ("My Child Is Changed") by contextualizing it within neoliberal discourses of self-responsibility, hyper-consumptive practices and the burgeoning therapy market. In the South Korean context, neoliberalization refers to an overarching principle of state and corporate policies that rendered labour precarious in the name of restructuring and flexibility (Song *New Millennium South Korea: Neoliberal Capitalism and Transnational Movements*). Further, the advanced liberal regime penetrated into individual personal life /career plans producing a dogmatic self-entrepreneurial ethos. In other words, the double wheels of the neoliberal construct in South Korea—macro level restructuring processes and the formation of the self-entrepreneurial subject (i.e., you can survive if you are individually smart)—magnified existent liberal ideology.

Since the Korean War and throughout the military dictatorship-led development era where political stability was low and social liberty was suppressed, there existed a liberal conceptualization of individual responsibility. However, while the self-made man/woman ideology is not new in South Korean history, neoliberal austerity measures, partnered with the ascendance of market-driven imperatives defining the social, has magnified conceptualizations of individual responsibility to a hyper level. In this regard, the Asian Debt Crisis that visited South Korea less than a decade after the end of the military dictatorship was anti-climactic since people's expectations of state accountability for subsistence and quality of living (through the welfare state) were crushed by neoliberal austerity measures. As a result, the expectation that people would be taken care of by the state through the welfare system was hardly achieved. Rather, individuals were continuously left alone and held solely responsible for their own security (Song *South Koreans in the Debt Crisis*). In this context, motherly responsibility to raise children as self-entrepreneurial—especially through education and market-driven therapy—has become more dire and imperative after the Asian Debt Crisis, particularly given the history of Korean motherhood in which public education has served as a springboard for upward class mobility (Park and Abelmann).

THE TV PROGRAM, "MY CHILD IS CHANGED"

The British series Supernanny has developed into a global phenomenon producing multiple international adaptations including a South Korean version, Supernanny Korea. South Korean populations, however, were already well familiar with a similar television series Uri ai ga dalla chôt ô yo (in short U-A-Dal, meaning "My child is changed"), which has enjoyed immense popularity. Although topically the television series Supernanny and U-A-Dal are similar, a closer examination suggests that the two are vastly different in their outlook and execution. U-A-Dal is not merely an imitation or adaptation of Supernanny, but a distinctively Korean development that reflects and shapes the emerging therapy market.

Until a decade ago in South Korea, the recognition of mental illness, and its treatment, was a tabooed subject. In sharp contrast, the recognition of mental illness and an expanding therapy market have now proliferated in South Korea alongside the neoliberal imperative for privatized responses to individual "pathology." Scholars now observe a wide-ranging awareness of mental health in South Korea including: stress ascribed as the primary cause of cancer (Nelson), the therapist being recognized as professional (Nahm), labour movements understood as trauma (S. Kang), and a discussion of past state violence against civilians (Cho). While this emerging awareness of mental health has produced relief for some by de-stigmatizing mental illness, the neoliberal marketization of therapy has also produced anxiety by establishing a normative imperative to seek privatized professional help.

This neoliberal marketization of therapy is reflected in U-A-Dal, which relies on the knowledge and expertise of various professionals who are trained in the areas of child development and psychology. The official website of U-A-Dal offers illustrious profiles of these experts from their educational background to published works and professional certificates. There is a need to emphasize the fact that these figures intervening in the intimate affairs of parenting are institutionally recognized experts. The emphasis on the professional status of these experts is indicative of their ambiguous status within the emerging field of psychotherapy in South Korea. In her examination of play therapy, Nahm notes the precarious position of play therapists and their blurring of the lines between psychology and mental health with education, social welfare, and child development. Nahm shows the struggles of play therapists in asserting their identity as legitimate professionals shaping public perceptions about "play" as work rooted in expertise rather than mere intuition. These struggles are augmented by the gendered nature of their work, as play therapists are predominantly female. Although intuition and flexibility are important characteristics of a play therapist, there is a tendency for the public to conflate intuitive expertise with maternal instinct. Due to these pressures, therapists need to differentiate their work from that of mothers by clearly presenting themselves as trained professional experts.

The need for this differentiation is reflected in U-A-Dal's portrayal of child development and therapy experts as distinct from parental figures and child caregivers. U-A-Dal severs the link between therapist and mother in order to present therapy as a legitimate professional service. The relationship between the expert and the family remains strictly professional. In fact, the expert merely states the diagnosis and treatment, and it is the Master of Ceremonies (MC) who engages in conversation with the parents. The MC, usually a beloved comedian or entertainer, placates the parents and shares their emotional response to the diagnosis. Thus, the role of the MC ensures that the expertise and professional status of the therapists are not compromised by the public's ambivalence or taboo towards therapy.

On the other hand, educational background or degrees have always been highly regarded in South Korea. University degrees have been a key component of upward class mobility in the post-Korean War period when such degrees led to stable employment (Seth). However, after the Asian Debt Crisis in the late 1990s, with the deregulated market and significantly reduced stable employment, the significance of regular degrees became less regarded. Entrepreneurialism gained more explanatory power in career development. A few new certificates that have become popular include physical and psychological therapists, social and care workers, teaching assistants, and real estate agents.

"EDUCATING" THE MOTHERS

Although U-A-Dal represents itself as a family project, U-A-Dal's main audience is mothers. Mothers are the primary subject. Fathers appear as an auxiliary subject. Their role is to acknowledge the expert's assessment and provide support for therapy. When the parents receive the diagnosis, both mother and father are present. During the treatment phase, however, fathers often disappear from the screen, and the show largely focuses on the mother and her implementation of the new treatment. In fact, many times the mother is not only responsible for carrying out the "proper" method of parenting, but also convincing both the child and father of these new methods. The father is usually included through a project that involves a special activity or event. These projects are often of a singular nature rather than involving a continuous everyday interaction with the child. Thus while the mothers' authority is de-legitimated by the experts' diagnosis, she is simultaneously expected to perform "good" motherhood by ensuring the "proper" treatment for her child is carried out.

It is noteworthy that representation (and practices to a lesser extent) of fathers' involvement in parenting is changing post-Asian Debt Crisis. Fathers appear in media and government policies as caring and warm parenting subjects (to their children). In a context where middle-aged patriarchs have lost their dignity through massive lay-offs during the Asian Debt Crisis, there has been a discursive/practical effort on the part of government and conservative society to uplift fathers' authority in the family. This new image is different from the pre-Crisis when normalized fatherhood meant not being intimate with their children partially because of long work hours and partially because of femininity/masculinity divisions that associate emotional attachment/care as feminine (Song *South Koreans in the Debt Crisis*). However, despite this larger media focus on fathers, mothers remain the primary caregivers in South Korea as reflected in the context of U-A-Dal. The mother is the one expected to be actively involved in the everyday treatment process. Although U-A-Dal is framed as a family project, in reality, the show mainly targets mothers and cultivates their need for expert advice, despite their presumed preexisting innate mothering abilities.

U-A-Dal features an array of children that display a range of problematic behaviors. Diagnosing and treating these problematic behaviors is at the core of U-A-Dal. The direct suggestion is that bad parenting leads to developmental issues. Given the neoliberal hyper-competitive South Korean job market, the presumed trajectory is that such issues will affect a child's life/career through poor formal education performances preventing access to good schools and consequently good jobs. In U-A-Dal, after a week of observation, the expert states her diagnosis of the child. Various psychological and developmental issues are often observed, such as hyperactive, aggressive, and antisocial behavior, along with fixation and attachment issues. Learning disabilities are also a frequent topic of discussion.

What is significant about this diagnosis is that even if there are no medical or "pathological" issues, the diagnosis often predicts that without an intervention at this critical time, further serious developmental problems will follow. Intervention and treatment usually involves additional experts who offer various forms of therapy within and outside the home. For example, play therapy is often utilized to introduce proper modes of socializing, through home visits and trips to therapy centres. Under the careful guidance of these therapists, parents are introduced to developmental psychology and the resources available in the market of psychological health and therapy.

U-A-Dal is concerned with children who exhibit "abnormal" or "deviant" behaviors. U-A-Dal educates parents at home to recognize these deviant behaviors from the developmental norm and become familiar with the language of child developmental psychology. U-A-Dal claims that part of being a "good mother" involves being able to recognize problematic developmental behavior and promptly seek expert advice. For example, in episode 309, which revolves around a 36-month-old boy who cannot speak, the father's failure to recognize the abnormal behavior of his child is a central moment (U-A-Dal, episode 309.) In response to video footage of his child unable to focus and follow directions from an adult during a play session, the father claims that he thinks his child is having a fun time. After viewing footage of a "normal" child's response to the play session, the father finally admits that there might be a developmental issue—the mother silently cries in the background. This admission plays a significant role in not only emphasizing the presumed complicity of the parents in exacerbating the child's delayed linguistic development, but also suggests that there may be other viewers who have yet to recognize the signs that their child is in need of help from a child developmental expert. Although the show focuses on the father's inability to recognize his child's issues, the mother is the one that is responsible for ensuring that the child receives proper therapy. Thus, the father receives the credit for diagnosis while the mother must do the actual work of change.

Although parenting and disciplinary techniques are introduced in U-A-Dal, its main focus is on educating parents about child development issues and available treatment and therapy options. For example, in the episode regarding language development, the viewers were informed of the proper stages of language development and given pointers about how to stimulate and encourage language development (U-A-Dal, episode 309). Similarly, in episode 255, which focused on a child who has impulse and attention issues, a range of therapy techniques were on display, such as music therapy and play therapy (U-A-Dal, episode 255). By watching how the therapy is carried out, viewers are not only able to learn simple methods they can use at home in order to enhance their child's attention span, but also become familiar and comfortable with the idea of specialized forms of therapy.

THE PRIVATIZED THERAPY MARKET

The popularity of U-A-Dal and its presence in public discourse reflects changing public perceptions regarding mental health and the subsequent emergence of a privatized therapy market. Although there are exceptions in which therapies are organized by government-sponsored programs for populations below the poverty line, the majority of therapies are practiced in the privatized therapy market. The range of cost for therapy varies from $150 to $500 per hour. For the case of U-A-Dal, the therapy cost for the program participants is sponsored by the broadcasting company and the volunteering of therapy experts during the process of episode production.

The therapists in Nahm's study also identify popular television shows such as U-A-Dal as having a large influence on public acceptance lessening stigma around therapy and leading to the growth of the therapy market and professionalization (Nahm). However, while therapy may no longer be stigmatized and has in fact become almost required, those undergoing therapy are further stigmatized should they not conform to the exacting standards of the treatment. Through its educational but entertaining format,

U-A-Dal alters perceptions of therapy from its negative associations with abnormality and illness to a family-friendly and socially acceptable means of improving mental health. At the same time, U-A-Dal maintains some forms of clinical and medical language to underline the professional legitimacy of the therapists. U-A-Dal highlights the seriousness of deviant behavior as a sign of developmental issues. However, it also carefully frames these behaviors along narratives of self-improvement, a story that is much more digestible to mothers interested in their child's development and performance—particularly in the realm of education. Normalizing the diagnosis and identification of deviant symptoms not only demarcates the boundary between normative and non-normative, but also guides how to care for self (or selves' extension, children) when "sick." Creating psychologically problematic subjects produces explanatory power in the general population by not simply identifying such subjects, but also properly treating them.

Such personal identification of "deviance" segregated from material social-structural realities, however, creates a further entrenchment of stigma for those unable or unwilling to transform accordingly. Thus, while such TV shows normalize therapy, they in turn require all individuals to constantly self-regulate within specific paradigms of constructed expertise revealing only one potential pathway to "success." Given how the current neoliberal climate in South Korea has increased competition for perceived scarce resources, such a psychologization[1] produces a powerful regulatory discourse necessitating individuals "cure" themselves. Thus, for those who do not become "cured" through highly expensive therapy programs, they are further identified and marginalized as "deviant."

The intensity of the public's interest in the link between therapy and education is made apparent in U-A-Dal's special episodes revolving around improving academic performance and study habits. For example, episode 159, the winter break special titled "mobŏmsaeng mandŭlgi p'ŭrojekt'ŭ (Strategies for Parents to Make Their Children Model Students)," addressed the audience's popular concerns and questions regarding children and their study habits (U-A-Dal, episode 159). The episode focuses on an eight year old who exhibits concentration issues and problems socializing at school. During the treatment phase, the child expert provides parents with a numerated list of tips and strategies to transform one's child to a model student. Strategies such as encouraging self-motivation, setting out short-term goals, and cultivating better parent-child and sibling relations can be carried out at home. Yet, U-A-Dal presents these strategies through psychiatric and therapy centres, in which parents are coached directly by therapy experts.

Therapy, thus, is not limited to abnormality and pathology, but is also applicable to "normal" children in improving mental health for maximizing their potential.

Thus, in such a hyper-competitive environment, the purchasing of therapy treatments operates as an additional market tool for advancing children's school performance, working alongside other mechanisms such as the highly financialized private education market. Education has been a heavily charged domain in relation to upward class mobility and individual success since the post-Korean War. The volatility of education has a long history in terms of connecting the processes of economic development with individual household success/failure in garnering social/symbolic capital (Seth). However, the "education fever" is not limited to public education. Private education, particularly for after-school learning, such as tutoring, once suppressed under the military dictatorship (ironically in the name of equity), has been gradually liberalized in the Democratization period since the late 1980s. Private education was further magnified in the post-Crisis neoliberal opening to foreign/global markets, especially through English education[2] and short-term experience in Anglophone countries.[3] It is not uncommon to hear that this kind of education fever (mostly through the zealous participation of mothers in the private education market) causes familial separation or even "divorce."[4]

THE EDUCATION WELFARE PROJECT

The way in which therapy is understood as an extension of private education is well demonstrated in our research on the Education Welfare Project in South Korea. The Education Welfare Project is a priority zone policy for shantytowns where children's educational quality is regarded poor in relation to their basic welfare conditions and familial care. Contradictory to the aim of the project, it ends up producing youth as psychologized subjects because it equates welfare for youth with "fixing" them psychologically so they can successfully adjust to school and perform well. The expectation is not just from the state government (that measures the success of the program through developmental psychological examination) or involved school social workers, but also largely from the parents' demand to improve their children's condition for bettering school performance. For example, school social workers will identify students who cause problems—because of absences or bullying other students—who are possibly deficient in their ability to concentrate (that is, have ADHD) or who have autism, all of which are to be cured through therapy. It also involves career counseling to assess student talents and behavioral patterns.

Most research literature on the Education Welfare Project measures success by higher scores, an increased ability to pay attention, and student satisfaction in school. Such measures of success do not consider the quality of working-class childrens' and adolescents' lives and whether the Project effectively reduces the class gap as initially intended. Parents in the shantytown are made aware of the effects of therapy through U-A-Dal-style media education. An advocacy program in welfare services provides therapies free of expense for children diagnosed with a behavioral disorder. It is not surprising to find that the majority of the researchers and evaluators of the Project have backgrounds in behavioral and developmental psychology.

A crucial consequence of the Project is the infiltration of a psychological model that has as its aim the "fixing" of behavioral and cognitive abnormalities in working-class neighborhoods. This fix is to be performed in particular through leading shantytown parents to join the highly expensive therapy market by accessing welfare benefits. The assumption is that this will maximize opportunities for a better future and class situation for their children. In this way, "good mothers" must accept the notion of their children's mental and psychological problems as identified by behavioral and developmental psychological specialists should they wish to access middle-class market resources. This acceptance marks a sea change during the past decade in Korea, particularly among the working poor. It breaks a taboo against recognizing family members as psychologized subjects in mental health terms. However, it has become feasible as a thin channel with limited social prospects: only through the linking of their children to a psychologized identity in the education system can families attempt to access the perceived promise of class mobility.

CONCLUSION

U-A-Dal demonstrates how mass media not only reflects but also makes more salient the mundane interests and practices of the psychological therapy market among mothers. Given societal pressure on mothers to engineer their children's future career success, therapy has become part of the everyday consciousness and practices of mothering in South Korea.

As revealed in the Education Welfare Project, the educated desire[5] and practices of mothers to utilize therapy for their children is not limited to middle-class motherhood. It is crossing class lines to make all mothers, particularly welfare mothers, accountable and burdened. Given the context of a hyper-competitive neoliberal environment where the purchase of services becomes the antidote to structural deficiencies, middle-class mothers feel increasing pressure to provide their children with all the identified market tools for success including therapy and private education. For welfare mothers, pressure to identify their children within the psychological realm is a matter of accessing resources for their material well-being and the livelihood of their children. Thus, only by proclaiming the "deviance" of their children, are welfare mothers able to access middle-class therapy resources constructed as necessary to their children's social and economic future. The psychological therapy market can be compared to the private education market in that it augments class divisions and places additional burden and responsibility for raising and educating children on parents, particularly on mothers.

NOTES

[1] See Rose for further discussion regarding psychologization
[2] See Park and Abelmann
[3] See Chun and Han forthcoming; and Y. Kang
[4] For geese family, see Abelmann; and Finch and Kim.
[5] Regarding "educating" mothers' desire, we build on Ann Stoler's notion of "educating desire", which she utilizes in her discussion of sexuality in the colonial context of Southeast Asia as a complement to Foucault's (western) History of Sexuality (1995). Although our research is not about colonialism or sexuality, we think the notion is useful because of the way in which psychologizing or pathologizing practices and desires are acquired through technologies of self (i.e., how to care and govern self) that Foucauldian scholars (including Stoler) theorize. The notion of "educating" is a conceptual tool, rather different from public or institutionalized education.

WORKS CITED

Abelmann, Nancy. *Intimate University.* Durham: Duke University Press, 2009. Print.

Cho, Hee Yeon. "Sacrifices Caused by State Violence under Military Authoritarianism and the Dynamics of Settling the Past during the Democratic Transition." *Korea Journal* (Autumn 2002): 163-193. Print.

Kang, Su Dol. *If I Were a President!* (Nae ka manil taet'ongnyông ira myôn!) Seoul: Saengka ûi namu, 2010. Print.

Kang, Yoonhee. "Any One Parent Will Do: Negotiations of Fatherhood among South Korean 'Wild Geese' Fathers in Singapore." *Journal of Korean Studies* 17.2 (2012): 269-297. Print.

Nahm, Sheena. "Between Stigma and Demand." *Human Organization* 68.4 (2009): 406-414. Print.

Nelson, Laura. "When the Personal Becomes Political, and Remains Personal: South Korean Women Confront Breast Cancer." *Journal of Korean Studies* 17.2 (2012) Print.

Park, So Jin and Nancy Abelmann. "Class and Cosmopolitanism: Mothers' Management of English Education in South Korea." *Anthropological Quarterly* 77.4 (2004): 645-672. Print.

Rose, Nikolas. *The Psychological Complex: Psychology, Politics and Society in England 1869-1939.* London: Routledge and Kegan Paul, 1985. Print.

Seth, Michael J. *Education Fever: Society, Politics, and the Pursuit of Schooling in South Korea.* Honolulu: University of Hawaii Press, 2002. Print.

Song, Jesook. *South Koreans in the Debt Crisis.* Durham: Duke University Press, 2009. Print.

Song, Jesook. Ed. *New Millennium South Korea: Neoliberal Capitalism and Transnational Movements.* London and New York: Routledge, 2010. Print.

Stoler, Ann Laura. *Race and the Education of Desire: Foucault's History of Sexuality and the Colonial Order of Things.* Durham: Duke University Press, 1995. Print.

U-A-Dal (Uri ai ga dalla chôt ô yo). 2011. Episode 309. Korea: Seoul Broadcasting System.

— 2010a. Episode 159. Korea: Seoul Broadcasting System.

— 2010b. Episode 255. Korea: Seoul Broadcasting System.

12.

"Education of Mothers" in Turkey

Discourses on Maternal Propriety and Neoliberal Body Politics on Motherhood

SEVI BAYRAKTAR

INTRODUCTION

Neoliberal mothering discourses in Turkey have amplified existent concepts of self-responsibility and morality as women are in constant negotiation with shifting narratives of maternal propriety and family formations. In the Turkish context, neoliberalism has strengthened existent ideas of "good" mothering through their placement within an accelerated economic paradigm. By producing and reproducing the ideas of "good" mothering, or promoting the idealized middle-class norms of being "proper" mothers, the productive Turkish economy participates in global markets through the regulated consumptive practices of mothers.

The 1980s were significant in Turkish history as the pervasive impact of globalization, and an expansion of neoliberal policies, combined with the post-coup restructuring of society. Because of the demands of the market economy, the state retreated from the social and cultural realms. However, with state abandonment, the neoliberal problem of "insecurity" ensuing from the fragilities of the market triggered the expansion of Non-Governmental Organizations (NGOs). Because of increasing structural problems due to neoliberal austerity measures, especially in urban communities, most of the NGOs became concerned with the provision of social services to poor and marginalized people living in the urban space. Therefore, the discourse of "empowerment" became targeted at the poor and marginalized segments of the population. By the beginning of the 1990s, mostly locally organized NGOs started to act to "share the state's burden" (Ipek). By the end of the 1990s the state was still participating in the ideological reproduction of the masses by using and directing the activities of the NGOs. Influences and capabilities of local governments have been rising in the 2000s, with NGOs increasingly engaging with local and community organizations.

In this context, poor, migrant, and working-class women have become the subjects of various education programs. Living at the margins of the urban space and within their own local networks, these women were seen as "not-yet" proper citizens nor part of the qualified labour force for the nation-state. National and international projects concerning the education of girls and women have been carried out by NGOs in Turkey in cooperation with state institutions with the aim of transforming families by investing in women.[1] The Mother-Child Education Program (AÇEP), which was conducted by the Mother-Child Education Foundation (AÇEV) in cooperation with Social Services and the Society for the Protection of Children (SHÇEK)[2] operating from 1993 to 2009, provides a strong example of state/civil society cooperation in producing regulating mothering discourses.

MOTHERS OF THE GAZI NEIGHBORHOOD

The Gazi Neighborhood—the site of the Mother-Child Education Program—is located at the height of the Gaziosmanpaşa District[3] within an area where revolutionary factions of left-wing organizations and politically active Alevi and Kurdish communities are living alongside Roma communities and migrants from Eastern Anatolia.[4] Therefore, the inhabitants of the Gazi Neighborhood are not only stigmatized by their marginalized ethnic and political identities within a nation-state discourse, but they are also imprisoned by poverty. Marginalization causes unequal job distribution in the workplace, and finding jobs in different parts of the city becomes often impossible.

The 75th Year Gazi Community Centre—where the education program for mothers was implemented—holds great significance since it is one of the most visible state institutions in the Neighborhood. The Community Centre was an institution of the Social Services and Child Protection Agency (SHÇEK), affiliated directly with the Prime Minister, or a State Minister nominated by the Prime Minister.[5] The Community Centres were located in needy suburb (gecekondu) areas with high migration rates "to integrate migrant people into society." The authorized officers of SHÇEK were responsible for controlling and supervising this "integration" as well as the other operations of the Community Centres. Hence, there were various educative programs being conducted in the Gazi Community Centre: Education of Mothers, Human Rights for Women, Reproductive Health and Family Planning Seminars, and Mother Training for Day Care Centres. In addition to its educative programs, the Community Centre was also used to financially assist the poorest families, although the amount of assistance did not reduce poverty.[6] This is consistent with a neoliberal agenda of state-governed "training programs" lacking structural support.

Therefore, going to the Community Centre meant getting "in touch" with the state and becoming "visible" in their relationships with the state, which requires certain vigilance on one's attitudes for the aforementioned reasons. Because state hegemony observes, judges, discriminates, and punishes, but also confirms, appreciates, and recompenses, it is important to consider both the sympathetic and the intimidating character of the Community Centre as a state institution.

At the Gazi Community Centre, every Wednesday thirty women gathered from 9 am to 12.30 pm to complete the Mother-Child Education Program (AÇEP). During this time, they played games, participated in mothering lectures, and shared their experiences according to the topic of the day's lecture. As "the mothers" of the Gazi Neighborhood, they were supposed to learn "proper" ways of mothering throughout the lectures. According to the Program mandate, homemaking skills were expected to improve alongside mothering. As part of the Program's activities, sometimes they would go to picnics, conferences, concerts, and museums located in different parts of Istanbul, where they were not only physically, but also socially and economically far-removed from the Gazi Neighborhood. Regarding the Program, the main objective was to "support 8-year education"[7] yet AÇEP aimed to educate mothers first: Every woman who had a 6-year-old child could participate in the program to prepare the child for school the following year. The 25-week program (September to June) was supported by educative materials, indoor and outdoor activities, and also regular home visits to "supervise and support the mothers' everyday practices with their children at home" (Sucuka 16).

DISCOURSES OF MATERNAL PROPRIETY

During the Education of Mothers, a particular "good mothering" prioritizing the independent, hard-working, self-criticizing, managing, consistent, and responsible citizen, was constantly reproduced. These meanings attributed to a "good mother" lead to its "other" as well: a "bad mother," who is not participating in the full-time care of her children, who is called lazy, irresponsible, inconsistent, and thus, "easy" in her mothering. These two contradictory conceptualizations of motherhood provide the basis for the notions of "successful" and "unsuccessful" mothering. The women were invited to participate in the reproduction of these good/bad mother dichotomies by taking sides, by desiring new types of subjectivities, and by making self-criticisms if there were any deviations from the desired "good mother," who was derived from the white, middle-class woman (Glenn). engaging in hyper-consumptive practices. Tapping into notions of neoliberal independence, "the mothers" were to think of themselves as individuals responsible independently for their practices of "good mothering" rather than as members of a larger family collective equally sharing the parenting.

SELF-RESPONSIBILITY

The neoliberal discourse of "responsibility" assumes individuals have enough power to improve their own capacities and life conditions. Disregarding social and political conditions, this discourse of "self-responsibility" leads to placing all blame on the individual whereby his/her decisions and actions lead to his/her deficiency in fulfilling norms. According to this mantra, regardless of social and political conditions, if a woman fulfills the norms and takes responsibility for her family, then she can become a "good mother." This discourse silences the women since in order not to be seen as "irresponsible," they do not talk about the material conditions of their poverty. For instance, an important component of a mother's responsibility is to take care of her children. However, there is no recognition if a working-class woman needs support for child care from her parents or from other women in the family. As the mother is supposed to be the only one responsible for child-rearing, parental help becomes inappropriate for the "consistent" development of the child. In this way, all the other (extended) family members such as grandparents, daughters-in-law, sisters, and neighbors are excluded from this realm. As it was advised in the classes:

> Do not allow the grandparents to intervene in your child-rearing business. Tell them "please, do not interfere, I know how to do it," and apply the correct way of child-rearing. You are the responsible ones. Do not allow anybody to take care of your children.

Hence, the mother was assumed as the only person who educated her children in a proper manner. In order to reach this objective, she should dismiss the grandparents and her female relatives from the business of child-rearing in the household as "nurture by anyone except the mother were automatically assumed to be dirty, incompetent and irresponsible" (Davin 92). In this way, she became deprived of talking, sharing, and questioning the manners of the grandparents at home. That left the woman wordless when facing patriarchal violence.

On the other hand, this approach endowed mothers with a certain "agency" against the constituted patriarchal relations among the women in extended families. Here, the "mothers" (as the "brides" having less authority in the extended patriarchal families) became able to escape from the authority of the senior women, especially of the mothers-in-law, by using this same responsibility discourse on child-rearing. By emphasizing that the "mother" should be solely responsible for child-rearing, a woman could have an opportunity to invalidate the patriarchal authority of the mother-in-law in this realm.

> [My child] is contrary. Why has this happened to her? Since her grandmother and grandfather were looking after her... She did not even want to come to the school [community centre] in the beginning. They [grandparents] used to tell me "don't make her cry; why do you take her to school?" They have spoiled her too much. Now they stopped spoiling.

This mother assumed that the "improper behaviors" of her child, which made him/her "unsuccessful," derived from the "improper behaviors" of the grandparents. In this case, going to school (the community centre) and "escaping" from the borders of the household, in which grandparents had the unquestionable authority, equipped her with an agency when facing the grandparents. Although they said, "Don't make her cry, why do you take her to the school?" she became able to disrupt the higher authority of the mother-in-law and the father-in-law by not doing so and going to the school instead. This sense of "agency" allowed the woman to get out of the power of the grandparents in the household.

The mothers in the Gazi neighborhood were happy to use this agency; indeed, they desired it. Therefore, they preferred to talk within a pedagogic language saying that "Having the indisputable knowledge on science of hygiene, nutritious cooking, house management, consumption, and so on, the mother must be the only responsible person to look after the children." In this way, they prevented the grandparents from using their power upon the mothers and exploiting them by using the children as a pretense. The woman claimed authority above everyone in "proper" child-rearing by calling herself the "educated mother." In this way, on the one hand, she became able to evade the grandparents' power at home, but on the other hand, she retreated from her relations with the neighbor women in this process. A "responsible mother" became isolated in the neighborhood but more powerful in the domestic sphere. Thus, any failure in this area seemed to be a part of her personal failure and lack of skill or of discipline. The Program Coordinator's definition of an "irresponsible mother" is as below:

> First, we call to the mothers' consciousness. Once we reach it, then, through self-control, they find morality at the end... This morality comes from the responsibility that these mothers do not have...

If the concept of "self-control" can be equated with "self-discipline," then these sentences can be interpreted as mothers *finding* "morality" through self-discipline. Moreover, as it is assumed that morality comes from responsibility, if the mothers are "responsible" they shall be moral as well. However, they have neither responsibility nor morality, according to the Program Coordinator, if they lack "discipline." Therefore, an "irresponsible" and an "immoral" mother with all other connotations of "impropriety" such as laziness, ignorance, and easiness, is also "undisciplined." In that sense, women, alienated from their actual political and economic conditions, are supposed to be responsible for the materialization of the ideal-home through disciplining themselves.

SELF-DISCIPLINE: "CONSISTENCY"

The term "consistency" was one of the most repetitive discursive terms used in the Education of Mothers Program. The term was defined as the mother's engagement of similar behaviors when faced with similar situations. For example, if a mother woke her child up to use the bathroom she had to repeat this act during the following days between the same time intervals. Similarly, if a mother did not allow her child to eat certain food, she should keep her stance even if her child started crying. This approach went with a sense of discipline applied by the mothers to the children, but more than that, it was referred to as mother's self-discipline.

When something went wrong in the household or in a child's life the aim was to "correct" the supposed "inconsistency" in the mother's behaviors; or, to correct the mother's lack of "self-discipline." Without talking about the power of the patriarchal authority at home, mothers lacked tools to explain their reasons for "inconsistency"; and hence, they become constantly self-criticizing: "It is my fault"; "It would be perfect if I woke her up"; "I have been neglectful…" These sentences were common among the women who could not teach their children good toilet habits. However, this mother's story was remarkable in this regard:

> I set my alarm clock up at 4 am for my child's toilet teaching. I had to do it in particular time intervals. The alarm rang. My husband woke up and he immediately began to dress up because he thought it was the time to go to work. I said [to him] that [the alarm rang] not for him but the child's toilet. Then, he got so angry with me, tore apart the child's toilet chart, which was a piece of paper that I had hung on the bathroom door. … I shut up and slept.

She could not wake her child up in the following days due to her husband's anger. She could be considered an "inconsistent" mother, as she did not repeat her actions with patience and persistence. She wanted to apply pedagogical teachings in her child's life, but her material and social conditions prevented this. Trying to be "consistent" she was violated at home; however, that did not prevent her from being criticized in the class on account of the fact that she was an "inconsistent" mother. The neoliberal focus on pedagogic tools divorced from material and social realities inevitably lead to further self-blame.

CONSUMING FOR THE FAMILY

Mothers were expected to consume generally, not for themselves but for the well-being of the family members. In that sense, what was offered as "beneficial" and "useful" for the family became important since a particular life-style was associated with these consumptive practices—a lifestyle demanding a particular class formation. The "pressure cooker" provides a good example. In order not to lose vitamins and proteins in the cooking process, a pressure cooker was highly recommended to the mothers. Moreover, this could be done "easily" as a pressure cooker could be "bought easily in installments" according to the teacher giving the lecture. In this way, the women who desired to be "good mothers" have learned their object of desire: a pressure cooker.

The purchase of a TV is another example of the embodiment of devotion. It was advised that if children had difficulties concentrating on their studies because the TV was always on in the living room, the mother should buy a small, extra TV to watch in her bedroom. That way the mother could watch TV without disturbing her child. Although some of the women said in the previous classes that they were living in the same room with the whole family, since economic deprivation prevented them from moving to a larger apartment, it did not change the prescribed TV location at home. Moreover, installments were again the recommended purchasing method. Also, purchasing an extra TV was evaluated as a kind of self-sacrificing gesture of the mother not only because she had to face her husband explaining their need for an extra TV, but also because she isolated herself in her bedroom so as not to disturb her child studying. Therefore, the mother would prove her self-sacrificing character as she considered her child's success above everything else, but at the same time could enjoy her "freedom" by purchasing a TV for herself. TV was positioned as a need rather than a want, requiring the purchase of a second TV over the option of not watching TV.

There were also other bits of information on the consumptive practices of the mothers. One of the recommendations was not to buy food sold on the streets. Instead of buying something from the street-sellers, whose products were assumed to be dirty (unhygienic) and unhealthy, a mother should go to the supermarkets, despite the fact that shopping from the supermarket was not a daily practice for the mothers living in the Gazi neighborhood. Apparently, when the lecturer used the word "supermarket" she thought about her own middle-class consumptive practices among which passing through a supermarket before going home was a casual activity. For the women living in the Gazi neighborhood, "grocery," where one could find packed/branded products, would be a correct word instead of "supermarket". Yet, by using the word "supermarket" a middle-class professional woman's fantasy came out, in which the mothers imagined themselves as the consumers of the supermarkets by shopping between shelves full of products waiting to be consumed.

Because of the presupposition that packed/branded products were made in sterilized and hygienic conditions, they were recommended as healthier than the homemade products sold on the street. In this way, the everyday consumptive practices of the women articulated with the needs of the global economy. For instance, it was advised not to buy ice cream on the streets, but to buy the packed/branded ones, which are sold in the supermarkets. Similarly, it was recommended that they should not buy ground beef from the butcher, who implied an image of "dirt" with his bloody apron and flies flying from one mass of meat to the other. The butcher was a traditional seller, thus, he signified a non-hygienic, dirty, and unhealthy way of producing and consuming. Instead, it was recommended to buy meat from the supermarket after checking its expiry date.

While local producers were evaluated as dirty and non-hygienic, the mothers were also contradictorily advised to consume domestic products. Once, there was a party in the classroom because of the nationally celebrated "Domestic Products Week" and the mothers brought in many different types of homemade food. On the one hand, the products of the local sellers were indicated as dirty, non-hygienic and unhealthy as opposed to the branded products sold in the supermarkets; but on the other hand, homemade products made by the mothers were assumed to be the best—the cleanest and the healthiest. The mothers were clearly articulated with the global economy as consumers, yet, they were encouraged to stay at home as their domestic labour was assumed to be more necessary than anything else for the health and hygiene of the family.

In these examples, women were called to consume with complacency as the consumption was practiced only on account of the family. The mothers were invited to imagine themselves in a middle-class household by consuming and desiring to consume certain products, which were recommended (and desired) by the "experts" giving lectures in the classroom. It was the bourgeois family fantasy of the experts/educators that the mothers were invited to participate in through their consumptive practices. However, consuming certain products, services and experiences, indicated a particular "life" which did not belong to the families living in the Gazi neighborhood.

It was, indeed, the idealized lifestyle of the middle-class educator who stops off at a supermarket casually after a workday, and takes off her modern-professional-woman shoes at the door just before she starts cooking with a pressure cooker. It seems that the mothers in the Mother-Child Education Program had no choice but to take their places in this fantasy.

The imagined perfect mother whom the Gazi women were encouraged to aspire represented a particular mother who set a romantic dinner table with flowers and candles, put separate spoons for each plate, and always served dinner with pleasure. In this context, the imperfections of the mothers (deviations from the "good mother") were seen as their personal failures since their personality was abstracted from the material and social conditions that they encountered in their everyday lives. Such a project often attempts to erase and recast class differences by consolidating a "good mother" modeled along middle-class lines (Shakry) although class-related conditions are determinant in a woman's everyday experiences. "Maternal perfectibility" or "imperfectability" is assumed to depend on personal potential and desire.

Although becoming the "good mother" was never possible, the time and energy required in attempting to approach this phantasmal image was a full-time job. The women participating in the Education of Mothers differentiated themselves from the upper-middle class women, who were closer to being imagined as the "good mother", living in bourgeois neighborhoods and having careers in business. Those women were labeled as "easy mothers" since it was believed professionals kept away from their children and did not put enough effort toward their family's needs, even if they hired paid-labour for housework and child-rearing. Thus, mothers were alienated not only to their own class, ethnic, cultural and political identities, but also to the other women coming from different segments of the society. In this way, any possibility for solidarity and collaboration among mothers became more and more difficult as women were individualized and left isolated both from the community and within their own families.

CONCLUSION

To sum up, the discursive field of the Education of Mothers reveals the extent to which neoliberal "good mothering" paradigms predicated upon white, middle-class motherhood become implicated in localized governance structures and negotiated within the diverse contexts of mothers' lives. This example reveals the extent through which such governance structures become segregated from social and material realities. Through the "technologies of self" (Martin et al.), by the promotion of self-controlling, self-criticizing, self-disciplining approaches, any deviance from the "norm" necessitates self-correction. In addition to the self-responsibility discourse, framing "I do" sentences encourages the subjects of these sentences to practice a constant self-policing. The discourse of individual responsibility on home and husband management through these self-governing approaches provide the woman an agency in the patriarchal structure of the extended kinship relations; however, these approaches also individualize and alienate the woman from her communal ties constituted with the other mothers.

The discursive field of the Education of Mothers exposes multiple technologies and "technologies of self" that attempt to govern families by investing and individualizing women in those families, and intervening in individualized family units. The state ensures its ideological reproduction among the poor marginalized masses of the society through these families, in which women become the pioneers of the state's ideological reproduction processes as long as they are called "the mothers." Since the time of this case study, there has been a recent shift as of 2013 in Turkey in which NGOs have less opportunity to "share the state's burden." The new policies and projects for governing families are increasingly directly state-oriented and focused on those living on the outskirts of the urban area and seen as politically whimsical segments of the population. A process of regulation once disseminated and made implicit is becoming increasingly explicit. Such government centralization represents a further amplification of neoliberal discourses governing "good" mothering, thereby increasingly regulating the lives of mothers (in particular marginalized mothers) in conflicting and ideological ways completely divorced from the material and social conditions of daily life.

NOTES

[1]The latest projects concerned with educating girls include Haydi Kızlar Okula (MEB-UNICEF, held by 2003), Kardelenler (ÇYDD-Turkcell, held by 2000), Baba Beni Okula Gönder (Milliyet Newspaper, held by 2005). These projects mainly targeted the poor, marginalized Kurdish girls from Eastern Anatolia "to transform them into reading, thinking, adjudicating individuals, and participant women in the labour force and decision making mechanisms" (for the RTL of *Baba Beni Okula Gönder* campaign, see

http://www.bbog.org/sss.html).

[2] The Social Services and Child Protection Agency was established in 1983 as an institution working as part of the Ministry of Health and Social Welfare; however, with a decree law in 1991 it became affiliated directly with the Prime Minister, according to code 2828. After its establishment in 2011, the Ministry of Family and Social Assistance centralized social policies eliminating SHÇEK as a state institution. The Mother-Child Education Program has been replaced with the Family Education Program centralized as Family Life Centres coordinated by the state.

[3] As of 2013, the Turkish Prime Minister Recep Tayyip Erdoğan declared this region the new gentrification area of Istanbul.

[4] Representations of both Kurdishness and Aleviness in the public space have been perceived as a threat to the national unity and homogeneity of the Turkish nation. In the socio-political history of the Turkish Republic, both Kurds and Alevis were welcomed to the public space only by denying their identities.

[5] When SHÇEK was eliminated as a state institution as of 2011, Family Centres replaced Community Centres in fulfilling the function of state regulation through the continuance of various educative programs including Family Education and Marriage Courses that have since replaced the Mother-Child Education Program.

[6] 2008 statistics of the Community Centre reveal 68 people (59 women and 9 men) received financial assistance from the Centre.

[7] The duration of compulsory schooling in Turkey was eight years until 2012 when parliament passed compulsory schooling being divided into three periods of four years each.

WORKS CITED

Davin, Anna. "Imperialism and Motherhood." *Tensions of Empire: Colonial Cultures in a Bourgeois World.* Eds. Frederick Cooper and Ann Laura Stoler. Berkeley: University of California Press, 1997. 87-152. Print.

Glenn, Evelyn Nakano, Grace Chang, and Linda Rennie Forcey. *Mothering: Ideology, Experience, and Agency.* New York and London: Routledge, 1994. Print.

İpek, Yasemin. "Volunteers or Governors? Rethinking Civil Society in Turkey Beyond the Problematic of Democratization: The Case of TEGV." Diss. Boğaziçi University, 2006. Print.

Martin, Luther H., Huck Gutman, and Patrick H. Hutton. Eds. *Technologies of the Self: A Seminar with Michel Foucault.* Massachusetts: University of Massachusetts Press, 1988. Print.

Shakry, Omina. (1998). "Schooled Mothers and Structured Play: Child Rearing in Turn-of-the-Century Egypt". *Remaking Women: Feminism and Modernity in the Middle East.* Ed. Lila Abu-Lughod. Princeton, New Jersey: Princeton University Press, 1998. 126-171. Print.

Sucuka, Nur. Ed. *7 Çok Geç! Erken çocukluk eğitiminin önemi Üzerine Düşünceler ve Öneriler.* İstanbul: Anne-Çocuk Eğitim Vakfı, 1999. Print.

13.

Affective Labour and Neoliberal Fantasies

The Gendered and Moral Economy of School Choice in England

ANDREW WILKINS

INTRODUCTION

Since the late 1970s/early 80s political and public policy opinion in England has been saturated with claims to the perceived waste and inefficiency generated through government intervention over the control and delivery of public services. As a corrective to such top-down bureaucracy, neoliberal ideologues insist that citizens should be "empowered" to pursue their own self-interest as a condition of their rights (and obligations) as consumers of public resources. The expectation is that market-driven reform will produce direct incentives for welfare providers to improve their services through appealing to welfare users as rational economic actors (calculating and discriminating).

School choice, for example, represents the translation of these ideas in the realm of education policy and practice with mothers summoned in the role of active, engaged consumers. A duty and condition of this role is that mothers know the "right" school for their child and link up their child's

needs with suitable forms of education provision. This necessitates the performance of "affective labour," including the utility of emotion and feeling
for the purpose of maximizing familial advantage. In this discussion I highlight how some mothers articulate emotive discourse as a framing for their
choice and in doing so seek to go against the grain of economical utility and
maximization through calculation. To conceptualize emotive discourse as
a form of resistance that exceeds the calculus of the market is problematic,
however. It can also be viewed as productive of neoliberal gains in terms
of generating self-governing subjects. To outline these issues I demonstrate
how emotion and feeling operate as discursive resources which feed into,
and which are products of, neoliberal governance.

REMAKING THE STATE

Although not formally introduced to British policy making until the 1980s
(specifically, the 1988 Education Reform Act), the blueprint for school choice first surfaced in 1977 when Stuart Sexton, who later went on to become
advisor to the Secretary of State in Thatcher's Conservative government,
advocated that parents should be granted freedom of school choice by application (Sexton). In fact, the historical and political forces that gave rise
to school choice are so diverse that they need to be examined as expressions
in the confluence of distinct economic and political rationalities, namely
monetarism and neoconservatism. Taking these two trends into consideration, I will analyze the policy of school choice as corresponding to the formation of a set of "political configurations" and "philosophies" (Hall 15)
geared towards the displacement of one political and economic settlement
(Keynesianism) and culminating in the birth of another (neoliberalism).

If we turn to the historical period in which school choice was arguably
first imagined—the mid-1970s—it is clear that a particular set of economic,
political, and cultural formations furnished its configuration as a policy
technology. After the Second World War, Britain enjoyed a relatively stable
period of affluence marked by an "unprecedented harmony between Ministers, sponsoring departments, institutions and the public" (Middlemas
342). Yet by the 1970s, British liberal economists and political conservatives
together with the support of the newly established right-wing think tank
Centre for Policy Studies (established in 1974) unleashed a torrent of anti-
statist rhetoric demanding that the traditional Keynesian method of using
government intervention to improve the demand for output and employment be overturned (Hirschman). The New Right replaced direct govern-

ment intervention in the form of structural supports with the new state role of setting the moral-religious tone for society (Brown). Through articulating and combining repertoires of "the people" and anti-collectivism (as against the state) together with traditional themes of family, nation, authority, standards, duty, and self-reliance (Hall), the New Right offered up a rhetoric that paved the foundation for the Conservative Party's landslide electoral victory in 1979. As Millar and Rose observe in *Governing the Present*, "These diverse skirmishes were rationalized within a relatively coherent mentality of government that came to be termed neo-liberalism" (Miller and Rose 211). In the 1990s Conservative leader and Prime Minister John Major introduced elements of managerialism and consumerism as mechanisms for guiding the delivery of public services (Pollitt). This had the effect of fortifying a decisive break with Keynesian consensus policies and, in particular, the model of citizenship engendered through post-war social policy (Lewis).

SUMMONING ACTIVE CITIZENS: NEOLIBERALISM AND THE ROLE OF AFFECTIVE LABOUR

Between 1944 and 1979 social policy in Britain was rationalized through a particular understanding of the relation between the state and citizen. This model of citizenship prescribed the entitlement that "citizens should enjoy a minimum level of rights (economic security, care, protection against various risks and so on)" (Johansson and Hvinden 106). From 1979 onwards, however, governments have ushered in a number of reforms that signal a shift away from these trends in welfare governance. Couched in the vocabulary of enterprise, marketization and self-responsibility, successive governments have sought to offset the perceived excesses attributed to state control over public sector organization through locating citizens and welfare providers in new modes of self-regulation—what can be concisely formulated as neoliberal or advanced liberal modes of governing.[1]

In this expanding neoliberal imaginary, individuals come to be constituted as bearers of consumer rights and pursuers of their own self-interest. Feelings and desires are reified into objects of consumption. The fulfillment of consumer-based obligations, such as the capacity and willingness to exercise choice and self-care, is defined as a condition for receiving particular rewards. Effective citizenship works as a form of political governance linking entitlement to the behavior of welfare recipients: "Without any choice, they are far more like the passive recipient than the active citizen" (Ministers of State 3.4.3). In the context of school choice then, "affective labour"[2] refers to how mothers as enforced "choosers" of education provision are governed through their capacity and willingness to utilize affect to maximize familial advantage. Thus, unlike in the Keynesian model where access to resources was predicated upon entitled need, neoliberal subjectivity predicates access to resources upon "proper" performance.

THE INJUNCTION TO CHOOSE

In the case of education, school choice represents the translation of neoliberal ideas into the realm of policy making and political discourse. Prior to the introduction of the 1988 Education Reform Act (ERA), local education authorities allocated each child a school place based on their geography and proximity to locally available schools. Subsequent to the introduction of the ERA, these powers were stripped away and parents were assigned obligations as active choosers (rather than passive recipients) of education services, "enabling" them to exit their local school system. While government documentation utilizes the gender-neutral term "parents," it is invariably "mothers" who are made responsible for this elaborate process of "school choice." Thus, such de-gendering through neutralized terms removes the increased labour required specifically by mothers that such an elaborate "choice" system necessitates.

The inability or "unwillingness" of mothers to choose a school for their child has not been overlooked by governments, however. To create "better-informed customers" (Ministers of State 3.4.3), the then Labour government set up local services in 2006-7 specifically designed to target and nudge those mothers who "find the system difficult to understand and therefore difficult to operate in the best interests of the child," or who are simply "unable or unwilling to engage with the process" (DCSF 2). This process of naturalizing an image of the willing and deserving "parent" as someone who operates "in the best interests of the child" (ibid) serves also to privilege emotion and affect as preferred strategies for securing competitive familial advantage. The active consumer is one "who mobilizes affects and emotions and governs itself through them" (Isin 232).

As for those mothers recognized as "willing" subjects, government information and advice sets out in no uncertain terms the conditions for exercising "reasonable" and "responsible" choice: "Armed with information about the schools in their area many parents can navigate the system successfully" (DfES 3.11). The use of the military metaphor (going "armed") is suggestive of the competitive educational space mothers are invited to survey and navigate in their role as consumers. In particular, it denotes a mode of engagement and relation to the self that is as much clinical and instrumental as it is social and cultural. To choose "responsibly," for example, is to engage in practices of long-term preparation and planning together with the exercise of certain skills, knowledge and orientations, all of which presuppose a network of equally shared and equally available dialogical competencies and socially appropriated behaviors. "Choice," therefore, is less an act of spontaneity than it is a behavioral adjustment to culturally acceptable values and politically mandated norms.

To refuse or "properly" engage with the logics of choice, therefore, is to run the risk of being relegated to the often demonized position of someone who is "passive" and "undeserving" (a particular offshoot of the government desire to constitute parents as "active"). This is because economical utility and instrumental calculation function as criteria for assessing the suitability of different schools. Refusal or inability to engage with the field of choice becomes synonymous with a perceived transgression of parental duties and responsibilities. Under neoliberalism, such duties and responsibilities increasingly take on the character of consumer-oriented dispositions with the economic *and* affective actor at its centre. This generates a "structure of feeling" (Williams) that is lived and negotiated (inhabited and performed) by mothers, often producing moments of anxiety. Some commentators observe choice as an obsession of the middle class (Hattersley), as something that inscribes and legitimates middle-class orientations and values.[3] This has implications for the ways in which mothers narrate and rationalize their experiences and enactments of choice.[4] However, rather than submitting to the economical utility prescribed by the dominant discourse of choice, mothers negotiate it in the context of interlocking and competing value systems and moral orders, often oscillating between antinomies of citizen and consumer, community and individual, and political and commercial (Wilkins, "Citizens and/or Consumers").

THE GENDERED ECONOMY OF SCHOOL CHOICE

In what follows I make explicit the dialogic struggle entered into as several mothers explain the meanings and representations expressed through their choice-making practices.[5] It is particularly salient that only mothers responded to the call to be interviewed. Indeed, as many British social policy analysts and sociologists of education observe, it is mothers who are expected to be responsible for linking together children's needs with agencies of service delivery.[6] By virtue of their ascribed role as primary caregiver of the child, it is therefore mothers who become the principle targets of neoliberal policies and practices of school choice. On this view it becomes possible to disentangle the generic language of school choice, with its appeals to consumer-based spectacles of need-satisfaction, from the concrete and embodied practices through which mothers experience and negotiate choice—what we might term the gendered economy of school choice. Indeed, the contradictions pertaining to some mothers' choice-making practices can be linked to the competing pressures they invariably confront as neoliberal subjects—economizing agents who also utilize affect to maximize familial advantage.

To demonstrate this I draw on a number of interviews I conducted with a group of London-based mothers (15 in total) during 2007. The purpose of this study was to better understand the different rationalities and values shaping school choices. To ensure confidentiality of all material, pseudonyms have been used to replace the real names of the mothers involved and any schools mentioned. I trace the contradictory discourses taken up as mothers negotiate framings of school choice on the basis of seemingly conflicting sets of demands, specifically the manipulation of clinical and affective responses.

School choice can be conceptualized in relational terms as straddling meanings and practices of neoliberal citizenship on the one hand (idea that citizens should behave as rational utility maximizers (consumers) who exercise choice between a given set of providers),[7] and behaviors and knowledge that necessitate the performance of affective labour. In this way it is important to be circumspect about the general applicability of Johansson and Hvinden's conceptualization of neoliberal citizenship as a stable and determinate reality. Instead, neoliberal citizenship might be better understood as lived and performed at the intersection of a range of competing rationalities and values, making it shifting and porous.

The point of the following analytical exercise is thus threefold. First, I suggest that the affective (the realm of private feelings and experientially driven values) is as important to the cultivation of neoliberal subjects as the utility of rational calculus. Moreover, I demonstrate the paradoxical situation confronted by many mothers whereby governments valorize expressions of affective labour while at the same time displacing it as trivial or secondary to the task of calculating risk through assessment. Second, I want to disrupt the narrow utilitarian notion of the chooser as primarily a "rational" agent through highlighting the emotional labouring underpinning choice, and I aim to do so without reducing emotion to something specifically unreflexive or corrupting of the rational senses (an idea which has gained scientific credibility in neurobiology studies and more recently influenced British government policy discourse) (Wilkins, "Libertarian Paternalism"). Instead, I want to highlight how emotive discourse can be understood to both describe and construct social reality (a useful formulation of emotion made popular by social constructivist thinkers and discursive psychologists).[8] Finally, I examine how mothers are encouraged both to utilize and demonize their emotional investment in choosing a school for a child, leading to the creation of a particular set of gendered dilemmas and tensions.

EMOTIVE DISCOURSE AND THE AFFECTIVE FRAMEWORK OF CHOOSING

As subjects of the parental "right to choose" (even though this "right" is mandated), parents are typically addressed through government, media, and popular discourses as potentially anxious and distressed subjects (British Broadcasting Corporation) However, this is an issue that affects mothers specifically, and is thus a product of a particular set of gendered dynamics and sensibilities. In circumstances where mothers (and their children) have been denied a place at their preferred school and wish to appeal against the decision, "experts" recognize that mothers become "emotionally involved" (Rooney 60) when summoned to present their case to an independent admissions panel. To increase the probabilities of success, mothers are encouraged to abandon the use of "vague emotional arguments" when formulating their appeal[9] and instead "uncover the truth" through "asking the right questions" and ultimately "win a [school] place" (Rooney viii).

In this framing, emotion is thought to occlude the successful performance of a rational position, one that is commensurate with the figure of the active, deserving citizen. Thus, striving for a maximum position entails the suspension or moderation of emotion through "rational" detachment from feelings held to be personal to the individual. At the same time and in contradistinction to this, mothers are encouraged to mitigate any potential risk in their choice-making by knowing the "right" school for their child—a huge emotional investment that relies on utilizing affect to maximize advantage and drawing on knowledge that is experientially proven. The process of choosing a school reveals a similar set of fractures, tensions, and oppositional thinking.

Mothers observe the prism of calculation to be a typical feature of choice, whether for themselves or others. But rather than fully commit to a clinical gaze, some mothers engage in routine practices of subordinating consumerist logics to emotional sensibilities, and do so in a way that problematizes cognitive accounts of emotions as reflecting automated, unreflective bodily responses.[10] The following extract is taken from an interview with Caroline, a single mother with young boys. When asked to give details on how she elected to choose a school for her eldest son, Caroline explained:

> Well it was an equal balance if you like between being quite cold and clinical and looking at the Ofsted reports[11] that was the research end of it, and there was the values end of it and actually how the children behaved, how they valued each other, the sort of values that they were given and whether there was a spiritual dimension to their teaching and their learning. (Caroline)

Caroline highlights the contradictory impulses embodied through her decision making and the conflicting values they give rise to. Caroline's desire to employ strategies that are "cold and clinical" can be closely approximated to a set of activities and orientations personified through the figure of the consumer. This might include the practice of pursuing technical means of estimating the quality of different goods and services through the utility of formalized reason. In this framing, intangible qualities such as feeling, emotion, and intuition are streamlined and rationalized to complement the de-humanizing core of a calculating framework of choosing. But rather than submit fully to the utility of one particular framework of choosing, Caroline indicates a preference for fusing seemingly disparate approaches, namely combining the practice of data crunching with what she describes as "the values end of it." The latter approach can be contrasted with a "cold and clinical" approach to the extent it mediates and redeems a sensualistic epistemology. In other words, it promotes understanding and knowledge based on experience, feeling, and affect. This is best captured through Caroline's concern with "whether there was a spiritual dimension to their teaching and their learning." In a similar vein, Pauline, a mother of three children, alludes to the de-humanizing aspects of a calculating framework of choosing:

I looked at league tables[12] (Interviewer: Did you find them useful at all?) No. I find them useful as in you could figure out the top sort of 10 per cent the next…My husband's a mathematician. Statistically the significance of one kid having a cold on one day in the top 100 schools can knock you ten places. It gave me an idea of where they sit in the world but it didn't really do much. I wouldn't change my child for five places or anything. (Interviewer: Was there anything missing from this information?) The nature of the school, the ethos, what kind of children go there because what we figured out was the older two schools seemed to recruit the kind of children and put personalities and certain personalities fit in best and I was actually looking for a match that would suit my son's work personality. (Pauline)

Pauline is hesitant about the utility of league tables as suitable criteria for judging whether a school is right for her child. She identifies their usefulness in terms of assigning school value based on "performance" and "quality" (e.g. the percentage of pupils gaining top marks) but attests to their contestability in terms of providing reliable and consistent measures of school "ethos." "Statistically the significance of one kid having a cold on one day in the top 100 schools can knock you ten places," Pauline remarks. A corollary of this is that Pauline relegates the cold and clinical approach to a reflex of maladjusted reasoning: "I wouldn't change my child for five places or anything." Important to Pauline are those intangible forms of distinction which have little expression in league table data. These include the school "ethos" and "what kind of children go there" (Pauline). By way of rendering intelligible these concepts, Pauline describes the affective labour performed through her actions, namely the emotional work of linking her son's needs with suitable forms of provision ("looking for a match", as she describes it). Kate, a mother of one child, relays a similar set of concerns and dilemmas:

I'm not really that fussed about league tables because I don't think they actually tell you what it's like for a child. So, for example, Moorgate Close [her son's primary school], which is always way down the league tables, but actually he is doing really well there. So it is more about him then it is about the school. (Kate)

Again, a cold and clinical approach is sidelined in favour of an emotional engagement with the perceived needs and personality of the child. These forms of engagement are typified through a child-centred discourse that serves to validate an image of the child as unique and special. The perceived needs of the child are constructed in psychosocial terms as isolated, incomparable and therefore beyond the estimations posited through a reductive (e.g. market-driven) model of choice-making. To compensate for this lack in the league table data, Kate highlights the importance of both understanding and knowing the needs of the child. "So it is more about him then it is about the school," Kate reminds us. Similar to Caroline and Pauline, Kate can also be captured positioning an affective framework of choosing as beyond the reifying mechanisms of the market apparatus. "I don't think they [league tables] actually tell you what it's like for a child," Kate explains.

Camilla, a mother of one child, draws on a similar set of discourses to explain her school choice:

> The higher the results and the better the results is, the more suspicious I am...I met a really good person and she said, you know, 'this school is about maintaining its reputation', and yes they may help children who perhaps have some difficulty learning, but that's not their emphasis. So that was quite truthful of her to say that and it made me think twice because it's all well and good getting your son into the best school, but if it's not meeting his needs. (Camilla)

The condition of successfully inhabiting and performing the role of the chooser and of the "responsible" mother is therefore powerfully shaped by the perceived individualized character of the child and his or her needs and personality. Choice is underpinned by the capacity to "know" the child and link their needs to suitable forms of provision through gainful knowledge and careful deliberation. Camilla, for example, echoes the desire to go against the grain of economical utility and maximization through calculation. She undermines the utility of projections based on "results" and "reputation" as insufficient or secondary to the task of finding the "right" school for her child. Camilla also demonstrates how gainful knowledge in a competitive educational marketplace is shifting and unstable. As mothers negotiate this difficult terrain of the personal and (utmost) impersonal, it is evident that knowledge and its utility are subject to conflicting forces and pressures. School choice can be seen as negotiated through the interplay of calculating and affective frameworks of choosing, each with their own set of rationalities, values, and social capital.

What is highlighted through each of the above extracts is the ways in which some mothers ascribe meaning and value to the practice of choosing a school for their child. They capture also among some mothers a pattern of uneasiness with the idea of using league table data to determine school choice. Instead, each mother articulates a preference for experience over expedience and the private world of feelings and values over the competitive world of risk-taking and calculating probabilities. Caroline contrasts a "cold and clinical" approach with the "values end of it," while Pauline and Kate together with Camilla question the utility of league tables as criteria for judging whether a school is "right" for a child. For Pauline and Kate, league tables rely on forms of school evaluation and testing that are numerically assessed and thus fail to capture the particularities and personality of the child. The suggestion here is that the child (and his or her needs) cannot be adequately communicated through the reifying mechanisms of the anonymous market apparatus. To illustrate this, each mother descriptively builds up an image of their child as unique. In contrast, a calculating approach with its emphasis on measurable standards is constructed in perfunctory terms as decontextualized, replicable, inauthentic, and superficial.

When viewed as a rhetorical device for positioning and accounting for the self (Wetherell), emotion here can be understood to function as a discourse much in the same way that formal rationality does—it makes available a set of familiar tropes to be used in the human activity of adjusting to or conversely resisting a given social reality, a way of validating particular representations of personal accountability. What emerges across each of the above extracts is a pattern of two perceived opposed realities: one mediated by the pressures and demands of the market, with its insistence on the calculation of probabilities, and the other linked with the concrete and lived practice of experientially knowing and engaging with the "needs" of the child. The discourse of emotion thus works on a practical and communicative level. It functions to individualize the child through a process of de-reification: the decoupling of the child from the phantom estimations posited through a formal rational model of choice supposedly devoid of content. Simultaneously, it works to undermine economic rationalizations of choice as abstract, generic, and alienating. The elevation of emotion in this way reflects a deliberate effort to index mothering practices through alternative forms of meaning-making not elicited through the clinical practice of economical utility.

With this in mind, we might want to rethink any dichotomy that engenders oppositional meanings of action and inaction, active and passive, the rational and the affective. The voices captured in this chapter highlight an often neglected feature of emotional labour—that emotion can be practical and practiced. At the same time, we should avoid reading these affective practices as transcending and therefore escaping the logic flowing from the market apparatus. Communicated through these emotive discourses and affective practices are meanings and representations that go against the grain of economical utility and thus can be considered in some sense oppositional. But they are also products of the power of the market. As Butler explains by way of Foucault, "the disciplinary apparatus produces subjects, but as a consequence of that production, it brings into discourse the conditions for subverting that apparatus itself" (100). The discourse of emotion can be usefully conceptualized in relational terms as inextricably linked with the discursive properties of the market apparatus—the child is anchored as unique *through* an appeal to the abstract and empty character of measurable standards. More specifically, the idea that each person is "special" feeds into, and is a product of, individualized neoliberal fantasies and dominant "good mother" imperatives that centralize the unique and demanding needs of the child.

CONCLUSION: GOVERNING THROUGH AFFECTIVE LABOUR

Taking school choice as my primary focus, I have explored two seemingly conflicting discourses—the rational and the affective—and traced how mothers articulate and combine these socially circulating repertoires in their ascribed role as "choosers." Mothers make use of a plurality of rationalities and frameworks when deciding on the "right" school for their child. Mothers are called upon to fulfill certain duties and responsibilities in their role as "consumers." But to "choose" is to inhabit the presumed requisite skills and knowledge pertaining to its successful performance. Mothers are encouraged to operate in "the best interests of the child" (DCSF 2) and to engage with the process of choice as responsible, discriminating agents regardless of material circumstances and daily realities.

A condition of this role, therefore, concerns knowing the perceived needs of the child and matching those needs to suitable forms of education provision. The practice by which mothers utilize calculation and affect to maximize familial advantage can thus be considered a set of relations, exchanges, and performances through which subjects are perceived as self-regulating and autonomous. Consistent with any regulating discourse, mothers are assumed to comply with such behavioral expectations (assuming they wish to be successfully positioned by official discourse as "deserving" parents). Mothers thus confront a set of injunctions around behavior and orientation in which the presumed educational needs of the child are decontextualized from the daily material and emotional realities of the mothers' and families' lives. Moreover, mothers must navigate a contradictory domain of intersecting positions and blurred boundaries, inevitably giving rise to uncertainty and even self-doubt over what constitutes "responsible" choice.

The lived practice of negotiating school choice produces yet another domain through which mothers are constituted through a moral economy as self-responsible, self-disciplined subjects. Given the competitive neoliberal framework placing undue emphasis upon education as a means for class mobility and social/cultural capital, taking on the ascribed role of "responsible mother" becomes that much more complex. For those mothers unable (due to structural constraints not mentioned in the self-responsible discourse) or unwilling to fulfill such behavioral obligations, the burden and anxiety of mothering is only intensified, in effect adding to the weight of uncertainty and strain already experienced.

NOTES

[1] See Duggan; Harvey; and Larner
[2] See Hardt and Negri, and Lazzarato
[3] See Ball, Bowe and Gewirtz
[4] See Reay, Crozier and James
[5] I use the term dialogic in a strictly Bakhtinian sense to refer to the interaction and interpenetration of opposites, the jostling or marrying of distinct rationalities and discourses—what Bakhtin terms "heteroglossia".
[6] See Graham; and Ribbens
[7] See Johansson and Hvinden
[8] See Harré and Wetherell
[9] Ex-chief school inspector Christopher Woodhead cited in Blinkhorn and Griffiths
[10] See Brafman and Brafman
[11] Ofsted (Office for Standards in Education) carries out inspections of state-subsidized schools on behalf of the British government. The aim of these

inspection reports (made available to parents and carers of children) is to maintain accountability and rationalize mechanisms of quality assurance in the field of education.

[12]League tables refer to a ranking system used in England to determine the performance of different schools through estimating the overall educational attainment levels for children attending primary and secondary schools. Schools are ranked on league tables according to the percentage of pupils gaining at least five A to C grades.

WORKS CITED

Bakhtin, M.M. *The Dialogic Imagination: Four Essays.* Austin, Texas: University of Texas Press, 1981. Print.

Ball, S.J., R. Bowe, and S. Gewirtz. "School Choice, Social Class and Distinction: the Realization of Social Advantage in Education." *Journal of Education Policy* 11.1 (1996): 89-112. Print.

Blinkhorn, A. and S. Griffiths. "I Won't Send My Child to a Sink School." *The Sunday Times, News Review,* March 23, 2008. p.12. Print.

Brafman, O. and R. Brafman. *Sway. The Irresistible Pull of Irrational Behaviour.* New York: Doubleday, 2009. Print.

British Broadcasting Corporation (BBC) "School Choice Causes Distress" 22 July, 2004. Available at http://news.bbc.co.uk/1/hi/education/3913853.stm [Accessed 7 June 2012] Online.

Brown, W. "American Nightmare: Neoliberalism, Neoconservatism, and De-Democratization." *Political Theory* 34.6 (2006): 690-714. Print.

Butler, J. *The Psychic Life of Power: Theories in Subjection.* Stanford, California: Stanford University Press, 1997. Print.

Department for Education and Skills (DfES). 2005. *Higher Standards, Better Schools for All.* London: HMSO, 2005. Print.

Department for Children, Schools and Families (DCSF). *Choice Advice: Guidance for Local Authorities.* London: DFES, 2006. Print.

Duggan, L. *The Twilight of Equality? Neoliberalism, Cultural Politics and the Attack on Democracy.* Boston: Beacon Press, 2003. Print.

Edwards, D. "Emotion Discourse." *Culture Psychology* 5 (1999): 271-291. Print.

Foucault, M. "The Ethic of Care for the Self as a Practice of Freedom: An Interview with Michel Foucault on January 20, 1984." *Philosophy Social*

Criticism 12 (1987): 112-31. Print.

Graham, H. *Women, Health and the Family.* Brighton: Harvester, 1984. Print.

Hall, S. "The Great Moving Right Show." *Marxism Today,* January, 1979, 14-20. Print.

Hardt, M. and A. Negri. *Empire.* Cambridge, Massachusetts and London, England: Harvard University Press, 2001. Print.

Harré, R. (ed.) *The Social Construction of Emotions.* Oxford: Basil Blackwell, 1986. Print.

Harvey, D. *A Brief History of Neoliberalism.* Oxford: Oxford University Press, 2005. Print.

Hattersley, R. "Agitators Will Inherit the Earth". *The Guardian,* Nov 17, 2003. Print.

Hirschman, A.O. *The Rhetoric of Reaction.* Cambridge, MA: Bleknap Harvard, 1991. Print.

Isin, E.F. "The Neurotic Citizen." *Citizenship Studies* 8.3 (2004): 217-235. Print.

Johansson, H. and B. Hvinden. "Welfare Governance and the Remaking of Citizenship" Ed. J. Newman. *Remaking Governance: Peoples, Politics and the Public Sphere.* University of Bristol, Bristol: Policy Press, 2005. Print.

Larner, W. "Neoliberalism: Policy, Ideology and Governmentality." *Studies in Political Economy* 63 (2000): 5-25. Print.

Lazzarato, M. "Immaterial Labour" Ed. M. Hardt and P. Virno. *Radical Thought in Italy: A Potential Politics.* Minneapolis and London: University of Minnesota Press, 1996. 133-147. Print.

Lewis, G. (ed.) *Citizenship: Personal Lives and Social Policy.* Policy Press: Bristol, 2004. Print.

Middlemas, K. Power, *Competition and the State. Volume 1: Britain in Search of Balance, 1940-61.* Macmillan Press: London, 1986. Print.

Miller, P. and N. Rose. *Governing the Present. Administering Economic, Social and Personal Life.* Policy Press: Cambridge, 2008. Print.

Ministers of State for Department for Health, Local and Regional Government, and School Standards. *The Case for User Choice in Public Services.* A Joint Memorandum to the Public Administration Select Committee Inquiry into Choice, Voice and Public Service, 2004. Print.

Pollitt, C. "The Citizen's Charter: a Preliminary Analysis." *Public Money and Management,* April-June, 1994: 9-11. Print.

Reay, D., G. Crozier, and D. James. "White Middle Class Parents and Urban Schools." London: Palgrave-Macmillan, 2011. Print.

Ribbens, J. *Mothers and Their Children: a Feminist Sociology of Childrearing.* London: Sage, 1994. Print.

Rooney, B. *How to Win Your School Appeal: Getting Your Child into the School of Your Choice.* Second edition. London: A & C Black Publishers, 2007. Print.

Sexton S. "Evolution by Choice." Eds. CB Cox and R Boyson. *Black Paper 1977.* London: Temple Smith, 1977. Print.

Wetherell, M. "Positioning and Interpretative Repertoires: Conversation Analysis and Post-Structuralism in Dialogue." *Discourse and Society* 9.3 (1998): 387-412. Print.

— *Affect and Emotion: A New Social Science Understanding.* London: Sage, 2012. Print.

Wilkins, A. "Citizens and/or Consumers: Mutations in the Construction of Meanings and Practices of School Choice." *Journal of Education Policy* 25.2 (2010): 171-189. Print.

— "School Choice and the Commodification of Education: A Visual Approach to School Brochures and Websites." *Critical Social Policy.* Special Issue: Inequalities and Images: Insights for Policy and Practice 32.1 (2012): 70-87. Print.

— Wilkins, A. "Libertarian Paternalism: Policy and Everyday Translations of the Rational and the Affective." *Critical Policy Studies.* Forthcoming.

Williams, R. *The Long Revolution.* Penguin Books: London, 1961. Print.

Section III: Neoliberalism and the Nuclear Family

14.

Redefining Single Motherhood

The 1990s Child Support Discourse and the Dismantling of the U.S. Welfare State

CELIA WINKLER

INTRODUCTION

As the number of women and children living in poverty began to rise in the early 1980s, U.S. scholars, policy makers, and activists focused on the effect of divorce and single-parenting in causing the "feminization of poverty" in America. It was common wisdom that following divorce, the standard of living of women declined, while men enjoyed an economic benefit. "The divorce revolution,"[1] far from liberating women, appeared to have plunged them into poverty. In order to address this disparity, a significant proportion of feminist legal scholars and women's advocates demanded increased attention to court-awarded child support and collections. Because women were disadvantaged in the labour market and devoted a greater amount of time and resources toward raising children, the assumption of equality upon divorce ignored the very real differences between men and women.[2]

Simultaneous with the rise of the feminist child support movement in the 1980s, Democrats joined with Republicans to pass "welfare reforms" that would strictly limit social assistance to the "truly needy" by increasing work requirements and surveillance, reducing incentives and deductions, and enhancing support collections from noncustodial parents (usually fathers) of children receiving AFDC (Aid to Families with Dependent Children) benefits. The net effect of these reforms, from 1981 through the end of the century, was to arrest an emerging public concern for the costs of care by reducing the state's assistance in the expensive work of raising children, repositioning responsibility onto the unsupported shoulders of the parents.

This chapter presents an analysis of the ideology and practice of child support enforcement as the solution to poverty in the U.S. in the era of neoliberalism, using a discourse analysis of congressional debates and other public documents. Neoliberalism in this context is to be understood as the political agenda that had the goal of replacing Keynesian economics with neoclassical economics' single-minded elevation of market forces, reduced government, "choice," and "personal responsibility"—an amplification of what C. B. MacPherson called "possessive individualism"—over notions of care, solidarity, and equality (MacPherson).

I argue that the 1990s U.S. discourse wedding welfare reform with heightened enforcement of private child support obligations presented at least three basic problems: (1) it enshrined the idea that the private heterosexual family unit was the only legitimate social and economic unit for the support of children, casting single mothers as quasi-wives and ignoring or stigmatizing those who could not or would not rely on the heterosexual family economic community; (2) by requiring women to rely on individual men for support, it discursively and materially placed on two individuals the entire burden of a system of discrimination and unequal distribution of wealth, ignoring economic inequality and the poverty of many men, and creating a stratified system of support for children and women's well-being; and (3) because it supported a gendered and stratified system of distribution, the emphasis on child support imposed a false universalism on women oppressed on the basis of class, race, and sexual orientation.

The heightened interest in child support enforcement in the U.S. should be seen within the context of the struggle over the welfare state. Locating the tasks of support and redistribution of wealth in the legal system on a theory of contract or status obligation rather than social rights vis-à-vis society, is consistent with the construction of the normative citizen as the "possessive individual" (Bussemaker and van Kersbergen 18; and MacPherson 263-267), and provided ideological support for the neoliberal "personal responsibility" discourse. Women's claims to citizenship were threaded through their status as quasi-wives. This distancing of the costs of reproduction from societal attention—in the labour market and the state—had the effect of promoting neoliberal hegemony by offloading all state and societal responsibility onto individual "delinquent" parents.

THE CONSTRUCTION OF THE CHILD SUPPORT DISCOURSE

Before 1984, the U.S. provided a two-track system to maintain children in lone-parent families: for middle-class families, private child support administered through the state courts and the means-tested AFDC (Aid to Families with Dependent Children) benefit for the poor.[3] Child support collections for AFDC recipients had been more of an afterthought than a consistent federal policy until the creation of the IV-D agencies in 1975 (Pirog and Ziol-Guest 950).[4] Many social workers had resisted increased collections, arguing that overzealous pursuit of child support from indigent fathers could harm relations between father and child (Krause 227-250).

In the early 1980s, Congress enacted significant changes in the AFDC program which reduced working mothers' eligibility for assistance and increased surveillance of the recipient family, justified by blaming "welfare moms" for the federal budget deficit, using the image of the "Cadillac welfare queen" Reagan had drawn on during his presidential campaign. The legislation also strengthened the rules governing child support collections, including automatic withholding of the obligors' federally issued checks (notably tax refunds) and exemption of support obligors from consumer debt withholding limitations.[5] The primary purpose of the collections was not, however, to benefit the family, but to recoup monies paid by the state (Pirog and Ziol-Guest 952).[6] Meager child support payments, when combined with women's low wages, were sometimes enough to make households ineligible for AFDC, but not significantly improve their standard of living. In many states, Medicaid (health care benefit) was tied to AFDC eligibility. Losing AFDC because the child support put the income over the eligibility threshold could mean that parents and children lost all health coverage.

Welfare regulations also brought harsh requirements for AFDC recipients to "cooperate" in collections and establishment of support obligations. A parent who refused to cooperate "without good cause" could lose AFDC eligibility. If paternity had not been established, welfare agency employees would interrogate applicants with humiliating and invasive questions about their sexual activity, and agencies brought paternity suits on behalf of the children even against the mother's wishes. In some cases, the fathers counter-claimed or brought separate suit for custody or visitation, but these mothers, poor by definition as AFDC recipients, were unable to afford an attorney and were unrepresented by the state agency. The agencies' sole interest lay in representing the state as assignee of the claim for child support.

The "good cause" for refusal to cooperate was frequently narrowly interpreted, limited to increased risk of physical, sexual, or emotional harm to the children or parent, or if the child was conceived as a result of incest or rape, and required corroborating evidence. If the mother had not sought help from authorities at the time of abuse or rape, this corroborating evidence was usually unavailable. If an applicant simply did not want to have anything to do with the other biological parent because the parent would be a negative influence on the family, good cause did not exist. Other mothers wanted to protect a cordial relationship with a father who provided care and resources for the children or other relatives but could not afford to pay child support.

In 1984, new legislation required the IV-D agencies to pursue nonAF DC cases in child support collections, in part to avoid costs incurred in other public assistance programs, including Food Stamps and subsidized housing. The welfare reform measures of 1981 had resulted in the termination of many working-poor women, but they were still eligible for other forms of assistance (Pirog and Ziol-Guest 952). This meant, however, that even middle-class mothers were able to count on the assistance of the state agencies, instead of using the much more expensive private counsel.

This incorporation of the interests of non-AFDC recipients in welfare state regulation was intensified in the 1990s as the public debates began to paint all single mothers with the broad brush of irresponsibility previously reserved for "welfare moms." The rising white out-of-wedlock birth rate appeared to alarm policy commentators, such as Charles Murray and David Blankenhorn, who laid the blame on AFDC, divorce, and single mothers as contributing toward poverty and a general relaxation in moral standards.[7] Commentators pointed to a six-fold increase in crime, use of drugs, and illiteracy among children born out of wedlock and blamed divorces among prominent media figures for the general moral decay, e.g. William F. Buckley, in a March 24, 1994, Firing Line debate: "Resolved: Welfare Does More Harm Than Good" (Steibel). From the demonized "welfare queen" as the lazy Cadillac driving fraud of the 1970s and 1980s, the moral panic over illegitimacy changed the public image of the "welfare mom" into the black, drug-addicted unmarried mother of numerous children of various fathers, who began her childbearing in her teens and continued on welfare for an average of 13 years (See, e.g., Norwood R-GA, 104 CR[8] H3333)—a category that was increasingly seen to encompass all single mothers.

The House Republicans' Personal Responsibility Act (104 H.R. 4), introduced in early January 1995 as part of the Republican "Contract with America," took aim at this archetypal "welfare mom," an image that came to encompass AFDC recipients and all other lone mothers. The primary purpose of the PRA was to eliminate the notion that the state had any responsibility toward poor families by explicitly stating that assistance was not an entitlement. With a preamble that blamed lone mothers for their own poverty, the Act contained provisions that would deny cash and other benefits to teenage unmarried mothers (but loosen eligibility requirements for teen married couples), put strict time limits on AFDC participation, and reduce work training and child-care assistance for mothers of young children.[9]

During the first two months of 1995, advocates for welfare recipients rallied to their defense and exposed welfare myths, showing, for example, that the typical mother receiving AFDC was 29, had two children and some work experience, used AFDC as a form of temporary unemployment compensation, disability benefit, or a subsidy for low wages, and concluded that women needed quality, subsidized child care, higher wages, and better work training (Spalter-Roth). In February 1995, the Council of Presidents of National Women's Organizations argued that the problem lay in labour market conditions, including discrimination, unstable jobs, and low wages, as well as the lack of educational opportunity, support services, child support, and punitive welfare regulations.

This perspective did not, however, gain much congressional following. In contrast, the Congressional Women's Caucus de-emphasized labour market conditions and concentrated on partially reconstructing the single mother as an unwilling and accidental welfare recipient who was the victim of the "deadbeat dad," reintroducing the image of the deserted mother and child that had been integral to the early century's crusade for mothers' aid (Gordon). Democrats criticized the Act for its failure to include any provisions on tougher child support collections, reiterating their disappointment that fathers' responsibilities for their children had been ignored in the general attack on the poor. In response to the vitriol leveled at lone mothers' alleged lack of responsibility, many Democrats stressed the importance of parental responsibility, arguing that if the mothers should be held responsible, so should the fathers. One of the prime movers for including support enforcement measures in the Act, a member of the Women's Caucus, Barbara Kennelly (D-CT) commented,

> All of us have heard the calls through the Halls of Congress for young mothers to be more responsible in regard to welfare reform. I completely agree. Shouldn't we also demand, equally loudly and clearly, that fathers be responsible.... Let's put that responsibility back where it belongs. Let's ensure that parents—both custodial and noncustodial—live up to their responsibilities. And let's make sure our children get the support they need and deserve. (104 CR H1035)

In a rare show of bipartisan agreement on welfare reform, a flurry of child support enforcement bills and amendments to the Act were introduced, all promising to get tough on "deadbeat dads." Only one group was exempted from this reconstruction of single mother as victim—women who refused to cooperate with support collections. Democrats and Republicans agreed that "benefits should be contingent on paternity establishment. At this time, there is no reciprocal obligation for welfare recipients to help the Government locate the absent parent" (Karen Thurman, D-FL, 104 CR H1032).

The Republican dominated House Ways and Means Committee integrated most of the proposed new provisions into the Personal Responsibility Act, although it was more "father-friendly" than the Women's Caucus proposal, offering funds to states to institute visitation enforcement measures. During the debate on the Act in late March 1995, Democrats and Republicans vied with one another on how tough they could be on deadbeat dads. Republicans argued that the child support obligation could be used to discourage out-of-wedlock births by holding up the spectre of lifelong child support payments.

Throughout the child support debate, the only visible mothers were the accidental welfare recipients—those who could conceivably cease receiving AFDC if collections were enhanced—and the negligent non-cooperators who had become the archetype of "illegitimacy." The invisible categories were the mothers who would really benefit from enhanced collections, many of whom were far from poor, and mothers who would not benefit at all, as the amount that could be collected, together with wages, would still be less than the grant amount—unless AFDC were terminated altogether.

The Republican "personal responsibility" agenda was the expression of neoliberal and neoconservative emphasis on private solutions for women's poverty and relied on the reawakening of the moral norm of the patriarchal family. Democrats, however, were not immune to casting the problem as private, although they were more likely to address questions of inadequate job preparation and support. Many Democrats favored increased support collection efforts, but saw them as insufficient to cure fundamental problems in the proposed Republican welfare cuts; they were "lipstick on the pig" (Obey D-WI, 104 CR H3627). However, throughout the 1995 "personal responsibility" debates, Republicans and many Democrats offered a conditional absolution from blame to lone mothers, but withheld it explicitly from non-cooperators and implicitly from those who could expect little or no child support from nonresident fathers. Moral rectitude for the lone mother, it seemed, depended on being tied to a man with money who abandoned her.

Although President Clinton vetoed the bill that eventually passed both House and Senate, the following year he signed into law a substantially similar bill, without many of the most problematic provisions penalizing teen and unmarried mothers (Geronimus 407-408). The new law, the Personal Responsibility and Work Opportunity Reconciliation Act (PRWORA), replaced AFDC with TANF, Temporary Assistance to Needy Families, and like the previous bill, contained the "sense of Congress" that the principal problem facing the U.S. was unmarried parenting, and marriage was "the foundation of a successful society, [and] . . . an essential institution of a successful society which promotes the interests of children." [10] The new benefit would be time-limited to a lifetime maximum of five years, eliminated any "entitlement" to benefits, giving significant discretion to the states to require paid or unpaid work, and tightened the "good cause" exemptions for cooperation with child support enforcement, while easing eligibility for two-parent families.

In the 1994 State of the Union Message, President Clinton had said, "We cannot renew our country when within a decade more than half of our children will be born into families where there is no marriage." It was the lack of a marriage—not the lack of help with the hard work of parenting—that was the problem, even to the most visible Democratic politician: "If we value responsibility, we can't ignore the $34 billion in child support absent parents ought to be paying to millions of parents who are taking care of their children. (Applause.) If we value strong families, we can't perpetuate a system that actually penalizes those who stay together."

PRWORA contained stiff, mandatory child support collection requirements and sanctions, including the suspension of drivers and trade licenses of the delinquent obligor—licenses that might be necessary for gainful employment. In both PRWORA and subsequent amendments, much was made of the support owing fathers, but nothing was said about assisting residential parents who could count on little child support because the obligated parents were poor. Instead, the bill concentrated on increasing the marriage rate, retaining the gendered construction of the child support system. For those who could not or would not rely on the marital or quasi-marital forms of distribution, there was workfare and eventually, when their sixty months of eligibility had run its course, nothing.

THE QUASI-WIFE

The normative family ideology of 1990s U.S. containing the basic logic of the child support discourse assumed that during marriage couples would form an economic community, sharing their collective resources and labour. The parents jointly contributed toward the well-being of children, whether through caretaking or paid work. This idealized community was constructed within the family economic system, according to prevailing notions of the proper roles of women and men in the family and society. Although women have an increased presence in the labour market and men are more likely to share in the care of children and the home, care remains gendered female, unpaid and invisible. The (feminine) unpaid care work still enables the (male) wage earner to pay the bills.

Assumptions about marriage were frequently reflected in justifications for employment practices that did not take responsibilities for the home into account, marginalizing women from the labour force and well-paid jobs. The hegemony of the male model in work, prompted by employer demands, meant that even "female" work did not respond well to workers' child-care responsibilities. These gendered wage and work structures reinforced the marital division of labour, marking the man as the breadwinner and the woman as the dependent care worker.

Following divorce, the norm of the married woman followed women into their single lives, and the family economic community was maintained primarily through child support and enforced in a way that it never was during the marriage. Far from ending the marriage, divorce laws maintained gendered expectations of behavior, with custody and support laws constituting the "regulation of the post-divorce family" (Thèry 78). The father in the normative description of the post-divorce family was not a caregiving low-waged father, but a football-tossing breadwinning male, and the actual practice of child support constructed the mother's interests as coterminous with the ability of the father to succeed in the economic marketplace. The mother was, in effect, a quasi-wife, both materially and discursively. As quasi-wife, the mother no longer had the duty to provide sexual or household labour for the father; her primary obligation was to provide the child's care, relying on the distribution of paternal income for well-being, in the legally constructed continuation of the family economic community, even for mothers who could not or would not rely on this community.

Prompted by this reality, many commentators criticized the divorce laws for their presumption of equality between husband and wife. Actual inequality, they argued, should be addressed through increased child support payments, property division, and a return to spousal support (e.g. Mason 49; Rhode and Minow 207). The adverse impact on women of the family economic system was solved by extending the economic community into single life, even when the parents were never married or where the idealized community never existed.

The policy emphasis on increased child support was predicated on the assumption of the ideal family economic community located within the gendered family economic system, posing the assumed well-being of women in marriage in contrast to their dramatic drop in income following divorce. In setting up the opposition between marital well-being and impoverished lone parenting, the ways that the gendered division of labour and gendered wage and work structures disadvantaged women during marriage were minimized, perpetuating inequalities and injustices woven into the family economic system itself. By relying on distribution between a breadwinning father and the caregiving wife, gendered expectations of role division and the relationship between family and society in larger social contexts remained unchallenged.

REDISTRIBUTION AND STRATIFICATION

The emphasis on child support re-crafted the public's perception of the causes for women's poverty to focus on the breakdown of the idealized family economic community. Through the construction of the post-divorce economic community by child support enforcement measures, some women were assisted, while others were harmed by the increased emphasis on child support collection as a solution to women's poverty. Lost in the common wisdom on the necessity of increased child support collections were reports and analyses that showed that the poverty of women of color frequently did not follow the same pattern as that of white women.

In a mid-1980s longitudinal study on household composition and poverty, Mary Jo Bane found that two-thirds of blacks who were poor after the break-up of a two-parent household had been poor before, compared to one-fourth of whites (Bane). Historically, the earned income of women of color had been essential to the economic well-being of their households, due to men's low wages. Furthermore, the two-parent household had not been self-sufficient under conditions of scarcity and cultural assault, relying on larger networks of extended and fictive kin (Dill 154, 165-167; Glenn 102-103). In short, poverty for women was not always due to single parenthood but frequently directly related to race and class, and a male partner's earnings could do little to relieve it because the men had low income themselves.

Scholars at the time knew that the benefit working-class women could derive from increased child support collections was small. According to one study by Garfinkel, Meyer and Sandefur, even if all child support awards were perfectly collected, there would have been only a 7% reduction in the "poverty gap" (the amount of income needed to bring family income to poverty level) for white families, and 2% for Black and Hispanic families. Using the Wisconsin standard for child support orders (17% of obligor's income for one child, and 25%, 29%, 31%, and 34% for additional children), perfectly collected, the reduction in the poverty gap for white families would have been 33%, and 22% and 17% for Hispanic and Black families, respectively (506). In addition, child support is usually collected more aggressively from low-income fathers than upper income fathers, in that in at least one study, low-income fathers were more likely to be ordered to pay more than the child support guidelines based on their income, while upper income fathers were ordered to pay less than the guidelines (Rettig, Christianson and Dahl 170).

Child support essentially attempted to redistribute income from one parent to another in order to balance the costs of raising children, in cash, time and other resources, including lost income. In 1990, the top 20 percent of U.S. families received 44.3 percent of the aggregate income, while the lowest quintile received 4.6 percent, and child support did little to remedy this, in many cases simply transferring income from one poor person to another. Child support collected from parents of children on AFDC also had the effect of removing money from low-income neighborhoods. Many low-income noncustodial parents contributed what they could to the upkeep of their children, bringing them clothes, food and toys, purchased from local businesses, which are viewed as "more authentic expressions of paternal love and responsibility and were assumed to have greater emotional significance to children than mandatory support payments" (Waller 112). But when the father is forced to pay the state agency directly, with only a portion of the payment returning to the mother, this means that the community loses (Garfinkel, Meyer and Sandefur 521). In fact, it may be said that the accepted principle for establishing a child's support rights based upon a percentage of the parents' income had an anti-redistributory message: children of wealthier parents deserve more than children of poor parents.

FALSE UNIVERSALIZATION OF WOMEN'S INTERESTS

The greatest benefit of child support enforcement in the U.S. inured to former wives of well-off men. Far less benefit went to former wives of poor men and mothers who had chosen not to have been any kind of wife. But, as we have seen, women who did not benefit were invisible—or worse—in the child support discourse. Further, some child support advocates argued that existing child support obligations should not be reduced as a consequence of any new family formation (e.g. Rhode and Minow 207). This approach set up an opposition between previous and subsequent wives and children and seemed to mirror the "family cap" rule; this rule, which by 2009 was adopted by over twenty states, most by 1998, denies additional assistance to families for children born while receiving public aid (National Conference of State Legislatures).

An additional problem with the universalization of the child support "solution" was that it did not address differences in families. Being "married" or being a "father" or "mother" may have very different meanings in different cultures. This is not only culturally constructed, by varying values and beliefs, but also materially constructed. In some cultures, the primary caretaker of children may usually be the maternal grandmother, or caretaking may be a responsibility shared among neighbors, friends, and other kin.[11] In communities where men's access to decent jobs has been limited, "kinship network" rather than "nuclear family" is usually a better descriptor of primary economic and social structures.[12] As late as 2010, about one-half of all custodial parents did not have a legal support order established. They gave numerous reasons, but at least one-third said that it was because the nonresidential parents were doing what they could, while about 17% did not want anything to do with the other parent (Grall 7).

The legal system, by defining responsibilities and rights as deriving from status as husband, father, or mother may not agree with the actual economic and social family formation as experienced by individuals, structured by beliefs and adaptations to material conditions. Where these conditions militate against conforming to the legally prescribed family form, the result can be social and economic exclusion. The discourse, then, constructed the interests of one relatively privileged group as representative of the interests of all women, even though the laws and their material and discursive effects could actually harm them, and defining those women who are not helped as deviant. In 1995, the nationally televised image of young, poor mothers blaming their poverty on the young, poor fathers of their children, gained a certain amount of social legitimacy in shifting the public blame from poor mothers to the poor fathers of their children. It is not uncommon for individuals to accept and endorse a poverty discourse that shape their lives as legitimate or illegitimate (Reid and Tom 402-403). However, in reconstructing their social legitimacy, these mothers advanced a cause that would benefit not them, for the amount these young men could pay would be negligible, but women from higher social and economic classes. It appeared that working-class women may have been in ideological service to middle-class divorced mothers.

However, this effect was most likely unintentional; it arose from a particular world view, informed by the life circumstances of the politically articulate divorced middle-class woman and her legal advocate. This more privileged mother was in a worse economic position than she was during marriage. She *did* struggle more to meet the everyday time and money costs of raising children. But the solutions she saw—and those her lawyer could effect with some small adjustments in family and collection laws—arose from within a specific space in the gendered and racially constructed class system. There may be several reasons why this relatively more advantaged group was taken to represent all lone mothers. First, those who benefitted most from child support payments—mothers of children of well-off fathers— may have been more articulate and have had greater access to venues where their voices could be heard. Second, it was an area where lawyers could be effective; the articulate and vocal legal community promoted its perceptions of the problems and solutions out toward the wider political discourse. And, child support, as privatizing the problem of women's and children's low income, was a comfortable fit with the 1990s neoliberal/neoconservative ideology.

CHILD SUPPORT AND NEOLIBERALISM

The privatization of income redistribution is entirely consistent with the classical liberal "possessive individual" that has marked the United States (and other Anglophone countries) since its inception. According to C. B. MacPherson, the ideology of the possessive individual maintains that "what makes a man human is freedom from dependence on the wills of others," and he owes nothing to society for his property, skills, and personality. He need enter into no relationship with any person, and all relationships are the bargained-for exchanges of a market society. Political society exists solely to facilitate the "orderly relations of exchange between individuals regarded as proprietors of themselves" (MacPherson 263-264). Carole Pateman shows that in the classical liberal conception of the individual, the citizen was the gendered husband/father who supported self and family with his own property. Because of their dependency, women and their children in the "traditional" family could not be possessive individuals; they were the "property" for which the possessive individual owed nothing to society, although they did have their own distinctive contribution to make as mothers (19).

Women's position within society was historically regulated through family law, which was constructed with this possessive individual and the dependent mother in mind. The essence of family law has been to define duties and rights by status rather than citizenship, and to regulate relations between individuals rather than between an individual and society. Women's rights, in classical liberalism, derived from their relationship with men. The mother and child were not really citizens in their own right but subsumed under the mantle of the father's citizenship. Their rights to well-being, if any, were derived from their status as his dependents (Brown 246-259).

When women began to rebel against this dependency/property status, classical liberal notions of equality demanded of them that they, too, become possessive individuals inhabiting a world based on market rationality instead of one focused on care. Of course, Pateman points out, this was and is impossible.

> On the one hand, to demand 'equality' is to strive for equality with men (to call for the 'rights of men and citizens' to be extended to women), which means that women must become (like) men. On the other hand, to insist... that women's distinctive attributes, capacities and activities be revalued and treated as a contribution to citizenship is to demand the im-

possible; such 'difference' is precisely what patriarchal citizenship excludes. (20)

That is, women's citizenship was either based on their adherence to the
model of the possessive individual (independent, market-based relationships), or on "women's distinctive attributes," which traditionally included
an emphasis on care, generosity, and cooperation. But this emphasis on care
and cooperation meant that they would need to be dependent, because they
unquestionably could not be independent of others' wills, needs, or demands. In the sequestering of the private, dependent, cooperative world
from the public, competitive world of market and state, dependency was
configured as a private female or infantile characteristic.

As caregivers for dependent children, doing the important, but unpaid,
work of raising the next generation, they would sustain a loss of income,
necessitating an income supplement in the form of marital distribution of
resources or assistance from the welfare state, in short, "dependency." Although familial dependency for women and children was acceptable, even
laudable, dependency vitiated the claim to citizenship. Instead, as an unarticulated member of a family, the dependent derived her claims through
the husband. Because women and children were subsumed into this entity,
represented by the male head of household, their identities, rights, and lib-
erties were derivative at best. When women's right to well-being are derivative of a breadwinner's property rights, women are distanced from the public sphere where the notions of ideal citizenship are created.[13] Concerns of
shelter, food, clothing, and care responsibilities are privatized within the local relationship. They are not a public matter. Accordingly, women's full
citizenship is not realized; she lacks the political rights that belong to citizenship. She lacks a public voice.

When dependency moved into the U.S. public sphere as "welfare," it retained its female or infantile character. Welfare was, for most of its history in
the United States, a form of "public patriarchy" (Walby 228-229), shaped by
deeply embedded patriarchal organizational and professional structures[14]
and other imperatives of the capitalist state, such as labour force control.[15]
Means-testing and other regulations have invaded privacy and stigmatized
and objectified the recipient, depriving recipients and potential recipients
of civil and political citizenship rights. "Welfare" tended to set apart those
who relied on it as somehow different from other women, without any clear
recognition that everyone is "dependent" on the state, society, and individuals in different ways and at different times (Fraser and Gordon 331-333; Lis-

ter 109-110).

Although the welfare state has been a means of social control, it was also potentially a site of struggles for economic democracy through which political and civil rights can also be strengthened.[16] As such, it could offer access to the public sphere, and a hearing for women's voices. Beginning in the 1930s, and intensified during the Welfare Rights Movements of the 1960s, the U.S. welfare state seemed to offer a means to "share in the social heritage" (Marshall 8) in the form of resources, services, and employment for working-class women. It also contained within it democratizing elements; the welfare state could give, in theory, a voice to every member of society. Formal political rights—that is, suffrage—alone have been insufficient to create economic democracy, increase working-class power, and solve gendered and racialized inequality, so long as the issues available for decision were limited to the requirements of capitalism. However, each time that a welfare issue found space in the public debate, the people to whom those issues were vital gained a little more substance to their political rights (Piven).

This promise was, however, cut short with the rise of neoliberal hegemony in the 1970s. Neoliberalism was the splicing of classical liberalism to neoclassical economics, that is, "possessive individualism" informed by radical forms of rational choice theory. The perfect society would be comprised of possessive individuals all exercising cost/benefit analysis without the interference of the state, its regulations, or especially its public benefit programs. Welfare would interfere with the workings of the market. Specifically, according to Sylvia Walby (11) neoliberal policies would require reducing state welfare spending, deregulation of worker protection, privatization of as many state functions as possible, and especially the "substitution of the market as an alternative form of governance to democracy..."

Neoliberalism's relationship to gender is contradictory. On the one hand, neoliberalism could easily accommodate the formal de-gendering of the law and legal language. No longer would we speak of the "single mother" or "deadbeat dad," but the "residential parent" and the "obligor." It would be important to nod in the direction of the lone father and equal-opportunity domestic violence, even though this "gender neutrality" covered over some very gender and class/race specific practices. However, all matters related to reproductive support—care of children, the home, the wage earner—must be the concern of the ideal individual alone. In addition, neoliberalism in the United States was in need of political allies, and these allies were found amongst social conservatives, notably the religious right.

This alliance set up some interesting contradictions, notably the conflict between the collectivism of religious conservatism and the individuation of classical liberalism. As society moved further toward privileging individualistic choice in the neoliberal consumerist framework, increasing isolation and alienation, it was no surprise that conservative actors committed deeply to social movements that seemed to reconstruct the private traditional family. The family became, in this world view, a singular unit that contained both sides of the equation. It was a site for cooperation and dependency, at the same time that it was an autonomous agent that could exercise choice. Lost in this construct was the caregiver, possessing only dependency, but neither voice nor choice.

The privatization of child support for low-income mothers accompanied the rise of neoliberalism in the 1970s, when we began to see an increased emphasis in the discourse on "family values," with the major spokespersons for neoliberalism using it at every turn. Returning responsibility for care and economic support to the privatized family was essential to the neoliberal agenda. It was not simply a matter of economics, but also of citizenship rights and control of the democratic state. The Welfare Rights Movement, the women's economic arm of the Civil Rights Movement, had begun to argue for the extension of social rights to women, in their combined role as mothers and workers, and not in their role as quasi-wives. Neoliberals saw a principal goal of welfare reform as reducing the power of interest groups and advocates to influence federal legislation. Martin Anderson, a chief bureaucrat of the Reagan administration, emphasized personal responsibility for support of dependents in his seven-point welfare reform plan (Anderson). The result was the child support enforcement reforms of the 1980s and the broad consensus in the 1995 House debates on the culpability of the deadbeat dad. Attention shifted from the inadequacy of wages, poor working conditions, work hours, and work supports, and centred on personal responsibility. If a mother could not support her children, it was the father's fault. If there was no father to blame (except if he was dead), that was the mother's fault.

In the revival of the "family values" discourse in the United States, attention was focused, not on society's duty to children, but on the parents. It was the parents' duty to stay together and support the children, regardless of their ability to do so or the cost to them on a personal level. The 1990s child support discourse sharpened this focus. Divorce became acceptable if and only if the parents continued in their gendered parental roles, the mother as caregiver/support recipient (mother/wife), and the father as the sole source of economic security. The feminist child support discourse did not directly challenge the essential content of this neoliberal hegemony, but could be considered an adaptation to the constraints it imposed. By transferring social responsibility to "the family," the neoliberal hegemony eliminated the democratic state as a site for political struggle over economic resources. If women were harmed by having to shoulder alone the time and money costs of caring work, feminist child support advocates asserted that the least the state could do was allay some of the worst problems caused by it, through redistribution between an individual who might be favored (a father) to one who is harmed (a mother). If economic relations and state policies located the sole responsibility for well-being in the private relationship, child support advocates argue that the least it can do is to give that relationship some rights. However, the private nature of that responsibility sustained no systematic challenge.

The idea that parents and children have a claim on society for economic or other forms of assistance disappeared behind the child support rhetoric. Women's solidarity was reduced to a postmodern irony: each case is heard individually, each mother pursues her own remedy against an individual father, but united by one solution patterned after a single situation—the quasi-wife of the upper income man. Collective solutions, on the other hand—state programs ensuring affordable, quality child care; union contracts protecting adequate wages, hours, and working conditions; paid parental leave—would have been more likely to create universals that attend to the "difference" posed by the woman who is not a quasi-wife.

CONCLUSION

Child support, while a necessary corrective to a gendered system of distribution of society's resources, poses problems of its own. In the debate on the state and the roles of women and family in society it carried a meaning unanticipated by its feminist supporters. The 1990s child support discourse in the U.S. affirmed the dominance of the heterosexual two-parent family as the sole legitimate social and economic form for the support of women and children through its discursive and material effects, actually harming women—and their children—who could not or would not conform to the hegemonic ideal. Child support itself is a defective system of redistribution of society's resources, often merely transferring income from one poor person to another.

Child support remains necessary, and probably will always be necessary on some level. However, if solidarity among women is to mean anything, it must mean that the problems of those with the most tenuous access to society's resources are honestly attended, not as a rhetorical device, but as the measure of the effectiveness of universal social policies. This suggests that a system of private economic distribution through marriage or child support, rent with enormous gaps through which millions of women and children fall, cannot be seen as the sole or even a primary solution for women's poverty. Instead, collective solutions are imperative that allow for difference within the politically contested framework of social rights and responsibilities.

Such a perspective necessarily calls up further debate—what sort of collective solutions, what are those rights and responsibilities? One frequently suggested solution is some sort of child support assurance common in many European countries. While some form of child support assurance would do much to help children of low-income parents, it would do little to address the situation where the mother does not wish to name the father or for some reason does not want the father in the life of the child. Even Sweden's maintenance support program (replacing the child support advance and supplement in 1996) requires parental cooperation.

Recognition for the validity of diverse family formations must be given. A more effective way to assist low-income solo parents may lie entirely outside the child support framework, with labour market, housing, child care, and cash benefits a preferable alternative, with child support enforcement and assurance a supplemental approach. The current universal solution— marital or quasi-marital distribution of resources—is a poor fit for those whose lives do not align with the quasi-wife mold. This is not to argue against the construction of universals—solidarity and effective social policy require some sort of universal—but that the construction of any universal purporting to define problems and solutions must consciously take difference into account. Instead of calling into service the emblem of the poverty-stricken lone mother to advance a solution applicable to the divorced wife of a middle-class man, it would have been more logical, effective, and solidaristic to address the problems encountered by women who could not expect financial support from the father in such a way that also benefitted the middle-class quasi-wife, and, indeed, all mothers and society as a whole.

NOTES

[1]See Weitzman for further reading

[2]See Fineman 26; Rhode and Minow 195; and Weitzman

[3]AFDC, Aid to Families with Dependent Children, was a means-tested benefit intended primarily for one-parent families. Originating as a form of support for children of widows and some other selected single mothers during the Great Depression as part of the Social Security Act, it was expanded to include even two-parent families, with several limitations. Over the years, various requirements were attached to receipt, from "suitable home" rules to work-search requirements. As a condition of receipt, mothers were required to name the father and cooperate in state efforts to obtain child support orders and payments. AFDC was eliminated in 1996, and replaced with the time-limited Temporary Assistance to Needy Families, retaining and augmenting the most stigmatizing and constrictive requirements.

[4]"IV-D" refers to section IV-D of the Social Security Act, which sets up the requirements and funding authorizations for the state agencies that pursue child support payments from non-resident parents.

[5]http://www.acf.hhs.gov/programs/css/employers/income-withholding retrieved July 31, 2012.

[6]A small "pass-through" of $50 of paid support was tacked onto the IV-D legislation in giving recipients $50 of the amount paid by the obligor, in an attempt to increase compliance. It should be noted that if an obligor paid several months of past-due support in a single month, it was common practice for agencies to "pass through" a single $50 payment for the month in which the support was paid.

[7]See Blankenhorn; and Murray

[8]All citations to CR refer to the 1995 Congressional Record, 104th Congress

[9]The Preamble to H.R. 4 read, It is the sense of the Congress that (1) marriage is the foundation of a successful society; (2) marriage is an essential social institution which promotes the interests of children and society at large; (3) the negative consequences of an out of wedlock birth on the child, the mother, and society are well documented as follows: (sixteen negative consequences, including crime, poverty, and poor school adjustment)

[10]U.S. Congress. House of Representatives. Personal Responsibility and Work Opportunity Reconciliation Act of 1996, HR 3734, Section 101. 104th Congress, 2d Session, 1996

[11]See Dill; and Glen

[12]See Collins; Stack; and Valentine
[13]See Hernes; Kittay 85-87; Lister 121; and Pateman
[14]See Acker; and Dressel
[15]See Piven and Cloward
[16]See Gough; Hernes; and Piven

WORKS CITED

Acker, Joan. "Hierarchies, Jobs, Bodies: A Theory of Gendered Organizations." *Gender & Society* 4 (1990): 139-158. Print.

Anderson, Martin. *Welfare: The Political Economy of Welfare Reform in the United States.* Stanford, CA: Hoover Institution, Stanford University, 1978. Print.

Bane, Mary Jo. "Household Composition and Poverty." *Fighting Poverty.* Eds. S.H. Danziger and D.H. Weinberg. Cambridge, MA: Harvard University Press, 1986. 209-231. Print.

Blankenhorn, David. *Fatherless America: Confronting Our Most Urgent Social Problem.* New York: Basic Books, 1995. Print.

Brown, Carol. "Mothers, Fathers, and Children: From Private to Public Patriarchy." *Women and Revolution: A Discussion of the Unhappy Marriage of Marxism and Feminism.* L. Sargent, ed. Cambridge, MA: South End Press, 1981. Print.

Bussemaker, Jet, and Kees van Kersbergen. "Gender and Welfare States: Some Theoretical Reflections." *Gendering Welfare States.* Ed. D. Sainsbury. London: Sage, 1994. 8-25. Print.

Collins, Patricia. *Black Feminist Thought.* Cambridge, MA: Unwin Hyman, 1990. Print.

Council of Presidents of National Women's Organizations. National Women's Pledge on Welfare Reform: Principles for Eliminating Poverty, read into the record by Rep. Patsy Mink, 104 CR H1684, February 13, 1995. Print.

Dill, Bonnie Thornton. "Fictive Kin, Paper Sons, and Compadrazgo: Women of Color and the Struggle for Family Survival." *Women of Color in the U.S.* Eds. M.B. Zinn and B.T. Dill. Philadelphia: Temple University Press, 1993. 149-170. Print.

Dressel, Paula. "Patriarchy and Social Welfare Work." *Social Problems* 34 (1987): 294- 309. Print.

Fineman, Martha. *The Illusion of Equality*. Chicago: University of Chicago Press, 1991. Print.

Fraser, Nancy, and Linda Gordon. "'Dependency' Demystified: Inscriptions of Power in a Keyword of the Welfare State." *Social Politics* 1 (1994): 4-31. Print.

Garfinkel, Irwin, Daniel R. Meyer, and Gary D. Sandefur. "The Effects of Alternative Child Support Systems on Blacks, Hispanics, and Non-Hispanic Whites." *Social Service Review* 66 (1992): 505-523. Print.

Geronimus, Arline T. "Teenage Childbearing and Personal Responsibility: An Alternative View." *Political Science Quarterly* 112 (1997): 405-430. Print.

Glenn, Evelyn Nakano. "Racial Ethnic Women's Labor: The Intersection of Race, Gender, and Class Oppression." *Gender, Family, and Economy: The Triple Overlap*. Ed. R.L. Blumberg. London: Sage, 1991. 173-200. Print.

Gordon, Linda. *Pitied But Not Entitled: Single Mothers and the History of Welfare*. New York: Press, 1994. Print.

Gough, Ian. *The Political Economy of the Welfare State*. London: Macmillan Press, 1979. Print.

Grall, Timothy S. Custodial Mothers and Fathers and Their Child Support: 2009 Consumer Income. U.S.B.o.t. Census, ed. Current Population Reports. Washington, D.C.: U. S. Department of Commerce, 2010. Print.

Hernes, Helga Maria. *The Dimensions of Citizenship in the Advanced Welfare State*. Ed. S. Maktutredningen. Vol. 15. Stockholm: Allmänna förl, 1988. Print.

Kittay, Eva Feder. *Love's Labor: Essays on Women, Equality, and Dependency*. New York: Routledge, 1998. Print.

Krause, Harry D. "Reflections on Child Support." *Child Support: From Debt Collection to Social Policy*. Eds. A.J. Kahn and S.B. Kamerman. Newbury Park: Sage Publications, 1988. 227-250. Print.

Lister, Ruth. *Citizenship: Feminist Perspectives*. New York: NYU Press, 2003. Print.

MacPherson, C. B. *The Political Theory of Possessive Individualism: Hobbes to Locke*. Oxford: Clarendon Press, 1962. Print.

Marshall, T. H. Bottomore T. B. *Citizenship and Social Class*. London: Pluto Press, 1992. Print.

Mason, Mary Ann. "Motherhood v. Equal Treatment." *Journal of Family Law* 29 (1990-91): 1-50. Print.

Murray, Charles. "The Coming White Underclass." *Wall Street Journal,* October 29, 1993. Print.

National Conference of State Legislatures. Family Cap Policies. Washington D.C. http://www.ncsl.org/issues-research/human-services/welfare-reform-family-cap-policies.aspx, accessed March 18, 2013.n Web.

Pateman, Carole. *The Disorder of Women: Democracy, Feminism, and Political Theory.* Stanford, California: Stanford University Press, 1989. Print.

— "Equality, Difference, Subordination: The Politics of Motherhood and Women's Citizenship." *Beyond Equality and Difference: Citizenship, Feminist Politics, Female Subjectivity.* Eds. Gisela Bock and Susan James. New York: Routledge, 1992. 1-31. Print.

Pirog, Maureen A. and Kathleen M. Ziol-Guest. "Child Support Enforcement: Programs and Policies, Impacts and Questions." *Journal of Policy Analysis and Management* 25 (2006): 943-990. Print.

Piven, Frances Fox. "Ideology and the State: Women, Power, and the Welfare State." *Women, the State, and Welfare.* Ed. Linda Gordon. Madison: The University of Wisconsin Press, 1990. 250-264. Print.

Piven, Frances Fox and Richard Cloward. *Regulating the Poor: The Functions of Public Welfare.* Updated edition. New York: Vintage Books (Random House), 1993. Print.

Reid, Colleen and Allison Tom. "Poor Women's Discourses of Legitimacy, Poverty, and Health." *Gender & Society* 20 (2006): 402-421. Print.

Rettig, Kathryn, Donna Hendrickson Christensen, and Carla M. Dahl. "Impact of Child Support Guidelines on the Economic Well-Being of Children." *Family Relations* 40 (1991): 167-175. Print.

Rhode, Deborah L. and Martha Minow. "Reforming the Questions, Questioning the Reforms: Feminist Perspectives on Divorce Law." *Divorce Reform at the Crossroads.* Ed. Steven D. Sugarman and Herma Hill Kay. New Haven, CT: Yale University Press, 1990. 191-210. Print.

Spalter-Roth, Roberta. "Welfare That Works: Increasing AFDC Mothers' Employment and Income." Testimony before the Subcommittee on Human Resources, Committee on Ways and Means, U.S. House of Representatives, 1995. (On file with author). Print.

Stack, Carol. *All Our Kin: Strategies for Survival in a Black Community.*

New York: Harper & Row, 1974. Print.

Steibel, Warren dir. "Resolved: Welfare Does More Harm Than Good." Public Broadcasting Network. 1994.

Thèry, Irene. "'The Interest of the Child' and the Regulation of the Post-Divorce Family." *Child Custody and the Politics of Gender.* Ed. Carol Smart and Selma Sevenhuijsen. New York: Routledge, 1989. 78-99. Print.

Valentine, Charles A. *Culture and Poverty.* Chicago: University of Chicago Press, 1968. Print.

Walby, Sylvia. "Theorizing Patriarchy." *Sociology* 23 (1989) 213-234. Print.

— *Globalization and Inequalities: Complexity and Contested Modernities.* Los Angeles: Sage, 2009. Print.

Waller, Maureen R. "Viewing Low-Income Fathers' Ties to Families through a Cultural Lens: Insights for Research and Policy." *The Annals of the American Academy of Political and Social Science* 629 (2010): 102-124. Print.

Weitzman, Lenore. *The Divorce Revolution.* New York: Free Press, 1985. Print.

All citations to CR refer to the 1995 Congressional Record, 104th Congress.

15.

"Who Is in Charge of the Family?"

Religious Mothering, Neoliberalism, and *REAL Women of Canada*

VANESSA REIMER

"The family alone, however, teaches the hard truths of moral values. In other words, it is the family which is the enemy of the State because it provides the formation of character which gives the young the ability to grow up to become independent, stable, functioning, and compassionate individuals."
—C. Gwendoyln Landolt. *REAL Women of Canada* newsletter, 2005

INTRODUCTION

Fundamentalist Christian morality has become so thoroughly intertwined with the political preservation of the "traditional" nuclear family structure that it may be difficult to distinguish one discursive paradigm from the other. Indeed, as feminist theologian Rosemary Radford Ruether contends, politically conservative Christians often portray themselves as restorers of what they consider to be the God-ordained Biblical form of the family which is, invariably, the white, middle-class, privatized family structure that gained prevalence in the nineteenth century (83). As such, in this essay I will explore how mothers who subscribe to fundamentalist Christian values may also be inclined to embrace conservative political ideologies that promote "the family" as a *privatized* institution through neoliberal socioeconomic policies. I also hope to further illuminate the complex implications that exist for Christian mothers when fundamentalist discourses render religious morality and conservative political ideologies to be unquestionably one and the same.

The discursive connection between neoliberalism and the preservation of "traditional family values" is not new to North American political rhetoric. Beginning in the 1970s and carrying on into the 1990s, political voices from the Right strategically attributed high interest rates, mounting national deficits, and massive debts to social welfare spending, rather than to the deregulation of international markets, which allowed businesses to cut wages and social welfare benefits in order to remain competitive (Chunn and Gavigan 736). These voices from the Right also attributed the "breakdown" of the nuclear family to the former welfare state, which was accordingly blamed for causing increased cases of single motherhood, divorce, women's paid employment, as well as the growing visibility of feminist and LGBQT activist groups—all of which were constructed as social ills (Chunn and Gavigan 22). These conservative voices accordingly argued that neoliberal socioeconomic policies were needed to stimulate economic growth. In turn, the role of federal governments in providing for citizens would have to be limited by shrinking welfare states and lowering labour costs. This socioeconomic restructuring ultimately resulted in tax cuts and the transferring of public responsibility to the private sector, in conjunction with establishing a discursive relationship between neoliberal policies and the restoration of traditional family values through the rhetoric of individual responsibility and privatization (Chunn and Gavigan 35; Madsen 26-29).

It is this discursive relationship between neoliberal socioeconomic policies and "traditional family values" that is of particular importance when considering the political affiliations of fundamentalist Christians. Within Christianity, as well as in other world religions, reliance on fundamentalist principles has become the growing solution to maintaining religious values within a changing mainstream society that is frequently perceived as being secular and disrespectful of historical traditions (Hardacre 129). Fundamentalist religious sects can thereby be understood as relying on literal readings of their canonical texts and accordingly emphasizing the maintenance of traditional gender roles within "the family" and society at large as a symbol of their religious commitments, in addition to constructing personal successes and failures as a measure of one's commitment to living a moral life. Along this trajectory, voices from the political and religious Right tend to demarcate poverty as a private moral failure linked with personal irresponsibility and disregard for religious morality, especially in the case of single mothers. Because fundamentalist Christian circles also rely on literal interpretations of the Bible to demarcate men's and women's roles within the domestic sphere and society at large, the notion of maintaining "the home" as a site of traditional morality becomes critically important during times of societal change (Colaner 98-99; Colaner and Giles 527-528).

"THE HOME"

Fundamentalist evangelical voices have been particularly prominent in bringing the Biblical hermeneutic concerning family values into the public sphere in response to feminist movements and LGBQT movements—both of which challenge the common sense ideologies that construct the patriarchal nuclear family as being unquestionably natural and universally desirable (Colaner 98; Vavrus 50). As these perceived social ills become increasingly visible, the need for "the home" to function as a private, moral haven that is separate from secular society becomes exceedingly crucial for many fundamentalist Christian families. This notion of "the home" can be further contextualized in the theory of religious subcultural strength which contends that, in historical and contemporary contexts, religions thrive when they provide clear beliefs and practices that strengthen group identity and distinguish one's religious subculture from the secular and religious alternatives (Gallagher 216). Combined with discourses of fundamentalism which render changes in family structures and the secularization of government to be morally deleterious, the result is a rhetorical emphasis on separation from, rather than engagement with, the immoral "outside world." It is thus likely that fundamentalist Christian circles may embrace neoliberal socioeconomic policies, at least in part, because they operate on the principle of maintaining a privatized homeplace without interference from secular government or societal influences. Such policies theoretically enable families to further separate themselves from a perceived immoral society, and this separation seems to be especially desirable when it comes to issues of social reproduction, and specifically issues of child-care.

MATERNAL THINKING

Because fundamentalist Christian circles place a crucial emphasis on the maintenance of patriarchal nuclear family values and gender roles, the onus to maintain this domestic privatization falls with particular weight upon the shoulders of fundamentalist Christian women who are mothers. Just as mothers are expected to perform the bulk of child-care duties within fundamentalist Christian families because it is believed to be their God-ordained role, women in turn function as the primary religious enculturators of their young children (Levitt 531-536). As such, these women have a particular stake in maintaining the privacy of the domestic sphere so that they can socialize their children into their religious value system with little interference from a society that they perceive to be "secular." To illustrate this point further, it is relevant to consider how this potential desire for economic and familial privatization is contextualized within Sara Ruddick's theory of maternal thinking. She contends that mothering and child-rearing practices must always be considered in the context of their history, culture, and material conditions, and she identifies three factors which govern maternal practice therein—preservation, growth, and acceptability (98). While the notion of preservation mainly refers to the physical care and nurturance of a child, those of growth and acceptability are more intricately tied to the mother's own peer group and its corresponding social values (102). As such, because women are regarded as the God-ordained primary caregivers and enculturators of their children within fundamentalist Christian circles, mothers will be subject to scrutiny and judgement when there is a "malfunction in the growth process" (98) of their children. Thus, these women may not only be perceived as inadequate mothers by their religious peer group should their children fail to fully reproduce its standards of acceptability, but these women may also be perceived as inadequate Christians because of this failure.

The discursive connection between neoliberal socioeconomic policies and ideologies of Christian morality is thus illuminated within a framework of maternal thinking. Historically within Canada and the United States the rhetoric of restoring traditional family values has been strategically linked to ideologies of individual responsibility and privatization, as well as to economic policies which incur this privatization through a shrinking social safety net and deregulated markets. These neoliberal policies have been implemented throughout the same decades in which the patriarchal nuclear family has seemingly diminished, while feminist and LGBQT movements have become increasingly visible. Collectively these societal changes pose a threat to fundamentalist Christian ideologies which perceive the white, middle-class, heterosexual, privatized family structure to be God-ordained. Thus, women who subscribe to fundamentalist Christian beliefs may value the neoliberal rhetoric of privatization because it will theoretically enable them to enculturate their children within a moral homeplace without secular State or societal interference. To explore this argument, I will now examine how the aforementioned discursive connections between fundamentalist Christian morality, traditional family values, and neoliberalism are evident in a selection of publications by *REAL Women of Canada* — a conservative Christian group who has been vocally opposed to LGBQT rights, feminism, women's reproductive choices, as well as Canada's now defunct national child-care program.

REAL WOMEN OF CANADA

The "real" in *REAL Women of Canada* stands for "Realistic, Equal, Active, for Life," and the group identifies as an NGO in special consultative status with the economic and social council of the United Nations.[1] It was federally incorporated in 1983, and it claims to represent a broad spectrum of Canadian women who, until its formation, did not have a public forum in which to express their views. A further look at the organization's website, however, reveals that this broad spectrum of women is comprised of those who oppose the "established feminist groups," thus constructing a dichotomy between feminists and the rest of Canada's women, with *REAL Women* presuming to speak for the latter.[2] As such, it identifies as an alternative women's movement which supports traditional family values. I will now briefly explain why critical discourse analysis is a useful method for understanding these "traditional family values" as they are constructed throughout *REAL Women*'s publications.

Feminist ethical frameworks, which seek to deconstruct and problematize sexism in its many forms, distinguish feminist research from other academic approaches. In this regard, discursive approaches to feminist research focus on the social construction and fluidity of power, particularly as it is constructed in the realm of cultural texts. Discourse analysis is thus largely concerned with the process of communication, and language can accordingly be understood as the primary force that produces and reproduces ideology (Leavy 98; Speer 784). I applied this research method to a purposive selection of *REAL Women*'s publications from 2004 to 2012 that are available on their official website. While *REAL Women* addresses a range of what it asserts to be problematic social issues, I focused on the recurring discourses of religion, women's reproductive choices, child-care, LGBQT rights, and feminism — all of which are connected either directly or indirectly with neoliberal policies that advocate for various facets of socioeconomic privatization.

PRIVATIZING CHILD-CARE

To begin, *REAL Women*'s garnered support for neoliberal policies is perhaps no more blatant than in its opposition to Canada's now defunct national child-care program. Canada's Liberal Party under Paul Martin began implementing a national child-care program in 2005, which would have cost $5 billion in tax revenue over a period of five years (Manu 242). When the Conservatives were elected to power in 2006 under Stephen Harper, they discarded the program and instead implemented the *Universal Child Care Benefit*, which would provide a maximum of $1,200 per year to families for each child under the age of six. This alternative program was implemented with the rhetoric of providing choices for parents to decide how they want to care for their children, even though the program has been criticized for its insufficient provisions and thus inability to really provide substantive choices for parents, and particularly for single mothers (Campbell 173-174; Manu 243-244). Its implementation was also in spite of the fact that there had been a steadily growing demand for regulated child-care spaces across the country (Madsen 55; Michalopoulos 466). *REAL Women* dedicates considerable space in its bi-monthly newsletter publications throughout this time period to the issue of child care, and the theory of religious subcultural strength and its discursive connection to neoliberal socioeconomic policies is profoundly evident in the organization's vehement opposition to national child-care.

This opposition is perhaps most tellingly expressed in a 2005 analysis written by *REAL Women*'s national vice president C. Gwendolyn Landolt, titled *Who is in Charge of the Family?*[3] Here she contends that the family is a community of love and solidarity that is best positioned to teach, among other things, the spiritual and religious values which are essential for the development and well-being of its own members. The family is also proclaimed to be a "haven in a heartless world" and the "cement that holds society together." These discourses meticulously echo the sentiments of Christian fundamentalism which construct "the home" as a necessary moral sphere where children can be socialized into the family's religious values that are otherwise devalued by a secular State and society. To emphasize this point, Landolt argues that the Liberal Party's national day-care program is the most recent example of the government's attempt to "interfere" in family life. She also equates this perceived interference with attempts made by Adolf Hitler and Joseph Stalin to destroy the family unit, since they regarded the family to be a dangerous threat to the power of the State.

By equating a national child-care program with the historical efforts of totalitarian dictatorships to eradicate the family unit in its entirety, a clear discursive connection is made: The State is a secular body that wishes to mould children into secular citizens that will fulfil its desired roles, although what these roles are comprised of, aside from being "secular," remains ambiguous. Therefore it is pertinent that the religious family maintains its ability to enculturate children in accordance with its values without interference from the secular State. The solution to this perceived problem is the privatization of the family, which can be ensured through neoliberal socioeconomic policies. As such, Landolt goes on to argue that the government exploits families by taxing them so heavily that they are left with little discretionary income, thereby forcing both parents into the paid workforce. She further contends that the strength and solidarity of the family is undermined by the government's "intrusion" in the personal decision making of the family. This discourse invariably echoes voices from the religious and political Right that blame excessive taxes and a large social safety net for unsustainable incomes, rather than the neoliberal policies that deregulate markets and thereby allow businesses to slash wages and benefits. As such, *REAL Women*'s solution to the problem at hand is not government intervention to remedy deregulated markets on behalf of its citizens, but further social and economic privatization through tax cuts.

This discursive connection between traditional family values and economic privatization is evident throughout various other *REAL Women* publications that discuss the child-care issue. For instance, alarmist rhetoric is used in a 2004 newsletter to argue that, should a national child-care program be implemented, Canada will turn into a "truly socialist country" in that the State, rather than parents, will be raising the nation's children.[4] Similarly, in a 2005 newsletter it is maintained that the elitist government is intentionally withholding its true political intentions behind the national child-care program from Canadians, and that the government wishes to make important decisions regarding child care on behalf of its citizens.[5] These discourses reinforce the supposed conflict that exists between the secular State and the moral family unit. Unsurprisingly, in a 2006 *REAL Women* post-election newsletter, the Conservatives' *Universal Child Care Benefit* is lauded as providing the needed opportunities for individual families to choose their child care options, including community care provided by religious organizations.[6]

REPRODUCING THE NATION

REAL Women's support for neoliberal socioeconomic policies, which are consequently informed by socially conservative and fundamentalist religious ideologies, is further solidified when the organization's views on child care are contextualized alongside its views on women's reproductive choices. While the organization's title directly identifies its "for life" stance, the root of the organization's anti-choice mantra arguably surpasses the issues of abortion and contraception. As such, nationalist rhetoric is adopted throughout *REAL Women*'s publications to discuss what it deems to be the culprit causes and dire consequences of Canada's declining birth rate. In this regard, Patrizia Albanese contends that nationalist discourse tends to construct women as symbols of the nation, as well as reproducers of it (829-830). Women of childbearing age are therefore expected to physically reproduce "the nation," not just by giving birth, but also by preserving the myth of ethnic "purity" by giving birth to the "right" kind of children. As such, women must also enculturate their children in accordance with the nation's traditions and values in order to preserve it and protect it from foreign influences. On the whole, then, nationalist discourse calls upon women to sacrifice their bodies, needs, and desires in order to perform motherhood for the sake of the nation, and it is women's collective duty to reproduce desirable citizens for the future (835).

REAL Women utilizes these tools of nationalist discourse throughout its publications which discuss Canada's dwindling birth rate. For instance, a 2011 newsletter titled *Canada's Birth Rate Rises at Glacial Speed*[7] opens with the proclamation that "No one can put their finger on exactly why Canadian women are so reluctant to give birth." It goes on to suggest several reasons why this may be the case, including the relevant possibility that women in the paid workforce cannot cope with large families. However, it concludes with the more prominent speculation that "Maybe it's the material nature of our times—when career goals and acquiring nice houses, cars and vacations are regarded as more important than children." Similarly, in a 2006 newsletter titled *Prosperous Canada is Dying*[8] it is argued that "[Canadians'] standard of living is going to have to be fundamentally changed to adjust to the fact that we just won't have enough workers to provide the money necessary to sustain Canadians at their present level of comfort." As such, the question is posed as to what factors have caused "[Canadian women] to go from a baby boom high of four children per mother in 1960 to our dismal 1.5 children today?" Here the birth control pill and legalized abortion are among the reasons listed, along with women's higher levels of education and career opportunities which provide them with "economic independence and an alternative to motherhood." That most of Canada's women (including mothers) who are employed in the public sphere for pay do not engage in fulfilling "career" work, but rather work out of necessity in part-time, temporary, contract, and low-wage positions without the possibility for sustainable maternity leave or affordable child-care—all the symptoms of neoliberal deregulation and privatization (England 138; Vavrus 58)—is not mentioned.

REAL Women's utilization of nationalist discourse thus becomes evident within these two articles: Canadian women are shirking their duty to the nation by pursuing careers and economic success rather than dedicating their "peak fertile years"[9] to having children. Along this trajectory, *Prosperous Canada is Dying* goes on to discuss the role of immigration in Canada's dwindling birth rate. Here *REAL Women* acknowledges that Canada does require immigrants to help amend the situation, however it further purports that immigration "is not the solution" to the larger problem at hand. It goes on to argue that "open immigration policies raise many other issues [...] such as national security, as well as the problem of family immigration that makes little economic contribution to Canada, while straining our social services and especially, our health care system." Here a dichotomy is established between "us"—those who belong in "the nation" of Canada as legitimate citizens—and the "other," who comes to Canada to reap the benefits without contributing to the nation's well-being in turn. It is then argued that "high immigration creates assimilation problems, especially in the major cities of Montreal, Toronto, and Vancouver to which immigrants migrate and where in 20 years' time, Europeans will become a visible minority." It is thus implied that an influx of immigrants will not only drain Canada's national resources, but also compromise the nation's mythical ethnic purity, since the possibility of Canadians from white European descent becoming a minority in large urban centres is constructed as a "problem." As such, it would seem that it is not "Canadian women" as a whole who need to produce more children, but *white* Canadian-born women whom *REAL Women* presumes to share its traditions and values.

Collectively, *REAL Women*'s nationalist discourses construct white, Canadian-born women as a culprit cause of the nation's future economic uncertainty. It is thereby interesting to note that, while *REAL Women* purports to speak for a "broad spectrum of Canadian women" who have been silenced by the feminist movement, it would seem that the majority of women in Canada do not share its views on women's collective duty to bear children, since they are not producing as many children as the organization deems to be necessary. The same can be argued of *REAL Women*'s religious beliefs, which the majority of Canada's "real" women clearly do not share. As such, in addition to women shirking their duties as citizens by failing to produce *REAL Women*'s desired number of children, religious discourse is also utilized to construct Canada's dwindling birth rate as a moral issue. To that end, a statement made by Pope Benedict XVI when addressing Canadian Catholic Bishops in May 2006 is quoted: "Canada's plummeting birth rate is due to the pervasive effects of secularism. No longer [...] is there trust in God's providence and care which helps couples to see the good in one another and human society and to trust in and hope for the future."[10] Furthermore, in a 2004 newsletter titled *The Future of Christianity in Canada*[11] it is argued that Evangelical Christianity and Catholicism will "save" Canada from its declining birth rate, and that "Members of these faithful churches are already turning their backs on the negative momentum created by couples who find it too strenuous, too expensive or too troublesome to raise children." It becomes clear, then, that women's "unwillingness" to bear many children is a direct result of secularism, consequently constructing women who do produce large families as moral, seemingly as long as these women are Canadian-born, Christian, and of white-European descent.

The discursive link between preserving "traditional family values" and increasing Canada's birth rate, as well as implementing socioeconomic policies that encourage privatized child care, accordingly becomes clear throughout *REAL Women*'s publications. It is the responsibility of individual Canadian-born women to act morally and dutifully by reproducing ethnically desirable future citizens for the Canadian nation, and it is consequently their individual responsibility to care for their children and enculturate them in accordance with the nation's "traditional" values, which *REAL Women* singularly equates with fundamentalist Christian values. The possibility of the modern, secular State interfering in this private, familial enculturation process accordingly poses a threat, to which neoliberal socioeconomic policies are posited as the ultimate solution.

In this regard, the religiosity of *REAL Women* is further revealed both blatantly and through the subtle rhetoric of morality throughout its publications. Some of the more obvious examples include an enthusiastic review of *The Next Christendom: The Coming of Global Christianity*,[12] a book that celebrates Christianity's growth in the global South as well as in predominantly Muslim countries. Similarly, a 2004 newsletter laments the abdication of the Lord's Prayer in public schools,[13] as another argues that it is a well-established fact that Christians in Canada are targeted for marginalization in the hopes of creating a Post-Christian society.[14] As such, in addition to these societal changes ushered in by the modern, secular State, traditional-religious families also require protection from two other immoral groups—"the homosexuals" and "the feminists."

"THE HOMOSEXUALS"

The perceived attack on traditional family values by "the State" is exacerbated in *REAL Women*'s numerous publications that discuss the interference of "homosexual activists" in the public school system. This sentiment is perhaps epitomized in a 2009 newsletter ironically titled *Intolerance*[15] where it is argued that there is a cultural struggle between those who support a secular, materialistic society, with no restrictions on sexual and other behaviors, and those who desire a society which respects the law, basic human rights and freedoms. In this case the former group refers to "the homosexuals" and their supporters, and the latter group ultimately refers to *REAL Women* and those who support its fundamentalist Christian ideologies, thus constructing an actively antagonistic relationship between the two. Similarly, in an analysis titled *How Same Sex Marriage Legislation Will Affect Our Future*[16] it is lamented that thousands of years of moral law have been overturned in the "culture war" that has granted the "homosexual lifestyle" legal and social acceptance. The article concludes with the dark contention that "the final struggle [...] is between the believers and the non-believers. Will man become a slave to the state, which will regulate his every thought and expression, and demand the abandonment of human reason and remove all moral restraints imposed by human experience?"

The relationship that *REAL Women* constructs between itself and "the homosexuals" is evident within these articles; the former is aligned with the rhetoric of morality, freedom and reason, and the latter is constructed as secular, materialistic, and enslaved to the State. Moreover, the antagonistic relationship that is presumed to exist between the two is revealing as *REAL Women* reinforces the need to maintain religious subcultural strength in the face of an opposition that actively seeks to eradicate Christian moral values. Along this trajectory, publications such as a 2004 newsletter titled *The Real Reason Why Homosexuals Are In Our Schools*[17] further illustrate *REAL Women*'s fear that children are being exposed to secular ideologies through LGBQT activist groups. Here it is implied that "homosexual activists" have strategically concocted a narrative about homophobic bullying being a problem in schools, an issue that *REAL Women* adapts a noticeably cavalier attitude toward, so that they can "infiltrate" the schools to spread their "propaganda." It thus becomes clear that *REAL Women*'s anxiety toward LGBQT groups is at least partially rooted in the latter's potential ability to influence children by engaging in the social reproduction process through the public education system.

Collectively, while *REAL Women*'s overt opposition to LGBQT groups does not directly incur the support of neoliberal socioeconomic policies, its connection to family privatization and the theory of religious subcultural strength is intricate as it is acute. The "homosexual activists" are rhetorically aligned with the modern, secular State, since the latter supports the former through its policies that undermine universal adherence to fundamentalist Christian ideologies. In conjunction with other secular influences such as LGBQT groups, the secular State assumes an actively antagonistic role in eradicating traditional family values. As such, the theory of religious subcultural strength infers the need for social and economic privatization in order to allow the religious family unit to protect its children from immoral outside influences, further illustrating the link between religious values and the imperative to support neoliberal policies that would provide opportunities for such privatization. This discursive connection is likewise apparent in *REAL Women*'s disparaging criticisms of feminism.

"THE FEMINISTS"

As previously mentioned, *REAL Women* establishes a dichotomous relationship between itself and feminists as it simultaneously claims to speak for "a broad spectrum" of Canadian women who have been silenced by the feminist movement. Its stance toward feminism is perhaps most vividly expressed in a 2009 newsletter which argues that the "militant bureaucrats" of the Royal Commission on the Status of Women have given millions of dollars of taxpayers' money to Canadian feminist groups in order to further the feminist ideology in schools, universities, government, and the courts.[18] Here *REAL Women* purports that "the feminists" use tax money to pay their own salaries and push their narrow agenda on the rest of the country, ultimately implying that they do not seek to serve the interests of "real" Canadian women. This reinforces the overlying dichotomy that *REAL Women* seeks to establish between itself and the "professional feminists," with the latter being disinterested in and disconnected from the well-being of Canadian women.

This discourse recurs throughout a number of publications that discuss the issues of child welfare and education, where feminist interests are directly aligned with those of the secular State. For instance, in a 2009 newsletter C. Gwendolyn Landolt blames feminists for the perceived social travesties resulting from the 1986 *Divorce Act*, which provided Canadians with the legal option of no-fault divorce.[19] Here it is argued that this act allows husbands to walk away from their wives and children, often leaving them to live in poverty, and that this act was the ultimate result of feminist initiatives. It is then stated that the low-income rates for female lone-parent families have been consistently above 50% since the 1980s when no-fault divorce came into effect, inferring a causal relationship between the two events. Landolt accordingly argues that the solution to the problem of child poverty is to strengthen marriage relationships, and she constructs feminism as the culprit cause of child poverty since it is also deemed to be the key force behind no-fault divorce. Similar to previously mentioned articles, this argument neglects to acknowledge the role that neoliberal socioeconomic policies play in creating child poverty by failing to ensure adequate wages and social welfare benefits to single (or partnered) mothers with children (Campbell 193; Madsen 25-26).

CONCLUSION

The purpose of this study is to generate a critical understanding of the types of ideologies that permeate fundamentalist Christian circles, and to reveal how political support for neoliberal policies is often intricately connected to the rhetoric of religious morality. Moreover, this connection is frequently communicated in absolute terms, so that it is seemingly impossible to be a "true" Christian while supporting socialist values, feminist values, or rights for LGBQT groups. These discourses place mothers who subscribe to fundamentalist Christian belief systems in a particularly precarious position— not only because fundamentalism leaves little space for women themselves to critique the political ideologies that are strategically aligned with Christian morality, but also because mothers are charged with the primary responsibility of ensuring that their children grow into individuals who are deemed acceptable within their religious peer groups. And so, as the secular "outside world" continues to defy the traditions of Christian fundamentalism, mothers may face mounting pressure to preserve the privatization of the home so that their children can grow into acceptable Christian adults without secular interference.

This is not to suggest that women who subscribe to fundamentalist Christian belief systems are victims of false consciousness. On the contrary, women can and do question, negotiate, and reject religious values that do not contribute to their spiritual growth. In this regard, while *REAL Women of Canada* may write and speak on behalf of its own members, it is problematic that this organization purports to speak for a broad spectrum of "real" Canadian women, let alone for most Christian women. *Real Women* constructs Christian morality within the narrow confines of fundamentalist theology and conservative political ideologies that take for granted a shared opposition to feminism and rights for LGBQT groups. However, this overlooks the existence of Christian feminist organizations, such as the American-based Evangelical and Ecumenical Women's Caucus, which integrate the core values of Christian canonical texts with feminist ethics and find them to be quite compatible.[20] This also overlooks the existence of feminist theologians, LGBQT Christians, as well as liberal Christians more generally who believe that their religious traditions and canonical texts need not be understood and applied in such absolute terms.[21] It is important for *REAL Women* to transparently acknowledge its specific religious affiliations, and to openly discuss how its understandings of morality intersect with its conservative political ideologies, rather than take for granted that the two are identical and inseparable. Doing so would duly complicate the problematic dichotomy that the organization constructs between elite secular feminists and the rest of Canada's "real" women.

The second purpose of this chapter is to emphasize the need for feminist academics and activists to understand and critically evaluate the complex discursive relationships that exist between political and religious ideologies within fundamentalist circles. Fostering such a critical examination is necessary when engaging in constructive dialogues with women whose world views are seemingly incompatible with a feminist ethical framework. Such dialogues with religious women who may or may not advocate for feminism are also increasingly necessary as fundamentalism becomes the growing solution for organized religion to cope with societal changes. The goal is not agreement, but understanding; because these women's lived experiences must be contextualized within their unique historical, material and ideological conditions if feminism's contentious political goal of solidarity is to continue its progression.

NOTES

[1] *REAL Women of Canada* official website home page
http://www.realwomenofcanada.ca/
[2] *REAL Women of Canada* official website "Our Views" page:
http://www.realwomenofcanada.com/page/ourviews.html
[3] *REAL Women of Canada* Analysis Report (n.d.):
http://www.realwomenofcanada.ca/publications/analysis-reports
[4] *REAL Women of Canada* newsletter titled Alert: National Day Care Plan (n.a. November-December 2004)
[5] *REAL Women of Canada* newsletter titled Propaganda On Childcare (n.a. March-April 2005)
[6] *REAL Women of Canada* newsletter titled Further Conservative Plans on Childcare (n.a. November-December 2006)
[7] *REAL Women of Canada* newsletter (n.a. July-August 2011)
[8] *REAL Women of Canada* newsletter (n.a. July-August 2006)
[9] *REAL Women of Canada* newsletter titled Canada's Birth Rate Rises at Glacial Speed (n.a. July-August 2011
[10] *REAL Women of Canada* newsletter titled Prosperous Canada is Dying (n.a. July-August 2006)
[11] *REAL Women of Canada* newsletter (n.a. July-August 2004)
[12] *REAL Women of Canada* newsletter (n.a. July-August 2004). See Jenkins for book reference.
[13] *REAL Women of Canada* newsletter titled The New Student's Prayer (n.a. November-December 2004)
[14] *REAL Women of Canada* newsletter titled The Future for Christianity in Canada (n.a. July-August 2004)
[15] *REAL Women of Canada* newsletter (n.a. November-December 2009
[16] *REAL Women of Canada* analysis (n.a. n.d.):
http://www.realwomenofcanada.ca/publications/analysis-reports/
[17] *REAL Women of Canada* newsletter (n.a. September-October 2004)

[18] *REAL Women of Canada* newsletter titled The Status of Women Must be Abandoned: An Egregious Abuse of Taxpayers' Money (n.a. November-December 2009)

[19] *REAL Women of Canada* newsletter titled *The Tragedy of No-Fault Divorce* (March-April 2009)

[20] Evangelical and Ecumenical Women's Caucus official website: http://www.eewc.com/about/

[21] For further reading see Mary Farrell Bednarowski's *The Religious Imagination of American Women* (1999), Ursula King's *Women and Spirituality: Voices of Protest and Promise* (1993), and Rosemary Radford Ruether's *Sexism and God-Talk: Toward a Feminist Theology* (1983); also see the official website for the Gay Christian Network

WORKS CITED

Albanese, Patrizia. "Territorializing Motherhood: Motherhood and Reproductive Rights in Nationalist Sentiment and Practice." *Maternal Theory: Essential Readings.* Ed. Andrea O'Reilly. Toronto: Demeter, 2007. 828-839. Print.

Bednarowski, Mary Farrell. *The Religious Imagination of American Women.* Bloomington: Indiana UP. 1999. Print.

Campbell, Angela. "Proceeding With 'Care': Lessons to be Learned from the Canadian Parental Leave and Quebec Daycare Initiatives in Developing a National Childcare Policy." *Canadian Journal of Family Law* 22 (2006): 171-222. Print.

Chunn, Dorothy E. and Shelly A.M. Gavigan. "From Mothers' Allowance to Mothers Need Not Apply: Canadian Welfare Law as Liberal and Neo-Liberal Reforms." *Osgoode Hall Law Journal* 45.4 (2007): 733-771. Print.

Colaner, Colleen W. and Steven M. Giles. "The Baby Blanket or the Briefcase: The Impact of Evangelical Gender Role Ideologies on Career and Mothering Aspirations of Female Evangelical College Students." *Sex Roles* 58 (2007): 526-534. Print.

Colaner, Colleen W. "Exploring the Communication of Evangelical Families: The Association Between Evangelical Gender Role Ideology and Gender Communication Patterns." *Communication Studies* 60.2 (2009): 97-113. Print.

England, Kim. "Home, Work and the Shifting Geographies of Care." *Ethics, Place and Environment* 13.2 (2010): 131-150. Print.

Gallagher, Sally K. "The Marginalization of Evangelical Feminism." *Sociology of Religion* 65.3 (2004): 215-237. Print.

Gavigan, Shelley and Dorothy Chunn. *Legal Tender of Gender: Law, Welfare, and the Regulation of Women's Poverty.* Oxford: Harcourt, 2010. Print.

Hardacre, Helen. "The Impact of Fundamentalisms on Women, the Family, and Interpersonal Relations." *Fundamentalisms and Society: Reclaiming the Sciences, the Family, and Education.* Eds. Martin E. Marty and R. Scott Appleby. Chicago: U of Chicago P, 1993. 129-150. Print.

Jenkins, Philip. *The Next Christendom: The Coming of Global Christianity.* Oxford: Oxford University Press, 2011.

King, Ursula. *Women and Spirituality: Voices of Protest and Promise* (2nd Ed.). University Park: Pennsylvania State UP, 1993. Print.

Leavy, Patricia. "Feminist Postmodernism and Poststructuralism." *Feminist Research Practice: A Primer.* Eds. Sharlene Hesse-Biber and Patricia Leavy. Thousand Oaks: Sage, 2007. 83-108. Print.

Levitt, Mairi. "Sexual Identity and Religious Socialization." *The British Journal of Sociology* 46.3 (1995): 529-536. Print.

Madsen, Lene. "Citizen, Worker, Mother: Canadian Women's Claims to Parental Leave and Childcare." *Canadian Journal of Family Law* 19 (2002): 12-74. Print.

Manu, Vera. Legislative Notes: Budget 2010 and the Universal Child Care Benefit: An Inquiry into the Gendered Nature of Childcare in Canada. *Canadian Journal of Women and the Law* 22 (2010): 241-246. Print.

Michalopoulos, Charles and Philip K. Robins. "Employment and Child-Care Choices of Single-Parent Families in Canada and the United States." *Journal of Population Economics* 15 (2002): 465-493. Print.

REAL Women of Canada Official Website. Home Page. Retrieved March 3, 2012 from: http://www.realwomenca.com/ Web.

REAL Women of Canada Official Website. Home Page. Retrieved February 18, 2013 from http://www.realwomenofcanada.ca/ Web.

Ruddick, Sara. *Maternal Thinking: Toward a Politics of Peace.* Boston: Beacon, 1995. Print.

Ruether, Rosemary Radford. *Sexism and God-Talk: Toward a Feminist Theology.* Boston: Beacon, 1983. Print.

— "Christianity in the Family: Ancient Challenge, Modern Crisis." *Conrad*

Grebel Review 19.2 (2001): 83-95. Print.

Speer, Susan A. "What Can Conversation Analysis Contribute to Feminist Methodology? Putting Reflexivity into Practice." *Discourse and Society* 13.6 (2002): 783-803. Print.

Vavrus, Mary Douglas. "Opting Out Moms in the News: Selling New Traditionalism in the New Millennium." *Feminist Media Studies* 7.1 (2007): 47-63. Print.

Christian Feminism Today Official Website. About EEWC-Christian Feminism Today. Retrieved March 20 2012 from: http://www.eewc.com Web.

Gay Christian Network Official Website. Home Page. Retrieved March 22, 2012 from: http://gaychristian.net/ Web.

16.

When Neoliberalism Intersects with Post-Second Wave Mothering

Reinforcing Neo-traditional American Family Configurations and Exacerbating the Post-Second Wave Crisis in Femininity

LYNN O'BRIEN HALLSTEIN

INTRODUCTION

Contemporary motherhood[1] in America is ensconced in what I refer to as a new post-second wave crisis in femininity that emerges when high-achieving women become mothers. While much has been written about the crisis in masculinity across disciplines[2] as a result of the gains brought about by second-wave feminism and the concurrent changes to gender roles and assumptions, little has been written about the contemporary crisis women face as second-wave beneficiaries and mothers: their lives are split between newfound gains in the public sphere as unencumbered women (women without children) and old gender-based, oppressive family-life roles in the private sphere that continue to place primary responsibility for child-rearing and care on women after they become mothers. In short, many women face a crisis after becoming mothers because the newfound gender equality they experience in the public sphere, particularly within educational and professional institutions, has not been met in the private sphere. Thus, contemporary women's lives are split between post-second wave gains in the public sphere and oppressive pre-second wave gendered-based roles in the private sphere.

In its foci on individual choice, personal responsibility, and privatization, neoliberalism intersects with the post-second wave context in ways that "resolve" the post-second wave crisis in femininity by reinforcing, encouraging, and further entrenching a neo-traditional family configuration —a "new" sophisticated-looking family configuration that continues to place the responsibility of child-rearing on mothers, ultimately erodes many of the gains in the public sphere that unencumbered women enjoy, and lays the foundation to exacerbate rather than resolve the crisis.

POST-SECOND WAVE MOTHERHOOD AND SPLIT SUBJECTIVITY

This chapter explores contemporary motherhood in neoliberal America by focusing on mothers who are both high-achieving and privileged: I address the lives of women who are highly educated and who have the various sorts of race, class, and heterosexual privileges that allow them to make the kinds of choices I discuss later in this chapter. Consequently, I am primarily talking about women who are high-achieving professional women who have graduated from leading colleges, earned graduate degrees, and pursued successful careers in their chosen fields prior to motherhood (Stone 22). Although I am writing about American women within an American context, I do draw upon some Canadian and British scholarship.

For high-achieving American women, the crisis in femininity emerges because contemporary motherhood is unfolding within a post-second wave context. When I use the term post-second wave, I mean to suggest "after second wave feminism" or "as a result of second wave feminism." By doing so, I also mean we live in a post-feminist context. Unlike much popular writing, I do not employ the term to suggest that all gender problems have been solved via second wave feminism, and, as a result, there is no longer a need for feminist thinking and political action. Rather, as does Angela McRobbie, I am suggesting contemporary motherhood is shaped by a post-feminist context where post-feminism is understood "to refer to an active process by which feminist gains of the 1970s and 80s come to be undermined" (*Post-Feminism* 255). One post-feminist hallmark is contemporary mothers' split subjectivity: women's subjectivity is split between second wave feminist gains in the public sphere and ongoing and patriarchal gender-based roles in the private sphere.

This contemporary split subjectivity is complex because it simultaneously reveals the gains and ongoing gender-based oppression that shape women's lives today. As gender roles and expectations have changed for both men and women in the public sphere, single or unencumbered—unencumbered with or from children—men's and women's lives are now "more similar," as long as both men and women adhere to the norms and institutional assumptions of professional organizations, including the male organizing systems that undergird professional institutions. However, becoming a mother fundamentally undermines this perceived similarity, and changes women's lives in ways that most often do not affect many men's lives after they become normative fathers. Indeed, feminist writers and scholars[3] have all shown that, even though second wave feminism opened up access to educational and professional contexts for at least already privileged women, women still have primary responsibility for child care and child-rearing once they have children. Popular writers,[4] for example, all argue that this is the case even when women work and across class lines. Ann Crittenden reveals that women's responsibility for child-rearing and care emerges even if a couple shared household labour before the arrival of a child. As she puts it: "Before the arrival of the first child, couples tend to share the house work fairly equally. But something about a baby encourages the resurgence of traditional gender roles" (25).

Another striking consequence of second wave beneficiaries' split lives is that most educated and class-privileged mothers either lay the groundwork for a professional career or establish a career before they become mothers. As Andrea O'Reilly argues, "Today, for the majority of middle-class women, motherhood is embarked upon only after a career is established, when the woman is in her thirties" (9). Susan Douglas and Meredith Michaels, in fact, suggest that most young women seem to ground this decision in the post-second wave choice to "do it all" or "have it all"—career and a family (5). Because many college-educated young women delay motherhood until their career is established, the post-second wave crisis does not emerge in earnest until they are in their early-to-mid 30s and well-established in the workforce. Many women today, particularly those who are college educated, middle-class and professional, may not encounter overt gender discrimination until they become mothers—as Crittenden puts it so well, "once a woman has a baby, the egalitarian office party is over" (88).

"HAVING IT ALL": THE WORK-LIFE BALANCE

For many American mothers, the crisis emerges after they become mothers and must suddenly negotiate societal pressures to "have it all," "juggle it all" and/or find "balance" between their roles as mothers and professionals. Peculiarly absent in discussions of "having it all" is the significant lack of societal structural supports. Thus emerges the so-called "work-life" balance dilemma: the struggle to "juggle" or balance work commitments in the public sphere in relation to child-rearing and care responsibilities in the private sphere. It should be noted that this issue of "balance" is a uniquely first-world dilemma based upon presumptions of a private/public dichotomy. Given the normativity of ingrained patriarchal nuclear family assumptions, women entering the workforce en-mass thus created a perceived crisis in America. However, while attitudes and perspectives on women's employment gradually transformed, "standard worker assumptions" and women's ongoing domestic and child-care responsibilities have not. Because women continue to be held responsible for domestic work, child-rearing, and child care, and affordable, reliable child care remains elusive in the public sphere, many mothers find themselves struggling on a daily basis to try to meet their obligations at home and at work.

As they struggle to "have it all" or "balance it all," many mothers also find themselves in a "new" neo-traditional family structure. Neo-traditional family configurations appear to be new and even progressive because many contemporary, privileged heterosexual families have both an educated and professional mother and father (Peskowitz). However, this post-second wave family configuration continues to be problematic since the basic foundation of pre-second wave family roles and responsibilities still hold in the private sphere once children arrive: mothers continue to be primary caregivers of children in this "new" family type, even when they work. Neo-traditional family configurations reinforce and support women's ongoing domestic responsibility, while also making visible that the "egalitarian office party" is over. A central question about neo-traditional families, then, must be addressed: If neo-traditional family configurations reinforce women's domestic responsibilities, why are so many contemporary American families, but especially mothers, opting for them?

DOUBLE ENTANGLEMENT: THE SEDUCTIONS AND ENTANGLEMENTS AMONG POST-FEMINISM, NEOLIBERALISM, AND THE NEO-TRADITIONAL FAMILY

To explore theoretically how neoliberalism actively encourages neo-traditional family configurations in the private sphere while also recognizing contemporary mothers' split subjectivity, I utilize McRobbie's concept of post-feminist "double entanglement." In terms of post-feminism, McRobbie explores how second wave feminist ideas and rhetoric are used to indicate equality has been achieved for women and therefore feminism is no longer necessary (*Post-Feminism* 255). Because McRobbie is interested in post-feminism's "doubleness," drawing on the work of Judith Butler, McRobbie's example of double entanglement is as follows:

> This [double entanglement] comprises the co-existence of neo-conservative values in relation to gender, sexuality and family life (for example, George Bush supporting the campaign to encourage chastity among young people, and in March 2004 declaring that civilisation itself depends on traditional marriage), with processes of liberalisation in regard to choice and diversity in domestic, sexual and kinship relations (for example, gay couples now able to adopt, foster or have their own children by whatever means, and in the UK and Canada, full rights to civil partnerships). (255-256)

Analyzing post-feminist "chick" films, McRobbie explores how double entanglement works in these films, so that the films can appear to be engaging in well-intended and well-informed responses to feminism for young women, while also repudiating a need for second wave feminism. Moreover, McRobbie argues, "Finally it suggests that by means of the tropes of freedom and choice which are now inextricably connected with the category of 'young women,' feminism is decisively aged and made to seem redundant" (*Post-Feminism* 255). McRobbie's interest is to explore how feminist ideas are entangled with conflicting ideologies and how ideologies coexist in seemingly contradictory currents.

INTERSECTING CULTURAL CHANGES: THE NEOLIBERAL AND POST-SECOND WAVE TURNS

Neoliberal principles became entangled with post-second wave feminist ideas because both emerged at the same time historically in the U.S. While debates remain about how, exactly, to define second and third wave feminisms and whether it is appropriate to describe the second wave as "over" or "continuing," I prefer to understand the second wave as "history," with both ongoing problems and possibilities for contemporary feminism. Indeed, drawing on the work of both Bonnie J. Dow and Sara Evans, I understand second wave feminism as feminism of the 1960s and through the 1970s that was primarily but not exclusively organized by and around white, middle-class women, and is generally marked as ending with the failure of the Equal Rights Amendment in 1982. Moreover, at least within White American feminism, the 1980s through the mid-1990s is viewed as the time when feminists began to live with the successes of and backlash against second wave feminist gains.

Undeniably, many feminists began to work within rather than outside institutions, in part, because they had gained access to the very institutions that had previously excluded them. This shift, however, was read by many—especially in popular media—as "the death of feminism" or signs of a kind of post-feminism that indicated that there was no longer a need for feminist activism because all gender "problems" had been solved. Writing in 1990, Mary Fainsod Katzenstein describes this shift differently: "As the 1990s begin, few feminists subscribe to the popular notion that the women's movement is dead. Yet we also know that the public face of the feminist movement is not the same. Marches, protests, and demonstrations are infrequent, press coverage is decreased and much of the drama is gone" (27). The forms of action that fueled the second wave had begun to be replaced by mobilization inside educational and professional institutions with ongoing attention to key feminist concerns in the 1970s: abortion rights, sexual harassment, date rape, pay inequities, women's double shift responsibilities, and care for the elderly (Katzenstein 27).

At the same time, however, the early backlash against second wave gains emerged, particularly during the 1980s. One of the primary reasons for this backlash was the conservative political and social climate that were the hallmarks of the Reagan presidency in the 1980s. Katzenstein summarizes this climate as follows: "The decade of the 1980s was distinctive for ten uninterrupted years of antifeminist, anti-liberal, self-identified conservative presidential administrations" (30). Harvey and other scholars[5] argue that neoliberal thinking and economic policy took off in earnest with Ronald Reagan's election in 1980. Neoliberal policies gained ground and accelerated through the 1990s, particularly in terms of reducing welfare and social policies (McRobbie *The Aftermath*). The neoliberal turn in America represents an ideological shift away from Keynesian economic policies, which saw the state playing an active role in market regulation and social provisions, to an emphasis on free markets, decreased state regulation, and a shift from the "public good" to "individual responsibility."

Two key consequences of the neoliberal focus on individualism and individual responsibility are an emphasis on freedom of choice and the fundamental assumption of the equal capacity of individuals to make fully "free" choices. As Harvey argues:

> ...each individual is held accountable for his or her own actions and well-being. . . . Individual success or failure is interpreted in terms of entrepreneurial virtues or personal failings (such as not investing significantly enough in one's own human capital through education) rather than being attributed to any systemic property (such as the class exclusions usually attributed to capitalism). (65-66)

Social problems are seen as outside the purview of the state and instead individuals need to take responsibility for solving their own "problems." This is most obvious in relation to the difficulties contemporary mothers face around caregiving. Thus, the neoliberal foci on individual choice, personal responsibility, and privatization all discourage social solutions for work-life concerns and instead encourage mothers and families to find their own individual solutions in the private sphere.

POST-SECOND WAVE BENEFICIARIES' INTERNALIZATION OF NEOLIBERAL IDEAS

American women who came of age at the centre of the intersection between the neoliberal and post-second wave turns have come of age within both post-second wave and neoliberal rhetoric and ideas. One consequence is that many contemporary mothers bring to bear neoliberal ideas when they face the post-second wave crisis in femininity. Addressing why many contemporary mothers in their 30s and 40s are apolitical and assume they must solve any difficulty they face as mothers on their own, Judith Warner's work reveals these connections well. Warner argues, "Good daughters of the Reagan Revolution, we disdained social activism and cultivated our own gardens with a kind of muscle-bound, tightly wound, über-achieving, all-encompassing, never-failing self-control that passed, in the 1980s, for female empowerment" (par. 12). Also raised to be independent and self-sufficient and deferring motherhood for a career as post-second wave beneficiaries, many contemporary mothers integrate second wave feminist ideas of female independence and self-sufficiency with neoliberal principles when the crisis emerges. Again, talking about contemporary American mothers, Warner argues, "They've been bred to be independent and self-sufficient. To rely on their own initiative and 'personal responsibility.' To *privatize* their problems" (italicized in original par. 21).

Another significant consequence of being "good Reagan daughters" is that these mothers blame themselves and/or hold themselves responsible for solving or addressing the contemporary crisis in femininity. Moreover, mothers do so because they have been disciplined to assume that the problems they face result from their own poor choices. As Warner argues, "Instead of blaming society, moms today tend to blame themselves. They say they've chosen poorly. And so they take on the Herculean task of being absolutely everything to their children, simply because *no one else is doing anything at all to help them*" (italicized in original par. 22). Feminist scholars[6] who explore neoliberalism and contemporary representations of motherhood also suggest mothers blame themselves when they fail to succeed in "juggling it all."

The language of second wave feminism that is most often invoked with neoliberalism is *choice*. In fact, recent feminist scholarship on the rhetoric of choice[7] also reveals the central role choice—contemporary women's ability to control reproduction such that motherhood is now considered a woman's choice—plays in contemporary women's understanding of motherhood and mothering. Moreover, in the context of high-achieving women's lives, Pamela Stone notes that many of the 54 women she interviewed relied on what she refers to as "choice feminism"—a form of third wave feminism that emphasizes individualism, personal choices, and personal agency—in describing their decision to quit working. As Stone reports, "choice rhetoric—phrases such as 'active choice,' 'professional choice'—studded their interviews, appearing in 70 percent of them and implicit in others" (113). Thus, the second wave rhetoric and ideas of reproductive choice have become intertwined with neoliberalism's understanding of choice and individual responsibility.

Much discussion has emerged in the popular press in the U.S. about motherhood and "having it all." A June 12, 2012, *New York Times* article, "Motherhood Still a Cause for Pay Inequity," implicitly addresses the post-second wave crisis women face and the ways that individual responsibility and choice are tangled up with contemporary motherhood. Noting ongoing pay inequity for women while also explicitly recognizing how much more similar men's and women's lives are in the public sphere, the author, Eduardo Porter, argues, "Most economists believe the gap between women's and men's wages does not stem primarily from employers paying women less than men for the same job...Much, though, is a result of the constraints of motherhood" (par. 6). Consequently, Porter suggests that obvious or overt gender discrimination is not the primary issue; rather, the primary issue is mothers' choices. As he puts it, "But outright sex discrimination has declined sharply, most economists agree. Today, women's career choice—constrained by the burdens of motherhood and family—account for most of the pay gap between women and men" (par. 11).

Equally revealing is the way the online responses to Porter's article invoked and used the rhetoric of choice and individual responsibility. While there were some nuanced and thoughtful responses, respondents, who addressed issues related to Porter's call for public policy changes to accommodate mothers, rejected the public policy suggestions and did so by drawing on neoliberal and post-second wave understandings of choice and individual responsibility in the private sphere. In addition to being grounded in the rhetoric of choice, "TS" (June 12, 2012, comment 3), for example, suggests, "If women want more successful careers, they should demand partners who will equally share domestic responsibilities. Dividing the burden of childcare is a personal choice made between the parents, and if one assumes more responsibility than the other, that parent's career will likely suffer. Why should any employer or coworker have to make up for that?" A grammatically incorrect comment by Anne Ingram also concurs that, because motherhood is a choice, professional institutions need not support working mothers. As she (June 12, 2012, comment 16) puts it: "My feeling is that if you have kids, [sic] that is your business. don't [sic] bring it into the workplace and make other people compensate for you. it's [sic] your choice and your problem." These comments are crystal clear: contemporary motherhood is women's choice—if any individual woman is having difficulty "juggling it all," it is her "choice and her problem," her personal responsibility to manage in the private sphere (comment 16).

As a result, because American motherhood is now founded on the idea that motherhood is a personal, individual choice for women, American mothers' relationship to contemporary society has changed. Writing about reality television and neoliberal ideas, Mary Thompson argues, "neoliberal ideologies that rely on notions of the individual, 'free choice,' and individual responsibility, have emerged as a new mode of expressing the changing relationships of the individual to 'neoliberal' society" (337-8.) Thompson's ideas also apply to contemporary motherhood: post-second wave women's contemporary relationship to society has fundamentally changed from one of maternal destiny to maternal choice. The implications of this shift are both freeing—unencumbered women's lives are more and more similar to unencumbered men's lives in the public sphere—and problematic—women's encumbered lives in the private sphere continue to be shaped by maternal responsibilities, responsibilities that are now viewed as women's "free" choice.

CONSEQUENCES OF THE ENTANGLEMENT: WHEN "IT JUST DOESN'T WORK"

Because motherhood is now fundamentally shaped by "maternal choice," I contend that the moment any contemporary mother decides "it just isn't working" is the moment when the post-second wave crisis in femininity emerges most clearly for that mother. Exploring how high-achieving women respond when "juggling it all" is "just not working" allows for a more complete understanding of how the intersection of neoliberal and post-second wave choice influence these mothers' lives and decision making and why the neo-traditional family configuration seems so "natural" or "normal."

Joan Williams, in *Unbending Gender,* has already begun to explore how and why juggling it all often results in "it just wasn't working." Drawing on Pierre Bourdieu's notion of habitus—the idea of embodied history that is so internalized that it becomes "second nature," and so it is forgotten—Williams argues:

> 'It just wasn't working'—this formulation encodes as choice an economy with work schedules and career tracks that assume one adult in charge of caregiving and one ideal worker, men's felt entitlement to work 'success,' and a sense that children need close parental attention. It encodes a habitus structured by domesticity, with default modes that set up power-

ful force fields pulling women back toward traditional gender roles. (38)

Williams reveals that a multilayered number of factors make it difficult to make juggling two careers and children work, while simultaneously cultivating domesticity, including women's caregiving responsibilities, and neo-traditional family configurations in the private sphere. Others scholars[8] address further the challenges ideal worker norms and intensive mothering raise for two-career-families-with-children and the barriers to mothers' empowerment.

Because contemporary American motherhood is founded on mothers' maternal choices, this shift to maternal choice obscures the ongoing gender-power structure in neo-traditional families that supports and further entrenches men's felt entitlement to career success. This is the case because upper class men in particular benefit from, what Karen Pyke calls, *the hegemony of the male career.* Drawing on the early work of Arlie Hochschild, Pyke argues, as does Williams, that the supremacy of the male career is founded on a patriarchal notion of gender differences, which "provides a rationale for husbands' entitlements that obscures the underlying gendered power structure. The logic is this: Because husbands are the main providers in their families, they ought to have certain privileges and rights that enable them to perform their duties" (533). As a result, men's careers are often privileged and prioritized over women's careers in heterosexual relations. Pyke argues, "The supremacy of the male career is most apparent in the marital arrangements of the middle to upper classes" because men are generally freed from the day-to-day responsibilities of child-rearing and care (533).

Even in our post-second wave context, the hegemony of the male career continues and, as a result, supports neo-traditional family configurations. Stone's work also explicitly notes the role of maternal choice in women's decision making about how to structure family life, and the ways that this configuration also supports the hegemony of the male career. In doing so, Stone recognizes that the "choices" women make are not "free" choices but are choices within gender constraints, male organizing systems in professional life, the privileging of men's careers, and women's caregiving responsibilities, even though the women with whom she spoke do not fully recognize these gender-power structures. As Stone puts it:

> While they couch them in the language of choice and privilege, the stories they tell reveal not the expression of choice,

but rather the existence of a choice gap, a gap that is a function of a double bind created primarily by the conditions of work in the gilded cages of elite professions. Married to fellow professionals, who face the same pressures at work that they do, women are home alone, and go home because they have been unsuccessful in their efforts to obtain flexibility [at work] or, for those who were able to, because they found themselves marginalized and stigmatized, negatively reinforced to trying to hold on to their careers after becoming mothers. (19)

Consequently, in detailing why high-achieving women "opt out" of their professional career in two-career couples, Stone suggests, "The fact that men's careers came first was the underlying and unspoken 'reason' women quit, but men's careers almost always come first; they come first in couples in which women continue working" (78). Stone concludes, "Women's own understanding of their decisions as implementing choice was further reinforced, as we saw earlier, by their husbands, who spoke repeatedly of giving their wives the 'choice' to decide whether or not to quit" (113). Although Stone does not say so specifically, this understanding of choice further entrenches the neo-traditional family structure because neither the hegemony of the male career nor women's caregiving responsibilities were ever questioned; both are habitus: embodied history such that both are "second nature." Rather, the only "questions" revolve around a woman's maternal choices: Should she have a career and have primary responsibility for child care and household labour or quit work and be home full time to meet her ongoing private sphere responsibilities?

When work-life decisions are framed around women's maternal choices, the male career hegemony—with its hidden privileges and ongoing gender-power inequalities—also becomes invisible in ways that further erase the problems of motherhood from the public sphere. Writing about media representations of race and neoliberal ideology, Thompson argues, "In the context of neoliberal ideology, the invisibility of whiteness and white privilege intensifies with the belief that race no longer matters and that achievement is equally obtainable to all who seek it. Success, in such a worldview, blind to structural inequalities and hidden privileges, is a matter of making good choices" (344). In a similar fashion, in the context of neoliberal ideology and post-second wave motherhood, the hegemony of the male career is also rendered invisible. As a result, to paraphrase Thompson, I am suggesting the invisibility of "maleness" as the norm intensifies the belief that gender oppression no longer exists and that professional achievement is equally obtainable to all who seek success, who make good choices. And as a result, many of the feminist gains of the 1970s and 80s come to be undermined because it is mothers rather than fathers who are leaving the public sphere when "it just isn't working."

The conflicting and intersecting neoliberal and post-second wave currents de-politicise the second wave feminist politics of choice by suggesting that the public sphere is no longer sexist; and, if the family is, then it is a result of women's choice to have and/or to make those sexist arrangements. These conflicting and intersecting currents also reinforce contemporary women's post-second wave split subjectivity. They work to reinforce the public-private split on which the split subjectivity and post-second wave crisis are built, while simultaneously denying any need for a feminist politics of choice to challenge ongoing gender inequities. Finally, it is for these reasons that the neo-traditional family configuration seems so "natural" or "normal," even though this family configuration is also the "Achilles' heel" of the maternal empowerment movement.

CONCLUSION

I have argued that the post-second wave and neoliberal turns intersect such that contemporary American society re-entrenches and "supports" the post-second wave crisis in femininity by offering the neo-traditional family as the private-sphere solution to the crisis. The neo-traditional family is the "easy" solution, because it asks the least of both society and public policy. The neo-traditional family configuration is a minimalist response to the post-second wave crisis in femininity in that it is the lowest-level "support" that the current U.S. context can offer American mothers. While the neo-traditional family is "logical" and "consistent" with the intersecting neoliberal and post-second wave principles of choice, personal responsibility, and privatization, I conclude by asking and answering the following question: If this minimalist approach continues, what might be the consequences?

American mothers are already facing a post-second wave crisis in femininity, and feminist scholars[9] have indicated there is a burgeoning social and economic crisis, one building around child care and domestic labour as more and more women try to negotiate mothering and professional life. In other words, because America has no public infrastructure to support mothers' child-rearing responsibilities, a variety of crises are brewing in the US. America is not preparing for the future by investing in the infrastructure needed to support family life; rather it continues to privatize and individualize caregiving and child-rearing. Moreover, offering the minimalist neo-traditional family as the solution to mothers' post-second wave crisis in femininity is creating disincentives for finding any other solutions for contemporary mothers. I close with Hall's warning and reminder:

> Women stand where many of these [defunded social and educational programs] savage lines intersect...cutting the state means minimising the arena in which women can find a voice, allies, social as well as material support; and in which their concerns can be recognised. It means reducing the resources society collectively allocates to children, to making children a shared responsibility, and to the general 'labour' of care and love. (Par. 12)

NOTES

[1]Following Adrienne Rich's groundbreaking distinction in *Of Woman Born*, I use the term *motherhood* to mean the patriarchal institution of motherhood, while I also use the term *mothering* to mean the potential mothering has to be empowering for mothers when they are able to define mothering for themselves. This essay, however, primarily focuses on how contemporary motherhood is being shaped by the intersecting and conflicting neoliberal and post-second wave turns.

[2]See Brooks; Dworkin and Wachs; Edwards; Katz; Kimmel; Malin; Messner; and Shugart

[3]See Crittenden; Hayden and O'Brien Hallstein; Hirshman; O'Brien Hallstein; O'Brien Hallstein and O'Reilly; O'Reilly 2004; Orenstein; Warner; Williams; and Wood

[4]See Crittenden; Hirshman; and Wolf

[5]See Bezanson and Luxton; Craven; Miller, Antonio, and Bonanno; and Vavrus

[6]See Kauppinen; Thompson; and Vavrus

[7]See Craven; Douglas and Michaels; Hayden and O'Brien Hallstein; Stone; and Vavrus

[8]See Douglas and Michaels; Hays; O'Brien Hallstein and O'Reilly; O'Reilly; and Warner

[9]See Crittenden, Folbre, Hays; and Vavrus

WORKS CITED

Bezanson, Kate and Meg Luxton. "Introduction: Social Reproduction and Feminist Political Economy." Eds. Meg Luxton and Kate Bezanson. *Social Reproduction: Feminist Political Economy Challenges Neo-Liberalism.* Montreal, Quebec: McGill-Queens University Press, 2006: 3-11. Print.

Brooks, Gary R. *Beyond the Crisis in Masculinity: A Transtheoretical Model for Male-Friendly Therapy.* Washington DC: APA Press, 2009. Print.

Craven, Christa. "A 'Consumer's Right' to Choose a Midwife: Shifting Meanings for Reproductive Rights under Neoliberalism." *American Anthropologist* 109.4 (2007): 701-712. Print.

Crittenden, Ann. *The Price of Motherhood: Why the Most Important Job in the World Is Still the Least Valued.* New York: Henry Holt and Company, 2001. Print.

Douglas, Susan J and Meredith Michaels. *The Mommy Myth: The Idealization of Motherhood and How It Has Undermined All Women.* New York: Free Press, 2004. Print.

Dow, Bonnie J. "Review Essay: Reading the Second Wave," *Quarterly Journal of Speech* 91.1 (Feb. 2005): 89-107. Print.

Dworkin, Shari L. and Faye Linda Wachs. *Body Panic: Gender, Health, and the Selling of Fitness.* New York: New York UP, 2009. Print.

Edwards, Tim. *Cultures of Masculinity.* New York: Routledge, 2005. Print.

Evans, Sara. *Tidal Wave: How Women Changed America at Century's End.* New York: Free Press, 2003. Print.

Folbre, Nancy. *Who Pays for the Kids? Gender and Structures of Constraint.* London: Routledge: 27, 1994. Print.

Galinsky, Ellen. "The Ongoing Struggle to Balance Career and Family." *The Diane Rehm Show*, Transcript. Retrieved June 26, 2012. <http://thedianerehmshow.org/shows/2012-06-25/ongoing-struggle-balance-career-and-family/transcript>. Web.

Hall, Stuart. "The March of the Neoliberals." *The Guardian Online.* Retrieved June 18, 2012.<http://www.guardian.co.uk/politics/2011/sep/12/march-of-the-neoliberals>.Web.

Harvey, David. *A Brief History of Neoliberalism.* Oxford: Oxford University Press, 2005. Print.

Hayden, Sara and D. Lynn O'Brien Hallstein. Eds. *Contemplating Maternity in an Era of Choice: Explorations into Discourses of Reproduction.*

Lanham, MD: Lexington Press, 2010. Print.

Hays, Sharon. *The Cultural Contradictions of Motherhood.* New Haven: Yale UP, 1996. Print.

Hirshman, Linda R. *Get to Work: A Manifesto for Women of the World.* New York: Viking, 2006. Print.

Hochschild, Arlie. *The Second Shift: Working Parents and the Revolution at Home.* New York: Viking, 1989. Print.

"Ingram, Anne." "Comment 16." "Motherhood Still a Cause of Pay Inequality." *The New York Times.* June 12, 2012. Retrieved June 12, 2012. <http://www.nytimes.com/2012/06/13/business/economy/motherhood-still-a-cause-of-pay-inequality.html?_r=1emc=eta1>. Web.

Katz, Jason. "Tough Guise: Violence, Media, and the Crisis in Masculinity." *Media Education Foundation.* Northampton, MA: Media Education Foundation, 1999. Print.

Katzenstein, Mary Fainsod. "Feminism within American Institutions: Unobtrusive Mobilization in the 1980s." *Signs: Journal of Women in Culture and Society* 16.1 (Autumn 1990): 27-54. Print.

Kauppinen, Kati. "Managing Motherhood: Empowerment and Neoliberalism in a Postfeminist Women's Magazine." Proceedings of the 5th Biennial International Gender and Language Association Conference IGALA. Victoria, University of Wellington, July 2008: 83-95. Retrieved 07/12/12. <http://www.victoria.ac.nz/igala5/igala-proceedings-book.pdf>. Web.

Kimmel, Michael. *Manhood in America: A Cultural History.* Oxford: Oxford UP, 2000. Print.

Malin, Brenton J. *American Masculinity under Clinton: Popular Media and the Nineties "Crisis in Masculinity."* New York: Peter Lang, 2005. Print.

McRobbie, Angela. *The Aftermath of Feminism: Gender, Culture, and Social Change.* Los Angeles: Sage, 2009. Print.

— "Post-Feminism and Popular Culture." *Feminist Media Studies* 4.3 (2004): 255-264. Print.

Messner, Michael *A. Power at Play: Sports and the Problem of Masculinity.* Boston: Beacon Press, 1992. Print.

Miller, Lee M., Robert J. Antonio and Alessandro Bonanno. "Hazards of Neoliberalism: Delayed Electric Power Restoration after Hurricane Ike." *The British Journal of Sociology* 62.3 (2011): 505-522. Print.

O'Brien Hallstein, D. Lynn. "Second Wave Silences and Third Wave Intensive Mothering." Amber E. Kinser Ed. *Mothering and Feminism in the Third Wave.* Toronto: Demeter Press, 2008: 107-116. Print.

O'Brien Hallstein, D. Lynn and Andrea O'Reilly. Eds. *Contemporary Motherhood in a Post-Second Wave Context: Challenges, Strategies, and Possibilities.* Toronto: Demeter Press, 2012. Print.

O'Reilly, Andrea. *Mother Outlaws: Theories and Practices of Empowered Mothering.* Toronto, Canada: Women's Press, 2004. Print.

Orenstein, Peggy. *Flux: Women on Sex, Work, Kids, Love, and Life in a Half-Changed World.* New York: Double Day, 2000. Print.

Peskowitz, Miriam. *The Truth Behind the Mommy Wars: Who Decides What Makes a Good Mother?* Emeryville, CA: Seal Press, 2005. Print.

Porter, Eduardo. "Motherhood Still a Cause of Pay Inequality." *The New York Times.* June 12, 2012. Retrieved, June 12, 2012. <http://www.nytimes.com/2012/06/13/business/economy/\-motherhood-still-a-cause-of-pay-inequality.html?_r=1\&emc=eta1>.Web.

Pyke, Karen D. "Class-Based Masculinities: The Interdependence of Gender, Class, and Interpersonal Power." *Gender and Society* 10.5 (Oct. 1996): 527-549. Print.

Rich, Adrienne. *Of Woman Born: Motherhood as Experience and Institution.* 2nd ed. New York: W.W. Norton, 1986. Print.

Shugart, Helene. "Managing Masculinities: The Metrosexual Moment." *Communication and Critical/Cultural Studies* 5.3 (Sept. 2008): 280-300. Print.

Slaughter, Anne-Marie. "Why Women Still Can't Have It All." *The Atlantic Monthly.* July/August, 2012. Retrieved June 26, 2012. http://us.mg4.mail.yahoo.com/neo/launch?.rand=370qhori9s962. Web.

Stone, Pamela. *Opting Out?: Why Women Really Quit Careers and Head Home.* Berkeley: University of California Press, 2007. Print.

Thompson, Mary. "Learn Something From This!: The Problem of Optional Ethnicity on American's Next Top Model." *Feminist Media Studies.* 7.1 (2007): 47-63. Print.

"TS." "Comment 3." "Motherhood Still a Cause of Pay Inequality." *The New York Times* June 12, 2012. Retrieved, June 12, 2012. <http://www.nytimes.com/2012/06/13/business/economy/motherhood-still-a-cause-of-pay-inequality.html?_r=1emc=eta1>. Web.

Vavrus, Mary Douglas. "Outing Out Moms in the News: Selling New

Traditionalism in the New Millennium." *Feminist Media Studies* 10.3 (2010): 335-352. Print.

Warner, Judith. "Mommy Madness (excerpted from *Perfect Madness*): What Happened When the Girls Who Had It All Became Mothers? A New Book Explores Why This Generation Feels so Insane." *Newsweek* Retrieved July 11, 2012. <http://www.thedailybeast.com/newsweek/2005/02/21/mommy-madness.print.html > Web.

Williams, Joan. *Unbending Gender: Why Family and Work Conflict and What To Do About It.* Oxford: Oxford University Press, 2000. Print.

Wolf, Naomi. *Misconceptions: Truth, Lies, and the Unexpected on the Journey to Motherhood.* New York: Anchor Books, 2003. Print.

Wood, Julia T. *Gendered Lives: Communication, Gender, and Culture.* 7th ed. Belmont: Wadsworth, 2007. 31. Print.

17.

Deserving Children and "Risky Mothers"

Situating Public Policy and Maternal/Child Welfare in the Canadian Context

PAT BRETON

INTRODUCTION

A predominance of international and national political discourses claim that children are the new strategic priority for global and local economies.[1] The rise of child rights and the increasing iconicization of the child in many global and national policy agendas reflect a professed concern for the plight of vulnerable and disadvantaged children in the global north and south. As mothers and their children experience the gendered inequalities of waged and unwaged labour in risky and unstable global economies, child welfare policy and practices claim to address childhood disadvantage in families. Central in such policy debates concerned with maternal and child welfare are western notions of an innocent childhood within the traditional nuclear family model. However, rather than reducing inequities and addressing childhood poverty as claimed, such initiatives further entrench inequalities leading to greater disadvantage for mothers *and* children.

This chapter explores how neoliberalism and the turn to child welfare and child rights in many global and national policies have influenced mother/child relations over the past two decades, localizing such policy agendas in the Canadian context. Here I examine policy implications for the welfare of mothers and their children amidst feminist concerns for the potential loss of gender claims against the state as mothers' issues are eclipsed in child-centric policy agendas that benefit neither mothers nor children.[2] How are nations investing in the deserving child citizen as the welfare state is restructured under neoliberalism? Where have mothers gone in policy over the past several decades when taking into account that women, as primary caregivers of children, have been the major recipients of welfare state investment? What are the gendered implications for maternal/child relations with the turn to the child in neoliberal policy?

FEMINIST CRITIQUES OF NEOLIBERALISM

Neoliberal philosophy, values, and principles have influenced many governments, geo-politics, and civil societies over the past two decades. While acknowledging the unevenness of neoliberalism globally and nationally, Raewyn Connell suggests that rather than a system, neoliberalism is "a large scale historical project for the marketization of social structures and practices" (Connell 33). According to neoliberal thinkers, individual human rights and freedoms are best protected where open competition, free markets, and unfettered trade agreements exist within a global economy.[3] Policy reforms under neoliberalism promote market liberalization, privatization, and deregulation to create and sustain open economies attractive to foreign investment.

Such market-driven individualistic language fails to acknowledge how individual rights are deeply embedded in social relations, and often unequal relations of power. International and national histories of capitalism, imperialism, and colonialism structure these social relations often producing and sustaining inequalities across gender, class, race, and national differences. Historically, in some countries, especially where advanced capitalist economies existed in the mid-20th C, the state has played a central role in addressing these structural inequalities through income and social supports provided through the welfare state. More recently under neoliberalism, the global trend of increased government funding to promote marketization and address the global economic crisis is also marked by state withdrawal from social welfare supports for families. As state budgets are brought into line and deficit reductions realized through the rollback of state supports for social welfare, many families are disadvantaged, particularly low-income single mother families. Feminist critiques of neoliberalism highlight how neoliberal values and the philosophy of market-driven individual rights have failed to advance and have eroded agendas and policies of social justice and equality. Arguing that the neoliberal project is embedded in masculinity politics (Connell 33), feminist challenges to neoliberalism flag the social and economic costs of neoliberalism for women, particularly mothers, across and within national borders.

THE NEOLIBERAL CONTEXT IN CANADA

In Canada, the 1990s marked a pivotal shift toward neoliberal political/economic policies. Federal policy agendas, shaped by globalization and the international priorities of trade deficits, security, and science and technology, have increasingly displaced national problems of deepening poverty, gendered wage gaps, and caring labour inequalities (Pal). Over the past eight years (2006-2013) of federal conservative party governance, the anti-government stance has resulted in the regionalization and privatization of social spending, downloading the responsibility of poverty and gendered caring inequalities to the provinces (Bezanson 96). The Canadian welfare state that has historically redistributed income to women and mothers, the primary providers of unwaged caring labour to children, the elderly and the infirmed, is shrinking (Bezanson and Luxton 4). As the state cuts welfare spending, women—particularly low-income, single mothers and their families who rely on income supports from the state—are most harshly effected. While women's increased participation in the paid labour force has provided some economic relief to families, mothers are increasingly burdened as they also carry the primary responsibility for children. As more women and mothers enter the labour force requiring more child-care supports, reduced state funding for child care and welfare has contributed to the commodification and privatization of publicly funded caring labour. For example, to fill the child-care deficit in Canada, the federal state grants working rights to "third world" migrant workers to provide low-waged caring labour to "first world" families, yet denies migrant mothers the right to bring their own children to the host country (Arat-Koc).

MARKET LOGIC

Contemporary neoliberalism can be defined by the "logic of the market" permeating not only politics and economics but all facets of social life (Brodie, cited in Braedley & Luxton 7). As the values, norms, and language of market rationality become embedded in everyday life, human rights, such as the right to an adequate standard of living and the right to the attainment of physical and mental health, less and less the responsibility of the state, become commodities available for purchase by individuals in the marketplace (Gideon 106). People are then bound together not as citizens in mutual caring relations, but as consumers with the values of self-interest and individual responsibility (Giroux 223). Families facing increasing financial hardship due to geo-political shifts to marketization now become individually responsible for purchasing their social, health, and welfare commodities and services.

There has been a cultural shift in popular consciousness reflective of a growing acceptance of neoliberalism (Connell 28). While Connell notes it is difficult to tell how deeply these neoliberal messages have penetrated people's thinking, she acknowledges a certain appeal of the marketing language of "personal freedoms" to younger people, used in advertising (Connell 28). The language of risk increasingly creates individual awareness of responsible citizenship within neoliberal values of self-discipline and individual responsibility as citizens are encouraged to become responsible risk-takers in this precarious political and economic climate (Gazso 48). Yet this discourse of responsible citizenship and consumer choice obscures structural factors and geo-political interests. How far can citizens really go to claim their rights beyond market-driven initiatives if they remain excluded from policy debates where international financial institutions such as the World Bank and the International Monetary Fund play a central role in establishing the agenda for social policy at a national level? (Gideon 96) Given such financial and economic neoliberal imperatives, how are the needs of children addressed in international and national policies?

THE DESERVING CHILD CITIZEN: NEOLIBERAL POLICY AND THE RIGHTS OF THE CHILD

In 1991, the United Nations Convention on the Rights of the Child (CRC) was ratified by one hundred and ninety-one nations. With the enshrinement of the rights of the child in a legal framework, the CRC represented a significant shift from a purely protection approach of children to a proactive approach to protect children as individual rights-holders (Holzscheiter 88, 114). Rather than objects of charity and benevolence, the new slogans of "child participation and empowerment" reflected the importance of giving children voice to express their views (Holzscheiter 86). While none of the nations who originally ratified the CRC have implemented the policy, the protection of children and their legal rights has been globally endorsed (Holzscheiter 87, 88). More than twenty years later, research indicates the hegemonic terrain of child rights and the neoliberal notion of the child as autonomous self has been widely accepted by think tanks, NGOs, and governmental agencies (Holzscheiter 87).

While concern for the rights and welfare of children warrants international and national attention within social justice agendas, individualistic rights-based policy initiatives and reforms for children are problematic in their claims of universal application. In doing so, they fail to account for different political, economic, and cultural contexts. Northern industrialized states, which dominated in the drafting of the document, successfully advanced western notions of childhood ideals within the nuclear family model (Holzscheiter 114). Here, according to the United Nations CRC, children, as rights-holders, are free of responsibilities, and childhood is dominated by education and leisure within a male breadwinner and female caregiver family (Holzscheiter 88). The western nuclear family model entrenched in policy not only de-legitimized non-western nations' family forms and notions of childhood, but also failed to account for the dual earner and single-mother families that increasingly dominate in many western nations. Additionally, while a few countries, such as the Philippines have since deployed the child rights framework to advance girls' rights, the predominance of the "gender-neutral child" in the CRC document potentially undermines current and future gender claims against the state (Croll 120; Holzscheiter 228, 232). In the drafting of the CRC, gender equality issues, such as female circumcision and child marriage/adolescent parenthood, which disproportionately affect girl children, were either not subject to deliberation, or were sidelined due to "cultural delicacy" (Holzscheiter 228, 232).

CHILD CARE IN CANADA

In Canada, while the discursive shift to the child in policy reforms can be traced to the 1980s where "children" were substituted for "families" in social welfare policy discourse (Jenson 193), a renewed emphasis on the child emerged in the mid-1990s at the same time as the drafting of the CRC. Child-care programs by the 1990s were almost exclusively framed in terms of the needs of the child, despite the gender equality claims advanced in the Royal Commission on the Status of Women in 1971 for a state-funded, universal and affordable national child-care program to support women caring for their children (Jenson 196). This turn to the child in Canadian policy under neoliberalism also marked the shift from the 1970s Keynesian welfare state that supported collective responsibility for those facing economic hardship, to the 1990s restructuring of the welfare state through spending cutbacks on universal social programs.[4]

Narrow child-specific public policies reflected a reduction of state involvement in, and funding for the unwaged caring work of children performed by mothers. With the introduction of the National Child Benefit in the mid-1990s, while the federal state maintained some presence in the lives of Canadian children and their families, it substantively reduced federal interest in and support for national child-care needs (Jenson). By 2006, the Universal Child Care Benefit (UCCB), introduced as a replacement for a national child-care program, provided a "taxable" cash transfer for child care to parents with children under six years of age (Bezanson). Employing the neoliberal discourse of "choice", the federal government under Prime-Minister Stephen Harper, promoted the program flexibility of this "taxable" cash transfer for child care that allowed parents to "choose" where and how they spent this money on their children's child care (Bezanson 98-99). However, instead of universalist and rights-based benefits for all families, as claimed by the government, the small, taxable and targeted payments of the UCCB reflected more of a residualist approach to child care, resulting in less child-care supports for the majority of families (Bezanson 109). Research indicates most mothers found that the UCCB cash paid for less than half and in some cases, only one day per month, of their child-care costs. Other mothers noted the increased taxes substantially reduced whatever minimal monetary benefit provided (Bezanson 99). Moreover, these cash benefits did not address the lack of available and affordable child-care spaces, nor contribute to improving the quality of existing child-care centres (Bezanson 106).

The 1990s restructuring of the federal welfare state and the withdrawal of federal level support for social welfare spending effectively downloaded most of the costs, risks, and responsibilities of caring for children to the provinces (Jenson). In the case of Ontario, when federal supplements for child care were received, the provincial government opted to invest in Ontario Early Years Plan, a program targeted at early child development. Rather than using the funding for universally accessible, high-quality public child care that would benefit all families, the Ontario government instead funded individualized, standardized, and privatized child development services (Vosko).

As both federal and provincial levels in Canada withdrew their policy supports for mothers and their children, the state instead funded targeted child-centred policies and programs claiming to address childhood disadvantage under neoliberalism. Child welfare policies to protect vulnerable children from abuse and neglect promote interventions and monitoring of children and their mothers by welfare authorities, particularly low-income, single-mother families. In these interventions, state workers assess the welfare of children by utilizing labour-intensive and costly child-care models and methods advanced by child and baby experts (Hays). Based on western notions of the innocent child and self-sacrificing mother centred on the children's needs, these maternal standards of child care are not easily met by most middle-class, stay-at-home mothers and often out of reach for low-income single mothers performing waged labour outside the home (Fox; and Hays 21).

Child apprehensions and the temporary and permanent removal of children by welfare authorities are increasingly utilized by the neoliberal state as solutions for childhood disadvantage, despite Canada's abysmal history of children abused and neglected while in state care in state-run group homes, foster family programs, and child institutions (Strong-Boag). For example, the state-sanctioned 1960s scoop of disadvantaged Aboriginal children from their Aboriginal families and their placement in non-Aboriginal foster homes and residential schools not only exposed children to abuse and neglect in state-run facilities and programs, but also contributed to maternal/child separations and familial and community breakdowns (Cull 148; and Strong-Boag). Despite this history of cultural genocide of First Nations by the colonialist state, between 1995 and 2001, the estimated number of Aboriginal children and youth apprehended from their families and placed in state care increased by 71.5 percent (Cull 152-153).

Recent child welfare policy and practice under neoliberalism reflects a "law and order" approach to child welfare within a rights-based discourse of child risk.[5] Operating from the "best interests of the child," these protectionist policies present the rights of the child in conflict with the mother's maternal rights to care for her child.[6] Risk assessment tools introduced by the child welfare state in the 1990s to assess children's safety and welfare in families created powerful and stigmatizing discourses of the at-risk child and the risky mother in policy and practice.[7] Forming the basis for increased state monitoring and surveillance of maternal/child relations, these risk assessments effectively blame mothers for the structural inequalities of gendered waged and unwaged caring labour. As child welfare research reveals, the use of scientific tools not only manufactures "bad mothers," particularly poor, racialized single mothers, but also reproduces the problem of child neglect as a personal problem of the mother (Swift).

RISKY MOTHERS: WHERE HAVE MOTHERS GONE IN POLICY REFORMS?

Has the turn to the child in local and global policies under neoliberalism eclipsed mothers' issues and their gender claims against the state? This narrow focus on the child had negative policy implications, particularly for mothers and their families on the margins of society, as the state was no longer addressing the structural gendered inequalities in women's waged and unwaged labour—the root of child poverty and disadvantage (Weigers). Furthermore, the retrenchment of the nuclear family as the unit of administration in social welfare policy often bound mothers to negligent and abusive partners.[8] By the mid-1990s, women's poverty and women's issues were made invisible through the focus on the child and the gender-neutral discourse of the middle-class, dual-parent nuclear family (McKeen).

More recently, the focus on increased state investment in narrowly defined child education and programs is also marked by the devolution of policy support and investment for non-working adults, and conditional and heavily monitored entitlements for unwaged women/mother caregivers (Jenson). Tracing the decline in public funding of adult income-support programs, research in three Canadian provinces from 1993-2004 reveals how neoliberal welfare reforms create the "responsible risk-taker worker citizen," while ratcheting down mother's rights and women's capacity to perform mother work (Gaszo). Mothers (and fathers) who are increasingly moved off social assistance and income-support programs unfairly encounter the risks and responsibilities of limited and precarious work resulting from unstable global markets without increased supports for their child-care labour (Gaszo). Despite the predominance of diverse family forms in society, retrogressive adult welfare policies under neoliberalism also retrench traditional norms of the nuclear family. Welfare authorities reinforce gendered notions of caring within the father breadwinner/mother caregiver model through increased monitoring and regulating of women's mothering, while active and participatory fathering becomes devalued within gendered notions of the male breadwinner (Gaszo 55-58).

CONCLUSION

Since the 1990s, global and national policy agendas shaped by an individualistic rights-based discourse of the deserving child citizen have led to reforms that effectively undermine maternal and child welfare. In Canada, state withdrawal from mother-specific social and welfare supports has compromised the capacity of mothers to care for their children, further destabilizing maternal/child relations and contributing to childhood disadvantage. Increasingly residualist and risk-based public policies that assume children live in nuclear families widen the inequalities of gender, race, and class, most harshly experienced by low-income single mothers and their children. Hegemonic notions of the deserving child within a rights-based childhood, and self-sacrificing mothers within notions of risky motherhood advanced in child welfare models, have only contributed to state-led child alienation and maternal/child separations in Canada. Although targeted and interventionist child welfare policy and practices claim to address childhood disadvantage, in effect they fail to address the gendered structural inequalities at the root of childhood disadvantage and the welfare of children within their families.

As governments prioritize financial and economic policies to address global economic instabilities, it becomes difficult to envision gender equality in a caring society supportive of maternal/child welfare. How then can the lives of mothers and their children be improved under neoliberalism? Social justice agendas for children can only succeed when the maternal/child unit is at the centre of global and national policy agendas (Greaves et. al). Publicly funded income supports for mothers working outside the home for wages and inside the home caring for children benefit all children and their families. Federal state policies for maternal/child welfare are required to support mothers from pregnancy to the child's development to adulthood through publicly funded, universally accessible national networks of child-care facilities, pregnancy, birthing and parenting centres, and baby and mom/parent drop-ins. Public reforms are also necessary to integrate the needs of pregnant and lactating moms and their playing children, in addition to bulky baby strollers and dirty diapers, in all public spaces and infrastructures such as transportation systems, playgrounds, communities, and workplaces.

Signs of maternal resistance are evident in this era of risky motherhood under neoliberalism. While acknowledging the predominance of a neoliberal ideology of rights-based individualism and the global marketization of societies, maternal/child and familial relations are the "irreducible barriers to the expansion of competitive individualism" that can powerfully resist the alienation of global commodification and marketization (Connell 36). Migrant mothers providing low-waged caring labour across national borders are demanding their individual and collective rights to raise their own children in host countries (Arat-Koc). In Ontario, mothers and their children are taking to the streets in "accountability marches" against the child welfare state demanding social justice for their families and their maternal rights to care for their children. The possibility exists for global activism by mothers with their children to exercise their democratic and maternal rights to raise, nurture, and love their children.

NOTES

[1] See Brodie; Jenson; and Lister
[2] See Brodie; and Lister
[3] See Braedley and Luxton
[4] See Jenson; and Vosko
[5] See Greaves et. al. 126; and Swift and Callaghan
[6] See Greaves et. al.
[7] See Swift and Callaghan 8; and Swift
[8] See McKeen; and Weigers

WORKS CITED

Arat-Koc, Sedef. "Whose Social Reproduction?: Transnational Motherhood and Challenges to Feminist Political Economy." Eds. K. Bezanson and Meg Luxton. *Social Reproduction: Feminist Political Economy Challenges to Neo-Liberalism.* Montreal & Kingston: McGill-Queen's University Press, 2006. 75-92. Print.

Bezanson, Kate and Meg Luxton. "Introduction." *Social Reproduction: Feminist Political Economy Challenges Neo-Liberalism.* Montreal & Kingston: McGill-Queen's University Press, 2006. Print.

Bezanson, Kate. "Child Care Delivered Through the Mail Box: Social Reproduction, Choice, and Neoliberalism." Eds. Susan Braedley and Meg Luxton. *Neoliberalism and Everyday Life.*
Montreal and Kingston: McGill-Queen's University Press, 2010. 90-112. Print.

Braedley, Susan and Meg Luxton. "Competing Philosophies: Neoliberalism and the Challenges of Everyday Life." *Neoliberalism and Everyday Life.* Eds. Susan Braedley and Meg Luxton. Montreal and Kingston: McGill-Queen's University Press, 2010. 3-21. Print.

Brodie, Janine. "Putting Gender Back In: Women and Social Policy Reform in Canada." Ed. Yasmeen Abu-Laban. *Gendering the Nation-State.* Vancouver & Toronto: UBC Press, 2008. 165-184. Print.

Connell, Raewyn. "Understanding Neoliberalism." Eds. Susan Braedley and Meg Luxton. *Neoliberalism and Everyday Life.* Montreal and Kingston: McGill-Queen's University Press, 2010. 22-36. Print.

Croll, Elisabeth, J. "From the Girl Child to Girls' Rights." Eds. Andrea Cornwall and Maxine Molyneux. *The Politics of Rights: Dilemmas for Feminist Praxis.* London and New York: Routledge, 2008. 111-124. Print.

Cull, Randi. "Aboriginal Mothering under the State's Gaze." Eds. D.M. Lavell-Harvard and J.C. Lavell. *Until Our Hearts Are on the Ground: Aboriginal Mothering, Oppression, Resistance and Rebirth.* Toronto: Demeter Press, 2006. 141-156. Print.

Fox, Bonnie. "Motherhood as a Class Act; The Many Ways in Which "Intensive Mothering" is Entangled with Social Class." Eds. K. Bezanson and Meg Luxton. *Social Reproduction: Feminist Political Economy Challenges to Neo-liberalism.* Montreal & Kingston: McGill-Queen's University Press, 2006. 231-262. Print.

Gazso, A. "Gendering the 'Responsible Risk Taker': Citizenship Relationship with Gender-Neutral Social Assistance Policy." *Citizenship Studies* 13.1 (2009): 45-63. Print.

Gideon, Jasmine. "Accessing Economic and Social Rights under Neoliberalism: Gender and Rights in Chile." Eds. Andrea Cornwall and Maxine Molyneux. *The Politics of Rights: Dilemmas for Feminist Praxis.* London and New York: Routledge, 2008. 95-110. Print.

Giroux, Henry. "Disposable Futures: Dirty Democracy and the Politics of Disposability." Ed. H. Svi Shapiro. *Education and Hope in Troubled Times.* New York, London: Routledge, 2009. 223-240. Print.

Greaves, L.,C. Varcoe, N. Poole, M. Morrow, J. Johnson, A Pedersen, L. Irwin. *A Motherhood Issue: Discourses on Mothering under Duress.* Ottawa: Status of Women Canada Policy Research Fund, 2002. Print.

Hays, Sharon. *The Cultural Contradictions of Motherhood.* New Haven and London: Yale University Press, 1996. Print.

Holzscheiter, Anna. *Children's Rights in International Politics: The Transformative Power of Discourse.* Houndmills, Basingstoke, Hampshire, New York: Palgrave MacMillan, 2010. Print.

Jenson, J. "Citizenship in the Era of 'New Social Risks': What Happened to Gender Inequalities?" *Gendering the Nation-State.* Ed. Yasmeen Abu-Laban. Vancouver & Toronto: UBC Press, 2008. 185-202. Print.

Lister, Ruth. "Children (But Not Women) First: New Labour, Child Welfare and Gender." *Critical Social Policy* 26.2 (2006): 315-335. Print.

McKeen, Wendy. *Money in Their Own Name: The Feminist Voice in Poverty Debate in Canada, 1970-1995.* Toronto: University of Toronto Press, 2004. Print.

Pal, Leslie A. *Beyond Policy Analysis: Public Issue Management in Turbulent Times* (Fourth Edition). Toronto, On: Nelson Education Ltd, 2010. Print.

Strong-Boag, Veronica. *Fostering Nation? Canada Confronts Its History of Childhood Disadvantage.* Waterloo: Wilfrid Laurier University Press, 2011. Print.

Swift, Karen. *Manufacturing 'Bad Mothers': A Critical Perspective on Child Neglect.* Toronto, Buffalo, London: University of Toronto Press, 1995. Print.

Swift, Karen J. & Marilyn Callaghan. *At Risk: Social Justice in Child Welfare and Other Human Services.* Toronto: University of Toronto Press, 2009. Print.

Vosko, Leah F. "Crisis Tendencies in Social Reproduction: The Case of Ontario's Early Years Plan." Eds. K. Bezanson and Meg Luxton. *Social Reproduction: Feminist Political Economy Challenges to Neo-liberalism.* Montreal & Kingston: McGill-Queen's University Press, 2006. Print.

Weigers, Wanda. *The Framing of Poverty as "Child Poverty" and Its Implications for Women.* Ottawa: Status of Women, 2002. Print.

Section IV: Countering Neoliberalism Through Maternal Activism

18.

Dancing without Drums

Using Maternalism as a Political Strategy to Critique Neoliberalism in Ibadan, Nigeria

GRACE ADENIYI OGUNYANKIN

"There is too much stress for the women. All men do is spend money, go out to play, and come back, meanwhile the woman is stressing about, 'what will this child eat?' She'd be dancing without drums in the middle of the night. That stress is enough for the woman." (Desola, interview by author, June 27, 2011)

"Lai si ilu, ko si ijo, lai si ijo ko si ilu" (Without drums, there is no dancing. Without dancing there is no drumming)
— Yoruba saying

INTRODUCTION

The above Yoruba saying explains the symbiotic relationship between drumming and dancing in Nigerian culture. However, Desola's reference to dancing without drums signifies that the woman is worried, and her state of restlessness means that far from being stationary, she is "dancing" with anxiety. Thus, "dancing without drums" refers to the intricate dance required of mothers in the struggle to make ends meet without having necessary access to urban social justice. I relate the phrase to this chapter on mothering and neoliberalism in Ibadan, Nigeria, because I examine the ways in which mothers resist and negotiate neoliberal imposition. I view dancing without drums as a defiant act, and I connect it to how low-income mothers in Ibadan employ maternalism as a political strategy. I engage with mothering in this chapter as the ability to care and provide for children in one's care. Mothering has been made increasingly difficult for low-income women in Ibadan as neoliberal policy has adversely affected them and exacerbated socio-economic disparities. Thus, women use mothering (dancing) to challenge the lack of socio-economic justice (drums) under neoliberalism in the city of Ibadan.

Drawing from my fieldwork interviews in Ibadan, I argue that neoliberal policies and the neoliberal urbanization project is posing challenges to low-income women in two realms that they consider key to good mothering: food and education. My fieldwork interviews were with 48 poor, low-income and middle upper class women in Ibadan, but I only focus on the data from the 32 poor and low-income women I interviewed as they are the ones who consistently highlighted the ramifications of neoliberalism on their ability to mother.[1] Based on these interviews and my own observations while in the field, I illustrate the ways in which maternalism gives strength to women in a patriarchal environment to challenge the neoliberal state and carve out political spaces that they would not otherwise have because they do not have political or economic clout.

I will examine three levels of resistances where the maternal is a site of political power by looking at their economic and political action. These three sites in which mothers critique neoliberal economic policy are individual action, collective action, and imagined action. My analysis of these resistances is informed by Lefevbre's concept of the "right to the city" which has been widely taken up by scholars as an alternative strategy to "address the growing disenfranchisement of urban inhabitants in the context of contemporary neoliberal policy making" (Fawaz 831). The "right to the city" involves inhabitants participating in decisions made about the use of urban space and prioritizing the rights and needs of the masses over the interests of the elite minority.[2] I thus posit that the struggle over urban space and the belief that the city should be a place where resources such as income and education are equally distributed propels mothers to contest and expose the contradictions of neoliberalism.

NEOLIBERALISM'S EFFECT ON MOTHERING

Many of the low-income mothers I interviewed believe that good mothering entails providing economically for their children. This belief has especially become more salient under neoliberal restructuring whereby social spending cuts have significantly relied on women to absorb macroeconomic shocks. By comparison to the middle-class mothers I interviewed, these mothers bear an increased burden in ensuring that their children have enough to eat and that their school fees are paid.

Neoliberalism was first introduced to Nigeria in 1986 through the implementation of the Structural Adjustment Programmes (SAPs).[3] As an import dependent country, the decline in world oil price affected Nigeria's foreign exchange, which went from $25 billion in 1980 to $7.2 billion in 1986 and thus led to a deficit in the balance of payment (CBN 1990.) Consequently, Nigeria became a highly indebted country and was part of the IMF and World Bank initiated debt rescheduling programme and conditionalities. This Structural Adjustment Programme promulgated the "discipline of the market [and] combine[d] privatization and liberalization with new forms of political governance" (Hoogvelt 176).

The SAPs comprised of four elements: mobilization of domestic resources; policy reforms to increase economic efficiency; generation of foreign exchange revenues through exports; and reduction of the active role of the state to ensure that it is non-inflationary. Moreover, the specific measures to achieve SAP objectives can be divided into two: stabilization measures (public sector wage freeze; reduced subsidies on basic food commodities, health and education; and devaluation of currency), and adjustment measures (export promotion, downsizing of civil services, economic liberalization and privatization) (Hewitt 296-308).

Neoliberal economic restructuring has significantly differentiated effects on men and women. Public sector cuts in social spending, intended to increase state efficiency and savings, have placed a greater burden on poor mothers whose gender roles require they take care of family needs and reproductive tasks, particularly when social spending no longer meets social needs. Mothers have consequently absorbed the economic shock of SAPs. Accordingly, this reliance increases women's productive, reproductive, and community roles (Moser) as it is assumed that "women could intensify their subsistence and domestic labour to offset the cutbacks to social reproduction in both the labour market and the state" (Luxton 39). Further, due to retrenchment, redundancy, and bankruptcy, many males are unemployed or do not have steady jobs; therefore, women are left to fill this gap.

The increased financial burden wrought by neoliberalism on mothers means that some of them have diversified their incomes and many work long hours. One woman pointed out to me that she works from 6am to 11pm. As such, the paid work of the women in the informal economy is difficult to balance with their unpaid work given their long hours. I saw that many mothers I interviewed while they were working have their young children around them. Some of these mothers also manage to cook for their children while they are working in their makeshift shop. These mothers' experiences under neoliberalism are what Sylvia Chant refers to as the "feminisation of responsibility and obligation," whereby "women are increasingly at the frontline of dealing with poverty...[and] the unevenness between women's and men's inputs and their perceived responsibilities for coping with poverty seem to be growing. In some cases, the skew is such that it has reached the point of virtual one-sidedness" (176). Some of the mothers alluded to the reversal of roles, stating that women, instead of men, have now become chief breadwinners:

> [women are] suffering o! They are suffering. Some have husbands. But the husband is not working. She's the only one who is working. Only the woman will be taking care of the children. (Remi, interview by author, July 28, 2011)

> But now where we are, it is women who are feeding the husbands because the husband does not have a real job... many men have become women and women have become men. So you see the lack of money in the city is what is making women do stressful jobs. (Ebun, interview by author, July 7, 2011)

It is important to note the reversal of productive roles does not translate to a reversal of reproductive roles. Women's productive work has increased, yet there is no parallel decrease in their reproductive work. In effect, there has barely been any rescaling in increasing men's participation in reproductive work to reflect the shift in women's participation in productive work.

When talking about the changes that have taken place in Ibadan over the years, the challenges mothers face daily, and their dislikes about Ibadan, most mothers said they can barely afford to feed their children because food prices have been going up at alarming rates. Increase in food insecurity can be attributed to neoliberal restructuring measures such as currency devaluation and increased importation of food, as well as the contemporary rise in global food prices. This change in food security was cogently expressed by Aanu:

> There is change [in Ibadan], since about 1973. Ibadan was so good to the extent that if we took 20 naira to the market, there will be so much food at home. Until 1979, if you bring 20 naira you will buy everything. Now if you bring 5000 naira to the market, it won't buy anything. (interview by author, June 27, 2011)

Some of the mothers said they sometimes rely on their social networks to help them feed their children. Other mothers mentioned that they and their children sometimes barely have enough to eat, while some mentioned that they sometimes forgo meals so that their children can eat. The mothers and their families have modified their diets and are buying cheaper food staples that are often not their desired choice or most nutritious option. Those who described having the most difficulty were the ones who were widowed or no longer with their husbands:

> May God not let us face challenges that is more than us. Part of it is that there is nothing to eat. That's one challenge. Part of it is that my husband is not taking care of the children. That's one challenge. (Titilola, interview by author, July 21, 2011)

> What I face is—let's say our daddy (husband) were alive—there are some days that we drink garri to go to sleep when there is no money—and it shouldn't be like that. Two are better than one—I will also be thinking ah if their daddy were alive—if their daddy were alive I would not be doing the work I'm doing. (Funke, interview by author, June 21, 2011)

The mothers also expressed their dismay with the retrenchment of the state in education matters. The education sector benefitted tremendously from Nigeria's oil boom in the 1970s. During this time, universal primary education was introduced and secondary and post-secondary education were heavily subsidized (Adejumobi 209). However, the economic crisis of the 1980s adversely affected government expenditure on education and has led to an increase in the privatization of education. Due to cuts in social spending, some complained that public education is not completely free, as explained by Funke:

Because if we say, "don't go to private school go to public school" when we now bring the child to public school the money they are collecting is almost the same as private school—and it shouldn't be like that. They said they should pay PTA money, pay for block, pay for toilet, pay for lesson, pay for everything. And it wasn't like that before. (interview by author, June 21, 2011)

Others enroll their children in private school because there are no public schools nearby, or because they want their children to receive a better education than what the poorly invested public schools can offer. It is important to note that there are different levels of private schools. The private schools that some of the women's children go to do not provide the same level of education as the private schools of the well-to-do children. These schools are only slightly better than the public schools. Unfortunately, some children are unable to finish high school or enroll in tertiary education because the mothers are unable to afford the fees and/or the examination fees that are required for enrolment. This is especially unfortunate considering that federal universities did not charge tuition fees before; now, higher education has become increasingly inaccessible (Uwakwe et al. 163). Yet other mothers who struggle to pay school fees are discouraged from continuing their investments as there are rarely any job opportunities available for their children once they finish their schooling (Okafor). The effects of neoliberal globalization on economies and labour markets compounded by the recent financial crises has led to "increasing precariousness in the labour market including job losses, reduced household incomes and reduced employment security as well as social protection" (Izuhara 2). Some also pointed out that the children of the poor are the "losers" in finding employment—as the Nigerian formal economy operates on a closed "network" basis.

Just as the low employment rates of husbands has affected male contribution to the household, and thereby affected women, the high unemployment rate of youths also has an effect on the women because it extends their mothering. Toluwanimi explained her experiences with mothering her adult children:

One is living with their 30-year-old child, 40 year old. When a child finishes from Poly[technic], uni[versity], finishes a master and does not find a job—will they be stealing? Will you not feed them? When one is taking care of a 40-year-old child at one's age, you know the city is not good. (interview by author, August 2, 2011)

Some women's mothering is also extended to their grandchildren. Zainab, for example, is a grandmother who experiences financial difficulty in caring for her grandchildren:

Some of my [grand]children are small ... It is hard! To spend money to care for them is something else. Some days, I don't find money to give them. And it might be compulsory that they, perhaps they've brought a bill, whatever I have is all I can afford. (interview by author, July 21, 2011)

For some women, extended mothering thus means they must continue to work into old age because the onus is on them to be "good" mothers.

LEVERAGING THE DISCOURSE OF "GOOD" MOTHERING AS A POLITICAL STRATEGY

A large majority of the mothers are employed primarily in the informal economy and out of those who are not, only two do not rely on the informal economy as a secondary source of income. Many of these women in the informal economy are street traders. Some of these street traders not only struggle to provide for their children as discussed in the previous section, their livelihood is also threatened by neoliberal urban beautification projects. These projects entail western modernist visions of what the city should look like.[4] The elite play a role in constructing this vision and as such cast street traders as deviants in urban public space (Brown, Lyons, and Dankoco 668). The urban is construed as the primary site for market-led economic growth, where capital interests prevail over citizen's needs (Vives Miró 3). As such, street traders, in certain urban spaces in Ibadan, are viewed as contravening planning and zoning ordinances. In short, urban planning in the Nigerian context, as guided by neoliberal policy, is anti-poor and promotes social and spatial exclusion (151).

During some of my interviews that took place on the sides of the roads in Ibadan, some of the women, as highlighted by my conversation with Victoria, expressed their fears regarding the government crackdown on street trading:

Victoria: … they should have mercy on us because it was we who voted for them—they shouldn't chase us. How we will eat (or our livelihood) is all we are looking for. They said they will chase all those on the side of the street.

One woman was also very vigilant throughout the duration of our interview, ready to run and hide if need be. She had briefly mentioned that government officials had come to chase them away previously but she returned because her livelihood was at stake if she complies.

Despite fears of being removed and possibly fined, economic necessity meant the mothers prioritized their access to the market. They were subversive to state policy because it challenged their roles as good mothers and their ability to provide for their children. One salient memory for me was while I was in a car with a civil servant who, when we passed by a particular woman street trader, expressed disappointment that the very woman she expelled just a few days prior was back in the same spot. The woman was the only street trader around[5] and therefore a highly visible target for "punishment." Yet I understood—based on my discussions with the mothers in my study—that women like her resist because they have children at home to care for.

Women also employ motherhood as a political strategy at the collective level. On August 4, 2011, while I was conducting interviews in the Yemetu community, I witnessed my first all women protest in Ibadan. There were at least fifty women (some had their children with them) who were marching towards the state government secretariat while chanting and carrying placards. The women were protesting against unfair police taxation. The police would not allow them to trade their goods unless they paid a particular sum of money, a "tax," to them. The women were calling the police thieves and made it clear that they refused to pay the police. They argued that the particular urban space where they conduct their trade should be tax-free because they need money to feed their children and pay their school fees. This protest reveals women's contestation of the power structures that lay claim over urban space in Ibadan. By engaging in this protest, these mothers are asserting their rights to the city and their rights to pursue their entrepreneurial economic interests for the livelihood of their families, which under non-contradictory circumstances would be complementary to neoliberal ideology.

Motherhood provides the most viable platform for low-income women to criticize the injustices of neoliberal policies. Given that Nigeria is a patriarchal society, women are often expected to limit their public voice and focus on being "good" wives and mothers, thus a claim to urban space based on gender equality would have likely not been taken seriously. However, these mothers deploy patriarchy to obtain voice and strive for political identity by highlighting that being a "good" mother and asserting a public voice cannot be mutually exclusive. As such, equality claims, made by women as mothers, to the city may be considered more acceptable and less confrontational as they are not necessarily challenging patriarchal norms but rather living up to the expectation to be "good" mothers. Moreover, from a socio-political economy perspective, the low-income women have little political influence and economic power—thus motherhood is the most viable base for resistance.

Women also articulated maternal resistance to neoliberalism at the level of their imagination, as revealed during the interviews. Most of the mothers I interviewed decried the exclusion of women in decision making to the detriment of the city, their socio-economic status and the future of their children. When I asked them whether the city would be better if there were more women in decision-making positions and/or when I asked them what they would do if they occupied a key post, the majority suggested that women would be better for the city either by describing women using adjectives that are normally associated with mothering, or by explicitly stating that because women are mothers they would do a better job caring for the city:

> The man is important too but a woman is important because she is very very caring. Women, we are mothers for the man. If there are no women, the city will not grow because a woman will know what's right at the right time. (Ebun, interview by author, July 7, 2011)

> …What the men cannot do, because, you know that the men they like enjoyment, that they would first take care of themselves first before they remember the city. But woman, a woman is someone who is kind. If a woman is in charge, in charge of the government, so, everything that is not in Nigeria, she will make sure it exists. Like free health care, will now exist. They will build schools. So they will take care of the city, if it is that there is no safety. Like how we said there is no toilet, no bathroom, they will do it all for us. Everything will go well.

Whoever doesn't have a job, will have a job. Whoever is lacking, they will take care of him/her. So there will be a major difference. (Mojisola, interview by author, July 15, 2011)

...women will even be better in politics. You can see the woman has a tender heart. They are not so rigid...and being a mother, passing through motherhood stage, taking care of children, you know, you should be able to know how to take care of the society you know the way you take good care of your children, you will take good care of them. You have the experience of taking care of the little ones and relating with people. Unlike the men, some of them don't have direct contact with the children...(Busola, interview by author, July 30, 2011)

Also when discussing the things that they would do, the women most often described what they would do for the people and the city within/from a mothering lens:

I will first focus on children. The students. The school fee that they are paying now it's too much. It's the rich that they want to be educated, they don't want the poor to be educated. There is too much suffering. Do you understand me? (Toluwanimi, interview by author, August 2, 2011)

[I will provide] free education. Government school—you know it was free before. They had free books. And the government helps out with that...when they had free books before, things were much easier...[I will be] taking care of students ... they should eat. Food that they eat in the morning, they shouldn't eat it in the afternoon. What they eat in the afternoon they shouldn't eat in the evening. [Diversifying the food] can bring good health/nutrition. It will deter sickness in the body of the children. But the food that they eat three times in a row, it will not have any meaning in their body.

It will be different. I will take care of people and I won't let those who finish school be doing nothing, I don't like it. I will create companies for employment...so their minds would be at rest. There would be no stealing or anything... I will [also] take care of [widows] because their burden is heavy.

338

The mothers focused on the detrimental oversight in excluding women from decision making. Thus, from a maternalist perspective, if mothers were in charge, neoliberalism would not have as deleterious an effect as it currently does in Ibadan, and even if it did, they would find a way to remedy it by caring the way mothers are "supposed" to. Within this patriarchal context, essentialist conceptualizations of mothering provide a viable challenge to the retrenchment of the state in social provisioning and neoliberal prioritization of the market over individual rights.

CONCLUSION

The neoliberal expectation that women will be "good" mothers—especially with regard to absorbing macroeconomic shocks and filling in the gap left by neoliberalism—is threatening to become an Achilles' heel to neoliberalism in Ibadan. The mothers have embodied the call to be "good" mothers to the extent that they have employed it as political strategy in a space that would otherwise eclipse poor women's voices. By working within the neoliberal and patriarchal rhetoric, mothers have been able to call in to question the neoliberal assumption that the market can solve socioeconomic disparities, as well as challenge the patriarchal prerogative to stifle women's voices and their claims to the city as equal inhabitants.

ACKNOWLEDGEMENTS

This research was carried out with the aid of a grant from the International Development Research Centre in Ottawa, Canada, to whom the author is grateful for support. For assistance in the field I would like to thank Dr. Wahab, Mr. Ayorinde, Mrs. Oladiran, Mrs. Oladepo, Mummy Sukurat, and Mr. Ojolowo. I am also indebted to Kate McPherson, Kehinde Adeniyi, and Lisa Boucher for their insightful comments during the writing of this paper.

NOTES

[1] For the remainder of this paper, I will refer to both poor and low-income women as low-income women.
[2] See Boer and Vries

[3] Although SAPs is no longer in effect, other forms of neoliberal market restructuring mechanisms are in place.

[4] See Brown, Lyons, and Dankoco

[5] There are some places in Ibadan that only have a few street traders, whereas there are others where street traders are highly concentrated.

WORKS CITED

Adejumobi, Said. "Structural Adjustment, Students' Movement and Popular Struggles in Nigeria, 1986-1996." *Identity Transformation and Identity Politics under Structural Adjustment in Nigeria.* Attahiru Jega ed. Nordiska Afrikainstitutet and Centre for Research and Documentation, 2000. 204-233. Print.

Boer, R. W. J., and J. De Vries. "The Right to the City as a Tool for Urban Social Movements: The Case of Barceloneta." The 4th International Conference of the International Forum on Urbanism (IFoU), Amsterdam/Delft. 2009. http://newurbanquestion.ifou.org/proceedings/

Brown, A., M. Lyons, and I. Dankoco. "Street Traders and the Emerging Spaces for Urban Voice and Citizenship in African Cities." *Urban Studies* 47.3 (2010): 666–683. Print.

Central Bank of Nigeria. Statistical Bulletin. Central Bank of Nigeria, Lagos. 1990. Print.

Chant, Sylvia. "The 'Feminisation of Poverty' and the 'Feminisation' of Anti-Poverty Programmes: Room for Revision?" *Journal of Development Studies* 44.2 (2008): 165–197. Print.

Fawaz, M. "Neoliberal Urbanity and the Right to the City: a View from Beirut's Periphery." *Development and Change* 40.5 (2009): 827–852. Print.

Hewitt, T. "Half a Century of Development." *Poverty and Development into the 21st Century.* Eds. T. Allen and A. Thomas. Oxford: Oxford University Press, 2000. 289-308. Print.

Hoogvelt, A. *Globalization and the Post-Colonial World.* Maryland: The Johns Hopkins University Press, 2001. Print.

Izuhara, M. "Introduction." *Ageing and Intergenerational Relations: Family Reciprocity from a Global Perspective.* Ed. M. Izuhara. Bristol, UK: the Policy Press, 2010. 1-13 Print.

Luxton, Meg. "Feminist Political Economy in Canada and the Politics of Social Reproduction." *Social Reproduction: Feminist Political Economy*

Challenges Neo-Liberalism. Eds. Kate Bezanson and Meg Luxton. Montreal: McGill-Queen's University Press, 2006. 11-44. Print.

Moser, Caroline. *Gender Planning and Development: Theory, Practice and Training.* London: Routledge, 1993. Print.

Okafor, E. E. "Youth Unemployment and Implications for Stability of Democracy in Nigeria." *Journal of Sustainable Development in Africa* 13.1 (2011): 358–373. Print.

Uwakwe, C. B., A. O. Falaye, B. O. Emunemu, and O. Adelore. "Impact of Decentralization and Privatization on the Quality of Education in sub-Saharan Africa: The Nigerian Experience." *European Journal of Social Sciences* 7.1 (2008): 160–170.

Vives Miró, Sònia. "Producing a 'Successful City': Neoliberal Urbanism and Gentrification in The Tourist City—The Case of Palma (Majorca)." *Urban Studies Research* 2011: 1–13. Print.

19.

Maternal Activism in the International Campaign for Justice in Bhopal (ICJB), India

REENA SHADAAN

INTRODUCTION

The Bhopal gas disaster is a telling account of the impact of neoliberal-driven development in India. However, Bhopal is also telling of the strength of mothers/othermothers that have emerged at the forefront of the movement for justice. Despite their activism spanning over two decades, these women have received little attention from social movement scholars. Using data from 27 interviews with top level leaders, community leaders, and rank and file participants, this study examines women's activism in one of the movement groups of Bhopal—the International Campaign for Justice in Bhopal (ICJB).

Similar to findings of other studies related to women's toxic waste activism,[1] there is a strong motherist justification underlying the women's activism. This is rooted in the impact of chemical exposure on children's health and women's reproductive health. It is as mothers/othermothers that many women locate their activism, and in the process they challenge patriarchal conceptions of motherhood as relegated to the private, "apolitical" sphere. Defining social activism as an extension of mothering was also found to positively influence activists' daughters. Such findings contribute to the growing data on maternal participation in popular movements.[2]

BHOPAL GAS DISASTER

Although neoliberal policies were only officially adopted by the Indian government in the early 1990s, the Bhopal gas disaster served as a forewarning of the destructive consequences of neoliberal-driven development. Deregulation and heinous corporate negligence coupled with the withdrawal of government from issues related to maintaining the public good produced—and continue to maintain—this disaster. In the case of Bhopal, environmental racism is also critical to the context. Chemical plants that produce toxic substances are routinely situated in low-income/racialized areas, placing the risks associated with such facilities disproportionately on these communities (Krauss 247). Similarly, the Bhopal-based Union Carbide India Limited (UCIL) chemical plant—a subsidiary of the American-owned Union Carbide Corporation (UCC)—was built in old Bhopal, the poorest subsection of Bhopal.

Bhopal is the capital city of Madhya Pradesh, located in central India. It is divided into three sub-sections: old Bhopal, new Bhopal, and a further area in the South. Large portions of the population of old Bhopal are migrants from neighbouring villages in Madhya Pradesh, displaced by projects touted as necessary for development, such as the Green Revolution (Sarangi 101). Old Bhopal, therefore, is not foreign to the destructive consequences of mainstream development, as many of these migrants were also those who were exposed to the toxic chemical compound methyl isocyanate (MIC) and other unknown gasses during the now infamous case of corporate crime by the American-owned Union Carbide Corporation (UCC), now owned by the Dow Chemical Company.

As a direct consequence of the gas tragedy, Bhopal has become the site of much social movement activity. The purpose of this chapter is to shed light on this social activism, and specifically maternal activism. It is mothers/othermothers who have emerged as a powerful force—or flame—in sustaining this movement for justice. Throughout the course of their activism, they have demonstrated remarkable strength and have challenged gender boundaries of behavior in old Bhopal as a result. Perhaps the most compelling illustration of their resolve is provided by one of their movement tactics—the *padyartra* (journey on foot). In both 2006 and 2008 they carried out a *padyartra* to Delhi—a 747 km distance from Bhopal. Movement leader, Champa Devi Shukla, discussed their arduous journey.

> ...all we had was two saris, one blanket, and we walked like this...We did not have anything to eat. We just kept walking. Wherever we stopped on our way to Delhi, we used to ask people around for help—for flour, rice...In places where we did not get any help, we used to sleep without food. We were 100 women and 25 children. When we had no food to feed our children, all the mothers got upset. They started pawning their jewellery. Even our footwear was completely damaged because of the continuous walk. None of us had money to buy new slippers...we wrapped our feet with the leaves of trees.

These words illustrate the strength and resilience of the women-activists of old Bhopal. Nevertheless, these women have to-date received relatively little attention in academic scholarship.[3] In effect, my first encounter with them led to my asking a number of questions: Why is it primarily women that are involved in this struggle? What are their motivations for engaging in activism? What are the roles they play in the movement? How has their involvement affected gender relations in the household/ community? These questions form the basis of my analysis.

INTERNATIONAL CAMPAIGN FOR JUSTICE IN BHOPAL (ICJB)

Using data gained from semi-structured interviews with 23 Bhopali mother-activists and four younger women-activists, the following will discuss maternal activism in the coalition group, the International Campaign for Justice in Bhopal (ICJB). This study involves women-activists who identify as being part of the Bhopal-based survivor/support groups that lead ICJB. This includes: (1) *Bhopal Gas Peedit Mahila Purush Sangharsh Morcha* [Bhopal Gas-affected Women and Men's Front]; (2) *Bhopal Gas Peedit Mahila Stationery Karmchari Sangh* [Bhopal Gas-affected Women's Stationery Worker's Union], (3) Children against Dow-Carbide, and (4) The Bhopal Group for Information and Action (BGIA).

ICJB is comprised primarily of women, most of whom are mothers-/other-mothers. Given the patriarchal context of their lives, being involved in this collective provides a central source of strength for these women. Gas-affected women are *othered* on several levels—as impoverished persons, as members of marginalized religious groups (in the case of Muslims and scheduled caste Hindus), and as women. The gas tragedy added the shared experience of post-disaster trauma, multiple deaths in the household, widespread illness/surging medical costs, increased levels of poverty, and governmental neglect. Amidst these multiple layers of shared injustice, social networks and community solidarity are important survival mechanisms. Resham Bi, an elderly activist whose husband died as a result of his exposure, maintained, "I cannot do anything on my own. Since we are all walking together and doing it altogether, that is why we have been able to do it." Shanti Bai, an activist who has been involved in the struggle for justice since the gas leak, maintained, "All my power comes from other women only. When I see them, I go ahead...I did not [feel powerful before getting involved] and now my power has come after seeing other women."

A MOTHERIST JUSTIFICATION FOR MOVEMENT PARTICIPATION

The adverse impact of the gas tragedy on children was a significant grievance expressed by the mothers/othermothers. As a direct consequence of the gas tragedy, there has been a large increase in congenital malformations, developmental disabilities, and reproductive health issues. In fact, 15 of the 27 women related a problem—stemming from their families or immediate communities—of relation to reproductive health.[4] Elderly activist, Omwati Bai, related the following regarding her two grandsons:

> [My grandsons] are disabled and they even faint while they are sitting. They often fall when they try to walk...When I think about their futures and their children in the future, I get worried. I even feel almost dead. If I am dead, who will give them water to drink? They can't even go to the toilet by themselves...Who will take these disabled children to the toilet?

The mothers discussed the negative impact on Bhopali children in general as influential to their participation. As maintained by community leader, Nafisa Bi, "Pain with our children is our anger. This is not only a question of our house; it is a question of all of Bhopal."

This is rooted in Collins's concept of *othermothering*—the long tradition amongst African American women of maintaining the wellbeing or mothering non-biological children in their communities. This is primarily rooted in the recognition of racial oppression as a force impeding the wellbeing and development of the African American community, and the need to develop community solidarity (particularly within poor communities) for the purposes of contesting and surviving amidst racial oppression. Similarly, othermothering in Bhopal is linked to class oppression. All the women I spoke to experience varying degrees of poverty, and linked their oppression vis-à-vis the Bhopal gas disaster to their class identity. Class oppression coupled with the debilitating impact of the gas tragedy, means that community solidarity is a necessity for survival. Othermothering is a necessary outcome of this.

Perhaps the most poignant example of othermothering stems from the Chingari Trust, a body that, amongst other initiatives, funds a school/rehabilitation centre for children with congenital malformations and developmental disabilities attributed to toxic waste exposure. Upon being awarded the 2004 Goldman Environmental Prize for their lengthy activism, movement leaders Rashida Bi and Champa Devi Shukla dedicated a large portion of their prize money to opening this centre. Rashida Bi discussed their decision.

> The award that we received, even from this we have created a flame. We thought that the money we have got should be given to Bhopal...We founded Chingari Trust and...started the work of rehabilitating the children who were affected by the poison of Union Carbide, because the government has done nothing for them and it was necessary for them to be rehabilitated...Women have already lived their lives, but there should be something for the children who are being born disabled.

Women's reproductive health also emerged as a significant grievance. Women's reproductive health is intrinsically linked to children's health; therefore, once the women began to speak about children's health, a discussion of their own reproductive health (or that of other women in their families and communities) ensued. Leela Bai, who has seen a slew of health-related problems in her household as a result of the gas tragedy, discussed this link in relation to her family.

Because of the gas, children cannot drink their mother's breast milk[5] and children are being born disabled... My own eldest daughter's daughter is so severely disabled... and now because of the gas, my youngest daughter has lost her fertility...I am completely fed up with her continuous treatment, so if we are that fed up, there would be many other people who are also fed up... That is why we thought the next generation should not face the problems that we are facing. That is why we are fighting this fight.

RECLAIMING MOTHERHOOD: THE PERSONAL IS POLITICAL

Bhopali women's motherist/othermotherist motivations for movement participation necessitates a discussion on the feminist strength of maternal activism. Rich's distinction between (*the patriarchal institution of) motherhood* and *mothering* is useful in framing the discussion.

> The term "motherhood" refers to the patriarchal institution of motherhood that is male-defined and controlled and is deeply oppressive to women, while the word "mothering" refers to women's experiences of mothering that are female-defined and centered and potentially empowering to women. (O'Reilly 2)

While (the patriarchal institution of) motherhood relegates women to the private/"apolitical" sphere, the act of mothering is potentially a space in which women can challenge patriarchal conceptualizations of motherhood.

Maternal activism is an example of mothering that challenges the patriarchal institution of motherhood. This is demonstrated in the process of political participation, i.e. the women-activists' rejection of mothering as an act limited to the private/"apolitical" sphere, and in their bringing formerly private issues (primarily reproductive health-related) to the public sphere through their activism. In 2008, when Bhopali mothers chained themselves to the railings of the Prime Minister's home in Delhi, carrying their children born with congenital malformations and made developmentally disabled by the toxins of UCC, they were in fact illustrating the feminist adage—the personal is political.

It is, therefore, the private-female-"apolitical"/public-male-"political" dichotomy that Bhopali women's mothering/social activism contests. This dichotomy is particularly pronounced in the context of old Bhopal, where the formerly prevalent practice of *purdah* literally kept women in the private sphere of the household. *Purdah* is the practice of secluding women from men outside their immediate families. Different forms of the practice are carried out by both Muslim and Hindu communities in primarily northern and central India. Although *purdah* is less common amongst poor women (given that economic necessity forces poor women out of their homes to engage in wage work), in old Bhopal many women did piece rate work in their homes allowing them to continue practicing the custom. The practice itself varies from community to community. In some cases women will wear loose fitting clothing that covers their face and body when leaving the home. *Purdah* can also manifest in stricter forms, such as disallowing a woman from ever leaving the confines of the home, although such stricter forms of *purdah* are much less common today.

Almost half of the 27 women practiced a form of *purdah* prior to the gas disaster. Some, such as leader Rashida Bi, practiced a very strict form. She said, "14 years after I got married, the gas disaster took place. Until then I had not even seen the roads and places in Bhopal." For many of these women, the rejection of *purdah* was the rejection of the construction of womanhood *purdah* represented—secluded and submissive. Rashida Bi went on to say:

> I did not know what power meant, but when I came out I recognized myself and came to know that even I can do something and fight. I can show and tell our sisters that the kitchen is not the only thing we have in our life. Our job is not only to give birth to children...We too have many things to do in our lives...The best part of life is to come out of the house, help others and show them the right path. That type of life is the best life.

The challenging of the public-male-"political"/private-female "apolitical" dichotomy is also apparent in the roles and responsibilities Bhopali mother-activists carry out as part of their activism. In ICJB, women make up a large part of the top level and community level leadership. As such, they are directly involved in both the strategic planning aspect of movement organization (e.g. decision-making with regards to campaign objectives, organizing campaigns/tactics, and so on), as well as in the frontline movement activities (e.g. community mobilization, acting as spokespersons, participation in campaigns/tactics, and so on). Activists also engage in confrontational protest tactics where they constantly clash with public authorities.

Ram Bai, an activist who has participated in numerous campaigns, said, "…now we are not scared of anyone and anything. We do not care if somebody scolds or beats us." This is the same woman who, prior to her activism, said, "I was not used to going out to buy things from the market. I used to feel that people would say something to me on the way if I went outside. I did not go out to buy vegetables, as I was not daring enough."

By virtue of this activism, mothers have positively impacted their daughters' construction of their identities. Safreen Khan (18 years old), Yasmeen Khan (13 years old), Sarita Malviya (17 years old) and Meera Morey (mid-20s) are prominent young activists.[6] Their activism, in large part, stems from their mothers' activist involvement.

> My mother used to say, "Gas leaked so they carry out rallies. This is why I go, so you should go as well". I didn't know this. Once I went with [my] mother…I came to know that usually more people come from outside…I felt that if people from other places and countries can join, why can't we people from Bhopal? (Meera Morey).

> In the beginning…I knew nothing…My mother spoke with the women [in the community] because we were newcomers here…The women told us that the gas leaked here, and there is an active organization. My mother used to go [to movement meetings] alone, and she used to say '[Sarita] come with me'…I started going to the meetings…I heard all these talks and after that I realized that it has been affecting our health. Then I decided that even I have to fight for this. (Sarita Malviya)

> …when [Safreen and Yasmeen] saw other people chanting slogans and saw the passion in them, they asked us, "What had happened?" We told them everything about the night of December 2nd in 1984. After this, these kids came in front too and joined us. (Nafisa Bi, mother of Safreen and Yasmeen)

CONCLUSION

Through their maternal activism, the women-activists of old Bhopal are redefining public discourse on the impact of neoliberalism. Using their knowledge/lived experiences and drawing from their gendered experiences as women and mothers, they remind us of its destructive consequences. In the process they challenge the public-male-"political"/private-female-"apolitical" dichotomy. For the women-activists, asserting their rights as women and mothers/othermothers is rooted in their experiences as women and mothers amidst patriarchy. They utilize the patriarchal power of essentialist maternal conceptualizations to claim their rights as women and mothers and in the process defy the very basis of such ideologies. In effect, the gender inequalities they experience emerge as a site of contestation even if this is not an explicit mandate of their movement activism. This work has drawn significantly from the knowledge and lived experiences of movement leader, Rashida Bi (117). It is perhaps her words that provide the most poignant description of Bhopali women-activists in the aftermath of the gas disaster:

> We are not expendable. We are not flowers to be offered at the altar of profit and power. We are dancing flames committed to conquering darkness. We are challenging those who threaten the survival of the planet and the magic and mystery of life. Through our struggle, through our refusal to be victims, we have become survivors. And we are on our way to becoming victors.

NOTES

[1] See Brown and Ferguson; Culley and Angelique; and Krauss
[2] This study is based on M.A. research conducted at York University (Toronto, Canada). As such, my gratitude goes out to my research supervisors, Sharada Srinivasan, Ph.D. and Eduardo Canel, Ph.D. Further, I would like to thank Bhopali survivor and activist, Sanjay Verma, for his support throughout the research process. Finally, my deepest gratitude to the women of old Bhopal. The inspiration I draw from them extends far beyond the scope of this research.
[3] With the exception of S. Mukherjee, who authored *Surviving Bhopal: Dancing Bodies, Written Texts, and Oral Testimonials of Women in the Wake of an Industrial Disaster*. New York: Palgrave Macmillan, 2010
[4] For medical studies on the impact on human reproductive health in the aftermath of the disaster see Pilgaokar and Sathyamala; Ranjan; Sarangi et al.; Shrivastava; and Varma 1987

[5]A 2002 study by Srishti and Toxics Link found contaminants in the breast milk of women in communities surrounding the abandoned Union Carbide factory.

[6]Ages at the time of the interviews.

WORKS CITED

Bai, Leela. Personal interview. 10 Jul. 2010.

Bai, Omwati. Personal interview. 20 Jun. 2010.

Bai, Ram. Personal interview. 22 Jun. 2010.

Bai, Shanti. Personal interview. 20 Jun. 2010.

Bi, Nafisa. Personal interview. 15 Jun. 2010. — Personal interview. 5 Aug. 2011.

Bi, Rashida. Personal interview. 2 Jul. 2010.

— "The Goldman Foundation Environment Award." *The Bhopal Reader.* Ed. Bridget Hanna, Ward Morehouse, and Satinath Sarangi. Goa: The Other India Press, 2004. 116-117. Print.

Bi, Resham. Personal interview. 14 Jun. 2010.

Brown, Phil and Faith I.T. Ferguson. "'Making a Big Stink'" Women's Work, Women's Relationships, and Toxic Waste Activism." *Gender & Society* 9.2 (1995): 145-172. Print.

Collins, Patricia Hill. *Black Feminist Thought: Knowledge, Consciousness, and the Politics of Empowerment.* Boston: Unwin Hyman, 1990. Print.

Culley, Marci R. and Holly L. Angelique. "Women's Gendered Experiences as Long-term Three Mile Island Activists." *Gender & Society* 17.3 (2003): 445-461. Print.

Krauss, Celene. "Women and Toxic Waste Protests: Race, Class and Gender as Resources of Resistance." *Qualitative Sociology* 16.3 (1993): 247-262. Print.

Malviya, Sarita. Personal interview. 17 Jun. 2010.

Morey, Meera. Personal Interview. 18 Jun. 2010.

Mukherjee, S. *Surviving Bhopal: Dancing Bodies, Written Texts, and Oral Testimonials of Women in the Wake of an Industrial Disaster.* New York: Palgrave Macmillan, 2010.

Pilgaokar, Anil and C. Sathyamala. *Distorted Lives: Women's Reproductive Health and Bhopal Disaster.* Pune: Medico Friend Circle, 1990. Print.

O'Reilly, Andrea. "Introduction." *From Motherhood to Mothering: The Legacy of Adrienne Rich's Of Woman Born.* Ed. Andrea O'Reilly. Albany: State University of New York Press, 2004. 1-23. Print.

Ranjan, Nishant, Satinath Sarangi S, V.T. Padmanabhan, Steve Holleran, Rajasekhar Ramakrishnan, and Daya R. Verma. "Methyl Isocyanate Exposure and Growth Patterns of Adolescents in Bhopal." *JAMA,* 290.14 (2003): 1856–1857. Print.

Sarangi, Satinath. "The Movement in Bhopal and Its Lessons." *Social Justice* 23.4 (1996): 100-109. Print.

Sarangi, Satinath, Tasneem Zaidi, Ritesh Pal, Diana Katgara, V. G. Gadag, Shree Mulay, and Daya R. Varma. "Effects of Exposure of Parents to Toxic Gases in Bhopal on the Offspring." *American Journal of Industrial Medicine* 53.8 (2010): 836-841. Print.

Shrivastava, R. "Bhopal Gas Disaster: Review on Health Effects of Methyl Isocyanate." *Research Journal of Environmental Sciences* 5.2 (2011): 150-156. Print.

Shukla, Champa Devi. Personal interview. 23 Jun. 2010.

Surviving Bhopal: Toxic Present, Toxic Future. Delhi: Srishti, 2002. Print.

Varma, Daya R. "Epidemiological and Experimental Studies on the Effects of Methyl Isocyanate on the Course of Pregnancy." *Environmental Health Perspectives* 72 (1987): 153-157. Print.

20.

It's Not the Meek Who Inherit the Earth

Low-Income Mothers Organize for Economic Justice in Canada

KATHERYNE SCHULZ

INTRODUCTION

Over the past twenty years, Canada has undergone massive economic and social changes that signal a fundamental shift away from the post-war Keynesian welfare state and toward a neoliberal governance model based upon market rationality, individualism, economic efficiency, and the establishment of supra national authority (Clarke). Globalization of trade and finance, the shift to lean production processes, deregulation and privatization has been accompanied by wholesale restructuring of social programs (Russell). Neoliberal governance has generated growing income polarization in Canada and elsewhere, intensified poverty for women, and has deepened the marginalization of disadvantaged groups, especially single mothers.[1]

Previously, corporations and the state were forced to assume some responsibility for social reproduction through progressive corporate taxation and the provision of universal programs such as health care, social insurance programs such as Unemployment Insurance, and social welfare programs.[2]

Policymakers in Canada have restructured state income security provisions so that the value of benefits has eroded while expenditures are redirected toward workfare style welfare programs (Russell). Labour market restructuring has deepened employment inequality across the country and this has affected low-income workers marginalized by race and/or gender the most deeply.[3] As restructuring shrinks the state income transfers and social programs that women rely on, responsibility for increasing amounts of unpaid caring labour fall on women's shoulders.[4] The impact has been particularly severe for low-income women, many of whom are further marginalized by race, immigration status, disability, and family status (United Way and CCSD). Lack of supports mean that low-income women are more likely to be excluded from paid employment and therefore have to rely on inadequate state income transfers; they spend more time engaged in unpaid work such as caregiving; and their needs are less likely to be met by service providers due to restructuring (Bezanson and Luxton).

Mirchandani and Chan use the term "gendered racialization" of poverty to describe the interaction of racism and sexism that leads to the economic exclusion of low-income women of colour, and to racist sexist stereotypes of women as undeserving "welfare cheats."[5] Many of these women live in poor neighbourhoods that have become increasingly racialized with high concentrations of immigrant residents whose needs cannot be met by underresourced community service agencies (Ontario Public Service Employees Union). Khosla's Toronto study also found that the unpaid work of low-income women of colour has intensified as funding and services are cut (Khosla). In Ontario, one example of this is the requirement that low-income single mothers participate in workfare programs. Single mothers who can make informal child-care arrangements are "free" to work for starvation wages in call centres for a minimal welfare top up (Little, "The Leaner, Meaner Welfare Machine"). Those who cannot get low-wage jobs are expected to do volunteer workfare placements or to act as informal child-care providers although they are in no position to care for multiple children (Community Development Halton).

Low-income single mothers need to organize for political change in order to reverse these punitive social policies and stereotypes. However, the challenges they face in terms of political participation and activism are poorly understood and rarely documented. While the U.S. literature contains a small but vibrant number of books about contemporary self-organizing by single mothers (Naples) in Canada their organizing activities have received much less attention. The only substantial scholarly contribution is

Little's 2007 article about single mothers' organizing in Ontario from 1968-1971 (Little, "Militant Mothers Fight Poverty").

A complex history of political engagement with important social policy implications can be uncovered by asking low-income, single mothers about their political experiences. Consequently, these questions are the focus of my research: How do low-income single mothers become engaged in political activism? What are the costs and benefits of activism? How is neoliberal restructuring affecting these women as activists? Activism in this context was broadly defined on a continuum from community work, to advocacy, to more militant direct action activities. I wanted to capture the overlap between women's work as mothers, activists, wage earners, and caregivers. Implicit in this approach is the recognition that real politics happen not only on the traditional public stage, but also in neighbourhoods and in women's homes, sandwiched between workfare jobs, school pick-ups, and visits to the welfare office.[6]

METHODOLOGY

My research was conducted in 2005 and it involved oral interviews with three low-income single mothers about their extensive experience as political activists in Ontario. This approach enabled me to get a more deeply contextualized and biographical perspective on the issues than would have been possible using other methods. The quotes in this article come from those interviews. All three women explicitly waived confidentiality because they saw my study as an opportunity for their political knowledge to be recorded and used to inspire other activists. The women were Josephine Grey from Toronto (June 15), Jacquie Thompson from London (June 18), and Cindy Buott from Peterborough (June 22). All three women knew each other through their work. Jacquie and Josephine have been economic justice activists for twenty years while Cindy has been an activist for a decade. Following the one-on-one interviews, I arranged for all of us to spend a weekend at a retreat where I conducted a group interview (July 16). I then wrote up my findings and each woman approved their life history and quotes, and provided comments on the research paper as a whole. This article is based on the critical knowledge and political insights that they shared with me.

PARTICIPANTS' LIFE HISTORIES

Josephine Grey

At the time of our interviews Josephine Grey was forty-five years old. She is a self-described mixed race woman of British, Jewish, and West Indian descent who was living with her four children in Toronto. Josephine told me that her childhood experiences of racism were key in developing her political consciousness. In the early 1980s, Josephine got involved in a food security group called Foodshare and started a coalition that led to the city-wide provision of hot lunches in schools. Subsequently she met Deborah Sharpe, a single mother and a National Anti-Poverty Organization (NAPO) board member, and the two women made deputations to the Social Assistance Review Committee hearings that were underway. In 1988, they co-organized an Ontario Poor People's Convention at Ryerson University. One of the convention recommendations was that a space run by low-income people should be created to support political organizing and so Low Income Families Together (LIFT) emerged as a poor people's advocacy group.

During the late 1980s, LIFT members conducted province-wide consultations on social assistance reform and in the 1990s Josephine helped design the Supports to Employment Program (STEP) which enabled over 100,000 women on social assistance to voluntarily enter the workforce. LIFT members also participated in the Ontario Social Safety Network and the National Anti-Poverty Organization. In 1995 after the Harris government was elected in Ontario, LIFT was denied access to provincial government funding. Despite this, LIFT coordinated a human rights audit and published a people's report to the United Nations about Ontario's violations to the covenant on economic, social, and cultural rights (Grey).

Jacquie Thompson

Jacquie Thompson is a white woman who lives in London, Ontario. She was forty-four when we did our interview and living with three of her five children. She has been an activist for over twenty years and a founding member of Low Income Family Empowerment - Sole-Support Parent's Information Network (Life Spin), a nonprofit, poor people's group. Jacquie said that she remembers becoming more politically conscious during the early years of being a single mother: She recalled:

> I didn't know about social assistance. I was living off of what

I could pick out of a strawberry field with my kid strapped to my back. I did whatever I could—cleaned houses, worked for a locksmith, wood working.

In the late 1980s, Jacquie started an informal mutual support group. Mothers would meet on weekends at Jacquie's place, a converted goat barn on a larger family farm, and bring their kids. In an interview with Tara McDonald, Thompson recalls:

> It didn't matter what you had, you shared it. The kids played while we worked... At the time there was no philosophical basis for it, there was no theory, it was just real. My place on the farm was a gift that was given to me and I invited people to share it. Then people would come and things would happen from there. (McDonald)

Over time the informal women's group evolved into Life Spin. Life Spin members do organizing and advocacy work with local, provincial, and national anti-poverty groups. Currently, the Life Spin office is located in a storefront property along with a free clothing store that is open to the public. Its operations include a community advocates' training program, advocacy support for social assistance recipients, and a Green Market Basket program that provides locally grown produce to low-income people.

Cindy Buott

Cindy Buott is a white, single mother who lived in Peterborough when we did our interview. She was forty-eight years old and living with her four kids at the time. Cindy worked as a nurse until she got into a car accident and became disabled. Cindy said her illness and her struggles to care for her children while on welfare shaped her decision to become more politically active. Cindy is a founder of Five Counties Low Income Families Together, a coalition group started by low-income people that merged with the Peterborough Coalition Against Poverty (PCAP) in 2002. Unlike Life Spin and the Toronto LIFT group, neither Five Counties LIFT nor PCAP had a formal structure outside regular meetings nor received government funding. Cindy has also participated in provincial and national anti-poverty organizations.

Cindy's organizing focuses on income security advocacy training, as well as mobilizing local low-income mothers struggling to deal with school authorities and Children's Aid. Cindy has also organized against Neo-Nazis and police harassment of First Nations and low-income people in Peter-borough. In 2003, the Peterborough Coalition Against Poverty organized a squat in an abandoned house and successfully mobilized residents to stop the demolition of local housing.

THE PROCESS OF BECOMING ACTIVISTS

My research found that a variety of factors encouraged the single mothers I interviewed to become politically active. Cindy linked her political en-gagement to the influence of her parents, and to her experiences as a single mother. She said that First Nations and anti-racist activism had been key influences, and that hearing Josephine speak motivated her to start a local low-income group. Josephine identified her experiences of racism as a child as formative, as well as the dissonance she experienced in having white par-ents who did not explain her heritage to her until adolescence as formative. Josephine told me that her friend Deborah Sharpe, who was "all about over-throwing capitalism," launched her political education. Jacquie Thompson told me that the main influences in her formation as an activist were the ex-periences she had with the other single moms who initially formed Life Spin and with Stewart Perry's writing on community economic development.

Jacquie, Josephine, and Cindy told me that they founded their low-income activist groups because more mainstream groups and services were failing to meet their needs as low-income single mothers. All three mothers talked about the important role other women have played in their political formation. Josephine was mentored by a community worker named Linda Dixon who also introduced her to Deborah Sharpe. Cindy was inspired to get involved in economic justice organizing by Josephine, while Jacquie became active through an initial process of collective consciousness raising with her mothers' group. These experiences highlight the importance of peer mentoring between low-income single mothers, as well as the role al-lies like community workers can play. Having space and time to share ex-periences and talk politics is crucial in order for low-income single mothers to become politically engaged.

Public consultations have also offered an important opportunity for marginalized mothers to participate in public policy debates and to work together. Just as the Social Assistance Review process in the 1980s created an opportunity for Josephine and Deborah to engage politically, the federal government's Special Senate Committee on Poverty in the 1960s provided funding for low-income people's participation and a focus for anti-poverty organizing efforts. Little writes "For the first time, a large number of low-income Ontario women, particularly single mothers, raised their voices in protest" (*No Car, No Radio, No Liquor Permit* 147).

In the 1990s, however, citizen participation was abandoned at both the federal and provincial levels in favour of closed-door policy making or what Battle and Torjman call social policy reform "through stealth" (53). Connell argues that neoliberal focus on markets and commodities influences political practices so that democratic participation and citizen mobilization are supplanted by advertising campaigns and "overt competition between the most effective slogans" (28). Collapse of public consultation has further eroded the meager institutional resources available to low-income mothers to challenge corporate interests and put forward their own political agenda.

Jacquie, Josephine, and Cindy's experiences also reveal that maternalist welfare policies facilitated single mother's political participation. Prior to workfare, single mothers on social assistance were not required to participate in full-time work or study because welfare recognized that lack of child care posed a serious barrier to employment. This meant that single mothers had more time to spend in their neighbourhoods caring for their children, building social networks, and participating in community affairs. Public housing subsidies and children tie single mothers to their neighbourhoods because of the challenges involved in changing housing, schools, neighbourhood services, and support networks. Mothers also learn over time about how local institutions such as schools, housing, and welfare offices are run, while lack of appropriate programs for their children, poor housing conditions, and inadequate welfare rates provide a real incentive to organize. My findings are consistent with Conway and Hachen's research into participation rates in low-income neighbourhoods which indicate that strong neighbourhood social ties, duration of residence, and having children are predictors of higher participation in neighbourhood groups.[7]

Just as lower wages and higher costs drain people's savings, workfare has drained away the labour power that single mothers used to provide as community workers and organizers in their neighbourhoods. Instead of securing improvements to schooling and housing or welfare benefits, low-income single mothers now spend their time meeting workfare requirements and dealing with caregiving crises.

THE COSTS AND BENEFITS OF ACTIVISM

Cindy, Jacquie, and Josephine told me that they chose to organize politically because it was one of the only ways they could use their skills that really made sense to them even though their political work is poorly resourced. Understanding welfare, housing, and child welfare policies helped them to defend their own rights. Engaging in collective political activities helped break down isolation, widened their social networks, and they earned them considerable respect in their communities. Jacquie, Josephine, and Cindy also spoke about the positive influence their activism has had on their children and their sense of pride in their children's political skills.

Activists' political work also advances the collective well-being of low-income people and their neighbourhoods. For example, Jacquie acquired knowledge about resources in her community through her own struggles with the welfare system. She told me that her phone would ring every night with women asking her for help so eventually she wrote a welfare manual because she got tired of repeating herself. Life Spin publishes and distributes the manual which is used both by poor people and local service providers to ensure that provincial welfare rules are applied fairly (Life Spin).

Cindy explained to me that she came up with the idea of protecting both her custody rights and her right to participate in direct action organizing by signing over guardianship of her children to their older brother. Cindy then shared this tactic with other single mothers in her community who were experiencing intense harassment by child welfare authorities in the mid-1990s. As a result, Peterborough's child welfare agency was forced to sit down with low-income mothers to discuss ways of providing support that did not involve child apprehension.

Activism can also lead to collective financial gains. Securing funds for programs such as the lunch programs Josephine helped create or the Green Market Basket Food program Life Spin founded puts state money into the hands of poor people. Challenging funding cuts and advocating for increased expenditures works to ensure that government funds flow into low-income communities. Without the self-organizing, research, and advocacy done by grassroots low-income people's groups, low-income people have no democratic political representation. Instead this role is filled by social service agencies whose knowledge and interests are not necessarily aligned with those of poor people.

During our interviews, Jacquie, Cindy, and Josephine clearly explained to me that activism carries with it very particular risks. Trying to juggle financial and caregiving responsibilities, in addition to political commit-ments, is extremely stressful. Authorities, neighbours, and even their own children may judge activist mothers for failing to spend time on more tra-ditional domestic activities. Political militancy may also have serious conse-quences ranging from barriers to employment and child apprehension, to incarceration and deportation for immigrant mothers. Jacquie, Cindy, and Josephine also spoke bitterly about the lack of resources for their activist work and the challenges they experienced in making alliances with more privileged activist groups and service providers.

THE IMPACT OF NEOLIBERAL RESTRUCTURING ON LOW-INCOME SINGLE MOTHERS' ACTIVIST WORK

Neoliberal restructuring has not only impoverished single mothers and their families; it is destroying the fragile political networks they have painstak-ingly built. Jacquie Thompson and Josephine Grey describe the situation:

> Jacquie: Smaller and smaller spaces. The room of your own became a thing of the past. Women were sleeping on pull out couches in their living rooms or someone else's... Their kids had to have bedrooms or CAS (Children's Aid Society) would take them, and they didn't have food. They just moved into smaller and smaller, more decrepit housing. The slumlords made a killing.
>
> Jo: Before CAS had all this stuff about prevention, and then all of a sudden it just became snatch and grab, snatch and grab.

In Toronto, the number of lone parent (*sic*)[8] families in higher poverty neighbourhoods has almost doubled between 1991 and 2001.[9] For single mothers, lack of resources, stringent workfare demands, increased child wel-fare surveillance, and intensified caregiving demands result in extremely high levels of stress and tension (Little, "The Leaner, Meaner Welfare Machine"). Neoliberal restructuring has shifted low-income single mothers' role from a pro-active struggle for additional resources to reactive attempts to manage without them:

> Josephine: It was pretty obvious the government didn't care what happened to people as a result of restructuring in my

neighbourhood when they took away the hospital, the disability office, and closed immigrant services. The largest riding of poor people in the country and you're going to move everything so nobody can get to anything! In my neighbourhood the reaction was to go into the drug trade, or to go into hooking...

Jacquie: And prove everyone poor is a criminal!

Josephine: Or throw themselves off balconies. We had an incredible suicide rate going on. What I found incredible was how the middle class, do-gooding population was in such a state of denial!

Josephine's and Jacquie's descriptions are supported by Bezanson and Luxton's study about the impact of restructuring on forty-one Ontario households (Bezanson and Luxton). She found that income insecurity was severely intensified, that no amount of economizing could enable people to overcome the serious economic challenges they faced, and that households headed by single mothers were the most affected.

Restructuring has meant that responsibility for social programs has been downloaded from cities to the under-funded nonprofit sector just when low-income people need community services most. Funding for nonprofits has been cutback and shifted from core to contract funding. Private donations aren't enough to compensate for state funding cuts and many agencies are too busy supervising workfare workers to train volunteers.[10] As a result, there are not enough services available and community members with complex needs are less likely to have them met. Khosla writes:

The failure to consider Toronto's growing population of women of colour and immigrant women...is a symptom that a deep democratic and social fissure is developing in our city. Take a look inside poor neighbourhoods however, and women's daily contributions are suddenly not so dispensable... The private space of home has already had to serve as the new workplace for many women with low-paying, piecemeal and contingent jobs. Now, homes are increasingly becoming makeshift hospitals, elder care, child care and recreation centres. (8)

Cutbacks and intensified demands on their time have made political participation extremely difficult for low-income women and especially single mothers. Jacquie, Josephine, and Cindy all said that after the Harris government cuts it became much harder to get women out to meetings. There was no funding available for transportation or child care, women were totally absorbed in "putting out fires", women lost their housing, or they lost their kids, they were pacified by anti-depressants, and in some cases they died. Jacquie and Josephine remark:

> Jacquie: They died because they couldn't feed their kids, they couldn't pay their mortgage, they had no dignity, they had no life—how do you deal with taking your kid to the food bank, when you're used to eating healthy, and (now you are) giving them Kraft dinner with worms in it? It was disgusting. Some women lost every bit of self-esteem and just gave up...

> Josephine: Even women who didn't get ill just weren't available anymore. They were constantly running from place to place, or standing in line. I'd run into women I used to go to meetings with and do (political) stuff with, and I'd be like, "How are you?" and it would be like, "Oh, well I got evicted from here and I'm going over there." All I could do was give them...a hand with the moving.

> Jacquie: Also people who were volunteering and doing community work for years, they couldn't because they were being sent off to workfare—the only way to get them to shut up and lay down was to ship them off to work somewhere for no pay.

These findings highlight the need for collective, organized resistance to neoliberal restructuring by poor people. However, funding changes have had a major impact on grassroots low-income groups just when their political leadership is needed most. Groups such as Life Spin, LIFT, and PCAP are very dependent on volunteer labour and women's volunteer leadership in particular. For example, Cindy became active later than Josephine and Jacquie when funding had already begun to dry up, so she was never paid for her organizing work and neither Five Counties LIFT nor PCAP ever received any government funding. This meant that Cindy's groups depended completely on volunteer labour and support from more affluent allies.

In contrast, older nonprofit groups such as Life Spin and LIFT never received core government funding, but they did receive piecemeal project funding from the provincial government and some charitable sources. This provincial funding grew under the NDP government in the 1990s and Josephine and Jacquie were paid (intermittently) for their organizing work. All of this changed with the election of the Harris government in 1995. Josephine explained to me that LIFT's funding was eliminated by the Harris government which "blacklisted" LIFT as an activist group and denied access to funding from the provincial government and its agencies. Subsequently, LIFT's budget dropped from a high of $700,000 in 1994 to $0 by 2001. During the same period, Jacquie struggled to find piecemeal funding for Life Spin as funding became more and more difficult to access. All three groups also relied on in-kind supports from their allies in the nonprofit sector in order to participate in broader provincial and national anti-poverty networks and to work on joint projects. Cuts to their allies meant that less money was available to extend to grassroots groups such as Life Spin and LIFT.

The funding cutbacks experienced by poor people's groups are part of a larger restructuring process undertaken by all levels of government over the past two decades. Neoliberal restructuring has cut funding to nonprofit groups and service providers, and drastically altered the funding rules. Under the contract funding system, nonprofits receive funding on a project-by-project basis and there are significant funding gaps. Funding takes longer to get, it is provided for shorter time periods, it is tied to creating joint projects with other organizations and to finding additional donors. The result is increasingly unstable funding with no money provided for administrative costs, despite funder demands for increasingly complex reports (Scott).

The contract funding model is based on performance-based budgeting.[11] However, measuring the success or failure of projects using outcome focused, quantitative methods such as counting clients "served" does not capture whether services are actually working for the people using them, does not promote service flexibility, and actually discourages service provision to people who require additional time and support. Restructuring is directing funding to large, centralized social service agencies at the expense of smaller, grassroots groups.[12] Richmond and Shields note that contractual agreements between the state and nonprofits focus on service provision at the expense of more political research and advocacy:

Advocacy through intermediary nonprofit organizations, under the rules of this new funding regime, has been actively discouraged (Laforest 8). Hence, other important roles served by the third sector, such as research and advocacy, are marginalized... The contract relationship can result in nonprofits losing their "political edge" and ability "to work for political change". This is hardly the kind of environment that is nurturing of a vibrant civil society... (6)

The shift to market-driven funding methods means that small, nonprofit groups such as Life Spin and LIFT cannot secure even small amounts of funding for self-directed research, advocacy, and training because of the amount of infrastructure needed even to apply. Furthermore, Josephine and Jacquie told me that restructuring has led to competition among community groups for access to remaining funding, and for ownership of community-based projects. Funding competition also leads to the appropriation of grassroots projects by larger organizations. Jacquie described one example of this:

> Our local food bank decided to follow the Green Market Basket model of locating their services in a variety of low-income neighbourhoods while the main food bank acts as a food depot. So now they have food bank branches. But what they're doing is corporate dumping of waste products for multinational food conglomerates instead of forming partnerships with local farmers the way we do.

> Then the food bank decided they should have fresh fruits and vegetables in the summer so they decided to attach a garden to each site. Now, there's nothing wrong with fresh food but who's going to grow it and are they getting paid? No, local seniors at the Church were asked to volunteer to do it for nothing. After one season, they realized how much work it was and they started asking why the people eating the food weren't helping to grow it! And now the growing work is done by people forced into it through workfare. In the end, the main food bank gets the funding instead of our grassroots program and they dictate the program without consulting...low-income people.

The point is that like everyone else, low-income mothers learn how to "do" politics through mentoring and practice. Learning about politics and becoming politically engaged are extremely difficult when access to spaces, mentors, and even small amounts of funding are eliminated, and when grassroots groups have to compete against much larger institutions for resources.

CONCLUSION

This chapter addresses three key themes that emerged in this study. The first relates to how low-income single mothers become politically active. Having space and time to talk with other mothers plays an important role in connecting women with peers and mentors who support political engagement. Furthermore, public consultation processes provided important opportunities for low-income single mothers to participate in public debates and to meet one another. Finally, in contrast to workfare policies, maternalist welfare policies allowed some time for political participation. Second, although low-income single mothers' political activism has been poorly documented, political participation offers substantial benefits to these women, their children, and their neighbourhoods. Defending their rights, creating social networks, sharing information, and learning new skills as activists increases income security and self-respect for women. Their children also benefit from their activities by developing their own critical skills. Low-income communities fortunate enough to include activist mothers make real gains in terms of government investment and the creation of spaces where developing poor people's political skills and knowledge is a priority. Third, neoliberal restructuring and cuts have impoverished low-income single mothers, intensified their unpaid work, and created an enormous strain on inter-personal relationships. This in turn has reduced the labour power available to grassroots low-income groups. Deep cuts to the nonprofit sector have eliminated funding for these groups including in-kind funding from their allies, and created adversarial relationships between local organizations. As a result, barriers to political participation for poor people, particularly poor mothers, have increased substantially.

Low-income single mothers have always faced major challenges in securing resources for self-organizing and as a result, their efforts often could not be sustained. But when resources can be found, low-income single mothers have demonstrated extreme political tenacity. In Toronto, although LIFT has lost its funding and its office, its members still meet and Josephine Grey continues to organize for food security in her community. In London, Jacquie Thompson's Life Spin group has its own space and is still running despite almost two decades of neoliberal attacks on poor people. In Peterborough, PCAP has been inactive over the past year, but plans are underway to restart it. Cindy Buott moved to Campbellford, Ontario, to be closer to her family. She continues to help low-income people in her community defend their rights.

Analysis of low-income single mothers' activist work shines light on the complex ways in which these women are excluded from political participation and on their strategies for resisting political and economic injustice. Low-income mothers' activism needs to be documented much more extensively in order to challenge stereotypes about poor people and political apathy, and to better understand the importance of activism and learning as strategies for women's liberation.

NOTES

[1] See Brodie, "The Great Undoing"; and Luxton
[2] See Brodie, "Globalization, Canadian Family Policy, and the Omissions of Neoliberalism"; Luxton; and Schragge
[3] See Luxton; and Thomas
[4] See Block; and Luxton
[5] See Mirchandani and Chan
[6] See Naples; Orleck; Pope
[7] See Conway and Hachen
[8] I do not use the gender neutral term "lone parent" in my writing because it masks the reality that the overwhelming majority of these "parents" are women. Thanks to Punam Khosla for this analysis.
[9] United Way of Greater Toronto and the Canadian Council on Social Development, 2004
[10] See Richmond and Shields
[11] See Burke, Mooers, and Shields
[12] See Khosla; Lailey; and Richmond and Shields

WORKS CITED

Battle, Ken and Sherri Torjman. "Desperately Seeking Substance: A Commentary on the Social Security Review." *Remaking Canadian Social Policy: Social Security in the Late 1990s.* Eds. Jane Pulkingham and Gordon Ternowetsky. Halifax: Fernwood Publishing, 1996. 52-66. Print.

Bezanson, Kate and Meg Luxton. (eds). *Social Reproduction: Feminist Political Economy Challenges Neo-Liberalism.* Montreal and Kingston: McGill-Queen's University Press, 2006. Print.

Block, Sheila. *Ontario's Growing Gap: The Role of Race and Gender.* Ottawa: Canadian Centre for Policy Alternatives, 2010. Print.

Brodie, Janine. "Globalization, Canadian Family Policy, and the Omissions of Neoliberalism." *North Carolina Law Review* 88.5 (2010): 1559-1591. Print. Rev. 1559 (2009-20

— "The Great Undoing: State Formation, Gender Politics and Social Policy in Canada." *Western Welfare in Decline: Globalization and Women's Poverty.* Ed. C. Kingfisher. Philadelphia: University of Pennsylvania Press, 2002. 90-110. Print.

Burke, Mike, Colin Mooers, and John Shields (eds). *Restructuring and Resistance: Canadian Public Policy in the Age of Global Capitalism.* Halifax: Fernwood Publishing, 2000. Print.

Clarke, John. "Living With/in and Without Neo-Liberalism." *Foccal* 51 (2008): 135-147. Print.

Community Development Halton. Social Assistance Reform Act: An Information Package. http://www.cdhalton.ca/publications/reports-list/340-social-assistance-reform-act-an-information-package, accessed October 30, 2012. Web.

Connell, Raewyn. "Understanding Neoliberalism." *Neoliberalism and Everyday Life.* Eds. Susan Braedley and Meg Luxton. Montreal and Kingston: McGill-Queen's University Press, 2010. 22-36. Print.

Conway, Brian and David Hachen. "Attachments, Grievances, Resources, and Efficacy: The Determinants of Tenant Association Participation Among Public Housing Tenants." *Journal of Urban Affairs* 27.1 (2005): 25-52. Print.

Grey, Josephine. "The Ontario People's Report to the United Nations: On Violations of the International Covenant on Economic, Social and Cultural Rights in the Province of Ontario." Toronto: Low Income Families Together, 1998. Print.

Khosla, Punam. If Low Income Women of Colour Counted in Toronto: Final Report of the Action Research Project "Breaking Isolation, Getting Involved." Toronto: The Community Social Planning Council of Toronto, 2003. Print.

Laforest, Rachel. "Funding Policy Capacity." Paper presented to the 30th Annual Conference of the Association for Research on Nonprofit Organizations and Voluntary Action. Miami, Florida, November 30, 2001. Print.

Lailey, Tonya. "The Ideology of a Hot Breakfast: A Study of the Politics of the Harris Government and the Strategies of the Ontario Women's Movement." M.A. thesis, Queen's University, 1998. Print.

Life Spin. Community Advocates Manual. London, 2003. Print.

Little, Margaret. "The Increasing Invisibility of Mothering". *A Life in Balance?: Reopening the Family-Work Debate*. Eds. Catherine Krull and Justyna Sempruch. Vancouver: UBC Press, 2011. 194-205. Print.

— "Militant Mothers Fight Poverty: The Just Society Movement, 1968-1971." *Labour/Le Travaille* 59 (Spring 2007): pars 41. http://www.historycooperative.org/journals/llt/59/little.html, accessed July, 15, 2012. Web.

— "The Leaner, Meaner Welfare Machine: The Ontario Conservative Government's Ideological and Material Attack on Single Mothers." *Making Normal: Social Regulation in Canada*. Ed. Deborah Brock. Ontario: Nelson Thomson Learning, 2003. 235-255. Print.

— *No Car, No Radio, No Liquor Permit: The Moral Regulation of Single Mothers in Ontario, 1920–1997*. Toronto: Oxford University Press, 1998. Print.

Luxton, Meg. "Doing Neoliberalism: Perverse Individualism in Personal Life." *Neoliberalism and Everyday Life*. Eds. Susan Braedley and Meg Luxton. Montreal and Kingston: McGill-Queen's University Press, 2010. 163-183. Print.

McDonald, Tara. *Building Foundations: The Early Years of L.I.F.E.S.P.I.N.* London: Life Spin, 2000. Print.

Mirchandani, Kiran and Wendy Chan. *Criminalizing Race, Criminalizing Poverty: Welfare Fraud Enforcement in Canada*. Black Point, N.S.: Fernwood Publications, 2007. Print.

Naples, Nancy. *Grassroots Warriors: Activist Mothering, Community Work, and the War on Poverty*. New York: Routledge, 1998. Print.

Orleck, Annalise. *Storming Caesar's Palace: How Black Mothers Fought Their Own War on Poverty*. Boston: Beacon Press, 2005. Print.

Ontario Public Service Employees Union. "Building Strong Communities: A Call to Reinvest in Ontario's Nonprofit Services." 2004. http://www. opseu.org/news/Press2004/feb202004.htm, accessed September 15, 2005. Web.

Pike Deborah and Katherine Scott. "Funding Matters For Our Communities: Challenges and Opportunities for Funding Innovation in Canada's Nonprofit and Voluntary Sector." Ottawa: Canadian Council on Social Development, 2005. Print.

Pope, Jacqueline. *Biting the Hand That Feeds Them: Organizing Women on Welfare at the Grass Roots Level.* New York: Praeger Publishers, 1989. Print.

Richmond, Ted and John Shields. "NGO Restructuring: Constraints and Consequences." Presentation to the 11th Biennial Social Welfare Policy Conference, University of Ottawa, 2003. Print.

Russell, Bob. "From the Workhouse to Workfare: Shifting Policy Terrains." *Restructuringand Resistance: Canadian Public Policy in an Age of Global Capitalism.* Eds. Mike Burke, Colin Mooers, and John Shields. Halifax: Fernwood Publishing, 2000. 24-49. Print.

Schragge, Eric (ed). *Workfare: Ideology or a New Underclass.* Toronto: Garamond Press, 1997. Print.

Scott, Katherine. "Funding Matters: The Impact of Canada's New Funding Regime on Nonprofit and Voluntary Organizations." Ottawa: Canadian Council on Social Development, 2003. Print.

Thomas, Mark. "Neoliberalism, Racialization and the Regulation of Employment Standards." *Neoliberalism and Everyday Life.* Eds. Susan Braedley and Meg Luxton. Montreal and Kingston: McGill-Queen's University Press, 2010. 68-89. Print.

United Way of Greater Toronto and Canadian Council on Social Development (CCSD) "Poverty by Postal Code: The Geography of Neighbourhood Poverty." Toronto: 2004. Print.

Epilogue

JESOOK SONG

The editor and contributors of *Mothering in the Age of Neoliberalism* have taken up risky subjects brilliantly and courageously. Both motherhood and neoliberalism tend to be subjects that rely on presumptions rather than building on meticulous historicization in local contexts, as Melinda Vandenbeld Giles (volume editor), acknowledges in her introduction. Mothering, in particular, has been a subject of avoidance within feminist intellectual discussions precisely because of the difficulty in addressing motherhood as a central subject without reifying hetero-normative family and gender norms that ascribe a particular mothering role and image.

Mothering in the Age of Neoliberalism provides a "countervision" (here, I am borrowing "countervision" from Christa Craven's Foreword of this volume). Rather than reproducing motherhood at the risk of essentializing, *Mothering in the Age of Neoliberalism* "recycles" the notion of motherhood similar to how Rosemary Marangoly George's edited volume, *Burning Down the House: Recycling Domesticity*, re-signifies or reclaims the presumed notion of domesticity as a critical window to challenge such presumptions. Further, *Mothering in the Age of Neoliberalism* makes a crucial intervention in the discursive topography of neoliberalism. Formal political economy fails to account for gendered labour, particularly mother's work (both waged or unwaged) as central to the entire economic, political, and cultural realms rather than being positioned in the name of maternal instinct or duty, or in a presumed segregated realm of (volunteer) care work. The concept of "women's work" has been undermined as the element of "reproduction" in formal political economy which highlights only "production."

The neoliberal framework is more disguising because it tends to brush off gender differences under the rubric of the "entrepreneurial self" encouraging the "empowerment" of women by promoting full-fledged wage markets including a sprawling care-work industry in the formal sector. This volume powerfully explicates such empty promises by showing the increasing poverty and burden on the shoulders of mothers. In sum, the conceptual contributions of this volume are to be admired: in particular, for "recycling" mothering/motherhood in feminist intellectual dialogues, and for intervening into neoliberal political economy through articulating motherhood's stakes in the new economy from various local historical contexts.

WORKS CITED

Marangoly George, Rosemary. Ed. *Burning Down the House: Recycling Domesticity*. Boulder: Westview Press, 1998. Print

List of Contributors

Grace Adeniyi Ogunyankin is a Nigerian-Canadian PhD candidate in Women's Studies at York University in Toronto, Canada. Her research interest is gender and the political economy of urban planning and development in Ibadan, Nigeria.

Patrizia Albanese is professor of sociology at Ryerson University in Toronto, Ontario, and President of the Canadian Sociological Association. She is co-author of *Youth & Society* (Oxford, 2011) and *More Than It Seems* (Women's Press, 2010); and author of *Child Poverty in Canada* (Oxford, 2010), and *Mothers of the Nation* (U of T Press, 2006). She is working on a number of research projects which focus on family policies and families under stress.

Gillian Anderson is a mother, feminist, sociologist, and a University-College Professor at Vancouver Island University (VIU) in Nanaimo, BC. Her broad areas of interest include the sociology of gender and family relations, social inequality, social policy and women's organizing for change. She and her family enjoy beachcombing and ferry watching.

Joanne Baker is Adjunct Senior Lecturer in the Department of Social Work & Human Services in the School of Arts & Social Sciences at James Cook University in Queensland, Australia. She has a background in social policy and women's studies. Her research interests cohere around the intersection of neoliberalism and feminism, particularly a feminist critique of individualizing logics and neoliberal subjectivity. She has published widely in this area. Joanne now lives in Vancouver, BC.

Sevi Bayraktar is a PhD student in the culture and performance program at the department of world arts and cultures/dance at UCLA. She completed her MA in sociology at Bogazici University in Turkey, where the study of motherhood education was her dissertation project. Her work has been published in Turkish as *Makbul Anneler, Mustakbel Vatandaşlar* [Proper Mothers, Improper Citizens] (Ayizi Yayınevi, 2011). Her current research involves the articulations of intergenerational and gendered transmissions of social memory with dance and movement among the urban Roma.

Katrina Bloch is an assistant professor of sociology at Kent State University at Stark. Her research examines the relationship between ideology and the social structure in the reproduction of inequality. She teaches courses on inequality, deviance, and research methods.

Pat Breton is a PhD candidate in Gender, Feminist and Women's Studies at York University in Toronto, Ontario. Her research interests are gender and Canadian public policy of unwaged caring labour, maternal/child welfare within the neoliberal state, and violence against women. Her work has been published in a Motherhood Initiative for Research and Community (MIRCI) journal issue. Pat has been involved in the Violence against Women sector for over fifteen years as an activist, front line worker and Executive Director. She lives in Flesherton, Ontario, but especially enjoys her Toronto visits with her daughter and granddaughter, Charlie.

Catherine Bryan is a PhD candidate in social anthropology at Dalhousie University. Her research focuses primarily on the small, unassuming town of Russell, Manitoba, and its connection to processes of capital accumulation, migration trajectories, and transnational fields of social reproduction (past and present). Her work is motivated by feminist political economy and an interest in labour, care, and migration. Originally from Winnipeg, she currently lives in Halifax with her partner and two year old son.

Megan Butryn is a graduate student in the Department of Sociology at York University. She is currently researching the negotiations of gender roles and feminist identities in the Christian church.

Angela Castañeda is associate professor of anthropology at DePauw University. Her research in Brazil, Mexico, and the U.S. explores questions on religion, ritual, expressive culture and the anthropology of reproduction. Her current project focuses on the role of doulas in birth culture. In addition to her work as a practicing birth and postpartum doula, she also volunteers as a Spanish childbirth educator in Bloomington, Indiana, where she lives with her family.

Jane Chelliah works in the UK public sector, is a voluntary CEO of a charity for women with Learning Disabilities; and sits on the UK Gender for Action, Peace and Security (GAPS) as the representative for UK-UN women. She has a particular interest in how Capitalism affects mothers.

Christa Craven is the chair of the Women's, Gender & Sexuality Studies Program and an associate professor of anthropology and WGSS at the College of Wooster. She is the author of *Pushing for Midwives: Homebirth Mothers and the Reproductive Rights Movement* (Temple University Press, 2010) and co-editor (with Dána-Ain Davis) of *Feminist Activist Ethnography: Counterpoints to Neoliberalism in North America* (Lexington Books, 2013). Craven has also published in journals including *American Anthropologist, Medical Anthropology Quarterly, Feminist Studies*, and *Feminist Formations*. She is the former co-chair of the Society of Lesbian and Gay Anthropologists (now the Association for Queer Anthropology).

Talia Esnard received her PhD in Sociology from the University of the West Indies, St. Augustine Campus in 2007. She is currently an Assistant Professor of Sociology in the Centre for Education at the University of Trinidad and Tobago. Her work explores gendered and socio-cognitive understandings and experiences of leadership, mothering, and entrepreneurship in the Caribbean.

Lynn O'Brien Hallstein is an associate professor of rhetoric in the College of General Studies at Boston University. She is the author of *White Feminists and Contemporary Maternity: Purging Matrophobia*, co-edited *Academic Motherhood in a Post-Second Wave Context: Challenges, Strategies, and Possibilities* and *Contemporary Maternity in an Era of Choice: Explorations into Discourses of Reproduction*, which won the Organization for the Study of Communication, Language, and Gender's 2011 Outstanding Book Award for an Edited Volume, and she has been published in *Quarterly Journal of Speech*, the *Western Journal of Communication, Women's Studies in Communication, Text and Performance Studies, Critical/Cultural Studies, National Women's Studies Journal, Feminist Formations*, and the *Journal of the Association for Research on Mothering.*

Louisa Hawkins is an MA student at Carleton University in the Sociology and Anthropology Department. Her research is inspired by her work as an Early Childhood Educator and private caregiver. She explores both child and elder care, with a focus on the social consequences of collective community caring.

Yoonhee Lee is a research assistant at the University of Toronto and recent graduate of the MA European, Russian, and Eurasian Studies program at the Munk School of Global Affairs.

Courtney Manion is a fourth year student in the Psychology Department at Ryerson University. She has worked as a research assistant for Patrizia Albanese on projects related to social/family policies and children and childhood. Courtney's research interests include an examination of the social policy surrounding childcare and the family.

Joseph (Joey) G. Moore is a father and activist. He is a University-College Professor of Sociology at Vancouver Island University. He has teaching and research interests in the sociology of work, urban environments and social movements. He is an organizer and board member with Car Free Vancouver and active in environmental justice issues.

Vanessa Reimer is a PhD candidate in York University's Graduate Program in Gender, Feminist and Women's Studies. She is the co-editor of Demeter Press titles *Mother of Invention: How Our Mothers Influenced Us as Feminist Academics and Activists* (2013) and *The Mother-Blame Game* (forthcoming in 2015). Her research interests include feminist studies in religion, girlhood, and mothering.

Katheryne Schulz is a white, working-class lesbian who lives with her partner Janet in Toronto. She is a doctoral student at the University of Toronto, and has been a community and trade union organizer for over twenty years. Katheryne's mother Pat was a low-income, single parent, and a radical writer and organizer.

Julie Johnson Searcy is a mother, doula and PhD student at Indiana University in the Communication and Culture Department and in the Anthropology Department. She is interested in the intersections between reproduction, medical discourse, disease and personhood. She plans to conduct her dissertation research in South Africa examining how the intersection of HIV/AIDS and reproduction troubles the boundaries between life and death.

Reena Shadaan is involved with the North American solidarity group of the International Campaign for Justice in Bhopal (ICJB). She received a M.A. in Development Studies from York University (Toronto, Canada), focusing her research work on Bhopali women's activism/empowerment in the aftermath of the Bhopal gas disaster.

Jesook Song is an urban and political anthropologist teaching in the Department of Anthropology at the University of Toronto. Her books include *South Koreans in the Debt Crisis: The Creation of a Neoliberal Welfare Society* (Duke University Press, 2009), *New Millennium South Korea: Neoliberal Capitalism and Transnational Movements* (edited volume, Routledge, 2010), *Living on Your Own: Single Women, Rental Housing, and Post-Revolutionary Affect in Contemporary South Korea* (SUNY Press, 2014). She also co-edited *Korea through Ethnography*, a special issue of the *Journal of Korean Studies* (November 2012), and published articles in journals such as *Anthropological Quarterly, Critique of Anthropology, Feminist Review, Gender, Place and Culture, Journal of Youth Studies, positions,* and *Urban Geography*.

Chikako Takeshita is an associate professor of women's studies at University of California, Riverside. She is the author of *The Global Biopolitics of the IUD: How Science Constructs Contraceptive Users and Women's Bodies* (MIT Press, 2012). She is working on her second book on surgical childbirth.

Tiffany Taylor is an assistant professor of sociology at Kent State University at Kent (USA). In her research, she examines a number of topics related to inequality. Her recent research focuses on policy implementation of programs for poor mothers in North Carolina and Ohio.

Melinda Vandenbeld Giles is a mother, feminist activist, and PhD candidate in socio-cultural anthropology at the University of Toronto. Her research involves working with mothers who are living with their children in Toronto motel rooms. Her work has been published in several Demeter Press collections and MIRCI (Motherhood Initiative for Research and Community Involvement) journal issues, in addition to the publication of a two-part series regarding mothers experiencing homelessness in Ontario for *Dispatches International*. She was a Research Associate for the University of Toronto Munk School of Global Affairs Comparative Program on Health and Society (CPHS) where she has two publications in their Working Paper

Series and is co-editor for the 2012-2013 CPHS Working Paper Series.

Andrew Wilkins is Research Fellow in the School of Education at the University of Roehampton. His core research interests are critical analyses of policymaking, statecraft, governance and neoliberalization. He is project leader for the ESRC-funded project SASE (School Accountability and Stakeholder Education, 2012-15) which examines issues relating to school governance and accountability in the current English school system. Andrew Wilkins serves as a member of the Economic and Social Research Council (ESRC) Peer Review College (2012-2014), co-convenor of the BERA SIG Social Theory and Education, member of the Paulo Freire Institute-UK Advisory Board, member of the International Editorial Board for Journal of Pedagogy, and core member of the Centre for Educational Research in Equalities, Policy and Pedagogy (CEREPP). He has been invited to review articles for *Educational Review, Journal of Education Policy, Critical Studies in Education, Gender and Education, School Leadership and Management, Journal of Gender Studies*, and *Journal of Community and Applied Social Psychology*.

Celia Winkler is associate professor of sociology at the University of Montana, receiving her Ph.D. from the University of Oregon and J.D. from Hastings College of Law (University of California) in San Francisco. She has been interested in women and the welfare state since working as a legal services attorney during the Reagan Administration, and compared the development of social policies affecting single mothers in *Single Mothers and the State: The Politics of Care in Sweden and the United States*. Her current primary area of research lies in citizenship theory in community participatory organizations, as well as examining women's labor force participation and wage inequalities.